ALSO BY DOUGLAS RUSHKOFF

Get Back in the Box: Innovation from the Inside Out

Nothing Sacred: The Truth About Judaism

Exit Strategy: A Novel

Coercion: Why We Listen to What "They" Say

ScreenAgers: Lessons in Chaos from Digital Kids

Ecstasy Club: A Novel

Media Virus! Hidden Agendas in Popular Culture

Cyberia: Life in the Trenches of Hyperspace

LIFE **INC**

LIFE **INC**

HOW CORPORATISM CONQUERED THE WORLD,
AND HOW WE CAN TAKE IT BACK

Douglas Rushkoff

 RANDOM HOUSE TRADE PAPERBACKS NEW YORK

The names and identifying personal details of some individuals have been changed to protect their anonymity. In such cases, only first names appear.

2011 Random House Trade Paperback Edition

Published in the United States by Random House Trade Paperbacks, an imprint of The Random House Publishing Group, a division of Random House, Inc., New York.

RANDOM HOUSE TRADE PAPERBACKS and colophon are trademarks of Random House, Inc.

Originally published in hardcover and in different form in the United States by Random House, an imprint of The Random House Publishing Group, a division of Random House, Inc., in 2009.

ISBN 978-0-8129-7850-6

Printed in the United States of America

www.atrandom.com

9 8 7 6 5 4 3 2 1

Book design by Christopher M. Zucker

TO YOU,
THE REAL PEOPLE ON THE OTHER SIDE OF THIS
CORPORATE-MEDIATED CONNECTION

CONTENTS

INTRODUCTION

Your Money or Your Life
A Lesson on the Front Stoop

I got mugged on Christmas Eve.

I was in front of my Brooklyn apartment house taking out the trash when a man pulled a gun and told me to empty my pockets. I gave him my money, wallet, and cell phone. But then—remembering something I'd seen in a movie about a hostage negotiator—I begged him to let me keep my medical-insurance card. If I could humanize myself in his perception, I figured, he'd be less likely to kill me.

He accepted my argument about how hard it would be for me to get "care" without it, and handed me back the card. Now it was us two against the establishment, and we made something of a deal: in exchange for his mercy, I wasn't to report him—even though I had plainly seen his face. I agreed, and he ran off down the street. I foolishly but steadfastly stood by my side of the bargain, however coerced it may have been, for a few hours. As if I could have actually entered into a binding contract at gunpoint.

In the meantime, I posted a note about my strange and frightening experience to the Park Slope Parents list—a rather crunchy Internet community of moms, food co-op members, and other leftie types dedicated to the health and well-being of their families and their decidedly progressive, gentrifying neighborhood. It seemed the responsible thing to do, and I suppose I also expected some expression of sympathy and support.

Amazingly, the very first two emails I received were from people *angry* that I had posted the name of the street on which the crime had occurred. Didn't I realize that this publicity could adversely affect all of our property values? The "sellers' market" was already difficult enough! With a famous actor reportedly leaving the area for Manhattan, does Brooklyn's real-estate market need more bad press? And this was *before* the real-estate crash.

I was stunned. Had it really come to this? Did people care more about the market value of their neighborhood than what was actually taking place within it? Besides, it didn't even make good business sense to bury the issue. In the long run, an open and honest conversation about crime and how to prevent it should make the neighborhood safer. Property values would go up in the end, not down. So these homeowners were more concerned about the immediate liquidity of their town houses than their long-term asset value—not to mention the actual experience of living in them. And these were among the wealthiest people in New York, who shouldn't have to be worrying about such things. What had happened to make them behave this way?

It stopped me cold, and forced me to reassess my own long-held desire to elevate myself from renter to owner. I stopped to think—which, in the midst of an irrational real-estate craze, may not have been the safest thing to do. Why, I wondered aloud on my blog, was I struggling to make $4,500-per-month rent on a two-bedroom, fourth-floor walk-up in this supposedly "hip" section of Brooklyn, when I could just as easily get mugged somewhere else for a lot less per month? Was my willingness to participate in this runaway market part of the problem?

The detectives who took my report drove the point home. One of them drew a circle on a map of Brooklyn. "Inside this circle is where the rich white people from Manhattan are moving. That's the target area. Hunting ground. Think about it from your mugger's point of view: quiet, tree-lined streets of row houses, each worth a million or two, and inhabited by the rich people who displaced your family. Now, you live in or around the projects just outside the circle. Where would *you* go to mug someone?"

Back on the World Wide Web, a friend of mine—another Park

Slope writer—made an open appeal for my family to stay in Brooklyn. He saw "the Slope" as a mixed-use neighborhood now reaching the "peak of livability" that the legendary urban anthropologist Jane Jacobs idealized. He explained how all great neighborhoods go through the same basic process: Some artists move into the only area they can afford—a poor area with nothing to speak of. Eventually, there are enough of them to open a gallery. People start coming to the gallery in the evenings, creating demand for a coffeehouse nearby, and so on. Slowly but surely, an artsy store or two and a clique of hipsters "pioneer" the neighborhood until there's significant sidewalk activity late into the night, making it safer for successive waves of incoming businesses and residents.

Of course, after the city's newspaper "discovers" the new trendy neighborhood, the artists are joined and eventually replaced by increasingly wealthy but decidedly less hip young professionals, lawyers, and businesspeople—but hopefully not so many that the district completely loses its "flavor." Investment increases, the district grows bigger, and everyone is happier and wealthier.

Still, what happens to the people who lived there from the beginning—the ones whom the police detective was talking about? The "natives"? This process of gentrification does not occur ex nihilo. No, when property values go up, so do the rents, displacing anyone whose monthly living charges aren't regulated by the government. The residents of the neighborhood do not actually participate in the renaissance, because they are not owners. They move to outlying areas. Sure, their kids still go to John Jay High School in the middle of Park Slope. But none of Park Slope's *own* wealthy residents send their kids there.

Our online conversation was picked up by *New York* magazine in a column entitled "Are the Writers Leaving Brooklyn?" The article focused entirely on the way a crime against an author could threaten the Brooklyn real-estate bubble. National Public Radio called to interview me about the story—not the mugging itself, but whether I would leave Brooklyn over it, and if doing so publicly might not be irresponsibly hurting other people's property values. A week or two of blog insanity later, a second *New York* piece asked why we should even care about whether the writers are leaving Brooklyn—seemingly oblivious of the fact that this was the very same column space that told us to care in the first place.

It was an interesting fifteen minutes. What was going on had less to do with crime or authors, though, than it did with a market in its final, most vaporous phase. I simply couldn't afford to buy in—and getting mugged freed me from the hype treadmill for long enough to accept it. Or, more accurately, it's not that I *couldn't* afford it so much as that I *wouldn't* afford it. There were mortgage brokers willing to lend me the other 90 percent of the money I'd need to purchase a home on the block where I was renting. "We can *get you in*," they'd say. And at that moment in real-estate history, putting even 10 percent down would have made me a very qualified buyer. "What about when the mortgage readjusts?" I remember asking. "Then you refinance at a better rate," they assured me. Of course, that would be happening just about the same time Park Slope's artificially low property-tax rate (an exemption secured by real-estate developers) would be raised to the levels of the poorer areas of the borough. "Don't worry. Everyone with your financials is doing it," one broker explained with a wink. "And the banks aren't going to just let everyone lose their homes, now, are they?"

As long as people refused to look at the real social and financial costs, the market could keep going up—buoyed in part by the bonuses paid to investment bankers whose job it was to promote all this asset inflation in the first place. Heck, we were restoring a historic borough to its former glory. All we had to do was avoid the uncomfortable truth that we were busy converting what were being used as multifamily dwellings by poor black and Hispanic people back into stately town houses for use by rich white ones. And we had to overlook that this frenzy of real-estate activity was operating on borrowed time and, more significantly, borrowed money.

In such a climate, calling attention to any of this was the real crime, and the reason that the first reaction of those participating in a speculative bubble was to silence the messenger. It's just business. The reality was that we were pushing an increasingly hostile population from their homes, colonizing their neighborhoods, and then justifying it all with metrics such as increased business activity, reduced (reported) crime rates, and—most important—higher real-estate prices. How can one argue against making a neighborhood, well, *better*?

As my writer friend eloquently explained on his blog, the neighborhood was now, by most measures, safer. It was once again possible to sit on one's stoop with the kids and eat frozen Italian ices on a balmy summer night. One could walk through Prospect Park on any

Sunday afternoon and see a black family barbecuing here, a Puerto Rican group there, and an Irish group over there. Compared with most parts of the world, that's pretty civil, no?

Romantic as it sounds, that's not integration at all, but co-location. Epcot-style détente. The Brooklyn being described here has almost nothing to do with the one our grandparents might have inhabited. It is rather an expensive and painstakingly re-created simulation of a "brownstone Brooklyn" that never actually existed. If people once sat on their stoops eating ices on summer nights it was because they had no other choice—there was no air-conditioning and no TV. Everyone could afford to sit around, so everyone did. And the fact that the denizens of neighboring communities complete the illusion of multi-culturalism by using the same park only means that these folks are willing to barbecue next to each other—not *with* each other. They all still go home to different corners of the borough. My writer friend's kids go off the next morning to their private school, those other kids to public. Not exactly neighbors.

Besides, the rows of brownstones in the Slope aren't really made of brown stone. They've been covered with a substance more akin to stucco—a thick paint used to create the illusion of brown stones set atop one another. A façade's façade. As any brownstone owner soon learns, the underlying cinder blocks can be hidden for only so long before a costly "renovation" must be undertaken to cover them up again. Likewise, wealth, media, and metrics can insulate colonizers from the reality of their situation for only so long. Eventually, parents who push their toddlers around in thousand-dollar strollers, whose lifestyles and values have been reinforced by a multibillion-dollar industry dedicated to hip child-rearing, get pelted with stones by kids from the "projects." (Rest assured—the person who reported this recurring episode at a gentrified Brooklyn playground met with his share of online derision, as well.)

Like Californians surprised when a wildfire or coyote disrupts the "natural" lifestyle they imagined they'd enjoy out in the country, we "pioneer," "colonize," and "gentrify" at our peril, utterly oblivious to the social costs of our expansion until one comes back to bite us in the ass—or mug us on the stoop. And while it's easy to blame the larger institutions and social trends leading us into these traps, our own choices and behaviors—however influenced—are ultimately responsible for whatever befalls us.

Park Slope, Brooklyn, is just a microcosm of the slippery slope upon which so many of us are finding ourselves these days. We live in a landscape tilted toward a set of behaviors and a way of making choices that go against our own better judgment, as well as our collective self-interest. Instead of collaborating with each other to ensure the best prospects for us all, we pursue short-term advantages over seemingly fixed resources through which we can compete more effectively against one another. In short, instead of acting like people, we act like corporations. When faced with a local mugging, the community of Park Slope first thought to protect its brand instead of its people.

The financial meltdown may not be punishment for our sins, but it is at least in part the result of our widespread obsession with financial value over values of any other sort. We disconnected ourselves from what matters to us, and grew dependent on a business scheme that was never intended to serve us as people. But by adopting the ethos of this speculative, abstract economic model as our own, we have disabled the mechanisms through which we might address and correct the collapse of the real economy operating alongside it.

Even now, as we attempt to dig ourselves out of a financial mess caused in large part by this very mentality and behavior, we turn to the corporate sphere, its central banks, and shortsighted metrics to gauge our progress back to health. It's as if we believe we'll find the answer in the stream of trades and futures on one of the cable-TV finance channels instead of out in the physical world. Our real investment in the fabric of our neighborhoods and our quality of life takes a backseat to asking prices for houses like our own in the newspaper's misnamed "real estate" section. We look to the Dow Jones average as if it were the one true vital sign of our society's health, and the exchange rate of our currency as a measure of our wealth as a nation or worth as a people.

This, in turn, only distracts us further from the real-world ideas and activities through which we might actually re-create some value ourselves. Instead of fixing the problem, and reclaiming our ability to generate wealth directly with one another, we seek to prop up institutions whose very purpose remains to usurp this ability from us. We try to repair our economy by bolstering the same institutions that sapped it. In the very best years, corporatism worked by extracting value from the periphery and redirecting it to the center—away from people and toward corporate monopolies. Now, even though that wellspring of prosperity has run dry, we continue to dig deeper into the ground for resources to keep the errant system running.

So as our corporations crumble, taking our jobs with them, we bail them out to preserve our prospects for employment—knowing full well that their business models are unsustainable. As banks' credit schemes fail, we authorize our treasuries to print more money on their behalf, at our own expense and that of our children. We then get to borrow this money back from them, at interest. We know of no other way. Having for too long outsourced our own savings and investing to Wall Street, we are clueless about how to invest in the real world of people and things. We identify with the plight of abstract corporations more than that of flesh-and-blood human beings. We engage with corporations as role models and saviors, while we engage with our fellow humans as competitors to be beaten or resources to be exploited.

Indeed, the now-stalled gentrification of Brooklyn had a good deal in common with colonial exploitation. Of course, the whole thing was done with more circumspection, with more tact. The borough's gentrifiers steered away from explicitly racist justifications for their actions, but nevertheless demonstrated the colonizer's underlying agenda: instead of "chartered corporations" pioneering and subjugating an uncharted region of the world, it was hipsters, entrepreneurs, and real-estate speculators subjugating an undesirable neighborhood. The local economy—at least as measured in gross product—boomed, but the indigenous population simply became servants (grocery cashiers and nannies) to the new residents.

And like the expansion of colonial empires, this pursuit of home ownership was perpetuated by a pioneer spirit of progress and personal freedom. The ideal of home ownership was the fruit of a public-relations strategy crafted after World War II—corporate and government leaders alike believed that home owners would have more of a stake in an expanding economy and greater allegiance to free-market values than renters. Functionally, though, it led to a self-perpetuating cycle: The more that wealthier white people retreated to the enclaves prepared for them, the poorer the areas they were leaving became, and the more justified they felt in leaving. While the first real wave of "white flight" was from the cities to the suburbs, the more recent, camouflaged version has been from the suburbs back into the expensive cities.

Of course, these upper-middle-class migrants were themselves the targets of the mortgage industry, whose clever lending instruments mirror World Bank policies for their exploitative potential. The World Bank's loans come with "open markets" policies attached that ultimately surrender indebted nations and their resources to the control of distant corporations. The mortgage banker, likewise, kindly provides instruments that get a person into a home, then disappears when the rates rise through the roof, having packaged and sold off the borrower's ballooning obligation to the highest bidder.

The benefits to society are pure mythology. Whether it's Brooklynites convinced they are promoting multiculturalism, or corporations intent on extending the benefits of the free market to all the world's souls, neither activity leads to broader participation in the expansion of wealth—even when they're working as they're supposed to. Contrary to most economists' expectations, both local and global speculation only exacerbate wealth divisions. Wealthy parents send their kids to private schools and let the public ones decay, while wealthy nations export their environmental waste to the Third World or, better, simply keep their factories there to begin with—and keep their image at home as green as AstroTurf.

People I respect—my own mentors and teachers—tell me that this is just the way things are. This is the real world of adults—not so very far removed, we must remember, from the days when a neighboring tribe might just wipe you out—killing your men with clubs and taking your women. Be thankful for the civility we've got, keep your head down, and try not to think too much about it. These cycles are built into the economy; eventually, the markets will recover and things will get back to normal—and normal isn't so bad, really, if you look around the world at the way other people are living. And you shouldn't even feel so guilty about that—after all, Google is doing some good things and Bill Gates is giving a lot of money to kids in Africa.

Somehow, though, for many of us, that's not enough. We are fast approaching a societal norm where we—as nations, organizations, and individuals—engage in behaviors that are destructive to our own and everyone else's welfare. The only corporate violations worth punishing anymore are those against the shareholders. The "criminal mind" is now defined as anyone who breaks laws for a reason *other* than money. The status quo is selfishness, and the toxically wealthy are our new heroes because only they seem capable of fully insulating themselves from the effects of their own actions.

Every day, we negotiate the slope to the best of our ability. Still, we fail to measure up to the people we'd like to be, and succumb to the tilt of the landscape.

Jennifer has lived in the same town in central Minnesota her whole life. This year, diagnosed with a form of lupus, she began purchasing medication through Wal-Mart instead of through Marcus, her local druggist—who also happens to be her neighbor. Prescription drugs aren't on her health plan, and this is just an economic necessity.

Why can't the druggist cut his neighbor a break? He's trying, but he's selling at a mere hair above cost as it is. He just took out a loan against the business to make expenses and his increased rent. The downtown area he's located in has been slated for redevelopment, and only corporate chain stores appear to have deep enough pockets to pay for storefront leases. It sounded like a good idea when Marcus supported it at the public hearing—but the description in the pamphlet prepared by the real-estate developer (complete with a section on how to compete more effectively with "big box" stores like Wal-Mart) hasn't conformed to reality.

Marcus's landlord doesn't really have any choice in the matter. He underwent costly renovations to conform to the new downtown building code, and needs to pass those on to the businesses renting from him. He took out a mortgage, too, which is slated to reset in just a couple of months. If he doesn't collect higher rents, he won't make payments.

Jennifer stopped going to PTA meetings because she's embarrassed to look Marcus in the face. As their friendship declines, so does her guilt about helping put him out of business.

Across the country in New Jersey, Carla, a telephone associate for one of the top three HMO plans in the United States, talks to people like Jennifer every day. Carla is paid a salary as well as a monthly bonus based on the number of claims she can "retire" without payment. Without resorting to fraud, Carla is supposed to discourage false claims by making all claims harder to register, in general. That's how Carla's supervisor explained it to her when she asked, point-blank, if she was supposed to mislead customers. She feels bad about it, but Carla is now the principal breadwinner in her family, her husband having lost a lot of his contracting work to the stalled market for new homes. And, in the end, she *is* preventing fraud. How does Carla sleep at night, knowing that she has spent her day persuading people to pay for services for which they are actually covered? After seeing a commercial on TV, she switched from Ambien to Lunesta.

One of the guys working on that very ad campaign, an old co-worker of mine, ended up specializing in health-care advertising because nobody was hiring in the environmental area back in the '90s. Besides, he told me, only half kidding, "at least medical advertising puts the consumer in charge of her own health care." He's conflicted about pushing drugs on TV because he knows full well that these ads encourage patients to pressure doctors to write prescriptions that go against their better judgment. Still, Tom makes up for any compromise of his values at work with a staunch advocacy of good values at home. He recycles paper, glass, and metal, brought his kids to see *An Inconvenient Truth,* and even uses a compost heap in the backyard for household waste. Last year, though, he finally broke down and bought an SUV. Why? "Everybody else on the highway is driving them," he explained. "It's an automotive arms race." If he stayed in his Civic, he'd be putting them all at risk. "You see the way those people drive? I'm scared for my family." As penance, at least until gas prices went up, he began purchasing a few "carbon offsets"—a way of donating money to environmental companies in compensation for one's own excess carbon emissions.

In a similar balancing act, a self-described "holistic" parent in Manhattan spares her son the risks she associates with vaccinations for childhood diseases. "We still don't know what's in them," she says, "and if everyone else is vaccinated he won't catch these things, anyway." She understands that the vaccines required for incoming school pupils are really meant to quell epidemics; they are more for the health of the "herd" than for any individual child. She also believes that mandatory vaccinations are more a result of pharmaceutical industry lobbying than any comprehensive medical studies. In order to meet the "philosophical exemption" requirements demanded by the state, she managed to extract a letter from her rabbi. Meanwhile, in an unacknowledged quid pro quo, she installed a phone line in the rabbi's name in the basement of her town house; he uses the bill to falsify residence records and send his sons to the well-rated public elementary school in her high-rent district instead of the 90 percent minority school in his own. At least he can say he's kept them in "the public system."

Incapable of securing a legal or illegal zoning variance of this sort, a college friend of mine, now a state school administrator in Brighton, England, just made what he calls "the hardest decision of my life," to send his own kids to a private Catholic day school. He doesn't even particularly *want* his kids to be indoctrinated into Catholicism, but it's the only alternative to the eroding government school he can afford. He knows his withdrawal from public education only removes three more "good kids" and one potentially active parent from the system, but doesn't want his children to be "sacrificed on the altar" of his good intentions.

So it's not just a case of hip, hypergentrified Brooklynites succumbing to market psychology, but people of all social classes making choices that go against their better judgment because they believe it's really the only sensible way to act under the circumstances. It's as if the world itself were tilted, pushing us toward self-interested, short-term decisions, made more in the manner of corporate shareholders than members of a society. The more decisions we make in this way, the more we contribute to the very conditions leading to this awfully sloped landscape. In a dehumanizing and self-denying cycle, we make too many choices that—all things being equal—we'd prefer not to make.

But all things are not equal. These choices are not even occurring in the real world. They are the false choices of an artificial landscape—one in which our decision-making is as coerced as that of a person getting mugged. Only we've forgotten that our choices are being made under painstakingly manufactured duress. We think this is just the way things are. The price of doing business.

Since when is life determined by that axiom?

Unquestionably but seemingly inexplicably, we have come to operate in a world where the market and its logic have insinuated themselves into every area of our lives. From erection to conception, school admission to finding a spouse, there are products and professionals to fill in where family and community have failed us. Commercials entreat us to think and care for ourselves, but to do so by choosing a corporation through which to exercise all this autonomy.

Sometimes it feels as if there's just not enough air in the room—as if there were a corporate agenda guiding all human activity. At a moment's notice, any dinner party can slide invisibly into a stock promotion, a networking event, or an impromptu consultation—let me pick your brain. Is this why I was invited in the first place? Through sponsored word-of-mouth known as "buzz marketing," our personal social interactions become the promotional opportunities through which brands strive to be cults and religions strive to become brands.

It goes deeper than that second Starbucks opening on the same town's Main Street or the radio ads for McDonald's playing through what used to be emergency speakers in our public school buses. It's not a matter of how early Christmas ads start each year, how many people get trampled at Black Friday sales, or even the news report blaming the fate of the entire economy on consumers' slow holiday spending. It's more a matter of not being able to tell the difference between the ads and the content at all. It's as if both were designed to be that way. The line between fiction and reality, friend and marketer, community and shopping center, has gotten blurred. Was that a news report, reality TV, or a sponsored segment?

This fundamental blurring of real life with its commercial counterpart is not a mere question of aesthetics, however much we may dislike mini-malls and superstores. It's more of a nagging sense that something has gone awry—something even more fundamentally wrong than the credit crisis and its aftermath—yet we're too immersed in its effects to do anything about it, or even to see it. We are deep in the thrall of a system that no one really likes, no one remembers asking for, yet no one can escape. It just *is*. And as it begins to collapse around us, we work to prop it up by any means necessary, so incapable are we of imagining an alternative. The minute it seems as if we can put our finger on what's happening to us or how it came to be this way, the insight disappears, drowned out by the more immediately pressing demands by everyone and everything on our attention. What did they just say? What does that mean for my retirement account? Wait—my phone is vibrating.

Can the hermetically sealed food court in which we now subsist even be beheld from within? Perhaps not in its totality—but its development can be chronicled, and its effects can be parsed and understood. Just as we once evolved from subjects into citizens, we have now devolved from citizens into consumers. Our communities have been reduced to affinity groups, and any vestige of civic engagement or neighborly goodwill has been replaced by self-interested goals manufactured for us by our corporations and their PR firms. We've surrendered true participation for the myth of consumer choice or, even more pathetically, that of shareholder rights.

That's why it has become fashionable, cathartic, and to some extent useful for the defenders of civil society to rail against the corporations that seem to have conquered our civilization. As searing new books and documentaries about the crimes of corporations show us, the corporation is itself a sociopathic entity, created for the purpose of generating wealth and expanding its reach by any means necessary. A corporation has no use for ethics, except for their potential impact on public relations and brand image. In fact, as many on the side of the environment, labor, and the Left like to point out, corporate managers can be sued for taking any action, however ethical, if it compromises their ultimate fiduciary responsibility to share price.

As corporations gain ever more control over our economy, government, and culture, it is only natural for us to blame them for the helplessness we now feel over the direction of our personal and collective destinies. But it is both too easy and utterly futile to point the finger of blame at corporations or the robber barons at their helms—not even those handcuffed CEOs gracing the cover of the business section. Not even mortgage brokers, credit-card executives, or the Fed. This state of affairs isn't being entirely orchestrated from the top of a glass building by an élite group of bankers and businessmen, however much everyone would like to think so—themselves included. And while the growth of corporations and a preponderance of corporate activity have allowed them to permeate most every aspect of our awareness and activity, these entities are not solely responsible for the predicament in which we have found ourselves.

Rather, it is corporatism itself: a logic we have internalized into our very being, a lens through which we view the world around us, and an ethos with which we justify our behaviors. Making matters worse, we accept its dominance over us as preexisting—as a given circumstance of the human condition. It just *is*.

But it isn't.

Corporatism didn't evolve naturally. The landscape on which we are living—the operating system on which we are now running our social software—was invented by people, sold to us as a better way of life, supported by myths, and ultimately allowed to develop into a self-sustaining reality. It is a map that has replaced the territory.

Its basic laws were set in motion as far back as the Renaissance;

it was accelerated by the Industrial Age; and it was sold to us as a better way of life by a determined generation of corporate leaders who believed they had our best interests at heart and who ultimately succeeded in their dream of controlling the masses from above. We have succumbed to an ideology that has the same intellectual underpinnings and assumptions about human nature as—dare we say it—mid-twentieth-century fascism. Given how the word has been misapplied to everyone from police officers to communists, we might best refrain from resorting to what has become a feature of cheap polemic. But in this case it's accurate, and that we're forced to dance around this "F word" today would certainly have pleased Goebbels greatly.

The current situation resembles the managed capitalism of Mussolini's Italy, in particular. It shares a common intellectual heritage (in disappointed progressives who wanted to order society on a scientific understanding of human nature), the same political alliance (the collaboration of the state and the corporate sector), and some of the same techniques for securing consent (through public relations and propaganda). Above all, it shares with fascism the same deep suspicion of free humans.

And, as with any absolutist narrative, calling attention to the inherent injustice and destructiveness of the system is understood as an attempt to undermine our collective welfare. The whistle-blower is worse than just a spoilsport; he is an enemy of the people.

Unlike Europe's fascist dictatorships, this state of affairs came about rather bloodlessly—at least on the domestic front. Indeed, the real lesson of the twentieth century is that the battle for total social control would be waged and won not through war and overt repression, but through culture and commerce. Instead of depending on a paternal dictator or nationalist ideology, today's system of control depends on a society fastidiously cultivated to see the corporation and its logic as central to its welfare, value, and very identity.

That's why it's no longer Big Brother who should frighten us— however much corporate lobbies still seek to vilify anything to do with government beyond their own bailouts. Sure, democracy may be the quaint artifact of an earlier era, but what has taken its place? Suspension of habeas corpus, surveillance of citizens, and the occasional repression of voting notwithstanding, this mess is not the fault of a particular administration or political party, but of a culture, economy, and belief system that places market priorities above life itself. It's not the fault of a government or a corporation, the news media or the entertainment industry, but the merging of all these entities into a single, highly centralized authority with the ability to write laws, issue money, and promote its expansion into our world.

Then, in a last cynical surrender to the logic of corporatism, we assume the posture and behaviors of corporations in the hope of restoring our lost agency and security. But the vehicles to which we gain access in this way are always just retail facsimiles of the real ones. Instead of becoming true landowners we become mortgage holders. Instead of guiding corporate activity we become shareholders. Instead of directing the shape of public discourse we pay to blog. We can't compete against corporations on a playing field that was created for their benefit alone.

This is the landscape of corporatism: a world not merely dominated by corporations, but one inhabited by people who have internalized corporate values as our own. And even now that corporations appear to be waning in their power, they are dragging us down with them; we seem utterly incapable of lifting ourselves out of *their* depression.

We need to understand how this happened—how we came to live for and through a business scheme. We must recount the story of how life itself became corporatized, and figure out what——if anything—we are to do about it.

While we will find characters to blame for one thing or another, most of corporatism's architects have long since left the building—and even they were usually acting with only their immediate, short-term profits in mind. Our object instead should be to understand the process by which we were disconnected from the real world and why we remain disconnected from it. This is our best hope of regaining some relationship with terra firma again. Like recovering cult victims, we have less to gain from blaming our seducers than from understanding our own participation in building and maintaining a corporatist society. Only then can we begin dismantling and replacing it with something more livable and sustainable.

LIFE INC

CHAPTER ONE

ONCE REMOVED: THE CORPORATE LIFE-FORM

Charters and the Disconnect from Commerce

If You Can't Beat Them . . .

Commerce is good. It's the way people create and exchange value.

Corporatism is something else entirely. Though not completely distinct from commerce or the free market, the corporation is a very specific entity, first chartered by monarchs for reasons that have very little to do with helping people carry out transactions with one another. Its purpose, from the beginning, was to suppress lateral interactions between people or small companies and instead redirect any and all value they created to a select group of investors.

This agenda was so well embedded into the philosophy, structure, and practice of the earliest chartered corporations that it still characterizes the activity of both corporations and real people today. The only difference today is that most of us, corporate chiefs included, have no idea of these underlying biases, or how automatically we are compelled by them. That's why we have to go back to the birth of the corporation itself to understand how the tenets of corporatism established themselves as the default social principles of our age.

There were three main stages in the evolution of the corporation, and each one further imprinted corporatism on the collective human psyche. The corporation was born in the Renaissance, granted personhood in post–Civil War America, and then, in the twentieth century, branded as the benevolent guardian and savior of humankind.

Most history books recount the development of the corporate charter as a natural, almost evolutionary step in the advancement of commerce. To a certain extent, this is true. After the fall of the Roman Empire, early Middle Ages Europe fell into disarray. Europeans lived in isolation from one another, dominated by self-sufficient and self-governing rural manors. Feudalism, as the prevailing political system came to be called, wasn't a particularly fun way to live—certainly not for the peasants who made up a majority of the continent's population. Landowning lords gave tracts of land to vassals in return for military allegiance. Vassals, in turn, ruled the peasant farmers, who were usually permitted to subsist on the remnants of their crops. Unlike in the Roman Empire, laws varied widely from place to place.

The lack of an overriding system of commerce left the lords out of a significant but growing business sector: the activity occurring between the people of different manors and beyond. By the 1200s, technological developments such as water mills and windmills as well as increased travel and commerce led to the resurgence of towns and cities outside the lord's direct control. Towns became centers for the manufacturing, exchange, and circulation of goods, and provided a stark contrast to the to-each-his-own way of life in the manors and villages. In their new urban setting serfs found legal freedom, opportunities for work, and a place to start afresh. Citizens of cities became known as "burghers," a term that spread throughout medieval Western Europe and provided the basis for the later word "bourgeoisie."

It was only a matter of time before the burghers would grow wealthier and potentially even more powerful than the aristocracy. Instead of depending on the ownership of a fixed tract of land farmed by peasants and protected by an expensive army of vassals, this new class of merchants and manufacturers could increase production, commerce, and acquisition almost infinitely. The marketplace where they transacted could grow as large as it needed to accommodate more and more trade, simply by spilling outside the city center. The town then naturally expanded around the new location, and this cycle would continue until the town would eventually blossom into a full-fledged city, which would in turn require more goods and commerce, and so on. Lords attempted to regulate all this trade and growth by controlling and taxing local markets, but people always found ways around these boundaries and restrictions.

One such boundary crosser was the merchant, who resurged in about the thirteenth century to serve as an intermediary between town and country, providing the first links in the chain connecting the movement of goods between producer, merchant, and retailer. On non-market days, cobblers, blacksmiths, and artisans were accustomed to selling their wares through the windows of their workshops. By allowing merchants to set up their own shops and sell these items for them, the artisans got more time to do what they did best. Shop owners did not specialize in actually making anything, but in generating profit through selling. Business for business's sake was born. Over the next few generations, along with the traders, moneylenders, and investors who backed them, these retailers would become the core of the urban bourgeoisie. While the nobility declined in land ownership, finances, and power—as well as numbers—this new class of pure merchants had access to international trade, investment, and an alternative economy.

Worse yet for the aristocracy, as merchants set sail they were to benefit from the vast resources of other territories. While the new bourgeoisie were becoming members of the fledgling global marketplace, the traditional aristocracy was essentially landlocked. What official authority they had left to offer their subjects was diminishing as rapidly as their wealth, influence, and numbers.

The aristocracy longed for a way to participate in the new economy—a way to invest that didn't put them or their good names at any risk. For their part, the new merchant class had certainly increased the speed and breadth of wealth creation—but this also made for a highly competitive and fluid business environment. Sudden wealth could be followed by a sudden wipeout if a single ship got lost at sea or a fire took down an entire workshop. Merchant businesses were still mostly family run, and rarely operated more than a few voyages before a shipwreck or other calamity took them down. They needed a way to institutionalize their success while they were on top, right after their ship had come in.

This is the landscape on which the Renaissance was to take place and a new way of conducting business was to emerge. The overriding priority was not to promote economic activity, global cooperation, or colonial expansion, but rather to freeze all this development in a particular position, and prevent the cast of characters at the top from changing too much over time. But locking down wealth was a lot harder for everyone now that so much innovation was going on—especially when success tended to come with a loss in competence. In fact, while the Renaissance is often celebrated for its emphasis on specialization and expertise, nothing could be further from the truth.

The division of labor is not the same thing as the specialization of labor. On the surface, it may appear that a society of merchants, managers, and various levels of laborers is more specialized than one of shopkeepers and artisans. But it was not to the manager's advantage to hire highly specialized laborers who could demand higher wages. Instead, managers standardized processes in order to hire the least qualified and most replaceable laborers around. Far from encouraging specialization, competence, or innovation, all this mercantile and industrial activity actually favored generalization.

As the population grew and the demands for goods increased, open land became privatized. This uprooted rural peasants, forcing them into the generic labor market. Previously, the life of a rural peasant had been below or altogether removed from money and the market found in urban centers. Peasants made do with what they could produce with their own hands and barter locally. It was a life of great limitation, but also of self-sufficiency. As the commercial economy spread, the peasant had to turn the only marketable skill he had—physical labor—into his means of survival. Evidence of this sort of wage labor can be traced all the way back to Portugal in 1253. Just like the Home Depot parking lot where Mexican immigrant laborers gather today, there were designated meeting places, usually a square at sunrise, where a foreman representing an employer would meet with day laborers and hire them right off the street.

Meanwhile, the managerial class sought to diversify itself as quickly as possible, undermining any specialization of its own. Once a low-level shopkeeper or wage earner had saved enough money to make the first step into more advanced levels of commerce, his first move was to commission the very work he used to perform. Then he began diversifying his wares and financial activities. The higher the capitalist was on the economic ladder, the broader and more varied were his investments and enterprises—and the more disconnected he was from his business's skills and the people performing them.

So both the aristocracy and the most successful of the mercantile class required a new mechanism through which they could invest their almost "generic" capital in the form of pure financial and legal power. This mechanism had to offer the ability to invest in a business with total discretion, anonymity, limited liability, passive participation, and little or no expertise.

Traditional family businesses, which shared labor, risk, and capital by blood ties, were no longer sufficient to the task. New kinds of laws, contracts, and standardized currencies would be required to extend these agreements to people of different families and regions. Florence, with its key location on the Mediterranean (as well as its widely accepted currency, the gold florin), became the birthplace of the first "limited partnership" firms. The precursors to full-fledged corporations, they distinguished between the liability of the firm's directors and of those who merely contributed capital, who would only be responsible for the amount of their contribution. Furthermore, contributors were not subject to being listed among the business partners, allowing noblemen, and even monarchs, to hide their commercial interests. The concept of the limited partnership quickly spread throughout Europe, funding daring investments from mines and plantations to colonialist adventures. Through this new opportunity for quiet and passive participation, the nobility became mad for investing.

As the operators of these huge projects sought to secure even more capital from a wider range of regions and social classes, they formed a more advanced form of limited partnership called the joint stock company, which could generate investment from shareholders on an open market. This broke business open, allowing for the creation of businesses by virtually anyone capable of getting investors. It almost heralded an era of business meritocracy, which would have generated unprecedented churn in the class structure. The wealthiest merchants were now as vulnerable to upstarts as the aristocracy.

Finally, the monarchy had something it could offer the bourgeoisie who threatened to unseat them.

A Child Is Born

Although monarchs might have lacked the vast financial resources of joint stock companies, they still enjoyed a structural advantage over any of them: central legal authority. Taking a cue from the Church, which had a tradition of "incorporating" groups of monks into single entities, royals exercised their authority to sanction a new kind of chartered body: the corporation. It was genius.

The corporation was not a business or a government entity, but a combination of the two. Its government supporters—the monarchs—had the authority to write the trade laws and grant monopolies; its business participants—the chartered companies—would enjoy the exclusive right to exploit them.

By granting a specific joint stock company a legal charter to do business, monarchs could give it a monopoly control of its business sector. So a shipping company that once competed with others for the resources of a set of islands now enjoyed exclusive, royally mandated control over that domain. No other corporation could do business in that region, and even locals or colonists would be prohibited by law from competing against the corporation extracting their resources or selling them goods. Another corporation would be granted monopoly control over glass production; another would win beer, and so on. By issuing corporate charters, kings could empower those most loyal to them with permanent control over their colonial regions or industries.

The joint stock companies' problem with competition from rising new businesses or local activity was solved. And in return for granting legally enforceable monopolies over particular industries and regions, monarchs got fiscal support and profit participation far exceeding the worth of any cash investment they could have made. As a Dutch lawyer explained in a letter describing the very first charter of this sort, for Holland's East India Company, "The state ought to rejoice at the existence of an association which pays it so much money every year that the country derives three times as much profit from trade and navigation in the Indies as the shareholders."

For merchants whose businesses previously lasted only as long as a single expedition, the arrangement offered a way to earn more permanent status, military protection from the Crown, and the right to exploit new regions and peoples with authority and impunity. Equally important, they could lose no more than their initial investment. The "limited liability" granted in a charter meant that a corporation's debts died with the bankruptcy of the corporation. And bankruptcy protection was granted by the state.

By inventing this virtual entity—the chartered corporation—the aristocracy and the bourgeoisie entered into a mutual codependency that changed the character of both. Through these first great trade monopolies, such as England's Muscovy Company of 1555, the British East India Company of 1600, or the Dutch United East India Company of 1602, monarchs found a way to extend their reach without the cost or liability of an official military expedition. Better yet: for the monarchs, the merchants running the corporation would now become loyal subjects, dependent on the Crown for their legitimacy, protection, and escape clauses.

The chartered corporation was a bold grasp for permanent rule and permanent wealth that constituted a stalemate between the two groups. The contracts that monarchs and mercantilists wrote not only stopped their own decline from power; they stopped time, locking in place a set of corporatist priorities that to this day have not significantly changed. Instead, these priorities work to change the world and its people to conform to the rules of corporatism.

People who had always engaged in business with one another would now be required to do so through monopoly powers. All lateral contact between people and businesses would now be mediated through central authorities. Any creation or exchange of value would have to be run through these centrally mandated companies, in a system enforced by law, controlled by currency, and perpetuated through the erosion of all other connections between people and their world. Moreover, the emphasis of business would shift from the creation of value by people to the extraction of value by corporations.

In the new corporate scheme, the profitability and authority of a company now depended on its *centrality*. The more powerful the king, the more dominion a chartered company could enjoy. Where successful companies once threatened the authority of the state, now they contributed to it. While earlier companies benefited from a landscape on which value could be created independently of established power structures, these new, chartered corporations were *part of* the established power structures. The more that currency, law, and belief systems favored trade conducted at a great distance and orchestrated by a central authority, the better off chartered corporations were. Merchants who originally came to power in a bottom-up fashion were now maintaining their positions through borrowed top-down authority. Their power was no longer earned in real time, but mandated by proxy; their business practices were no longer dependent on value created but value extracted.

Meanwhile, and almost certainly unintentionally, the abstract and independent nature of the corporation gave it a life and agenda of its own. The more such corporations came to dominate business and finance, the more that legal and social systems evolved to serve them. Most of the business and finance innovations of the early corporate era—inventions we still look on fondly today—were really just ways of preserving and extending the reach of this new business entity.

The health of a corporation was understood purely in terms of money, as measured by the new accounting technique of double-entry bookkeeping. Any transaction resulted in the debiting of one account and the crediting of another. This made achieving a favorable balance of trade the highest priority, and fostered a zero-sum-game mentality among all participants. International trade became a fierce competition between states for positive balances, which led to wars unlike any seen before.

Where armies and navies had for most countries consisted of temporary forces raised to wage a specific conflict, the emergence of corporations with long-term agendas now necessitated full-time professional armed forces. This, in turn, led monarchs to raise sufficient quantities of hard currency to support their militaries. Corporations were happy to pay the levies for military protection—as long as they gained more influence over state policies protecting them from competition. And thus the cycle reinforced itself.

As businesses and states alike began to see the world through the lens of corporatism, places became "territories," people became "laborers," money became "capital," and laws became "game rules." For this was the embedded bias of the charter itself: to maintain the *central authority* of the state while granting *monopoly power* to the corporation. Corporatism. Real things, such as human beings, land, and resources, only mattered insomuch as they kept the credit side of the balance sheet bigger than the debit side. The underlying bias of corporatism would be that everything, and everyone, could be colonized for a profit. Anything and anyone would be incorporated, as long as they increased the power of a central authority that in turn promoted the monopolies of its chartered corporations.

The rise of European imperialism itself can be attributed to this new perspective. Thanks to the distance and limited liability offered by the new corporate entity, the people enacting policies and making decisions were effectively removed from any personal connection to the repercussions of their actions. The less liable for and connected to their choices, the less responsibility they felt and culpability they incurred. Besides, corporations outlived any human individual or monarch, anyway.

My Oppressor, My Hero

By the seventeenth and eighteenth centuries, monarchs were unflaggingly catering to the merchant corporations that fed them. Whenever state favoritism became too overt and subjects or colonists revolted, monarchs eased restrictions on the people and promoted their favorite corporations' interests through preferential taxes and duties instead. Everything went through corporations; even the Pilgrims' famous voyage to America was made on a chartered British East India Company ship, the *Mayflower*, which was actually on its fourth such trip to the continent. The corporation had already claimed—and been granted—the entire American coast. Successive waves of colonists were appreciated solely for their capacity to enhance the credit column of the ledger back home.

The East India Company lobbied vigorously for laws that would help it quell any competition from the colonists. This was a particularly easy sell since the royals and governors they were lobbying also happened to be shareholders. Laws forbidding colonists to actually fabricate anything from the resources they grew and mined made self-sufficiency or local economic prosperity impossible. "An Act for the Restraining and Punishing of Pirates" defined the import of tea from anyone other than the Company as smuggling. The Townshend Acts of 1767 and the Tea Act of 1773 helped the Company unload a surplus of tea accumulated in British warehouses by removing all barriers to trade as well as granting tax exemptions. "No taxation without representation"—the rallying cry that led to the Boston Tea Party—wasn't about voting as much as about Britain's passage of tax laws to the exclusive benefit of the East India Company. The American Revolution itself was less a revolt by colonists against Britain than by small businessmen against the chartered multinational corporation writing her laws.

This is why the founders so carefully limited the reach and scope of corporate power in newly independent America. Corporations were to be chartered by states, not by the federal government, so that their actions could be governed locally by those affected. Corporations were also required to demonstrate that they had a specific beneficial purpose other than making money—such as getting a bridge built or a waterway opened. Having fought against a foreign megacorporation, the founders understood the dangers inherent in the kind of centralized economic authority demanded by corporatism. Just like Adam Smith, they hated big government and big corporations alike, envisioning the ideal business landscape characterized by locally scaled firms and farmers, unencumbered by large, dehumanizing monopolies. Thomas Jefferson considered "freedom from monopolies" one of the fundamental human rights. James Madison praised self-sufficiency and appropriately scaled enterprises: "The class of citizens who provide at once their own food and their own raiment, may be viewed as the most truly independent and happy. They are more: they are the best basis of public liberty, and the strongest bulwark of public safety." It was as if they meant to reverse the effect of the Renaissance-conceived corporate charter.

Still, due largely in part to the tremendous Revolutionary War debt, early American politics was dominated by a division over whether or not the United States, like European nations, should have a strong central government that was also capable of granting corporate charters and running a bank. Jefferson argued unsuccessfully against Federalists George Washington and John Adams for the Bill of Rights to include "freedom from monopolies in commerce" and to forbid the creation of a permanent army. This back-and-forth continued for the next century. One administration or Congress would pass laws favorable to corporations, and then the next would attempt to rescind them. But because they could live on indefinitely, corporations simply waited for conditions to change, made what progress they could, and then waited some more.

The second great phase in the evolution of the corporate life-form would take place under Abraham Lincoln, who had built his legal career fighting on behalf of the Illinois Central Railroad, and then used the privilege of free rail travel the job afforded to keep his presidential-campaign costs low. With Lincoln's help the railroads won the right to break unions, hire immigrants for up to a year by paying for their passage to America, and—most important—enjoy strong contractual advantages that people didn't have. According to successive pieces of legislation he signed in the early 1860s, if a corporation broke a contract with another corporation, it was still to be paid for the portion of the contract it had fulfilled. But if a human being broke a contract with a corporation, he was entitled to no payment whatsoever. The playing field itself was changed to give corporations rights that people lacked.

The only privilege corporations were still denied was that of personhood itself. If only corporations could get a court to consider them people, they would be entitled to all the rights that real people got in the Constitution and the Bill of Rights. The rail companies understood this well, and fought for the "personhood" argument in every court case they entered—whether it applied or not. The passage of the Fourteenth Amendment, written to guarantee the rights of citizenship to former slaves, gave corporate lawyers the legal framework to make their cases. For reasons historians can't quite articulate, the Amendment uses the phrase "persons" instead of "natural persons." Corporations argued that this was because it was meant to include their own, non-natural personhood. In their opinions, justices repeatedly scolded corporate lawyers for attempting to exploit a law written on behalf of emancipated slaves. But the corporations had patience, and opportunistically sought out every leak and crack in the system.

Finally, in 1886, in a legal maneuver that has yet to be conclusively explained, a Supreme Court clerk with documented affinity for corporate interests incorrectly summarized an opinion in the headnotes of the decision on *Santa Clara County v. Southern Pacific Railroad Company*. The clerk wrote, "The defendant corporations are persons within the intent of the clause in section 1 of the Fourteenth Amendment to the Constitution . . . which forbids a State to deny to any person within its jurisdiction the equal protection of the laws." There was no legal basis for this statement, nor any discussion about it from the justices. From then on, however, corporations were free to claim the rights of personhood. The more precedents that were established, the more embedded the law became. Over the next twenty-five years, 307 Fourteenth Amendment cases went before the Supreme Court. Two hundred eighty-eight of them were brought by corporations claiming their rights as natural persons.

The elevation of corporations to personhood was accompanied by a slow, corresponding devolution of human beings to something *less* than personhood. Corporations were bigger than people, lived longer, had more money and more influence. The biases programmed into them four centuries earlier, however—to thwart local activity, prevent competition, and disconnect people from their resources and competencies—remained the same, regardless of the circumstances. Traditionally, the distance between corporations and the people or territories they exploited was a matter of geography, class, and race. But America was *already* a colony, and its people had been raised on an ideology of equality, freedom, and agency. The Industrial Age gave corporations a new way to create the illusion of a preordained social order: the machine.

Originally, the steam engine was developed as a means of sucking water out of mine shafts in order to get to the coal beneath. Until the abolition of slavery, American industrialists saw no role for this contraption in agriculture or industry, where the human body was still the primary energy source. When slavery became untenable, a reconfigured steam engine rose to the occasion, accomplishing with coal what used to be done with indentured muscle, and what we now call the Industrial Revolution began. Coal allowed for the mechanized factory, the locomotive, and, perhaps most important, the steamship. With coal-powered boats, newly industrialized Western nations—predominantly Britain—were capable of distributing their manufactured goods to their colonies, as well as enforcing military superiority and the trade policies that went along with them. Legislation required the colonies in India to use mechanized looms, for example, so that the ready availability of human labor in that region could not compete with England's mechanical replacements.

The increased mechanization of labor in the United States, where freedom was supposed to rule, proved a bit more troublesome. Machines now controlled the rate at which people worked, and the assembly line further reduced the autonomy and humanity of workers by relegating them to a single, repetitive task. Early industrialists, such as Andrew Carnegie, Henry Ford, and particularly John D. Rockefeller, were constantly on guard for labor unrest, and not averse to resorting to violence when necessary. It was a bad strategy. Union busting only provoked progressive newspapers to attack the industrialists, leading to further unrest, more violence, ugly interventions by the National Guard, and even some legislation against corporate power.

As an alternative to overt repression, the industrialists sought to develop a cultural ethos more simpatico with corporate prosperity. In their new world picture, machines became the model for society, and people were the cogs within it—increasingly disconnected from their own sense of technical expertise or whatever unique contributions they might make to the process of production. They were replaceable. The function of the industrial corporation was to extract value from people's work, for the economic benefit of the nation. This meant disconnecting people from the wealth they might be creating through their labors, and substituting a less costly sense of satisfaction or, at the very least, compliance.

So leading industrialists funded public schools—at once gifts to the working class and powerful tools for growing a more docile labor force. They hired education reformers, like Stanford's Ellwood P. Cubberley, to design a public school system based on a Prussian method that sought to produce what he called "mediocre intellects . . . and ensure docile citizens." Cubberley modeled our public schools after "factories, in which the raw product [the children] are to be shaped and fashioned . . . according to the specifications laid down."

Still, a public school system alone didn't guarantee a compliant population—not when intellectuals, artists, philosophers, and labor-union organizers still seemed to emerge from its ranks and so easily foment dissidence wherever they went. Henry Ford, in particular, identified this ability to breed discontent with the Jews—not the real Jews people might know as neighbors, but the more abstract Jews and Jewish ideology thought to be running and ruining the world. The anti-Semitic diatribes Ford published formed the foundation for the anti-Semitism incorporated by Hitler into his book *Mein Kampf.* Hitler even quoted Ford, with attribution. And though Ford might have been more vocal about the need to eliminate Jews than most of his fellows, he was hardly alone in his support of Nazi-style fascism. American corporations from General Electric to the Brown Brothers Harriman bank either funded the Nazis directly, or set up money-laundering schemes on their behalf. Though well financed, this effort to order the world by force would fail.

While Henry Ford was busy compiling his perverse pamphlets on the power of industry and the Jewish obstacles to corporatism, brighter propagandists with even loftier goals were still working on behalf of government. Although he had run for reelection to the presidency in 1916 on a "peace" platform, Woodrow Wilson eventually decided that America needed to get involved in World War I. With the help of some of the first practitioners of the new science of public relations, including a young Edward Bernays, he formed the Creel Commission, whose job was to change America's mind. It worked, and it served as the model for what would become known as mass communications.

Bernays and his cohorts, just like Ford, honestly believed that the masses were too stupid to make decisions for themselves—particularly when they involved global affairs or economics. Early public-relations specialists were convinced by Freud (Bernays's uncle) and a century of savage wars that human beings could never overcome their bestial instincts. Instead of letting them rule themselves, an enlightened and informed élite would need to make the decisions, and then "sell" them to the public in the form of faux populist media campaigns. This way, the masses could believe they were coming up with these opinions themselves.

But particularly after the perceived failures of the League of Nations and two world wars to lay the groundwork for a peaceful world order, Bernays and those of his ilk no longer believed that this enlightened élite was to be found in the chambers of government, or that this was even the power center from which to direct the mob. Bernays turned instead to the boardrooms of corporations. If democracy is a sham, why bother to prop up its impotent leaders? Consumers are easier to please than citizens, anyway: simply get people to believe in corporations as the great actors of civilization, and in consumption as the surest path to personal fulfillment.

Besides, the more influential the public-relations industry became in the electoral process, the more corporate funding was required to put anyone in office. By the late 1940s, it was already very clear which way the power was flowing: toward a corporately governed industrial society that had much less to do with politics than it did with commerce and capital. So the public-relations industry eventually turned

its back on an already cynical version of democracy, and focused its efforts on supporting an institution it believed really did stand a chance
of organizing the savage world with far less messy voter intervention:
the corporation.

This was not a devious plan, but a hopeful model for controlling
human beings and their unpredictable group behavior, as well as keeping an economic engine in motion without an all-consuming war to
motivate our production and resource extraction. As the nation's best
engineers and economists unanimously agreed after World War II, the
tremendous strides made in wartime technology simply had to be retooled for a postwar era. Although everyone from computer scientists
and the Frankfurt School to President Eisenhower warned of the dangers of a military-industrial complex promoted through mass spectacle, the engines of production could not be slowed for the specious
priorities of civically engaged workers or an artwork's "aura."

The disconnections inherent in industrialized culture would thus
extend beyond the division between management and labor to include
the distance between consumer and producer. The rise of factory-
made products and a rail system to transport them meant that consumers no longer knew exactly where their goods came from or, more
important, the people who made them. The "brand" emerged to serve
that function, to put a face on the oats, beverages, and automobiles we
bought, and eventually elevating them from commodities to icons.
The new corporatism would use television to stoke desires, and factories to fulfill them.

Mass media stimulated the new mass market and created a sense of
trust between people and the corporate-created brands that were bidding for their attention. Marketing through media also became a kind
of science, ruled by the same principles and ethos as the factory floor.
Everything from spokesmodels to theme songs were tested on sam-
ples of potential consumers for their efficacy in eliciting a positive response. This made us all, in one sense, parts of the machine. Goods
were developed by industrialists, manufactured in factories, shipped
via rail or interstate highways, and then sold to consumers whose ap-
petites were already whetted by commercial television. The more dependent Americans and our economy became on this model, the more
America remodeled itself to its demands.

Suburbs such as Levittown, New York, guaranteed that each family
would own an individual house, car, and entertainment system. And

the more individualized consumers became—the more separated in their own suburban homes, isolated from their communities and totally self-reliant—the more stuff they would need to buy. Independence from one another meant increasing dependence on the companies that served us.

For those who might yet remember—or, worse, talk openly about—better times, a new ethos was developed that valued the future over the past, and progress over nostalgia. Public-relations and advertising chiefs borrowed the most persuasive features of the spectacles staged by their Nazi counterparts—and in some cases employed some of the very same architects—to stage new spectacles on behalf of the American corporation.

World's Fairs in 1939 and again in 1964 offered the experience of a future America where a benevolent corporation would address every need imaginable. AT&T, GM, and the U.S. Rubber Company sponsored utopian pavilions with names such as Pool of Industry and the Avenue of Transportation. Corporations would take us into the automobile age, the space age, and even the computer age. No matter the sponsor, the overarching message was the same: American-style corporatism would create a bright future for us all.

The intelligentsia played along. Former socialist academics and Nazi expatriates alike were finding easy money in the form of research grants from both the military and industry if they recanted their prior socioeconomic theories and promoted the new corporatism. Many of these academics, like James Burnham, professed the benefits of an industry-led "American Empire," which, like the Roman Empire that conquered Greece, would "be, if not literally worldwide in formal boundaries, capable of exercising decisive world control." Freshly graduated psychologists, now willingly in the service of marketers, conducted the first "focus groups" to determine how and why people buy things. Slowly but surely a new definition of self as "consumer" penetrated the mass psyche.

The scores of economic, management, urban-planning, and marketing theories to emerge from this effort were almost invariably geared toward making one part or another of the industrial machine work more efficiently: motivate production, stimulate consumption, assimilate impediments. No matter how humanistic in their wording, or how focused on giving people what they *really* wanted or needed, these techniques were only "creative" in their ability to tweak the great engine of commerce. They all came down to manufacturing, shipping, and selling more stuff for greater profit and in less time.

As a result, our physical, commercial, spiritual, and personal accomplishments came to be valued only insofar as they could serve the market. And while the market may be as good a model as any for human interaction, the corporate terrain did not represent a level playing field or a "free market" in which value might be created from anywhere. Remember—in spite of its individualistic mythology of open competition, the landscape of corporatism was first cultivated during the Renaissance, when local currencies were outlawed in favor of centralized money. In the United States, in an assumption of centralized value creation that reached a crescendo under the Nixon administration, the Federal Reserve won the authority to create money by fiat, based on nothing but faith in its own corporate chutzpah.

The massive potential of computers and networking, technologies developed in many cases by engineers hoping to decentralize the very power structures funding their projects, was quickly recontextualized as a market opportunity—the beginning of a "long boom"—and appropriated as NASDAQ's stepchild. New rules for a new economy were invented, in which people's ability to access interactive technology for free or to create value independent of any corporation could be understood as the power of the network to leverage what were formerly "externalities." The dot-com boosters sought to reconcile the incompatibility of an abundant, decentralized media space with the legacy of a scarce, centralized monetary system. Everything is "open source," except, of course, money itself.

Instead of serving to reconnect us, our technologies now serve to disconnect us further, reducing our contact to virtual prods and pokes. Meanwhile, corporations are finding online a path toward incarnation: Chase and Coca-Cola build avatars in online environments such as the Second Life "virtual world" that are as real as we are. Sometimes more so, especially as our life and status online dictate or even supersede our life and status in the former real world.

The institutions of last resort, be they religious or nonprofit, are themselves in the thrall of the marketing techniques employed on behalf of their corporate rivals. Instead of presenting alternatives to totalitarian corporatism, they conclude that "if you can't beat them, join them." Religions hire consultants to re-brand them in the image of MTV, while charities refashion themselves into for-profit corporations seeking "social-philanthropy" money as sexy to venture capital-ists as an Internet IPO (initial public offering of shares). Even those who seek to overturn what they see as the corporate hegemony succumb to the logic of corporatism in their campaigns.

It's not just that the landscape is sloped toward corporate interests, but that our own beliefs and activities are directed by corporate logic. When those of us alive today have no memory of a world that functioned in any other way, how are we to think otherwise? Like kids with a radio dial that plays nothing but Top 40 songs, we have adapted to the music that we hear, and choose our favorite tunes and pop heroes from the available menagerie.

With no other choice available, we grow up partnering with corporations for our very identities. A kid's selection of sneaker brand says more about him than his creative-writing assignments do, and is approached with greater care. Our ability to actually do anything about, say, greenhouse-gas emissions is based entirely on the extent to which we can trust Toyota's claims about developing a car that cleans the air as it drives. Our feedback and participation are managed by customer service, empowering us as consumers by infantilizing us as human beings. This dependency augurs a regression on our part, and a transference of parental authority onto our corporations that recalls our ancestors' allegiance to emperors and high priests.

While some corporations may serve as our accepted public enemies, others quickly step in to embody our dissent. Ford's contention that it knew the one right car for every American was countered by GM's repackaging of its cars in personalized brands for each of us. As much as Microsoft frightens us by echoing the tactics of chartered monopolies, Apple and Google excite us by presenting the illusion of a bottom-up, people-centered alternative. We hate Nike and love Airwalk, hate Hummer and love Mini, hate Nabisco and love Hain, hate A&P and love Whole Foods. Or vice versa.

But we all love corporations.

Role Reversal

The last century of media-enhanced public relations set in motion something the founding fathers simply couldn't have imagined: a corporate sphere in cahoots not only with a corrupt government, but with the people. *We* are the new collaborators, engaging with one another and the world at large through these artificial actors. As we do, our behaviors become increasingly predictable, our lives more predetermined, and our awareness of alternatives to corporate-enabled autonomy diminished. It's just the way things are and—as far as we can tell—have always been.

The more disconnected and predictable we become, of course, the less *alive* we are by all measures that matter, and the more our corporations take on a life of their own. On the synthetic landscape of corporatism, corporations are the indigenous creatures and we are the aliens. They function better than we can, because our laws—even our roads, neighborhoods, and political processes—are written to favor their activity over our own. We must work through them rather than through each other, which only worsens our disconnected predictability. We surrender our agency, losing the free will that makes us human. We have reversed roles.

The landscape of corporatism favors the selfish over the social, the brand over the product, and the central over the local. This is why our search for solutions has been so stunted; we look for nationally branded answers to problems that can be approached only on a local or a personal level. We are drawn to solutions that offer the same instant gratification as consumption, the same frictionless immediacy as high-end salesmanship. Political leaders have all the emotional power—and insubstantiality—of the tested images on which their campaigns are based. As long as we experience the world from the perspective of its corporate conglomerates, we will remain oblivious to the activity and opportunities still available to us on a human scale. We will continue to fight on a battlefield that was created to benefit corporate actors while disempowering and dehumanizing real people. And the longer we limit our activity to this synthetic sphere, the further we mistake this artificial landscape for the territory on which we are to act.

The corporation is a significant but invented institution—and the impact of its invention on our relationship to one another and the world around us was as significant as the invention of an abstract God. For while it might be said that the invention of monotheism purposefully disconnected us from the forces of nature, the invention of the corporation purposefully disconnected us from one another. And while religious institutions and mythologies may have dominated the social, political, and economic landscapes for the first thousand or so years of civilization, it's corporations and their mythologies that direct human activity today.

Corporatism depends first on our disconnection. The less local, immediate, and interpersonal our experience of the world and each other, the more likely we are to adopt self-interested behaviors that erode community and relationships. This makes us more dependent on central authorities for the things we used to get from one another; we cannot create value without centralized currency, meaning without nationally known brands, or leaders without corporate support. This dependency, in turn, makes us more vulnerable to the pathetically overgeneralized and fear-based mythologies of corporatism. Once we accept these new mythologies as the way things really are, we come to believe that our manufactured disconnection is actually a condition of human nature. In short, we disconnect from the real, adapt to our artificial environment by becoming less than human, and finally mistake carefully constructed corporatist mythologies for the natural universe.

By tracing the development of the great disconnect and unearthing the misconceptions supporting it, we will enable ourselves to come to terms with how we reconnected to an artificial landscape sloped in favor of corporations and away from our own agency—or why we behave against our better natures in the name of self-interest. Luckily, if we can call it that, the real world is finally diverging too far from this false model for the illusion to be sustained. The reality in which we actually live is crumbling; the barbarians are at the gates and the muggers are in Park Slope, while the wealthy are still arguing about the impact on property values.

Instead of using this opportunity to reconnect to our world and our potential to create value from the bottom up, we argue about how to restore and refinance the very corporations whose purpose is to disempower us further. If we can forget about the Dow Jones Industrial Average for long enough to remember who we are and what value we might truly bring to this world, we may just be able to take back the world we have ceded to a six-hundred-year-old business deal.

CHAPTER TWO

MISTAKING THE MAP FOR THE TERRITORY

Colonialism and the Disconnect from Place

The World According to Trump

"Hello, New York!!!"

We're in New York, but we could as well be anywhere. Still, the crowd of several thousand people cheers, as if the master of ceremonies really cared where the traveling pyramid scheme organized by the Learning Annex called Wealth Expo has set up shop for the weekend.

"Do you want to make money right now?"

"Yes!"

"I can't hear you!"

"YES!!!"

"Everybody get up and raise your arms!"

Over two thousand people—most of them black—rise from their folding chairs as if from the pews of a Southern Baptist church. Water leaks from the glass roof of the Javits Center as it echoes with their collective cheer.

A siren wails, and a dozen girls in tight tank tops with the word "FUN" stretched across the breasts bound onto the stage. Two parts

Hooters waitress to one part auto-show model, the girls begin their trademark "money dance." *Oh, I wanna be rich*, they sing—or probably lip-synch. *Oh! Oh! I want a pie in the sky!*

The couple seated next to me has heard it all before. Still, Charles and Sandra rise dutifully if slightly less spiritedly than their peers, and pump their arms into the air as directed. It's the second day of the conference, and the two-hundred-dollar admission price they've paid seems a bit less like the steal they'd imagined it to be. Instead of buying access to the seminars and information they need to get rich quick, they've bought access to pitches for other, more expensive seminars where this information will presumably be delivered.

Charles and Sandra—a middle-aged black couple dressed less conspicuously than most of their peers at the event—aren't even particularly interested in real estate, the topic of the current pitch. They're just interested in making back some of the money they lost to unexpected (but, as they'll learn, not unexploitable) calamities over the past few years. I met them out in the exhibits area, where Charles had just charged up a thousand dollars to buy a Barron's investment package. The best I can tell, he bought a password that will grant him access to the "insider" pages on the Barron's website. The energetic young salesman explained to Charles that he was purchasing more than mere information—"It's a system." That's the big word here: "system." "A system to give you an insider's edge to what's high, what's low, who is selling, who is buying . . ."

In a real-time display of buyer's remorse, the corners of Charles's mouth turn downward in the same moment that his credit card is swiped. I ask him if he's having second thoughts. "Hell," Charles says, parroting the salesman's pitch. "With this accessibility I can make a thousand dollars back in one trade. And they said if I changed my mind, I can just sell this access to someone else for a profit!"

"That's the spirit, hon," says Sandra, as she tugs him toward Keynote Hall, where Jack Canfield, the author of *Chicken Soup for the Soul*, a frequent *Oprah* guest, and now an officially approved proponent of "The Secret™," is scheduled to speak. "I want Charles to see this. It'll give him a winner's attitude," she explains to me. "He's been so depressed since the fire."

Fire, flood . . . their story is typical of the Wealth Expo attendees. Charles and Sandra ran a successful fish restaurant near Atlantic City, New Jersey, for over twenty years. They came back from their

annual August vacation to learn that faulty wiring in the kitchen's re-
frigeration system had torched the place. "We didn't own the building," Charles told me. "We had no equity. I'm fifty-two years old; do
I want to do this all over again?" Sandra's supplemental income as a
"jazzercise" instructor was wiped out just a few months later when
the basement studio hosting her classes was flooded and closed. The
salary she should have collected for her work was lost to the company's
bankruptcy settlement, which favored the dance school's mortgage
lender, not its employees.

For the past six months they've been living on savings and credit-
card advances. And now they're in the Javits Center with thousands of
others in virtually the same situation, learning how to make a fortune,
"no money down." Except, of course, to buy the expensive systems
teaching you how.

The systems all seem almost interchangeable. Although Canfield
has been delayed, Than Merrill, the star of A&E's *Flip This House,* has
flipped his time slot and taken the stage. Like many of the speakers,
Merrill is an ex–pro athlete. He graduated from Yale and went straight
to the NFL and a $200,000 season before an injury forced him to leave
football. He had to start again "from scratch," he explains, "and so
can you!" He's a good-looking guy—white, wealthy, and winning. (In
fact, except for George Foreman, all the speakers today are white, even
though the vast majority of their audience is not.)

"Are you ready?" he asks. "Everyone up on your feet, turn to the
person beside you, give them a high five and say, 'I am ready!' " Along
with the rest of the crowed, Charles and Sandra follow his orders.

"I spent hundreds of thousands of dollars on my education, and
now you can use that as leverage. What did I learn? Go after the pre-
foreclosure lists, find the fire-damaged properties, the divorce lists,
bankruptcy lists, tax-lien lists. Go after these people *before* they are
selling, *before* they're in foreclosure, and you can flip the properties
within the same day to make a profit."

Then it gets a little weird. Merrill starts throwing CDs and DVDs
into the audience. "Do you want to know my number one secret?"
he keeps asking. "It's in this DVD!" Then he flings it at the spectators, who fight over it like fans scraping for a fly ball in the Fenway
bleachers. He invites a young black man onto the stage and grasps his
shoulders. "Are you happy now?" he asks. The man looks down, embarrassed. Then, giving his charge a shove that could make a crippled

man walk again, Merrill shouts, "You WILL be happy when you make thirty-nine hundred dollars an hour!" The man starts to dance and takes a DVD as the crowd cheers.

Sufficiently convinced of their own burning desire to catch a disk, the new believers gladly pay for the system. Girls at tables around the perimeter of the room accept credit cards from the willing throngs. From what I can tell, the main course is $1,297. But the girls are also encouraging people to sign up for Merrill's special one-day event next month, at which even more secrets will be revealed.

Sandra is one of the first standing in line for Merrill's course. She spends the rest of their weekend's budget and then some, maxing out her last credit card on the DVD.

"What about Canfield's course?" I ask. It's the one she said she came for.

"Isn't fate strange?" she says. "This is the one I must've been *meant* to get."

"Besides," her husband tells me, as if reassuring himself at the same time, "we're getting an 'Expo-only' discount. We could turn around and sell this for two thousand." (I checked on a few online auction sites, where the entire package is available from other former students for $349 "or best offer.")

I spoke with dozens of conference-goers that afternoon, and their stories were all essentially the same. An illness, divorce, fire, or flood had suddenly changed their circumstances for the worse. Too leveraged or indebted to adjust, or already living hand-to-mouth, they had lost their businesses and homes, and were now desperately seeking a way out of mounting debt. On hearing that the famed real-estate and reality-show maven Donald Trump had been paid a million dollars to share the secret of wealth, they flocked to the Javits Center and paid two hundred dollars each to start a new life under the benevolent tutelage of Trump and the other Learning Annex stars.

Instead of being taught how to get wealthy, however, they were persuaded to stretch their credit-card balances just a bit further to purchase "wealth systems" that would teach them how to take advantage of people who had suffered unexpected illness, divorce, fire, or flood. People like themselves. In a feedback loop within a feedback loop, they were paying to get lists of fellow unfortunates.

As if passed over by the headlines, this mania is occurring in late 2008, well *after* the real-estate bubble popped. These are the very victims of the predatory lending practices and frenzied "flipping" that undermined whatever legitimacy there might have been to this sector of the economy in the first place. They don't realize that they're simply being trained to serve as the dupes in yet another Ponzi scheme.

"I'm looking for partners," explains Merrill. "We are looking for joint ventures."

It's not just talk. Merrill may be making a few hundred thousand dollars selling his DVD package today, but that's not the entirety of his or any of the other instructors' business plans.

No, the real economic activity is occurring in a large, windowless room in the middle of the convention floor. Finding it feels like coming upon the sports-betting area in a Las Vegas casino: Céline Dion is nowhere to be heard, and the garish spectacle has given way to race-track seriousness. Men and women of all shapes and sizes, colors and clothing styles, sit staring at newsprint pamphlets and listening to an announcer calling off numbers as if he were leading a Bingo game.

Turns out this is a real-estate auction, where numbered parcels of land, foreclosed homes, and mystery properties with undisclosed problems or unknown liens are announced and then bid upon by the new crop of amateur speculators. People who have lost their houses are bidding on foreclosed properties as a way of generating the wealth they need to one day own a house again. This is what those courses are teaching them how to do.

The seminars themselves are just rallies—motivational meetings to give this crowd the faith they need to take additional leaps into debt. By indoctrinating these masses into the wealth-building mythology of Trump, the Wealth Expo pumps just a little more air into the still-deflating real-estate bubble, giving the real-estate sharks on stage one more audience of patsies on whom to prey.

It would be easier to dismiss this carnival of land selling and re-selling if it were just an isolated, bizarre corner of our corporatized society—some amusing, if pitiable, subculture covered in a lifestyle magazine. But it's just an extension of the central and accepted operating premise of land valuation today. For, in addition to sales pitches from George Foreman, the self-help guru Tony Robbins, and The Secret teachers, the Wealth Expo is offering a keynote address by former Federal Reserve chairman Alan Greenspan.

Greenspan is only too happy to confer legitimacy upon the Learning Annex event, as well as the real-estate speculation it has been invented to invigorate. Sure, he's careful to distance himself just a bit from the proceedings. He appears by satellite instead of live, and makes sure he isn't photographed actually interacting with the convention's many victims. But he knows what he's there for, and delivers on his brand.

A soap-opera star interviews the economist.

"With the ups and downs of the real-estate market—do you still think real estate is one of the best investments for investors nowadays?"

"Over the long run, unquestionably. We are going through a testing period."

"Other than telling everyone to get your book, *The Age of Turbulence*, what would you give New Yorkers as advice for investing in this coming year?"

"Well, I think investing in my book is not a bad idea to begin with." The crowd laughs.

"I think that sums it up! You're such a great mind. A great and powerful world leader. One of the most powerful world leaders. Amazing! It's like having the answers to the test!"

It's hard to know whether Greenspan is simply hawking his book or attempting to salvage a housing market that went bad under his watch. After all, it was Greenspan who refused to rein in the predatory-lending industry, under the rationale that exercising any regulatory pressure would put the Fed in the improper role of protecting people rather than the economy. Or maybe he really is a true believer, and sees his audience less as dupes than as a necessary species of bottom-feeders in the overall economic ecosystem. At the very least, that's what he's pretending to believe.

What Greenspan certainly does understand—however inscrutable his feelings about it—is that this Wealth Expo isn't just a microcosm of the housing market; it *is* the housing market.

Our relationship to the land on which we build our homes and grow our food has become abstracted to little more than a premise for the exchange or collateralization of credit. The land is no longer a place, but a placeholder on a balance sheet. And the more disconnected from the reality of its actual use, health, and inhabitants we get, the easier it is for us to exploit it for short-term gain, whatever the long-term environmental or collateral damage. Just as it's easier for Greenspan to make his own sales pitch to the impoverished via space satellite, it's easier for us to destroy our world from a distance.

The Wealth Expo represents just the final stage in a series of abstractions that began with the emergence of chartered merchant corporations in the 1400s. As these corporations mapped the uncharted regions of an expanding globe, they reduced a world of people, cultures, and ecologies down to one of slaves, commodities, and economies. If it couldn't be represented on the map or the balance sheet, then it didn't exist. Over the centuries that followed, these maps and ledgers became the new territories—which were themselves mapped and charted for the derivative value they could generate, and so on, and so on. As mortgages were themselves mortgaged and then mortgaged again, the thing we used to think of as real estate became anything but real.

We'll have to retrace our steps in order to reverse this process and return to earth.

Prince Henry and the Navigators

Until late in the twentieth century, European schoolchildren—particularly those in Portugal—were taught that the great Prince Henry single-handedly invented blue-water sailing when he taught his seamen how to navigate beyond sight of the shore. Henry of Portugal's greatest achievement, according to those officially chronicling his exploits in the early 1400s, was to help sailors overcome their fear and superstition to sail south of Cape Bojador on the African coast. This opened unprecedented opportunities for trade, making Portugal one of the great colonial powers. Henry was later credited with opening a school of navigation at Sagres, personally teaching courses to sea captains, and studying astronomy and the oceanic arts until his death. His story was told and retold so many times and in so many contexts over the centuries that a nineteenth-century German geographer eventually dubbed him Prince Henry the Navigator—which he is called to this day.

Alas, Henry wasn't a navigator at all. He rarely traveled by ship except as a passenger on short routine voyages. He started no school, taught no sailors, and studied no stars. The very notion that until Henry sailors would have been forced to navigate by hugging the shore is itself preposterous. Sailors of all ages avoided the coasts, which were fraught with perils, and have successfully navigated in deeper waters beyond the sight of land for many centuries.

Henry did not personally expand exploration of Africa's coasts—he did just the opposite. For Henry was no sailor but rather one of Portugal's first corporatist monarchs. He issued a charter in 1443 that, instead of opening Africa's coast past the Cape of Bojador, prohibited sailors from going past it without his permission. So, contrary to corporatist mythology, Henry's charters didn't enable seafaring; if their journeys required approval, then apparently sailors were already more than willing to explore on their own. It was the Portuguese monarchy that, like the other kingdoms of the early Renaissance, sought to rein in the advancing class of ship merchants, and lock down deals that would help them monopolize any gains made.

Henry the navigator might as well have served as the prototype of today's heroic CEO: a dry-land monopolist praised for his seafaring adventures, a calculating politician praised for his hands-on, can-do attitude, and a greedy opportunist lauded for his farsighted philanthropy. Almost all media profiles of modern-day business figures perform a similar alchemy. Still, while they may not be able to take credit for oceanic travel, Henry and his royal peers can claim responsibility for transforming an era of exploration and trade into one of exploitation and monopoly.

On one level, these monarchs can't really be blamed for their reductive approaches to new territories. Advances in the sciences had led to a rationalist—or rationed—stance on nearly everything. Reductionism promoted a fragmented view of the world, biased toward studying how constituent elements operated rather than how they might interact. The monarchy's slow but eventually wholehearted acceptance of cause-and-effect logic and scientific observation might have been great for curbing magical thinking and superstitious activity, but it could just as easily be abused to categorize foreign peoples the way a biologist might categorize any "inferior" species, and foreign places as wilds to conquer.

Royals went map crazy. Cartography was as much the rage in the Renaissance as MapQuest and Google Earth are today. Nearly every ship had a cartographer aboard to map new regions of the world and, of course, label them as belonging to whichever kingdom had chartered the voyage. Mapping a territory meant documenting one's control of it—whatever the reality might have been on the ground. Eventually, the mapmaking fetish turned inward as well, as monarchs attempted to map the entirety of Europe and determine who owned exactly what. By 1427, a Danish cartographer working in Rome had developed the first known map of northern Europe. In 1507, the voyages of the Florentine seaman Amerigo Vespucci resulted in the first maps of "America," showing two distinct continents separated from Asia.

With the physicality of the world represented in maps, and the exploitation of these maps arranged by charter, monarchs were at least two steps removed from the results of their actions—actions already undertaken with a cool logic defined by scientific rationalism. This disconnect characterized the colonial era, and determined the bias with which we treat our physical surroundings to this day. Place became property.

At home in Europe, this abstraction meant a completely new approach to land ownership, as the seigneurial system gave way to active trading. Why should we care that control of land in late-medieval Europe shifted, at the dawn of the Renaissance, from "feudal" to "market" control? For the peasant working the land, this turned out to be a significant distinction. In the feudal societies, land was rarely traded; it simply passed down from generation to generation. Peasants generally stayed put, and often had as much claim on the land they worked as the fief or lord who controlled it.

The market for land was a relatively new concept, and really developed more as a vehicle for capital—an investment opportunity for the burgeoning class of merchants and bankers. Merchants were making more money through their businesses than they could reinvest in them, while landowning monarchs were falling further behind. By selling their lands, the aristocracy could participate in the new market; meanwhile, merchants could acquire property, which was both a safe investment and an opportunity to earn social distinction. Common lands, which might have been owned by lords but were open for grazing or even agriculture by any commoner, became increasingly "enclosed" or fenced in. These tracts were no longer pastures, but parcels.

As the market in property grew to account for more and more of the woods, pastures, and moors on which peasants worked, land—and the labor done to it—became more a commodity than a system of interdependence. Unlike the hierarchy of lords and vassals who both owned and depended on the active use of the land by its laborers, the people buying and selling these parcels related to them as deeds to be sold for a profit as soon as the market allowed. Peasants moved from place to place, enjoyed less implicit and explicit authority over the lands they worked, and found their labors becoming part of the same commodity markets.

Of course, the people living in newer territories had it even worse. Aboriginal people who weren't simply massacred were treated with about the same respect as any other natural resource, and enslaved by expanding colonial empires. And while historians are at pains to decide whether the merchants or the monarchs chartering their voyages and settlements are more to blame for the inhumanity of colonialism, it was the charter itself, and the rules of engagement it demanded, that generated the disconnection from place permitting this exploitation and that remains with us today.

Remember, while the merchant class was rising in wealth and status, the aristocracy was stuck. This is because merchants were participating in manufacturing, trade, and other expanding businesses while nobles merely owned things. Their assets were stable, but static. In a growing economy, standing still meant falling behind. Charters gave the aristocracy a way to invest in opportunities that could bring their assets to life, and to do so on a playing field where they had the power to write the rules and, in Henry's case, their mythologies as well.

The discovery of the New World may have, for a short time, created a sense of endless frontiers. But to asset-hungry corporatists, Magellan's 1519 voyage around the world also accomplished just the opposite: it conveyed that the amount of land on this planet was bounded. There was only so much of it, making it scarce enough, at least in theory, to conform to the rules of the market. And those rules were rigged by the corporate charters spelling them out.

As investors in their corporations' projects and competitors in the fast-growing global marketplace, monarchs hoped to extract as much value as possible from their colonies, and to do so as quickly as possible. It was in the interests of both early corporations and the monarchs legitimizing them to colonize as much of the earth as possible over the next few centuries.

Charters gave corporations the authority to take military action, while granting monarchs distance from the real and political consequences of this violence. Corporate monopolies enjoyed exclusive dominion over a region, and in return gave the authorizing monarch a disproportionate share of returns. Colonists, still subjects of the kingdoms from which they came, were as bound by the charters as the corporations on whose behalf they were written. Mercantilism didn't give them the opportunity to build businesses, only to extend monopolies owned by others. No sooner would a market arise than it would be usurped by the corporation. It was a closed system, created to maximize the extraction of a colony's human and resource value. This was true whether the regions considered themselves colonies or not.

The English East India Company ignored whatever markets already existed in the regions where it did business. They used their financial and military clout to deal directly with the laborers whose goods they wished to purchase, bypassing all involvement with local markets, and dissolving local cultures and business relationships in the process. In Bengal, for example, the East India Company provided its own looms, factories, and materials transport, slowly putting the local businesses that provided these services out of business. Incapable of maintaining even a local presence, Bengal's internal weaving industry became utterly dependent on an international company that could define its own terms. Similarly, when the Muscovy Company realized that it was supporting local business in Russia by purchasing rope, it opened up its own cordage factory. But what might have looked at first like an employment opportunity for devastated workers quickly vanished, for Muscovy employed an entirely English workforce.

These arrangements did not always make strict financial sense—certainly not for the local economies involved. That's why they were enforced not by the market, but by arbitrary laws written by monarchs to favor the activities of the companies in which they were either directly or indirectly invested. American colonists were permitted to grow cotton, but not to make clothing from it. It had to be shipped to England for manufacture, and then purchased back in finished form. This was not economic efficiency, but economic exploitation. Charters gave corporations the exclusive right to vertically integrate anything they needed onto the credit side of the balance sheet, no matter the cost to the territory. The only thing they had to fear was revolution—but to attack a chartered corporation meant facing the army of the empire that underwrote it.

It was these seventeenth- and eighteenth-century equivalents of no-bid contracts to Halliburton that led Adam Smith to write *Wealth of Nations*. While celebrated today by corporate libertarians as philosophical justification for free-trade policies, the book was meant as an

attack on the scale and effects of chartered monopoly. By arguing—
now famously—that "self-interest" might promote a more just society, he was speaking in the context of an economy already heavily
tilted against individual human agency. "By preferring the support of
domestic to that of foreign industry," Smith explains of the average
person, "he intends only his own security; and by directing that industry in such a manner as its produce may be of the greatest value, he
intends only his own gain, and he is in this, as in many other cases, led
by an invisible hand to promote an end which was no part of his intention."

Smith *assumes* that people would be biased against international
trade, naturally preferring the security offered by sourcing goods
locally—and that his readers would agree with him on this point. Like
the founders of America, who may have differed on almost everything
else but this, Smith saw economics as characterized by small, scaled,
local economies working in interaction with one another and guided
by the enlightened self-interest of individuals. This was not a reaction
to "leftist" regulations on corporate power, but against the unfair
practices of early transnational corporations, which were operating on
a level completely removed from the real affairs of people and the
proper stewardship of resources.

Of course, eventually real people in real places stood up against corporations and the governments behind them—the American Revolution was just one of the first in a long series of anticolonial movements
that included the birth of many American, Asian, and African nations.
While governments of the modern era might never be permitted to
charter monopolies from afar quite as directly again, corporations
didn't forget the methodology of remote control.

Over There . . .

At the end of World War II, it became clear that the last of the official
colonies—such as Ceylon, the Ivory Coast, and Burma—would be returned to local rule. The problem for locals, however, was that their
economies and social infrastructures had been devastated over a century or more of corporate exploitation. They couldn't just start over.
They needed a hand. Of course, the former colonial empires were
willing to lend it—for a price.

To be fair, most European nations were having their own problems in the late 1940s. The only one of the allies that had made it through the war without significant damage was the United States. Foreseeing the need for a postcolonial world order, the Allied nations sent delegates to a meeting at a hotel in Bretton Woods, New Hampshire, in 1944 to figure out a new global monetary system. The U.S. was in a position to leverage its authority as Europe's military savior and the only surviving industrial economy to promote its own fiscal agenda: free markets and monetary leadership. Everyone else's currencies would be pegged to the dollar, and the world would enjoy open markets, which benefited the U.S., as the economy poised to grow the most. The meeting established the International Monetary Fund, set up the World Bank, and laid the foundations for an international trade pact that was finally implemented fifty years later by George Herbert Walker Bush and Bill Clinton as the World Trade Organization.

Through the World Bank and the International Monetary Fund, lender nations would be in a position to assist developing nations with huge injections of cash. By accepting the loans, however, borrower nations would be obligated to open themselves to rules of free trade as established by the international lending community at Bretton Woods. This made them vulnerable to a new style of the same old colonialism.

Taking a loan meant opening one's ports to foreign ships, and one's markets to foreign goods. It meant allowing foreign corporations to purchase land within a country, and to compete freely with any domestic company. Nations would not be allowed to impose restrictions on what sorts of goods could be imported, or which resources could be extracted. In short, taking a loan from the IMF meant losing all forms of "protectionism." And while protectionism has been cast, in free-market terms, as a fear-based reaction to the healthy and necessary functioning of the market, there are instances when nations might simply be attempting to protect their real territories and people from the tyranny of the balance sheet. For, even if every currency in the world was in some way pegged to U.S. money, not every gain and loss proved to be measurable in dollars and çents.

For one, the economic globalization negotiated in Bretton Woods has given wealthy industrial nations the ability to pass environmental liabilities on to poorer nations. As documented in several of David Korten's books on corporate power, wealthy nations actually take credit for this exploitation of poorer ones on the grounds that they're bringing them prosperity.

Japan, for example, financed and constructed a copper smelting plant in the Philippines to produce cathodes. The Philippine Associated Smelting and Refining Corporation (PASAR) was built on four hundred acres of land sold to the company by the government at giveaway prices. PASAR is now a prosperous multinational, and in dollar terms the local economy is bigger than it was before. This same case study is regularly cited as a global free-trade success story: Japan now has a ready supply of copper without any of the environmental damage associated with its production, and the gross domestic product of the Philippines has been increased.

But the Filipinos actually living in the area are sick and jobless. Plant emissions, including boron, arsenic, and heavy metals, have polluted local water, poisoned fish, and sickened residents. The contamination of the land has made it impossible for them to return to subsistence farming, and their government is busy repaying Japan and the IMF for the loans that built and subsidized the plant.

Because the gross domestic product of an exploited area invariably goes up, case studies like this are used as evidence of how IMF practices and free trade provide necessary assistance to developing nations. Using these metrics, the more pollution a project can generate, the more environmental remediation and medical costs will be rung up, increasing the GDP even further. In purely corporatist terms—which are the only ones most of us physically removed from the effects of our actions have to go on—pollution is good.

By lending money to developing nations, wealthier nations can force them into agreements that "grow" their economies while sapping them of their ability to take care of themselves. In order to repay ever-increasing debts, poorer nations must dedicate increasingly larger tracts of land for export crops. They grow food that their own citizens quite literally cannot afford. Since their acceptance of loans means allowing corporations from other nations to purchase land, debtor nations lose their best farmland to wealthier foreign farm conglomerates anyway. Locals who used to farm for subsistence now must farm that same land for day wages, if it is farmable at all.

Through the use of loans with binding free-market provisions, powerful nations and the corporations they support have restored the grip that chartered monopolies once had over these same regions.

Their policies are analogs of those of their predecessors: the same exploitation of land from a distance, only removed another degree.

Consider the strategy of any typical early chartered corporation. In 1602, the Dutch Crown sanctioned the United East India Company to conquer territory and exploit resources in the Pacific. The Company's scheme was to acquire lands in Indonesia by lending money to cultivators and then dispossessing them when they failed to make payments. This was made easier by trade policies that guaranteed the farmers' failure. The Company got the Dutch to prohibit cultivation of the most profitable export crops—like cloves—on land not already under Dutch ownership. Loans failed, and more collateral in the form of land passed into Company hands. Indonesians lost access to the most fertile land, and were ultimately forced to buy their rice from United East India at the artificially inflated, monopoly-supported prices. The local economy was devastated as more land and labor were surrendered to the corporation.

As if borrowing from the United East India Company playbook, modern corporations leverage the power they've been granted through free-trade agreements. Where old-school colonialism was enforced with gunships, the new school uses bank loans, currency, and membership in the international community. The World Bank and the IMF impose policy prescriptions on the nations to whom they lend money, all geared toward opening their markets to the interests of foreign corporations. When they fail to make their mortgage payments, these nations are subjected to "structural adjustments" that increase the resources they must commit toward repayment of the debt. As a result, debt payments made to the World Bank calculated as a percent of total government budgets have doubled each decade in Latin America and Africa. More loans lead to more collateralization, which in turn leads to more losses.

Eventually, as with a restaurant in hock to the mob, all productive assets and resources end up owned by foreign corporations and devoted to export production in order to repay the loans. Public services and utilities are taken over by foreign corporations and run for a profit. The World Bank serves as the loan shark, financing corporate missions at the expense of developing nations, while the IMF plays the menacing debt collector—backed by First World armies and their intelligence agencies.

One step further abstracted from the land and resource-management techniques of their predecessors, modern corporations exploit a sloped monetary policy to lend scarce currency to nations who pin their hopes for advancement on participation in the global economy. Only too late do they realize that this participation is limited to providing labor, resources, and land to some of the very same corporations from whom they were liberated half a century before. These loans turn out to be *anti*developmental, increasing dependence on imported technology, driving people off their lands, polluting them, and making subsistence farming impossible. And adding insult to injury, today's corporations retell these stories on their websites and in quarterly reports as evidence of the economic opportunities they offer the rest of the world. But just because GDP has gone up, things back here in the real world have not necessarily gotten better.

The World Trade Organization, finally established in 1995, is testimony to just how universally accepted these practices have become in the developed world—and just how dependent we are on them for our lopsided prosperity. This wasn't a Republican idea or a Democratic one, but a corporatist mentality that patiently waited for acceptance. Widespread protests by disparate groups of environmentalists, labor activists, and others who understood one or more of these points were ridiculed by most American, British, and German media as the work of unfocused, untidy, and uninformed people, afraid of the globalized future.

What these protesters understood all too well, however, is that WTO policies aren't moving us forward at all, but sending us back into history. Indeed, we might as well be in the colonial era: the WTO plays the role of the monarchy, writing policies as favorable to today's multinationals as their forerunners' charters were to the corporations in which they invested. For who is in the WTO, ultimately? Board members of the banks and conglomerates who benefit from its policies.

As long as the pollution and labor unrest are "over there" somewhere, and only represented in terms of the profit they generate for one corporation or another, they are good for the bottom line—or, at worst, collateral damage to people who were probably killing each other in tribal wars, anyway. This is their path toward participation in the global marketplace.

Defenders of the free market—including editors of financial publications from *The Economist* to *The Wall Street Journal*—deride any critique of these development strategies as jingoistic, ill-informed, and protectionist. They like to cite David Ricardo's 1817 theory of comparative advantage, which most of us were taught as freshmen in Econ 101. I had the pleasure of learning it in a Princeton lecture hall with a thousand other college freshmen from the left-leaning former Fed vice chairman Alan Blinder, and it goes something like this:

The theory of comparative advantage shows how trade can benefit all parties as long as they produce goods with different relative costs. It's easy to see that if Country A makes shoes faster, and Country B makes hats faster, then everyone in Country A should make shoes, and everyone in Country B should make hats. But what if Country A makes both shoes *and* hats faster than Country B? The people in Country B should still go ahead and produce whichever item they are relatively better at, and Country A should make the other item.

So even if the U.K. can make cars and dresses less expensively than Italy can make either one, it's still more efficient for Italy to make whichever one of these that Britain produces less efficiently. Let's say it's dresses. When the two nations trade their stuff, both do better. For every man-hour the U.K. spends making cars, it earns more value to trade for Italy's dresses than it would if it made dresses for itself. It's better to have everyone in the U.K. doing the thing they do best, and then trade with other countries that are doing what they do best.

Corporations use the theory of comparative advantage to justify the way they do foreign trade and, moreover, to explain why building cars and trucks over in Mexico or Brazil doesn't really take away jobs from people in Detroit or Birmingham. The domestic workers simply need to be "retrained" to do what Westerners do best (whatever that is), and then everything will be okay.

A closer look at Ricardo's theory, however—the kind of look offered by a teacher like Blinder—reveals that it depends on a set of preconditions. The equations work out only if you've got full employment in both nations. It's not more economically efficient to do international trade if it ends up decreasing employment in the more efficiently operating industrial economy. Furthermore, Ricardo himself argued that his theory works only if the trade between the two nations is balanced—something the United States has not enjoyed with, say, China for over a decade.

In today's corporatized global marketplace, Ricardo's work is all but obsolete, and the examples he used to prove his point have little or nothing to do with the way comparative advantage is universally applied. Ricardo showed how the climate in Portugal made it relatively more efficient for the Portuguese to make wine than for the English to do it. The Portuguese vintner enjoyed soil more conducive to growing grapes, and was much less likely to lose his crop to bad weather. It made sense, under these circumstances, for the British farmer to convert his fields to pasture for sheep. He could export wool to Portugal in return for the wine—and both could fully employ their workers in these pursuits. Even if the Portuguese farmer could have raised sheep more efficiently than the Brit, he's better off doing the thing that he's *relatively* better at. More total wine and sheep are produced, lowering everyone's costs. Trade is good, especially if it allows nations to specialize in what they do best, or what their natural endowment allows.

The comparative advantage argument no longer holds when you're talking about a car manufactured in ten countries, each with its own exchange rates. Comparative advantage applies to balanced national economies trading with one another. Trade agreements like the North American Free Trade Agreement (NAFTA) and the General Agreement on Tariffs and Trade (GATT) are more about creating "integrated economies," whose national boundaries no longer pose any obstacles to the corporations who transcend them. The United States is not trading with China at all. Wal-Mart is leveraging what *used* to be comparative advantage by sourcing products in China and selling them in the U.S.—where nothing but credit is produced in return. And what is a Mercedes manufactured by Beijing Benz-Daimler-Chrysler Automotive Corporation, Ltd., anyway? Who exactly is trading to whom?

The tasks sent overseas are simply the ones whose greater costs— environmental damage and health risks—can be externalized to the natives of the country where they are being performed. Labor is treated as a commodity. Is the terrain of China or the Philippines more suited to environmental damage? Are the people there better at getting cancer? Of course not. Unlike comparative advantage, externalizing costs is not about giving people the jobs that they do best, or using land in a manner consistent with natural climate and topology. It's more a matter of giving the lowest-paying and most dangerous jobs to people who don't have the means to complain—or who are so far away that we couldn't hear them if they did. International trade offers a means for businesses to circumvent democratic oversight, regulation, and labor laws. In the process, corporations externalize the longer-term costs of their operations to nations who have no choice but to absorb them. The credit column of the corporate balance sheet remains intact.

Those on the other side of the trade have little choice in the matter. They are debtor nations, whose loans have been restructured by an IMF with only corporate interests or misapplied international trade theories in mind. A free-trade landscape sloped to the interests of corporate colonialism leads to what progressive economists call a "race to the bottom." Nations compete to offer the best prices and the fewest obstacles for corporations to come set up shop. If this means preventing unions from forming, lowering environmental standards, or even subsidizing the construction of factories, so be it. With no minimum standards established between them or through international regulation, whoever stoops the lowest wins the contract.

This downward leveling supports the West's consumption via credit while inhibiting local production of goods by developing nations for their own use. The cost of basic staples like food and clothing go up, as local consumers are now forced to compete against those in much wealthier nations for the same products. The net result is that the disparity of wealth and standards of living between the rich and poor nations gets worse, not better.

People living in the developing world might take heart in the fact that corporate colonialism no longer distinguishes between the localities it undermines. The phrase "race to the bottom" was first used, in fact, by Supreme Court Justice Louis Brandeis in 1933 to describe the way American states were falling over themselves to attract corporate business. Just like developing nations undercutting each other's labor and environmental interests to win factory contracts, U.S. states were busy rewriting their charters and laws to the benefit of companies who incorporated there. Delaware eliminated most corporate tax, while New Jersey limited its citizens' ability to challenge corporate behavior.

Corporations in the United States, England, and most other market-driven Western nations now operate at home with the very same colonial aggression they applied overseas—if we can even refer to today's corporations as having "home" nations anymore. And domestic localities still fall over each other to win their business, either too confused or too corrupt to act in their own best interests.

In the 1970s, for example, Moore County, North Carolina, began working hard to attract businesses from the Northeast, with promises of corporate tax breaks, lax environmental standards, and a compliant, union-free workforce. The county finally won the privilege of hosting a Proctor Silex plant by floating a $5.5 million bond to finance water and sewer services for the facility—even though many residents in the region were themselves living without running water or basic services. Predictably, in 1990 the company moved to Mexico, which was offering more competitive terms. Moore County was left with toxic waste, eight hundred unemployed workers, and tremendous public debt for having subsidized the company's plant.

In 1993, South Carolina bent over backward to secure a plant from BMW. *BusinessWeek* and other publications praised the state for its progressive policy toward competing with Mexico for automobile-manufacturing jobs. South Carolina promised to help BMW externalize its costs by subsidizing inexpensive mansions for executives, good golf courses, cheap labor, low taxes, and limited union activity. The state raised $2.8 million to send engineers to Germany for training. When BMW indicated its preference for a particular thousand-acre parcel on which over one hundred homes were already located, the state spent another $36.6 million to purchase all of them for subsequent destruction. South Carolina then leased the site back to BMW for one dollar per year. Winning the BMW factory is estimated to cost taxpayers $130 million over thirty years.

It's not only our production that we subsidize on behalf of corporations, but our consumption as well. Remember, in addition to extracting resources from the colonies they controlled, chartered corporations also held monopolies over what the colonies could buy and from whom. The more corporations could control the laws and tax policies of the regions where they were operating, the more they could externalize the costs of selling just as they did the costs of manufacture. Today's corporate-favoring legal framework permits domestic companies to behave in an analogous fashion.

Wal-Mart may be the easiest and most obvious target for us in this regard, but that's for a very real reason: its practice of colonizing new regions for stores amounts to a scorched-earth policy that leaves financial and social ruin in its wake. Wal-Mart monopolizes new territory by pricing items below cost and rendering local merchants incapable of competing. Once the competition goes out of business and the community is dependent on Wal-Mart, the corporation raises prices to more profitable levels. Free and fair competition, as defined by the market, favors the company with more money to burn.

Although Wal-Mart enters new regions promising gainful employment and an expanded local tax base, the opposite usually occurs. A Congressional Research Service report found that for every two jobs created by a Wal-Mart store, the local community ended up losing three. Furthermore, the jobs created were at lower wages (an average of under $250 a week), fewer hours, and reduced benefits. A majority of Wal-Mart employees with children live below the poverty line, qualifying for public welfare benefits such as free lunch at school. Seventy percent of Wal-Mart employees leave within the first year of employment, and do so—according to a survey that Wal-Mart itself conducted—because of inadequate pay and lack of recognition for their work. Other studies have shown that, as a result of the increase in social services spent on the families of Wal-Mart employees, the net effect of a new store is to place a greater financial burden on the taxpaying community.

In spite of a huge "buy American" campaign, Wal-Mart purchases 85 percent of its merchandise from overseas, and is consistently associated with sweatshop scandals, from Kathie Lee Gifford's clothing line and Disney's Haitian-made pajamas to child-produced clothing from Bangladesh and Wal-Mart–brand apparel manufactured by underage Chinese workers in New York City sweatshops. So maybe it's not even in Americans' best interests to be manufacturing for Wal-Mart, anyway.

There's nothing new in attacking Wal-Mart for poor corporate citizenship. There are plenty of organized protests and lawsuits under way, as well as at least some action on the part of the company to correct this impression and perhaps even its own behavior. What's more important to recognize here is that Wal-Mart's activities do not appear to be the result of conscious choices by a mean-spirited board of human directors who have any real relationship to the communities in which they operate. Rather, Wal-Mart's relationship to the world seems to be directed by the sort of charter written four hundred years ago for trade monopolies. The company's practices—abroad and at home—erode regional stability and self-sufficiency in order to conduct the long-distance trade at which Wal-Mart excels. Wal-Mart turns its home territories into colonies, robbing them of their ability to generate value for themselves and creating greater dependence on the colonial empire.

Wal-Mart's relationship to place has become so abstracted that the company views even its own stores through the conquistador's eyeglass. Like temporary forts built solely for purposes of territorial conquest, any one of them can be abandoned at any time. For example, it is deemed efficient by Wal-Mart to open two stores very close to each other if this quickly and most completely puts local merchants out of business. Once a monopoly over the region has been established, Wal-Mart can close the less profitable of the two stores. Residents will then pick up the externalized costs of fuel to travel to the farther one. As of 2000, by utilizing this strategy, Wal-Mart had already left behind twenty-five million square feet of space. In one Kentucky town, the abandoned Wal-Mart was eventually torn down at taxpayers' expense, according to the corporation's own website. After peaking at more than two new stores per day in 2005, Wal-Mart still planned to open 212 stores in the U.S. in 2009, despite the credit crisis.

Wal-Mart's behavior is not terribly mysterious. What's more puzzling is the widespread acceptance and patronage of this company and its peers by people who actually live in the wake of their damaging effects. While regions with very strong advocates for the environment, labor, local commerce, or health may have been successful in limiting the spread of the "big box" chains to their neighborhoods, the vast majority of American and, now, European counties have succumbed to or even welcomed their own colonization by international branded retail stores.

Our readiness to surrender the territory on which we live shouldn't surprise us all too much, for we were already treating our neighborhoods as anything but real places.

CHAPTER THREE

THE OWNERSHIP SOCIETY

Real Estate and the Disconnect from Home

Neighbors Become Homeowners

When I was a child, we lived in a middle-class urban neighborhood, a workingman's section of Queens, New York. It wasn't fancy or even particularly quaint, but I do remember—surely romantically and inaccurately—how the tiny yards of our "semiattached homes" were all connected to create one big one. Every Friday evening, someone would light the big barbecue grill at the end of our dead-end block and launch a weekend-long cookout. I don't know who, if anyone, that grill belonged to, but pretty much any kid could show up with a hotdog or a drumstick and one of the grown-ups would make sure it was cooked right.

As my father moved up the career ladder we moved out to the suburbs: bigger houses, better schools, and brighter prospects. But all that stood out to my seven-year-old sensibilities was that in our new neighborhood each family had its own barbecue grill in the backyard, and that each backyard was separated from the others by a fence or a high hedge. The houses weren't even attached. Families would compete via patio landscaping, grill size, or cuts of meat. The Millers ate porterhouse, while the Portnoys grilled nothing but filet mignon. Now, instead of barbecuing with the Joneses, we were barbecuing against them—or at least apart from them—in a typically suburban status war. The fun was gone from the barbecue, even though market metrics would have registered a huge increase in grill popularity. By the time I was a teenager, we didn't grill at all anymore. We had more money, more land, and more stuff, but we seemed to be experiencing less of what made our poorer neighborhood more, well, fun.

My family was just one of many making the exodus from the city to the suburbs over those decades. Getting out of the city was a sign of having "made it." To my parents, it surely felt as though they had finally earned the right to make an independent, conscious decision of where and how to live. Of course, they had merely succumbed to the agenda of a more contemporary breed of speculators, who saw in the creation of the suburbs a path toward turning what had been worthless land into an investment opportunity. Their efforts might not have succeeded, however, were they not so well matched to the twin requirements of the new industrial base. Manufacturers required a class of consumers anxious to buy all the goods—especially automobiles—that factories were churning out. But they also needed a class of workers satisfied with the bounty their labors could earn them. The new suburbanites would be both.

Before the twentieth century, suburbs were anything but a desirable place to live. The only people who lived on a city's outskirts were those who couldn't afford to live in town. In preindustrial cities, many of the outer dwellers were employed carrying urbanites' garbage and sewage beyond city limits. After transporting their last wagon of waste safely to the fields, it only made sense that they should sleep there instead of traveling back to town. In the 1700s, the suburbs of Paris were home to those too poor to pay the taxes collected at the city gates. In the same period, Londoners spent over a century trying to halt the rise of "base tenements" outside the city—an effort complicated by the growing demand for unclean businesses like soap-making and tanning that were conducted there. In America, the suburbs were considered so inferior that the word "suburb" was used as a pejorative. Emerson wrote of "suburbs and the outskirts of things," while Nathaniel Parker Willis complained that compared with England, America had "sunk from the stranger to the suburban or provincial." Philadelphia's first suburb was created to house businesses condemned from the city proper, such as brothels and slaughterhouses.

The other chief inhabitants of the suburbs were slaves and former slaves. In the 1800s, they lived in alleys in and around their masters' city homes. But the squalor disturbed the wealthy, who then established the "living out" system. Slaves moved to "suburb sheds" beyond city limits so that the wealthy could rehabilitate the alleys behind their homes for their own use. This strategy made sense in walking cities, since everyone had to get everywhere else by passing through areas in the open air. The rich didn't want to walk through anything particularly unpleasant or unsettling on their way to work or the market.

By the late 1800s this all began to change. The Industrial Revolution enabled the segregation of commercial areas from wealthy residential areas. Thanks to steam ferries, cable cars, and the first commuter railroads, people who could afford to began to put considerable distance between their work and home. Cities began to turn inside out as suburban despair and center affluence was replaced by center despair and suburban affluence.

Where once an executive had a stake in the conditions surrounding the factory he commanded and the homes in which his workers lived—if for no other reason than their proximity to his own home—now he could hop on a streetcar and leave the filth and noise behind him at the end of the day. This distance promoted a new attitude toward labor, one shared by the wealthy industrialists who sought to bust unions, bilk workers, and increase profits. Labor unrest only exacerbated this urge to retreat to a home that was both a refuge and a fortress.

Progressive-minded journalists wrote well-meaning accounts of how the masses were "sinking into degradation and misery," unwittingly fueling the flight of the wealthy to the safe haven of more distant dwellings. In February of 1894, *Godey's Lady's Book* justified this retreat, arguing that "society is not friendly," and that every man required a home to serve as "a little bulwark against the outside world, in which those matters personal to himself should be carried on privately." The pursuit of happiness thus moved from the public realm—a cooperative urban landscape—to the private realm. People sought to become spectators to society, shaking their heads in disbelief as they read the evening paper, rather than true participants. They disconnected from public space and purchased their own private spaces instead. Their abstention from public life made them all the more ravenous for sensationalist depictions of what they had left behind:

strangers became criminals, political activity became sinister conspiracy, and cities became pits of depravity.

To serve this new market, savvy real-estate developers invested in property that could provide the wealthy with guaranteed distance from the urban poor. Developers gauged in which direction railways or other commuter services might be implemented, purchased cheap land, and then waited—or lobbied—for transport to be provided.

The first suburbs, like Brooklyn, gave wealthier workers the opportunity to live with the pleasantries of small-town life on tree-lined streets with the amenities and employment opportunities of the city. Before long, these first suburbs were themselves clanging with streetcars. Grand Army Plaza—now a major interchange, but originally a public park—was surrounded by a bluff of land to keep out the noise from streetcars and the surrounding buildings. The very same bluff today serves to keep the clamor of cars within Grand Army Plaza from disturbing residents of the buildings around it. The transportation industry that first enabled people to escape the noise of the city eventually enabled the smoke, clatter, and frenzy of urban life to follow them out to Brooklyn.

Although steam railroads were originally intended for long-distance travel, by the end of the nineteenth century the railroad industry had completed its transcontinental lines and was looking for new sources of revenue. By building stations in rural areas close to cities, they created lines for new populations of suburbanites. They kept fares high (the annual rate for a Westchester commuter in 1853 was forty-five dollars), which kept these new suburbs limited to the desirable people who could afford it. This was fine with the land developers, who sought to maintain the investment integrity of the lands they were selling, which depended entirely on the social class of residents. The Long Island Rail Road, which was originally intended as the beginning of a much longer link from New York to Boston, turned out to have more value as a commuter line to suburban Newtown, Maspeth, and Flushing, in what was even then called "unabashedly the instrument of real-estate speculators."

By this time, suburban development was less a matter of finding new places where workers could be housed comfortably than stoking demand for new and more fashionable places for the wealthy to live. One advertisement for the Boston and Lowell Railroad proclaimed "Somerville, Medford, and Woburn present many delightful and healthy locations for residence, not only for the gentleman of leisure, but the man of business in the city." Suburban developers reciprocated by including railroad timetables in their listings, and reminding potential homeowners that every lot was "within a few minutes walk of the station."

But the development of each new, healthy suburb wreaked havoc on the ones closer to the city. Early suburbs became little more than the places through which newer, wealthier suburbanites commuted to get to and from work. The worse those places looked, the more justified any suburbanite felt for traveling all the way past them to get to the safety and peace of home. Home took on a whole new meaning.

Until this point, the word "home" had never really referred to the unattached dwelling we think of today when we hear it. Home was the town or city a person came from—not the structure in which he lived. A household, noted the French historian Philippe Ariès, was a production unit supporting apprentices, journeymen, and retainers as well as spouses and children. "Much of life was inescapably public; privacy hardly existed at all."

As the household business gave way to the corporation and the factory, and as the streets where children played became the streets where they were run over by streetcars, the family home became a refuge from the perceived ills of a society beyond anyone's control. The more families who left the city to build houses, the more cities became characterized by those left behind: the poor.

The increasingly desperate flight from cities was reframed for suburban exiles as the attainment of the American Dream. While *Godey's Lady's Book* and the "domestic science" texts of Harriet Beecher Stowe and Catherine Beecher created the mythology of woman as queen of the house and competent homemaker, other writings depicted an equally compelling role for men to fill, utterly dependent on the attainment of a private home. Walt Whitman wrote, "A man is not a whole or complete man unless he owns a house and the ground it stands on." *The American Builder* magazine amplified this view into a sales pitch in 1869: "It is strange how contentedly men can go on year after year, living like Arabs a tent life, paying exorbitant rents, with no care or concern for a primary house." The Baptist minister Russell Conwell's infamous lecture "Acres of Diamonds," reportedly delivered over five thousand times between 1900 and 1925, equated home ownership with righteous living: "Introduce me to the people who own their own homes around this great city, those beautiful homes with gardens and flowers, those magnificent homes so lovely in their art, and I will introduce you to the very best people in character as well as in enterprise in our city. . . . A man is not really a true man until he owns his own home, and they that own their own homes are economical and careful, by owning the home."

From the perspective of the *Communist Manifesto* coauthor Friedrich Engels, however, this indebtedness was just the yoke that capitalists needed to keep labor in line. Home ownership, and the mortgage it required, would be "chaining the worker by his property to the factory in which he works." This possibility for social programming was not lost on real-estate speculators or the many businesses looking to the suburbs for a way to create a highly compliant middle-class society. As the president of Provident Institution for Savings in Boston explained, "Give him hope, give him the chance of providing for his family, of laying up a store for his old age, of commanding some cheap comfort or luxury, upon which he sets his heart; and he will voluntarily and cheerfully submit to privations and hardship."

So the suburban home was as much a symbol of luxury as it was a real luxury. It was less important for this new life to provide actual satisfaction as for it to produce a class of people who *behaved* as if they were satisfied. So much the better if they believed that true satisfaction was just one more paycheck, and one more purchase, away. Our social programmers were learning how to keep us on the edge of a true climax of consumer satisfaction. For us to remain goal-oriented, the suburban ideal had to remain unattainable—always one step away.

Only the very wealthiest Americans owned the kinds of estates on which the suburbs were pretending to be modeled. The "great country estate" was actually a Renaissance ideal, proclaiming and maintaining a person's political and social position. The Renaissance's new focus on individuality meant that an accomplished gentleman required a place set off and apart from everyone else. A room within one's city home was no longer enough. Moreover, country estates served as an early form of branding and publicity. A newly wealthy family could display its land acquisitions by creating a country estate of size and grandeur corresponding to its holdings. Much as Donald Trump tags his buildings with ostentatious gold letters spelling his name, the new élite built country estates to trumpet their investments in order to gain political and financial leverage. Again, it had less to do with land as a place than property as a commodity. And even then, it was less about the land's value as a real asset than as a sign of a family's healthy balance sheet—an advertisement for assets held somewhere else.

Whether or not America's new homeowners had a conscious grasp of the history they were imitating, their prefigured ideals came straight from the storybooks. As far back as 1839, the *Encyclopedia of Architecture* explained that the inspiration for the proper American house with a spacious manicured lawn was the Renaissance Italian villa. Yards were not really for play or recreation as much as for identifying the separateness and privacy of each home from the world around it. By the 1880s, these practices were codified in property deeds, which included mandates for "setback" (the amount of distance between a house and the street) and sometimes even landscaping.

The overt call to Renaissance values reached a peak at the beginning of the twentieth century, as the first totally planned suburban communities, such as Llewellyn Park, New Jersey, and Riverside, Illinois, offered their nouveau-riche residents the opportunity to live in houses that emulated the country estates of British gentlemen and châteaus of French aristocrats. This imagery did more than sell houses; it promoted a lifestyle of consumption.

Each home was to be its own fiefdom. Self-sufficiency was part of the myth of the self-made man in his private estate, so community property, carpools, or sharing of almost any kind became anathema to the suburban aesthetic. The sole exception to this rule was country clubs, whose steep dues and competitive, fraternity-like bidding process maintained a sense of exclusivity to what was, at its core, a sharing of expense by men very much poorer than the nobles they were imitating. But they did the best they could. To complement their conspicuously consumptive country homes, men formed conspicuously consumptive country clubs, where they played conspicuously consumptive games of golf. How better to demonstrate one's control over vast property than to waste it?

Of course, the entire lifestyle was based on a charade and exploitation. Just like the Renaissance retreats on which they were modeled, suburban homes depended on the labor of unacknowledged legions of workers. In Boston's Brookline, for example, 10 percent of the taxpayers controlled 70 percent of the assessed property. The other 90 percent of the taxpayers were people who served them as landscapers, domestic servants, construction workers, painters, and groomers. These were the suburbs' real denizens.

Soon, however, they too were to be included in at least some version of the suburban home. The best suburbs won their own suburbs, with subdivisions between subdivisions, each containing people of a different social status. Unlike the city, where people of different classes lived side by side, the suburbs not only put distance between individuals but between *sorts* of individuals. The better insulated neighborhoods were from one another, the more carefully real-estate values could be controlled.

Élite suburbs now sought to distinguish themselves financially from the cities around which they had developed. Where early suburbs often welcomed annexation by cities, now suburbanites were determined to maintain control over their uniquely privatized neighborhoods. What better tool than incorporation? By incorporating, suburban towns like Boston's Brookline or Chicago's Oak Park allowed for easier discrimination against minorities, and a sense of true, legally ordained distance from the multiethnic confusion and moral compromise of the city. They were also relieved of the tax burden of social services for the poor. This made them even more desirable.

By the twentieth century, the kind of money that could be made developing a single successful suburb was well known to both railroad barons and real-estate speculators. The economist Richard Hurd showed them how the value of land would go up as a function of its convenient commutation distance to a central business district. Transit tycoons shifted their emphasis from providing good transportation for people to manipulating the value of undeveloped farmland. They built rail lines to the subdivisions they owned, while passing over those of their competitors. They never even intended for their rail services to be profitable; tracks were a loss leader for the real-estate sales they enabled. Neighborhoods and commuter lines were not natural phenomena that sprang up around the needs and activities of people. They were master-planned developments aimed at delivering land-speculation profit.

The automobile might have changed all this, but it actually served to accelerate the conversion of place to property. Henry Ford, for all his faults, saw owning the automobile as an inalienable right. He believed that cars should be cheap enough for any worker on his assem-

bly line to own. What he and his counterparts at General Motors required, however, was a compelling reason for owning one. The suburbs gave them one.

The problem was that, unlike railways, cars required public space
to operate. Who would build, and pay for, all the roads? Although it
might have seemed logical for drivers to pay the tolls and taxes
required to maintain automobile thoroughfares, this would have dis-
couraged people from buying cars in the first place. Instead, the automobile companies, as well as tire manufacturers, oil companies, and,
of course, land developers, pressured the government to pick up the
tab. While GM's role in dismantling the city streetcar has been over-
stated, the company did identify the cities where trolley systems were
vulnerable, and then created competitive lines that put them out of
business. Once this was done, GM would convert the new system into
a bus line—serviced by GM's buses. Then GM would divest itself of
the company. This practice spurred the transition from city streets
that served pedestrians, merchants, and kids along with trolleys, to
roads that served the automobile.

By the end of World War II, most people finally had enough money
to consider buying an automobile. But car production had been increasing twenty times faster than highway construction. In order to
get more asphalt for its cars, the auto industry needed to persuade the
government to develop land and roads at a pace that matched the output of its car factories.

Mirroring the techniques of the railroad barons of the century before, GM's lobbying group crafted legislation that made highways
federally funded and controlled. Their justification was that highways
were a national defense issue—required to move troops around the
country in case of an attack. Conveniently, this made the secretary of
defense, Charles Wilson, responsible for highway acts. Wilson was a
major GM shareholder, and former president of the company. (When
asked at his confirmation hearing about a potential conflict of interest,
he famously answered, "I thought that what was good for our country
was good for General Motors, and vice versa.") Thanks to GM's policy influence, highways would become a national priority, controlled
far away from where they were actually built.

Municipal governments had no say in the design of the highways
that passed through them. Federal road engineers were not particularly concerned with anything but the efficiency of long-distance

travel, and didn't bother to consider the effects of their constructions on the people who lived around them. Huge swaths of territory were considered only for their value as rights-of-way, not as places in themselves. Neighborhoods were uprooted, divided, and demolished. Local governments that attempted to resist were quickly and decisively neutralized by the courts.

The resulting highways displaced hundreds of thousands of people and further drove down property values in the cities. According to Senator Gaylord Nelson, 75 percent of federal transportation spending has gone toward highways, while 1 percent has been spent on mass transit. Urban-planning masters such as Robert Moses developed highway schemes intended to keep undesirable people from traveling into desirable neighborhoods. In just one of many examples, Moses built highway overpasses with only nine feet of clearance in order to prevent buses from getting through. This was intended to keep poor black people from traveling from the city to the new suburbs, while also making the purchase of a car a prerequisite for residence.

So public funds would be used to render public space more accommodating to the most private of vehicles, and less suitable for habitation by the public at large. Meanwhile, public streetcars and other mass transit would remain classified as "private investments" ineligible for subsidies and dependent solely on their own operating profits. They couldn't keep up. Americans witnessed a cascade of streetcar-company bankruptcies and came to believe that mass transit was on the way out. This pressured people to buy cars and learn how to use them before it was too late, which only accelerated mass transit's downward spiral. In most suburbs to this day, getting to work—or anywhere, for that matter—means owning and operating a car.

Today, most of us look back on the triumph of the car and the automotive suburbs as the natural march of progress. A new technology can naturally render older ones obsolete. As people make money, they might naturally seek greener pastures and more land for themselves. As a country and the cities within it grow up, they naturally convert more land into residential areas. But none of these seemingly natural phenomena were natural at all. Corporations wrote business plans aimed at attacking the viability of mass transit; they leveraged their political influence to enact policies that undermined municipalities' ability to control their own land use; and, perhaps most significant, they promoted a myth that success in America should be equated with self-sufficiency, privacy, and property.

The suburbs became dependent on the automobile, and dedicated increasing amounts of space to parking spots, garages, and intersections. Towns once planned to accommodate walks to the train station were now expanded horizontally across rail lines. Houses were built farther apart and front porches gave way to garages and back decks. Suburbs extended as far from the city as their developers could win asphalt roads from the government. The daily commute grew longer and less social; where workers and their bosses might have once traveled the same train but gotten off at different stops, now everyone traveled in separate vehicles. Suburban town centers, such as they were, deteriorated as foot traffic declined. This devastated local businesses, while making chance encounters with neighbors less likely. Lifestyles were developed around the needs of a corporate product, rather than the other way around.

Scores of other corporations learned to support and exploit the suburban propensity for ownership and self-sufficiency. In 1935, General Electric sponsored architectural competitions for model homes that used as many GE appliances as possible (one architect incorporated seventy-six of them). Over the next two decades, women's magazines such as *Ladies' Home Journal* glamorized the latest household products as well as the push-button control over life they offered. Life in the suburbs became about buying things, installing appliances, and making improvements.

The very premise for the suburbs was to turn more of the real world into a market opportunity, so it shouldn't be surprising that it provided such a terrific canvas for successive layers of marketeering. Just moving to the suburbs made people more dependent on products, and less able to share. The automobile suburbs were even more highly stratified and homogeneous than their predecessors. The only way to distinguish oneself, entertain oneself, or take care of oneself was by buying oneself a factory-built product.

Perhaps no other shift better epitomizes our disconnection from the real, and our change from human actors to agents of corporatism. It's more than a little reminiscent of the shift away from feudalism and the emergence of a real-estate market during the Renaissance. Neither had anything to do with people's real need for land, and everything to do with excess capital's need for a place to grow. In both periods, peo-

ple who actually used and lived off the land were displaced by speculators who merely owned it, and then residents whose use for it was ornamental or self-promotional, at best.

Just as those early members of the bourgeoisie helped redefine
public land as private property, speculators of nineteenth- and
twentieth-century America created what we now call the suburbs out
of land that had no previous market value. The agenda of the real-
estate speculators drove both land-use policy and the psychology of
home ownership. While some people may have had a natural desire to
leave the city and live a pastoral life, the overall shift in land use that
created the suburbs was almost entirely directed by the needs of capital, not people.

It was only a matter of time before the people living in the suburbs
began to experience their homes as property, too.

Place Once Removed: The Mortgage

It all started innocently enough. America was still in the midst of the
Great Depression, and the expansion of home ownership appeared to
solve a number of the nation's problems. The new suburbs boosted
the real-estate market, created construction jobs, and stimulated the
consumption of manufactured goods. The new suburban lifestyle,
meanwhile, quelled labor unrest and made more people feel like they
were on a path toward attaining the American Dream. Even displaced
blacks were being shunted into new housing projects. What's not to
like?

All the research indicated that everyone would be happier in the
new scheme. The social theorists on whom the U.S. government
relied—whose work was funded mainly by the corporations benefiting from their findings—cited home ownership as the surest path to
becoming part of the consumer class. Home owners had a stake in the
nation, as well as a new kind of obligation: a loan to pay back. This
meant they worked harder—both to make money to pay down their
mortgages, and to acquire more stuff for their homes. And, assuming
the economy worked the way it's supposed to, this would engender a
more compliant and eager workforce, momentarily satisfied with what
it had and consistently desirous of more. It sounded good on paper,
anyway.

Herbert Hoover convened the President's National Conference on Home Building and Home Ownership to help him figure out how to get people into their own new suburban houses. Their main recommendation: long-term, amortized mortgages. If people could pay back the cost of a house over fifteen or thirty years, they would be empowered to live beyond their present means, and committed to earning steadily well into the future. The Federal Home Loan Bank Act of 1932 created a credit reserve for banks to pump more funds into the housing market. But the banks were still too traumatized by repeated "runs" on their liquidity. The mortgage terms they came up with were so restrictively risk-averse that only three out of the forty-one thousand applications they received ended up being approved.

After a few fits and starts, Franklin D. Roosevelt managed to do a bit better. He began with a characteristically federal effort called the Resettlement Administration, which simply relocated poor people to cheap land, then knocked down slums and put parks in their place. They built three towns this way, from scratch, but they went way over budget and the whole project was scrapped for lack of additional funds.

His penchant for federally funded projects notwithstanding, FDR realized that an effort of this magnitude required the massive, decentralized power of the free market. Instead of simply paying for towns to be built, the federal government would create agencies, laws, and codes that favored construction and home buying by millions. As a result, the needs of the market came to define the fabric of suburban reality, at the expense of all other priorities. It was built into the rules defining building, zoning, ownership, segregation, and class mobility. Eventually, the market and the landscape would actually change places. Instead of exploiting the market to build the suburbs, the suburbs would be exploited to build new markets. This was not about constructing a nation; it was about repairing an economy.

To begin with, FDR's Home Owners Loan Corporation changed America's relationship to mortgages. Prior to the HOLC, a mortgage was a stigma. More like turning over one's "property cards" in a game of Monopoly, a mortgage had always been something a person took out after owning a property and then going into debt. It was a bank's way of helping customers get through bad times. Although home loans became more popular during the speculative bubble of the late '20s, by the Depression many of those were going into default. The

HOLC helped people refinance their loans without going into foreclosure, and offered special low-interest loans of its own to help people buy back houses they had already lost.

More significant, the HOLC figured out how real-estate markets worked, and systemized an appraisal methodology that would help banks, lenders, and home owners guarantee the investment value of their properties. People were not about to take out mortgages to buy homes in neighborhoods that might go down in value. Banks were not inclined to lend the money, either. The long-term financial commitment of a thirty-year mortgage meant ensuring that the main characteristics of a neighborhood remained stable over time.

Instead of measuring this stability in terms of civic participation, church membership, community reinvestment, or local volunteerism, the HOLC evaluated neighborhoods through more familiar statistics: age, jobs, income, housing materials, and, most of all, race. The new, mathematically justified system for classifying neighborhoods became known as "red lining." The scheme used colors, letters, and numbers to code the desirability and investment value of different neighborhoods. Green was the best—a homogeneous, perpetually high-demand area, occupied by white businessmen and professionals, with no Jewish infiltration. Blue was next, for desirable areas that had already reached their peak. Yellow was for neighborhoods in decline, and red was for those already fallen. "Full decline" meant that black people already lived there.

The methodology assumed that all neighborhoods would decline as structures aged and progressively poorer people moved in. Appraisers learned to see any mixing of races as a sign of instability and impending price drops. This logic trickled down to home owners who were tied to big mortgages and had more of a stake in the value of their property than the quality of their lives or, least of all, the eradication of their prejudices. Besides, recognizing the precursors to a neighborhood's infiltration by blacks or Jews meant getting out in time to win a good price for one's home and pay back the mortgage. Getting out too late could mean owing more on a house than it was currently worth. Thanks to the way the federal government promoted home ownership, suburbanites learned to become more racist as a means of financial survival.

It wasn't enough just to turn races against one another for the sake of a housing market tilted toward real-estate speculators. The very design of the neighborhood had to incorporate this bias toward segregation and isolation for the sake of price stability. These practices were fully institutionalized by 1934, when the Federal Housing Administration was set up, ostensibly to jump-start the construction industry and put people back to work. The sole strategy of the FHA, however, was to insure long-term mortgages: a bank would still make the loan, but the FHA would back it up if the borrower defaulted—much as the Fed is now insuring the "liquidity" of failing predatory mortgage lenders. It worked as planned. Over the next decade, housing starts went up more than sixfold. Loans were so plentiful that it became cheaper to own than to rent.

But the biases of the new system were very specifically aimed against shared property, renovation of existing homes, or any racial interaction. Separated single-family structures got better mortgage terms than multifamily dwellings. It cost more to borrow money for home repairs than for the purchase of a new home. Worst of all, the FHA rules heavily favored the strict segregation of neighborhoods, going so far as to recommend that deeds include clauses legally preventing black occupancy.

These rules dictated the physical characteristics of the real world. In one startling example, white families settling at Eight Mile Road outside Detroit in 1940 ended up surrounding a black neighborhood. Neither blacks nor whites could be approved for mortgages until a developer built a concrete wall between the areas. After that, the whites were able to get mortgages. This FHA-mandated discrimination was rejected by the Supreme Court in 1948, but the publicity around the ruling only made builders more aware of such clauses, increasing their overall popularity. Once the private sector came in to take over the government's role of guaranteeing loans, they used the same race-based and divisive techniques, which had already been institutionalized for them.

From the available evidence, it appears that all FDR hoped to do was create jobs and new public housing by demonstrating "to private industry the feasibility of large-scale community planning efforts." But the marriage of these private and public housing efforts ended up producing projects that reflected the worst of each. The Public Works Administration and the U.S. Housing Authority lent money to private corporations for slum clearance, while giving local municipal governments authority over whether and where to build public housing. No one wanted a housing project near his own community, so the corporations and municipalities used the financing to tear down any slums near expensive suburbs and rebuild them as projects back in the city. Urban decay got worse, and the suburbs got even more segregated. If money had been put toward rehabilitating existing slums instead of tearing them down and building new ones, it might have created fewer construction jobs and lower profits, but it would have also prevented this very rapid redrawing of the residential map for the benefit of white suburban property values and the developers who exploited them. Instead, the attention to zoning and its implications for a family's net worth heightened Americans' sense that a house wasn't simply a place to live, but an asset to protect by any means necessary.

Finally, the FHA was expanded to include a Veterans Administration to take on the problem of how to compensate World War II veterans and integrate them back into America's economy and society. If Europe after World War I was any example, widespread resentment among veterans could lead them to turn to unions or, worse, communism. As Jack Hardy, the national commander of the American Veterans of World War II, warned, "It is likely that a desperation born of unmerited privation, inexcusable in this country, may create an acute and dangerous rift between veterans and the political management that makes such conditions possible."

The resulting GI Bill used everything that had been learned so far about the suburbs to plan communities that could safely domesticate both GI Joe and Rosie the Riveter, as quickly as possible. Developers built hundreds of thousands of small single-family houses, for which the government issued mortgages at whatever prices builders demanded. Housing starts boomed from 114,000 in 1944 to 937,000 in 1946 to a high of 1,692,000 in 1950. The sheer volume and scale of these projects and the speculative wealth they created led to the dominance of bigger players who gobbled up independent builders. By 1949, only 10 percent of firms were constructing 70 percent of new homes. Central funding by the government had corporatized the building industry.

Island Trees, Long Island—as "Levittown," the most famous development of the homebuilders Levitt and Sons, was first called—brought Industrial Age management and scale to home construction. Where houses were once built individually by skilled carpenters, the Levitts' twenty-seven-step system used separate crews for each job, assembling pre-made components with power tools. Only 20 percent to 40 percent of construction tasks required skilled labor.

Essentially a federally chartered corporation, Levitt and Sons enjoyed exclusive rights and discount rates on land secured by the government. And just like authorized monopolies of the colonial era, the Levitts arrived on a site and then learned to make everything they needed. The company refused to buy nails, concrete, or even appliances from regional vendors, purchasing all its materials from its own subsidiaries, which employed low-wage laborers. It even grew its own lumber.

As a return on its investment, the federal government got to dictate the basic template for all the houses. The FHA used this opportunity to design houses and communities that reinforced the nuclear family while discouraging the congregation of larger groups. The recommended house plans were for four- and five-room Cape cottages. The houses were uniform—intentionally interchangeable. The five models offered at Levittown varied only in color and exterior window arrangement. Variations less expensive to deliver could have been offered, such as rotating the position of the house on its axis, or changing colors and textures in the interior. But this would have defeated the underlying agenda of uniformity; the homogeneity of the houses was supposed to engender a culture of conformity.

Advertisers readily joined in the establishment of a four-room Cape house as the new symbol of the American Dream. Ads for everything from automobiles to radios featured young families standing in front of nearly identical Cape houses. A print spread for the Lee Rubber and Tire Company in 1943 showed a small family in front of a Cape house, with a church and a factory hovering above and the words "THESE ARE FUNDAMENTAL." A lifestyle in which conformity meant happiness had been defined and celebrated as payback for the sacrifices of war.

Conformity shouldn't be confused with solidarity. The houses and families within these subdivisions were equal, but separate. The architecture promoted nuclear-family values and gender-based roles for parents. As delivered, there was no room for relatives or even large parties—just the essential activities of a small family. The Cape houses had kitchens in the back, from which moms were to watch kids play in the backyard. In the front yard of each house were a lawn, landscaping, and four fruit trees to be tended by Dad. As William Levitt himself promised his government patrons, "No man who owns his own house and lot can be a Communist. He has too much to do." He meant this quite literally.

The homes also begged for owners to expand them. The footprint of each house was a scant seven hundred fifty square feet, barely enough space for one bedroom, much less the two or three required by a single family. But the houses were set on a minimum of six thousand square feet of land—two thousand more than zoning rules required for this size home. People were supposed to add on. Attics were also designed to accommodate the addition of dormers to create two additional bedrooms. The culture of do-it-yourself magazines and how-to books was born, as the men of these new suburbs expanded their houses—often buying materials and tools from the Levitts.

The design of the Levittown house intentionally demanded its owner's time while fueling his pride in ownership. Not that he would have had much to do in Levittown, otherwise. At the request of the FHA, all recreation spaces in town were for the exclusive use of nuclear families, while traditional male meeting places—bars, firehouses, gas stations—were conspicuously absent.

Levittown and other FHA-sponsored, master-planned, corporate-built communities provided "entry-level" homes for hundreds of thousands of Americans, mitigated civil unrest, and housed World War II veterans who certainly deserved a fair shake. But the plan came steeply sloped toward promoting individual home ownership over all other social priorities.

By making a house available to every white lower- to middle-class American, the FHA and its chartered corporations made home ownership a basic right—the first rung on the ladder to success. A private house went from being a status symbol to a middle-class prerequisite. Now, instead of buying a house to show that one had arrived in life, a successful man needed to buy a *bigger* house to make a more relative point. Home buying and selling, or "trading up," became the way to earn status. And because doing well meant moving up and out, any gains in status were at the expense of community.

Although it launched an era of home ownership as private enterprise, Levittown was itself made possible by a massive government subsidy. Even though a lion's share of the money ultimately ended up going to the Levitt brothers, without those subsidies the vast majority of residents never would have become home owners on their own. Not that its current residents would approve of any such government dole-out today. The middle-class white inhabitants of Levittown are among the first to put out yellow ribbons in times of war, and remain staunch supporters of conservative economic policies. Virtually unaware that their own home ownership was made possible by a huge government intervention, they do not seek welfare for themselves or support it for anyone else.

Having paved over the country with an American Dream represented by the single-family house and a single-family life, one of the most centralized government efforts in American history succeeded in creating a population utterly convinced of the primacy of home ownership and the deep connection between the value of their houses and that of their life's work. For all their supposed concern for the beauty and quality of their houses, 1960s suburbanites treated them more as assets than as homesteads—always ready to sell out and move up to the next level.

This was not a mere unintended consequence of government-backed housing mortgages, or some free expression of human nature for a private dwelling in which to hole up with one's family. The combination of government power and corporate monopoly ingrained an ideal not just in the minds of people, but in the very landscape in which they lived their lives. This, in turn, made a constructed mythology seem like a preexisting condition of our world—or, at the very least, a fundamental premise of a free civilization. Going into debt, distancing ourselves from our neighbors, and striving for conformity became equated with freedom.

Like any myth, this ideal was created independently of any experiential evidence beyond our own enduring dreams. This is what made it so easy to use a second time in completely different circumstances.

Twice Removed: No Money Down

"Let me first talk about how to make sure America is secure from a group of killers. People who hate—you know what they hate? They hate the idea that somebody can go buy a home. They hate freedom, that's what they hate."

—GEORGE W. BUSH, *Remarks on Home Ownership to the Department of Housing and Urban Development, June 18, 2002*

Just as George W. Bush told Americans to respond to the 9/11 attacks by shopping, he claimed that terrorism was an effort to undermine the freedom to be a home owner. In one sense, he was right. Home ownership, and the vast consumption of materials and energy it requires, forces some pretty exploitative foreign-policy maneuvers. This makes people in those resource-rich places as mad as natives were at the practices of the colonial empires exploiting them two hundred years ago.

It's a little harder to see exactly how the ideal of home ownership has also been used to exploit the supposed home owners. Just a couple of years ago, those of us attempting to warn friends against taking out questionable mortgages were ridiculed as conspiracy theorists. Didn't we understand that real estate always goes up? Or that home ownership was the only way to guarantee one's retirement? That the longer you wait to buy a house, the further out of reach that house was going to get?

The question of whether to become a home owner gave way to the much more presumptive "How are we going to get you *in*?" While government promised to encourage home ownership as a way of improving participation by poor people in the economy, banks came up with increasingly clever mortgage products that postponed the real cost of buying a house well into the future.

It all became clear to me as I sat at the kitchen table with a legal pad one summer evening, attempting to figure out just how much it was going to cost me to buy the overpriced apartment that my real-estate agent and mortgage broker assured me I could afford. True enough, if I had put down my life savings and then taken out the interest-only mortgage, I would have been able to make my payments for at least the first five years of the loan. At that point, although the mortgage would "reset" to a different rate of interest, all I had to do was refinance the loan and start again. Of course, "interest-only" meant that throughout those first five years I wouldn't have actually paid back any of the principal at all.

"What if interest rates are higher in five years?" I asked.

"The increase in the home's value will offset it," the mortgage broker responded.

"What if the house—for some reason—doesn't go up in value?" I asked.

"Houses always go up in value," she responded.

"But what if the mortgage resets to a rate I can't pay?"

"Everybody has these mortgages, now. Banks can't set the rate so high that everyone defaults. They won't make anything that way."

That very night, depending on this logic, I agreed to put in an offer for an apartment I could not afford. The next morning, I couldn't help but conclude that I was about to ruin my family's financial prospects for a very long time, and withdrew it. When I shared the news with my friends—about how "the man" had almost gotten me into the system—they almost universally chided me. "Grow up, already," said one good friend. Some of the others weren't so kind. Why was I trying to scare them about their own mortgages? Did I really think everyone with an interest-only loan was in trouble? How *dare* I imply that their houses might go down in value? (I ended up moving to a little town up the Hudson River and purchasing a whole house for about a quarter the price.)

Over the time I've been researching and writing this book, I've seen my suggestions that the mortgage industry was about to bilk consumers of their life savings go from fringe conspiracy to front-page news to global credit crisis. Just how and why so many of us bought into the scam, however, still remains essentially misunderstood.

Unlike the postwar housing boom, the great push for home ownership in America and Britain since the early '90s had nothing to do with creating a more compliant working class occupied with the tasks of taking care of a house and incapable of questioning their plight or even gathering to discuss it. This had already been accomplished. And segregation had been so complete that those still incapable of participating in the dream of home ownership could only imagine how much better it must have been than life in the projects.

The recent real-estate investment craze—much like the property craze back in the Renaissance—was more about finding investment vehicles for excess capital. It wasn't the prospective home owners with so much money to burn; it was banks and speculators. Regressive tax policies and new, cheap sources of labor in Asia had put even more wealth than usual in the hands of corporations and the very rich, and they needed new asset classes for all of it. Between the dot-com bust and the Enron scandal, the stock market was no longer a great place to stage a pyramid scheme. But the real-estate market, with its seemingly secure foundation in physical places, was still ripe for an extended boom and bust cycle.

Investment banks knew better than to invest in land. The last thing they wanted to be involved in was the buying and selling of real property—especially since its value had already been inflated by decades of mythmaking. No, the land would be at the very bottom of the pyramid. Instead, they invested in mortgages *other* people took out to buy land.

As Alan Greenspan eventually explained it to *Newsweek* magazine, "This particular problem was an accident waiting to happen. The euphoria that existed in the expansion of the housing-market bubble induced investors around the world who'd had a huge buildup in liquidity—largely because of the lower real long-term interest rates that occurred as a consequence of the end of the cold war—to invest in something with a higher rate of return. And, lo and behold, the sub-prime mortgage market provided it."

The housing bubble had little to do with buying pressure, and everything to do with an excess of capital looking for people who might borrow it. In Greenspan's words, "The big demand was not so much on the part of the borrowers as it was on the part of the suppliers who were giving loans which really most people couldn't afford." Mortgages were less about getting people into property than getting them into debt. Someone had to absorb the surplus supply of credit.

To generate more demand for loans, mortgage sellers would have to offer products to people who had never considered home buying before. This meant higher-risk consumers. Since they had lower credit ratings, they would have to pay higher rates of interest. More profit for the lender. Because these borrowers were generally less educated and less experienced with complex banking products, they were also less likely to fully grasp the implications of adjustable rates—often buried deep in mortgage documents only presented at closing, when there's no time to read through them. Other high-risk mortgage candidates included home owners who could be induced to "move up" to bigger properties, and "flippers"—who bought houses with almost no money down hoping to resell them at a profit before the first payments came due.

Banks found willing customers in the U.K. as well, where a "spend now, think later" psychology had already permeated the culture, and the average person had 2.8 credit cards. Unlike the Continent, where going into debt was still frowned upon and real-estate markets were tightly regulated, England had witnessed a real-estate boom even bigger than the one in the U.S. Those without real estate wanted to be among the home owners, who had passively watched the value of their properties triple in less than a decade. Bankers blame Britain's obsession with home ownership on an "island mentality" in which land is seen as a more precious asset than elsewhere. But even then, it was less about borrowing enough money to own a piece of the island than to have a piece of it to sell. By the late 1990s, Citigroup and Capital One had come to their rescue, introducing a wide assortment of suspect lending products to Britain as the country's regulators sat idly by. Within a few years, Britons were spending more than they earned, achieving an average household debt-to-income ratio of 1.62—even greater than that of Americans' 1.42. As of this writing, 6 percent of British home owners have been using their credit cards to pay their mortgages. As anyone who has ever used one credit card to pay off another surely knows, such a situation doesn't last for long.

Banks sought to mitigate their own risk in two ways. The first was to change what happened if a customer defaulted on his loan. Between 1997 and 2005, banks and credit agencies spent over $100 million lobbying to change bankruptcy laws in the United States. The main purpose of the 2005 bankruptcy bill they fought for was to make it harder for private citizens to win the same bankruptcy protections that corporations enjoyed. And declaring bankruptcy no longer absolved a person of his debts; under Chapter 13 he would still be responsible for them, along with additional penalties, forever. This made even the riskiest of loans a surer bet.

Banks also lobbied lawmakers to overturn rules that prevented them from engaging in both investment- and commercial-banking services. With the suspension of the 1933 Glass-Steagall Act (and the associated Bank Holding Company Act), banks won the ability to make loans and then underwrite their sale to other people and institutions.

In the old days, a bank made its money on the mortgage payments: it would write a loan to a customer, and the customer would pay it back. In the new scheme, a typical loan would be written by a mortgage lender—like Countrywide or New Century. A bank would then agree to provide the actual money for the loan, in return for the underwriting contract—the business of packaging the mortgage company's loans and selling them to others. These big bundles of loans would include both "subprime" mortgages and regular ones, minimizing the appearance of risk. The bank had much less of a stake in whether a loan was ever really going to be paid back. Its profits depended completely on the spread between the cost of writing the loan and the earnings from selling it.

And to whom were these bundles of unrecognizably mashed-up mortgages ultimately sold? Quite often, to you and me. Our pension funds, municipalities, and money-market accounts were made up largely of these "mortgage-backed securities." Many of the more responsible institutional buyers had strict portfolio constraints that should have prevented the acquisition of these high-risk assets. But credit-rating agencies including Moody's and Standard & Poor's gave mortgage-backed securities AAA status and delayed lowering their ratings long after they knew them to be composed of lower-quality loans. Goldman Sachs and other investment banks understood the ensuing problem so well that they began betting against the very mortgage-backed securities they were underwriting!

We were taking out mortgages we couldn't afford because they were camouflaged to look as if we had a reasonable chance of paying them back. Banks then changed the bankruptcy laws so that we could not get out of our obligations once the rates changed. Lastly, they sold us back our own mortgages, shifting back to us any of the risk through our money-market accounts and pension plans.

It wouldn't have worked if buyers hadn't themselves been disconnected from these homes as places to live, and already seeing them as investments to be sold. "Flip this house" became a renovation philosophy, with each improvement to a kitchen or a bathroom measured less in the utility it offered than its effect on resale value or capital-improvement-tax exemptions. "I really wanted white appliances," a home owner in Montclair, New Jersey, told me during the housing boom, "but if we sell I know the stainless steel will get us a better price." Was she planning to sell? No. But, as she liked to put it, "you never know." Now that the market has crashed, she's stuck polishing the thumbprints off stainless-steel appliances she doesn't like.

She's in a better position than many of her neighbors. Although her house isn't worth what it was last year, she didn't borrow money based on its falsely inflated market value. Engaged in a new form of serfdom—only bound now to banks and mortgage lenders instead of to lords—her more highly leveraged neighbors pore over the business section of the newspaper each day looking for some sign that the government will soon step in to "freeze" their mortgage rates where they are before a scheduled adjustment hits. Of course, freezing a mortgage rate may help an individual stay in his house, but it won't help the pension fund or municipal project depending on that interest to stay solvent. Selling their homes now won't even help. Thirty-nine percent of Americans who bought homes in 2006 owe more on their mortgages than the homes are worth. By contrast, of those who purchased their homes in 2003, only 3 percent now have "negative equity."

The government's cure for what is being called a "liquidity crisis" is to add liquidity to the system. Through lower interest rates or direct bailouts, the Fed gives more money to the lending institutions, re-creating the problem that got us here in the first place: a supply-side glut of money. This may calm Wall Street (long enough for institutional investors to sell their assets, anyway) but it has no positive effect on Main Street, where homes are still going into foreclosure at record numbers. When federal guarantees of the banking industry were first put in effect after the Great Depression, they were coupled with tough regulations on banks preventing them from making risky investments with government-backed credit. As the banking system was deregulated and privatized, financial institutions were freed to engage in increasingly leveraged schemes—but the government did not take back its promise to back them up with what could only be considered the people's money.

That's the downside of having turned our homes into assets, subject to the ebb and flow of a speculative marketplace. Step by step, place became property, property became a mortgage, and mortgages became derivative investments. The government entrusted corporations to build a new social order right into the architecture of our homes and the master plans of our suburbs. The resulting neighborhoods promoted pride in the family unit and the property it owned over any civic virtue or lived experience. The more abstract our relationship to home and hearth, the more dependent we became on metrics such as real-estate appraisals to gauge our happiness and social station. The appraisal map became the territory. How else to know you're in a good neighborhood, or that you've "made it"? It wasn't enough for a house to provide shelter and comfort in the real world; it also had to be a good growth investment in a manufactured one. It wasn't enough for a neighborhood to provide good schools, water, parks, and neighbors; it also had to be a racially stable "blue" zone, with very little income variation and, ideally, some good press.

We behaved like corporations ourselves, extracting the asset value of our homes and moving on with our families, going into more debt and assuming we'd have the chance to do it again. As long as prices went up, it seemed as if everyone was simply doing better. The speculative marketplace into which we had entered was part of an economy much bigger than all of us home owners put together: the highly leveraged, barely regulated world of investment banks. The enthusiasm with which we embraced our skyrocketing home values was more than matched by the greed of lending institutions flush with cash to capitalize our suspect mortgages.

Although lawmakers and the Fed had sufficient warning about widespread unscrupulous lending practices and the impending disaster in the housing market, they did nothing to avert it. Why? Mr. Greenspan and the federal government put a higher priority on promoting "financial innovation" and the "ownership society." Besides, Greenspan says he believed that any problems would remain "local" and not systemic, which is why he felt no qualms about encouraging what he called "innovative" lending products even after home owners had begun to default, and the ratings on mortgage-backed securities had begun to fall.

While the value of housing doesn't usually collapse across an entire country at once, when these cycles do end, failures feed on one another. Once the cost of borrowing changes, property owners begin to default and all the best-laid plans for neighborhood-as-investment dissolve: houses empty of their occupants and are often taken over by vagrants. Declining tax bases lead to cuts in police and other social services that would normally address these problems. Crime and truancy increase, and property values continue their downward spiral. Homes, now worth less, become increasingly difficult to refinance at better terms. This, in turn, leads to more foreclosures, and so on.

Government, somewhat sensibly, tries to stay out of the way while the market corrects itself. Even sympathetic congressional leaders understand that to bail out consumers who bought houses more expensive than they could afford is to reward careless speculation. But when the financial institutions backing these faulty mortgage products begin to fail, government is there with a check. The federal government exchanges real money in the form of Treasury notes for bad money in the form of mortgage-backed securities. The highest-paid brokers at Bear Stearns keep their jobs, even if the logo on their letterhead changes to J. P. Morgan, and their bonuses are reduced for a few years while the dust settles.

The fiction is that the money just "vanished." Financial newspapers and cable-TV business channels say that the value of holdings has been "erased" by market downturns, but it hasn't been erased at all. It's on the negative side of one balance sheet, and the positive side of someone else's. While Goldman Sachs was underwriting mortgage-backed securities of dubious value, it was simultaneously *selling them short*! (The firm bought "puts" on mortgage bonds, which go up in value as the bonds fail.) The trader John Paulson earned himself $4 billion and his funds another $15 billion in one year by betting against the housing market. For help predicting the extent of the downturn, Paulson hired none other than Alan Greenspan as an advisor to his hedge fund. The Fed chairman who encouraged the housing bubble even after it began to crash is now cashing in on the very devastation his policies created. The money did not disappear at all. It merely changed hands. The land was just a medium for the redistribution of wealth.

The extent to which people search for a figure or an institution to blame after a crash is matched only by our refusal to recognize the disaster in the making. Try telling people that their home values are inflated while the market is still going up, and they're likely to treat you as if you were committing treason. Afterward, experiencing themselves as the victims of a cleverly orchestrated scam, everyone is ready to review the records and dole out the blame. But forensic analysis of faulty mortgage instruments and unforeseen market corrections only tells a part of the story. Worse, it distracts us still further from the social crisis at hand by recontextualizing it as a market phenomenon. After all this, we're still most worried about the money?

Indeed, the most debilitating social symptoms—the ones responsible for laying bare the social ties of real community—actually surface during a boom, not the eventual bust. Yes, neighborhoods get "better" as houses are renovated, fancy restaurants move in, and prices go up. If it's the city, the newspaper's real-estate section invents a new name for a district—some combination of syllables meant to please brokers advertising on the same page. Higher rents soon outprice the artists and students who made the place newsworthy in the first place. Bodegas give way to boutiques, next-door neighbors send their kids to private schools across town from one another, and decals from security companies start showing up in ground-floor windows.

If it's the suburbs, then all sorts of new rules begin to issue from the town council, limiting grass height, reducing to one the number of families that can live in a single home, and closing businesses that stay open at night attracting the "wrong" element. Property taxes rise beyond the reach of anyone but the target demographic, and the desired homogeneity sets in. Membership in civic organizations, volunteer groups, and local libraries goes down, fences and gated developments go up.

In both city and suburb, whatever once contributed to community and connected people is slowly replaced by the real-estate market's simulations of what community looks like. The centrality of mortgages and property valuations to our experience of home detaches us from the values that once connected us to the actual places where we lived. For the most part, we see the value of our experience through the computer window of our banking software—this era's equivalent of the double-entry ledger. When we do go outside, our ability to make a more meaningful connection to place has been lost to a simulation that is itself tilted toward the needs of the market.

We reconnect, all right. But to the wrong thing.

The New Old Urbanism

By day, the illusion is almost convincing.

People of all ages stroll down a cheery Main Street, window-shopping. An elderly couple slowly circles the fountain in the town square while another, decades younger, sits on a well-shaded park bench and bottle-feeds their infant. A teenager carefully parallel parks in front of a quaint clothing shop with a "sale" sign on the door, while his girlfriend bounds into the Colonial-style storefront.

Above one shop, a middle-aged man in a bright yellow T-shirt sits on his apartment's terrace drinking coffee and reading that morning's edition of the *Charlotte Observer*. A postal worker with a mailbag over her shoulder passes by on a bicycle and shouts up to him. He waves and smiles, takes another sip of joe, and goes back to his paper. Another Saturday morning in a typical, perfect American town.

It's really not until the place empties out at night that Birkdale Village, North Carolina, begins to look more like a stage set. The proportions are just too perfect. No matter where you stand, the angles between the buildings line up as if they were intentionally placed to provide you with a perfect perspective and vanishing point. Sprinklers quietly activate, spraying a thin mist onto the landscaped meridians, zone by zone. Mexican landscapers hop off trucks to manicure the shrubbery; the last of the shops turns off the lights; and the final few residents—themselves as much a part of the illusion as the dwarfs inhabiting Disneyland—return to the condos they rent over national-chain tenants such as Talbots, Sunglass Hut, and the Gap.

Only then might you notice that Birkdale isn't really a town at all, but a mall. What by day appeared to be rows of separate little buildings are really separate little storefronts along the faces of just a few really big buildings. These structures are bounded on two sides by parking lots so immense that they prompted an Urban Land Institute report on the potential environmental damage to surrounding areas by their water runoff. Almost everyone—more than 99 percent—inhabiting Birkdale by day has driven there from somewhere else. They aren't Birkdale Villagers at all, but shoppers, diners, and moviegoers.

"I certainly would never build a mall," declares J. Michael Dunning, a principal architect at Shook Kelley, the firm charged with designing the whole place. Dunning is a tall, sandy-haired man in his mid-forties, with a muscular build, clear eyes, and an earnest face. He walks through Birkdale with the critical gaze of a designer let down by the builders, retailers, and real-estate developers who were charged with making his dream a reality. "That white band is no good," he says, referring to the thick white horizontal stripe going around all the buildings so that merchants' signs will all be at a uniform height. Of course, a real town wouldn't have a white stripe running across it. "They made these so cheap," he says, knocking on a white column with a hollow thud. "It's plaster over foam. Not like anybody uses real limestone anymore, but this isn't even the *good* plaster over foam."

Dunning had hoped for more. He intended Birkdale Village to be just that—a village, with residences, stores, sidewalks, offices, and everything else that makes up a real town. To a great extent, he succeeded: the fifty-two stores and fourteen restaurants in this outdoor complex are accessible by sidewalks, and even have parking spaces in front of them. Over the stores, three hundred twenty apartments with forty unique floor plans house people committed to making Birkdale their way of life. One of them even posts glowing daily observations to his Coffee at Birkdale blog about the community, its members, and their cars. Of course, he's also a local real-estate agent.

Birkdale was meant to serve as an antidote to the dislocation of the regular suburbs, and an application of a theory known as New Urbanism to the real world. The approach was first pioneered by the urbanist Jane Jacobs, a vocal critic of the land-use policies of the 1950s. Jacobs believed that the common practice of separating residences from businesses dislocated people from the real, vibrant spaces of more naturally developed towns and destroyed any opportunity for community. She often held up Manhattan's Greenwich Village as an example of a thriving urban community. Its confusing streets exemplified the delightfully messy mixed use she so admired. Keeping stores and workshops adjacent to schools and homes allows for random interactions between people and keeps the sidewalks busy and safe late into the night.

It's hard to plan a town from scratch according to the principles of New Urbanism. Greenwich Village happened over a couple of centuries. Birkdale Village had to happen a lot faster. Its two institutional investors and lending banks needed to recoup their $82,500,000 sooner than a regular city might have generated such returns. Real towns, though they often had a master plan, were built around some actual production like farming, shipping, mining, or manufacturing. Stores, schools, and libraries emerged to serve the growing population.

In Birkdale's case, this sense of community would be promoted by conscious top-down master planning instead of any natural bottom-up evolution. Everything would be built at once, but made to look as if it came into being naturally over a long period of time. If Dunning succeeded, his streets would imitate the usage patterns of a real town and promote the kinds of random interactions one might experience there—all while looking as unplanned as possible.

While real towns were built around industries, the only industry in Birkdale is shopping. If it was to succeed, Birkdale needed to be built all at once and then opened all at once—lest a majority of shops and apartments stood empty while others attempted to conduct business. You can't just open part of a town when that town is supposed to seem like a preexisting "destination," whose charm and attraction is based

on its vibrancy and cohesiveness. The whole place needed to be activated at the same moment—every store leased, and as many apartments as possible rented *in advance*. Only then could the ribbon be
cut, and Birkdale set into motion.

Dunning is the first to admit that he bent the rules of New Urbanism to fit the realities of his development situation. "Strict New
Urbanism is dogmatically sustainable and ecologically friendly development. But there are market forces, developer mind-sets, retail
mind-sets, and economic realities that don't always merge easily with
what we'd really like to happen," he says. While Dunning first conceived Birkdale as a real residential community with a few small
shops, its financiers required a level of funding that only big anchor
stores could provide. The ratio was gradually tilted in favor of commercial space, making the remaining residences less a functional town
than an ornamental addition. ("Look, honey," a shopper says to her
husband as she notices the apartments over Victoria's Secret, "people
live here!")

The big box stores demanded the big parking lots, visibility from
the "major arteries," and the humongous signage already familiar to
the automotive American consumer. Where Jacobs had always advo-
cated building towns around the needs of people instead of the needs
of cars, Birkdale was being constructed at the intersection of NC-73
and I-77, a ribbon of highway that *is* Birkdale's natural environment,
forcing many concessions by this walking town to the primacy of the
automobile.

For all their town's compromises, however, Birkdale's residents are
dedicated to their community, and see in it the qualities they've come
to identify with home: a Starbucks with friends, a well-stocked magazine rack at Barnes & Noble, and a decent dentist's office (just next
to the Pier 1). Parking is easy, the sidewalks are clean, and everything
looks just like it does on *Gilmore Girls*. Having spent most of their
lives in some of the worst automobile suburbs ever built, they see
Birkdale as a throwback to an earlier, more innocent time, when people talked about the weather and just hung out in one another's company. They're not stupid consumers. The residents I met are well
aware of the effort being made to simulate town life. They appreciate
it, and mean to play their part.

Although it was built *for* them instead of *by* them, and they rent instead of own, Birkdale's residents have taken psychological possession

of their town. When North Carolina state agencies ordered Birkdale to shut its fountain off during the drought affecting the entire Southeast, residents came out and staged a demonstration. "And they didn't just say, 'Turn on the fountain,' " recounts Dunning. "They said, 'Turn on *our* fountain.' That's how you know it is a real community. They took ownership of the public space."

Of course, the "public space" to which Dunning refers is actually private space, owned by the shopping center. And the single example of community activism we can credit to its citizenry is demanding the right to waste valuable water during a drought in order to preserve Birkdale's self-image as a town living in harmony with its physical surroundings.

It's hard to blame Birkdale's residents for loving their town, however it came to be. No, it's not a real community; they don't make anything, they share no interdependencies, there are very few families, no one owns their home, and the rate of turnover is as high as that of any other prefab condo village. At best, they buy stuff from the stores their friends work at—stores actually owned by corporations headquartered a thousand miles away, selling products shipped from an even greater distance. Instead of a family living over the store it owns, employees—if they're lucky enough to be able to afford it—rent space over the retailers for whom they work.

Most of the residents work elsewhere, and return to the mall in the evening for dinner out and to sleep. Coming home to Birkdale is like returning to a cruise ship or a resort hotel. Yes, they get to know their neighbors because they're eating in the same restaurants and buying stuff from the same shops. They consume together, and enjoy one another's company, but have none of the other ties that build community.

As one local real-estate agent confided, "When the next 'village' goes up, most of these people will check out and won't look back. They may even move on as a group." But compared with the suburban wasteland of the '50s through the '80s, this is paradise. It is an opportunity to reconnect to place, to experience the street as something in its own right rather than just a way to get somewhere else. Towns like Birkdale—and there are a few dozen now in full swing—refocus people on how they're living instead of just where they're getting, and create destinations off the highway where the most jaded automotive suburbanites can get a taste of what it's like to walk around outside with other people.

Isn't reconnecting to a fake town better than not connecting at all? Although the New Urbanism aesthete will deride the people of Birkdale for responding to the cues embedded in its absolutely planned and artificial re-creation of small-town life, where does such orthodoxy get us? Is Birkdale just a cynical application of watered-down New Urbanism to make the Gap look and feel more like a local business? Or does it help transform the otherwise alienating landscape of the suburbs into a healthier, more potentially social setting?

Perhaps it is the latter. But these master-planned faux villages would stand no chance at all of endearing themselves to people who weren't already, and by design, disconnected and alienated from the places where they live. By installing national chains and superstores as their foundational institutions, mall towns redirect our dormant instincts for civic and social connection to the brands sponsoring all this supposed renewal. It's not an American Legion, a public library, or a war memorial gracing Birkdale's most prominent locations, but an Ann Taylor and the fittingly named Banana Republic.

Just because a century of misguided social engineering has sterilized our urban and suburban landscapes doesn't mean that corporations offer the best hope of restoring a social fabric. To the companies paying for it, New Urbanism is the latest in a long series of efforts to take advantage of the deadened suburbs and crumbling, crime-ridden cities. With the civic sector quite literally zoned off the map, the corporate sector is free to remake the territory in its own image. The results are prettier and sometimes even more fun, but any creation of meaning and value comes from the outside in. To participate means to buy.

The campaign to spawn corporate life on an otherwise barren suburban landscape began with the theme stores and restaurants of the 1950s. Department stores in the city were already entrancing consumers with elaborately concocted themes for each department. At Macy's, men's shoes were sold in a paneled room that looked like an English gentleman's den, staffed by men with intimidating accents. A Cinderella-themed bridal shop at Wanamaker's compelled a young woman to compensate for the less-than-storybook reality of her upcoming matrimony by spending money on veils and sachets. Each department was a world unto itself—an architecturally rendered dream with the singular purpose of stimulating desire and a sense of unworthiness.

Stores in the suburbs had the even greater agenda of overcoming the utter utility of their surroundings. Sitting off a highway or on the main road connecting two unrelated residential areas, these freestanding buildings had to advertise their themes to people whizzing by in passenger cars. So carpet stores erected giant statues of Arabian princes, while Chinese restaurants took on the exaggerated shapes of the buildings Hollywood uses to depict the Orient. Once inside, customers were treated to theme experiences that contrasted with the otherwise generic Americana to which they were accustomed. The Chinese restaurant offered a self-contained black-lacquered and paper-lanterned world that bore no more resemblance to China than the horseshoes on the wall of a steak house had to cattle ranching, but such simulacra gave weary suburbanites ways to identify their experiences and who was providing them.

This consumption was desocializing. A family might travel a whole day by car to visit just two or three of these simulated meccas, leaving at least one member dissatisfied. The only public space encountered between shopping experiences was the highway.

An Austrian architect named Victor Gruen saw a better way. Having foreseen the loss of cultural values Americans would suffer as a result of this decentralized shopping experience, he envisioned a way to re-create Main Street and the civility it promoted. His innovation, what we now call the shopping mall, was first introduced in 1956 to an affluent suburb of Minneapolis called Southdale. The Southdale Center brought together dozens of different retailers under one climate-controlled roof. Gruen believed that malls could be more than "selling machines," and included a post office, a library, and club meeting rooms in his original plans for Southdale. Little did he suspect that his vision would be co-opted by people he would later call "fast-buck promoters and speculators" who exploited the self-contained atmosphere of the shopping mall for its purely commercial potential.

While individual mall stores offered their own theme environments, the design of the mall as a whole proved even more compelling to early mall-goers. Studies showed that shoppers went to the mall for the mall itself. They thought malls were beautiful, and wanted to behold the spectacle. Many people said they enjoyed the sense of "escape" they felt there. Stimulated by sound and light, they were distracted from their daily worries. Lonely suburbanites said they felt less isolated, and the overworked experienced a pleasurable "loss of time."

Follow-up researchers, using video cameras to capture shoppers' faces, discovered something even more interesting: shortly after entering a mall, a person's expression went blank. The jaw dropped, the eyes glazed over, and the shopper's path through the mall became less directed. This phenomenon, named the Gruen Transfer, was defined as the moment when a person changes from a customer with a particular product in mind to an undirected impulse buyer. Clearly, the tenants at the mall preferred the latter. In spite of Gruen's original intentions, his mall gave retailers an unprecedented opportunity to use place to disorient consumers even further.

Retail architects developed a subspecialty called "atmospherics," the science of manipulating shoppers' senses to make them buy more. They discovered that obscuring the time of day led customers to spend more time in the mall. Forcing people to make three turns when walking from the parking lot into the mall led them to forget in which direction they had parked the car (and you thought it was just you). Without this sense of an anchor, customers walked around more aimlessly. The floors in the corridors were made of harder materials than the floors in the stores, subtly encouraging tired shoppers inside. Studies on smell led corporations to concoct trademarked scents for each of their store brands. Muzak's research teams developed sound tracks capable of making people chew food faster, try on more clothes, or spend more money.

By the 1990s, retailers were exploiting more than just the five senses, and moving on to a higher order of behavioral manipulation. Stores for teenagers were all put in one section of the mall, so that kids could be more easily isolated from their parents and targeted without adult interference. Companies with names such as Envirosell used security camera tapes to analyze many kinds of consumer behavior. Bigger sales counters make people feel self-conscious about purchasing only one small item; if a woman is accidentally "butt-brushed" by another shopper while stooping over to inspect an item, she won't buy the item; people tend to move to the right when entering a store rather than to the left. These studies led to theories about how to sell more stuff to more people in less time.

As environmental manipulation became more overt, consumers couldn't help but notice their moods changing. An afternoon at the mall used to be an exhilarating experience. Now, thanks in large part to all the psychological manipulation going on, it was draining. The stores' aggressively dehumanizing designs became overwhelming, and the promise of the mall as a social substitute for Main Street was revealed to be a farce. As the film director George Romero satirized them in the horror flick *Dawn of the Dead*, mall-goers were zombies: dead people who mindlessly flocked to the mall each weekend as if the stores inside were capable of instilling them with life again. Only a suburban teenager with no place to go could justify an afternoon at the mall to hang out with friends—and even then, only ironically. Smoking pot at the Space Port arcade is as much a rebellion against mall culture as it is participation in it. Educated city dwellers and wealthy suburbanites alike found it increasingly difficult to justify a weekly trip to the mall as an enriching experience for themselves or their children.

Developers came up with a new approach to address these concerns and more: the theme mall. By representing a mall in the architectural language of authentic cultural history, the designers of shopping centers could aspire to the pretense of restoration. Dilapidated landmarks like Boston's Quincy Market and New York's South Street Seaport were revitalized as shopping centers. Instead of buying stuff at Toys "R" Us, parents could take their kids to Ye Olde Toye Shoppe for the same piece of Chinese plastic displayed in a quaint oak barrel instead of a plain metal shelf. The Gruen Transfer needn't be divorced from an overarching theme; it worked even better when it was disguised as an all-encompassing and historically justified architecture. Patrons thought they were visiting a theme-park museum when, of course, they were really just visiting a mall.

For most visitors the connection felt real enough—at least compared with whatever else they were getting in their home neighborhoods and office parks. These projects were hailed as successes from nearly all corners. Landmarks were being restored, and the uniqueness of place was being celebrated. Urban-renewal advocates issued reports showing how these projects lowered crime in the streets, relieved residents of boredom, and increased tourism.

Theme malls served as a compelling enough proof-of-concept for developers to attempt the Gruen Transfer on an even greater scale: they would transform whole districts into master-planned shopping environments. Instead of requiring people to get to a mall, why not just bring the mall to them? Las Vegas served as the model for self-contained urban environments where simulations and real life become indistinguishable. To walk (or drive) the Strip at night is to pass seamlessly from one neon-lit corporation's resort to another. The cumulative effect overpowers the senses just like a mall, Gruen Transfer and all, only outside in the fresh air. But Las Vegas is an anomaly—or at least it used to be. What happens when this approach to space is applied to the real world?

A walk through the recently renovated Times Square offers the answer. I watched a family of tourists emerge from *The Lion King* onto a restored Forty-second Street as well lit as the most lumen-rich stretch of the Vegas strip. Neon signs at regulated heights and sizes bathe the streets, cars, and people in rich hues of red and green. The mother's jaw drops first, but soon the whole family is in Gruen Transfer, transfixed by the video screens and fluorescent moving billboards. The youngest son breaks free of the trance long enough to drag his hapless parents into the Disney Store, located strategically next to the theater.

Times Square has been turned into a Las Vegas–style simulation of itself, only located where the real Times Square used to be. To be sure, Disney, Virgin, MTV, Condé Nast, and the dozen other major media conglomerates who paid to transform a seedy porn district into a flourishing theme park have done the city a great service. Although they received tremendous tax incentives for agreeing to take up residence in Times Square, they also accepted a great risk. Thirty years of strenuous municipal government intervention couldn't fix this neighborhood. Three years of corporate activity did.

Aesthetes continue to complain, longing for a remembered Times Square that may never have actually existed. But the local, living culture of New York and the unpredictability of the real world have been sacrificed to a planned environment where the designers exercise absolute control, and where the values of media conglomerates—once limited to the TV or movie screen—become those of the real world. Only the very biggest companies can afford to rent or buy space, erect the mandatory illuminated signs, and then participate in the manipulation of the throngs who pass through.

When I finally caught up with that family leaving the Disney Store, I tried to ask them questions. They ignored me, and headed straight for a cab. When I pressed them for a comment about their experience of Times Square, the father finally said, "Leave us alone. We don't live here." True enough. No one does—not even the people who do.

It's hard to complain about one's town getting cleaner, safer, or more prosperous. But the Disneyfication of Times Square systematically excludes anyone but the largest conglomerates, setting in motion a dangerously exclusive approach to land use in general. The clean is favored over the messy, the predictable over the live, and the corporate over the small. As an old waterfront section of Brooklyn called Red Hook reached advanced stages of gentrification last year, all of a sudden people began to question the appropriateness of that strip of thirteen Mexican, Honduran, and Caribbean food vendors who once added so much authentic character to the area next to the playing fields. Shouldn't those concession positions be auctioned off to the highest (corporate) bidder? At the very least, they needed to be moved to make space on that spot for an Ikea—just one of the corporations looking to touch down in Brooklyn's latest consumer district.

This corporatization of cities and towns reduces their natural ecologies, oversimplifies the processes by which real places develop, and tilts everyone's priorities and behaviors toward the companies responsible for their planning. The more a town or city skews itself toward wealthy consumers, the harder it is for real culture to take place. Rents go up, making it impossible for young people and artists to afford to live there. Warehouse lofts are renovated into expensive co-ops. New residents and businesses lobby city governments to close noisy clubs and other night spots where creative culture most often pollinates, and the result is less of the art, music, and culture that once made a place worth living in. The simulations with which real culture is replaced aren't just worse from an aesthetic point of view. They are worse because they exist solely to promote behavior that improves the profits of the corporations manufacturing them. But GNP for the rebuilt areas does go up, and—under the logic of corporatism—we have no choice but to record it as another success story.

Finally, as with Birkdale Village, corporations abuse the logic of New Urbanism to develop mall towns from the bottom up. These are not genuinely diverse communities in the spirit of Jane Jacobs's West Village, but selling machines as fastidiously constructed to induce spending as the most manipulative shopping mall. Just because they don't have roofs doesn't mean these faux villages are any less self-contained than the Southdale Center. Residents exist in a perpetual Gruen Transfer, consuming as a mode of existence, and utterly incapable of distinguishing between the stores in which they live and the real world they left behind. If there were any question about Birkdale's intended effects on its residents, consider the design firm Shook Kelley's new corporate tagline: "It's all consuming."

But as we're about to see, the people who grow up on this remade landscape end up becoming something altogether worse than mere consumers.

CHAPTER FOUR

INDIVIDUALLY WRAPPED

Public Relations and the Disconnect from
One Another

The Self Is the Source

"We're trained in our society to give, but to feel uncomfortable taking or receiving. But if you don't take, you are denying another person from giving."

Three of the women smile and two others half-nod, glazed over. But the younger one in the corner still appears unconvinced by the life coach leading the session.

"What's that really mean, Eileen?" Amy asks. "Greed is good?"

"Well, sure," answers Eileen, a middle-aged and middleweight woman in a chocolate-brown pantsuit. She doesn't appear to realize that Amy was quoting from the movie *Wall Street*. "That's not how they put it, but yes. We have to learn to accept the bounty that life offers. It's the key to seeing self as source. Remember, you make the world around you with your thoughts. If you aren't ready to accept, then how can the universe give you anything you want?"

Eileen's holding today's meeting in her apartment, a nondescript garden condominium outside Grand Rapids, Michigan. I found her while researching former Amway sales representatives for what I thought was going to be a chapter in this book on multilevel marketing networks. But Eileen's not interested in talking about her past failures as a Silver Producer level Amway distributor. She's dedicated to sharing her newest passion, free of charge, with the women who responded to her Internet notice for practitioners of The Secret—the latest and greatest "quantum-based" self-improvement system known to humankind, according to its practitioners and promoters—who are often the very same people.

Most simply, *The Secret* is a self-help DVD and companion book synthesizing the pitches of a few dozen of today's most prominent self-help gurus. Its creator, an Australian named Rhonda Byrne, claims there's a single truth underlying all the spiritual systems and get-rich-quick schemes of her many peers. It's more ancient than the Bible and has been intentionally hidden from human beings for just as long. The great secret? Positive thinking or, in The Secret's parlance, "The Law of Attraction." Like attracts like. Abundance is a state of mind: Think healthy, and you'll be healthy. Or—more to the point—think rich and you'll get rich.

The Secret is spirituality reconstituted for the "me" generation. As self-contained and utterly artificial as Birkdale Village, The Secret masquerades as a time-honored and diverse set of insights. And like the faux New Urbanist shopping mall, the underlying purpose of The Secret is to make money. Most of the spiritual teachers in The Secret are wealth-seminar leaders who display the book's logo on their ads and websites. The Secret has certainly worked wonders for its marketers: as of this writing, more than two million DVDs have been sold, and the book hit number one on the *New York Times* Best-Seller List of hardcover advice books.

While positive thinking no doubt has its benefits—from the placebo effect to good old self-confidence—The Secret tries to justify itself not only in the language of pop psychology but also in that of modern physics. According to the book, happy thoughts will do more than affect behavior. The Secret claims that interrelatedness of matter and energy—Einstein's $E = mc^2$—allows people to change reality to their liking by changing the way they think about it. Thought is presumably the energy in this schema, and reality is the matter. For most, however, this potential for quantum transmutation is limited to attracting more marriage prospects into their bedrooms, or money into their personal bank accounts.

Eileen puts the law of attraction into practice on pretty much every physical surface of her home. Handwritten signs and Post-its proclaim affirmations such as "THE UNIVERSE ADORES YOU" and "YOUR MAN IS ON HIS WAY." A $10 million check from Eileen's bank account, written to Eileen, is stuck to her refrigerator under a green "S" magnet—most likely the closest one she could find to a dollar sign. Over her gas fireplace hangs a collage of images she has clipped from catalogs and magazines representing the things she is in the process of attracting to herself. Female models smile as they drive expensive cars, frolic in the waves with muscular male models pretending to be surfers, or sit with baby models under trees. The classic cultic goals: wealth, sex, fertility. In what might easily be a coincidence or simply the ethnographic bias of Eileen's favorite magazines, none of the pictures contains any black people, even though Eileen herself is African-American.

"Vision walls really work," Eileen assures her group. "There was once a man who wanted a multimillion-dollar mansion. He made a vision board, and kept it even after he made his millions. One day, he was looking at it hanging in his bedroom, and he realized he was *living* in the *exact house* he had clipped!"

"Then there was the woman who really wanted to get married," chimes in Sharon, a thirty-something unemployed former sales rep (she never told me of what) and recent convert to The Secret. "She started buying wedding magazines and clipping pictures of rings, flowers, dresses. She started acting like she *was* married already. And not only did she get married, the ring her fiancé proposed to her with was the exact same as the one she'd clipped for her board."

Think it, clip it, get it. In a process that's one step more pathetic than working to get the things they see in advertisements, practitioners of The Secret put the ads up on their walls and then wish really hard for what's in them. They turn the pictures in ads into idols to be worshipped. And to prove to themselves that they believe in the system enough to get it to really work for them, they must enlist others in The Secret as well. When not enlisting newcomers, they must meet regularly with other believers to keep the buzz of the belief alive. To stay psyched, so The Secret can work its positive magic.

That's the real reason for meetings like Eileen's: to proselytize The Secret—spreading the new word while supporting one another in buying more of the featured teachers' books and courses. It's a win-win for all concerned that mirrors the relationship of a corporation to its chartering monarch. Top-shelf self-help gurus—*Men Are from*

Mars, Women Are from Venus author John Gray, *Chicken Soup* founder Jack Canfield, *Conversations with God* creator Neale Donald Walsch— get new life pumped into their waning careers, while the new self-help brand gains instant credibility from their participation. As if in full disclosure, they are all willing to teach the fine arts of logrolling and bootstrapping to anyone who will listen and pay. Secret is as Secret does.

While The Secret isn't itself a multilevel marketing scheme (or MLM), it has become the sales pitch and rationale for many others. Three of The Secret's best-known officially sanctioned self-help gurus, Canfield, Bob Proctor, and Michael Beckwith, teamed up on a Secret-inspired get-rich MLM called the Science of Getting Rich. For $1,995, anyone can join. The only prerequisite to getting rich this way is that you have to really want it enough to get all your friends to want it, too.

"Kids, when they want something, harp on it, focus on it, and obsess over it until they get it," Eileen explains. "A child whines, 'But you promised!' " The women laugh. "Kids have the freedom to *want* what they *want*. And that's what the vision board reminds you. To really want means to be able to fully visualize and then through that, to really live."

"What if you don't get what you want?" The quiet one in the corner—the one in her twenties who, at least by outward appearances, would have the least trouble attracting a mate or landing a job—has finally spoken up. "If you don't get what you want, is that because you didn't attract it?"

"Right, Amy," says Eileen, nodding. "At least not yet." Eileen claims to be a graduate of the University of Michigan Business School's "Life Coach" program. No such program exists, but she does have an undergraduate diploma hanging in her bedroom office. If she really had attended a Life Coaching program, this is probably the kind of moment she would have trained for.

"So, if you're a mom in Iraq with a starving baby," Amy goes on, pursuing her line of questioning, "and you just can't get out, does that mean you're not wishing hard enough?"

"We get what we want," Eileen says. "So let's all think good thoughts."

"But what about the Holocaust?" Sooner or later it had to get there.

"I can't really answer that," Eileen says. "But I know there were people in the Holocaust who did want to survive and they lived."

"Just like there are people with cancer who lived because they really wanted to," adds Sharon.

"How? By putting pictures on the wall of people who are healthy?" Amy asks.

"That's part of it." Eileen is fumbling with her papers now, trying to move to her next planned part of the meeting. "They took responsibility for their disease, and visualized a way beyond it."

"And the ones who didn't live? They didn't want to survive badly enough?"

"Look, it's not all those *other* people you should be worrying about right now. You're here to make *your* life better. Start with your*self*. The rest will follow. We attract what we are. The self is the source."

Amy's concern for others may be quaint, even well intentioned— but in the logic of The Secret, it's just an obstacle to manifesting her true self and attracting the partner, health, and wealth she deserves. Updating the rationale of the American Calvinists, who believed that wealth was an indication of God's approval, The Secret's practitioners equate personal success with having achieved scientific and spiritual harmony with the greater universe. All it takes is being enthusiastic and clear enough to manifest it—to attract all this good stuff to one's *self*.

The Secret isn't a fringe cult, but a mainstream global phenomenon. Its teachers show up regularly on *Oprah*'s schedule right between Barack Obama and Michael Moore. That's because the philosophy is not an aberration at all, but the culmination of several centuries' dedication to promoting the self over pretty much everyone and everything else. The Secret simply gives people permission to be as selfish as they can tolerate, and to internalize the language and symbols of advertising into one's life as core guiding principles.

The self-absorption and self-interest dominating our values today is not mere happenstance, but the result of a century of public-relations campaigns, advertising, and social engineering waged against collective action, altruism, and even good government. Just as we were disconnected from place and reconnected instead to a map biased toward corporate interests, we have been disconnected from one another and led to behave instead as individuals and through corporatist ideals.

The rise of the self went hand in hand with the rise of the chartered corporation and the central authorities it anchored. Only a world steeped in this false notion of a wholly sovereign individual could have generated the bourgeois merchant class of self-made men threatening the static power of the aristocracy. Likewise, the subsequent elevation of chartered corporations was dependent on highly individualized laborers and, eventually, customers who competed with one another for wages and riches. The more disconnected people became from one another, the more easily they could be manipulated. Unions of workers and functioning communities of citizens threaten the power of corporations, while individuals out for their own interests behave more like corporations themselves. The social concerns that make collective human behavior multifaceted and complex get smoothed out as people take actions directed by the much simpler calculus of the market. This makes people entirely more predictable, better targets for advertising, increasingly more isolated from one another, as well as more dependent on central authorities to create both value and meaning.

It's not as if a king conspired with the head of a chartered corporation to concoct the notion of individuality. (It wasn't until the heyday of public relations in the 1920s that anyone consciously tried to promote individual freedom as a cynical means of social control.) But the elevation of individual personhood to a literary and social ideal took place as part of the same wave of rationalism that brought us chartered corporations, colonialism, and the Industrial Age. This was a new framework for how society could work and grow, funded and promoted by those who were growing rich and powerful by using it. We have to understand at least the very basics of how this notion, individuality, was invented in order to dismantle its inappropriate and automatic application today.

Self-made Man

Although the ancient Greeks had a strong concept of the individual in relationship to the state, the family, and the gods, it wasn't until the Renaissance that the notion of a full-fledged person with a truly free and effective will was born. Nearly every major Renaissance innovation in some way celebrated or further refined these new notions of self, perspective, experience, and agency. And, at least in retrospect, nearly all these terrifically self-affirming beliefs and practices foreshadowed a bit of the self-obsession of our own era. In those first visions of the self-sufficient Renaissance Man, we get an inkling of the self-as-source logic in The Secret. It just took us five hundred years to get here.

Even today, when we look back on the Renaissance—or at least when we try to remember what they told us about it in high school—we recall it as the era of humanism, perspective painting, and rational scientific inquiry. What may not occur to us so readily is that all of these ideas were inspired by a renewed sense of the importance of an individual *self* perceiving and acting on the world. "Humanism," a term first coined in 1808 to identify this Renaissance trend, refers not to some sort of humanitarian impulse, but to the solipsism and self-absorption characterizing the era's religion, art, and science.

Humanism's founding father, the fourteenth-century Italian poet and scholar Francesco Petrarch, believed that only by looking within could a person guarantee his own salvation. At the time, this was a liberating idea. Instead of depending on the decree of an external authority, a human being could enter into a deeply personal relationship with the rest of the chain of being, God included. Grace was no longer bestowed by God, but achieved by the individual. Man had his own self-directed and divine function in the cosmos.

Da Vinci's classic Renaissance drawing *Vitruvian Man* (a man standing in two overlapping positions, creating both a square and a circle) remains perhaps the quintessential image for this humanism. Based on the specifications set forth by the ancient Roman architect Vitruvius, da Vinci's image depicts an idealized human form, perfectly proportioned to the elemental shapes of geometry. Although the portrait doesn't actually succeed in its quest (the human shape does not so readily conform to easy ratios) it does convey a new mechanistic, science-based understanding of the world, as well as man's divine place within it. The function of an individual human being was seen as analogous to the working of the universe: man was a complete and autonomous being—no more a creation than a creator.

Man's new abilities to cocreate the universe rivaled those touted in The Secret. In his influential "Oration on the Dignity of Man" (1486), Giovanni Pico della Mirandola hypothesized that after God made all the creatures, He realized He wanted to make just one more being—one capable of actually appreciating all of God's many creations. But God had used up all the links in the great chain of being, from worms all the way up to angels. With no place of his own, man would instead learn from and imitate all the existing creatures. As long as man uses his intellect and contemplates his existence through philosophy, he will ascend the chain of being toward the angels. Pico's belief system was almost New Age physics in its assertion that human thought could change reality. Indeed, by exercising his free will, man could change himself and his very place in the cosmos. Man's capacity for self-transformation through thought is the only constant in the universe.

This idea inspired many poets and artists to think about how man might break free of the chain of being altogether. Christopher Marlowe's infamous sorcerer-scientist Doctor Faustus explicitly rejects the dependent, medieval way of thinking about scholarship. In his opening soliloquy, he lists all the academic disciplines, rejecting them all for the limits they place on his quest for true knowledge. Instead of studying traditional authorities, Faustus pursues individual inquiry, observation, and experimentation. In the course of the play, he is damned for his great insult to the order of being—leading us to wonder whether the playwright was cheering the modern spirit of individuality or warning us of where it might lead. At the very least, the play introduces what theater historians generally consider to be the first true individual character with a complete and independent will. Faustus's ambitions as an individual trump all other story elements. He is the first character utterly in charge of his destiny, and capable of transforming himself and his world.

Just being able to think as an individual, to experience an interior consciousness, was a major step. Dr. John Dee, considered a sorcerer in his day, amazed crowds simply by being able to read without moving his lips. He could silently read a page and then answer questions about it because he had the ability to create an internal mental picture formed by the words—a skill inconceivable to those unfamiliar with an internal mental experience.

Perspective painting was as much a celebration of the individual as it was of the geometry enabling the "separation of planes" and "vanishing points." The object of perspective painting was to imitate the orientation that a single human observer would have on the scene being depicted. Perspective painting meant that one's perspective mattered. Sometimes, of course, it mattered too much. Real science waned in the early Renaissance as philosophers became increasingly convinced of their own ability to change matter and reality through their will or vision. Humanism held that nature was no longer an authority, but a result of various animistic forces—of which human agency might be among the most important. But the primacy of the individual and observation paved the way for the rationality and enlightenment that would eventually follow the Renaissance.

René Descartes' famous proclamation *"cogito, ergo sum"* (I think, therefore I am) extended the supremely first-person focus of the Renaissance. For Descartes, man was a transcendental figure, existing in and of himself. Building on the logic of Petrarch, Descartes concluded that man could know the world around him only by using perception and deduction. But instead of resorting to animism, Descartes turned to the logic of science. His Cartesian coordinate system described space and movement within it purely in terms of an x, y, and z axis. This led to maps with latitude and longitude lines, as well as analytic geometry and calculus.

The invention of the printing press turned reading, literature, and Bible study from a group activity into an individual one. Instead of listening to a priest read from a sacred manuscript, people (at least the rich ones) could now read from mass-produced texts. To read individually meant interpreting texts as an individual. The gentleman sat in his study alone, reading great works and developing his own perspective.

To read one's Bible without any intermediary meant developing one's own concept of God. At least as much as any other social influence, this heightened sense of individuality enabled the Protestant Reformation. If each person could enjoy a personal relationship with God, there was no need for an institution to mediate. The new Protestantism, beginning with Martin Luther's revolutionary Ninety-five Theses, held that the faith of a lone individual transcended everything else. Though they were to prove themselves as violently intolerant as any previous religious institutions, Protestant churches laid the foundations for the "personal relationship" to God many Christians, particularly evangelicals, aspire to today.

Finally, the Renaissance notion of the individual with his own unique perspective led to the Enlightenment ideal of democratic self-government. The citizens of an enlightened society do not need a monarch or other father figure doing their thinking for them. A person's conscience was a better arbiter of good and evil, right and

wrong, than any external authority. Human beings began their elevation from peasants to subjects to citizens, as their individual perspectives and choices were deemed increasingly relevant.

Enlightenment, individuality, and agency are all beautiful concepts, but they came along with new allegiances to larger, depersonal-
ized, and abstract institutions. The clean, universal truths associated
with Renaissance-inspired ideals kept people's eyes and attention
upward, and off one another. This is how Enlightenment enthusiasts
could simultaneously own slaves, how ardent supporters of democracy
could ignore the rights of women, and how the tyrannical theocracy of
John Calvin could use adherence to Biblical texts as an excuse to torture people for dancing or drinking on the wrong day of the week.

Of course, the reason this worked so well in the context of emergent corporatism is that corporations and the newly colonial nations
they supported were also abstract entities—especially in comparison
with the local institutions people had been used to dealing with before. A person with a local sensibility understood his role within the
fabric of his farming community or village relationships. Now people
were supplying commodities to more centralized business institutions, or even to the great shipping expeditions. Yes, their autonomy as
individual businesspeople had increased, but their relationship to one
another as members of a local business community diminished. Instead of seeing themselves as members of their village or ward, they
began to see themselves as subjects of national monarchies. Most local
currencies were outlawed and replaced by mandatory use of the national coin—which could also be taxed more easily. Likewise, while
Protestantism liberated parishioners from the control of their local
priest and the hierarchy in Rome, it replaced this authority with the
mass-produced text of the mechanically replicated Gutenberg Bible.

We became nations of individual subjects, relating to distant and
highly controlled entities instead of through the people who might
have once represented these interests. But how does an individual relate to a national identity, a king, or a large chartered corporation? He
doesn't. He relates instead to the brand created for that entity.

The brand was born to give corporations and nations alike the ability to relate directly to the Renaissance's new individuals. The brand
functioned as a human face, employing icons, mythology, and symbols
as substitutes for the features of real people. The brand replaced peer-
to-peer human relationships with abstract, top-down ones. And be-

cause they were designed for and by the institutions they represented, they were also biased in their favor.

While there's some evidence of what we could call branded imagery as far back as the Bronze Age, the modern idea of branding might best be credited to King Louis XIV's famed finance minister Jean-Baptiste Colbert. The Dutch, English, and Portuguese had invested heavily in navies and protecting their trade routes, but the French of this era were still heavily committed to regional ground armies and inexperienced in sea battles. They lost their bounties to pirates and their land claims to colonial rivals. France just couldn't keep up with the heavy competition for resources in the New World, and began to run a trade deficit.

Colbert realized that France's only alternative was to rely on domestic production and sell French goods to the rest of the world. "French fashions must be France's answers to Spain's gold mines in Peru," he said. Colbert envisioned a France capable of competing with the rest of the world not through the acquisition of territory and resources, but through style. He needed a way to make French exports seem special for their own sake, and took it upon himself to invent what we now think of as luxury goods.

Colonialism had already done half of Colbert's job for him. People throughout Europe were already accustomed to awaiting the treasures of spices and silks that merchant ships brought from faraway lands. All Colbert had to do was establish France as the tastemaker—the best place for the natural resources of other lands to be ground, wound, fabricated, or assembled into the latest and most fashionable products imaginable. "With our taste," Colbert explained, "let us make war on Europe, and through fashion conquer the world."

Colbert set in place strict and well-publicized manufacturing rules on French goods. Merchants who violated the rules of manufacturing, brewing, or bottling were pilloried. He used trade surpluses to support the development of high-quality national industries, which in turn led to more trade surpluses. Tax-financed roads, rails, utilities, professional schools, and corporate subsidies still characterize French industry today, and account for the nation's oft-noted resistance to global free markets. It's not anti-Americanism or even an anti-globalist sentiment at its core, but a commitment to a more managed market that can maintain a trade surplus through the quality of goods rather than the quantity of resources. But it was no less corporatist in its design: instead of striking a deal with chartered colonial corporations, the French monarchy struck a deal with domestic mercantile capitalism. Instead of sailing merchant ships under a French flag, the country exported the perfumes of Paris in decorated bottles under the French brand. A stamp of approval from the appropriate French ministry or the Court of King Louis XIV meant that a jar of caviar, a bolt of silk, or a case of wine bore the official mark of French luxury.

That's why Colbertism, as it came to be known, may finally have had less to do with making than marketing. The important thing was for people in France and around the world to treat France's exports *as if* they were the highest quality available. And as Colbert readily admitted, this had less to do with any intrinsically superior attribute than with fashion. It was about style, not substance. Public flogging of errant perfumers was meant to publicize the French commitment to quality more than enforce it.

Always ready for a cross-promotional opportunity, Colbert tried to get the king to live at the Louvre. But Louis preferred Versailles, so Colbert was forced to improvise. The clever minister turned the palace into a showcase for French wine, Champagne, cuisine, furniture, mirrors, and, most of all, fashion. After all, visiting dignitaries were trendsetters in their own countries, and represented a terrific avenue for word-of-mouth marketing across Europe. Keeping his monarch in a removed and controlled setting allowed Colbert to craft a narrative for the French people as well: Versailles housed a benevolent leader who served the people's interests by subsidizing and branding the nation's vast corporate sector. Even through the bloody revolutions to follow, the French people maintained a belief in the power of the state to control unregulated markets and guarantee some level of fairness.

Throughout the four centuries since Colbert's invention of French luxury, branding has done roughly the same things, in roughly the same ways: it has created a mythology that elevates either a central government, a centralized corporation, or some combination of the two. And under the guise of promoting the station, style, or stature of individuals, it actually makes them more dependent on abstract ideas and institutions, more accessible to centralized image-making and storytelling than they were before. And more disconnected from one another.

Branding defined and redefined individuals as subjects, citizens, workers, consumers, and eventually shareholders, always counting on the power of image and myth to stir people's hearts more effectively than other people ever could.

Mass Productions

The Industrial Age forced colonial powers to engage in similarly nationalist forms of public relations. The British East India Company extended its reach and power into India and China by promoting opium use and then overthrowing addicted leaders. The great Opium Wars were fought and won, forcing China to accept British import of the debilitating drug, and helping England maintain a favorable balance of trade. Elsewhere on the continent, in spite of violent protests, Indian rug weavers were mandated by law to use British mechanical looms, devaluing personal skill and creating dependence on the corporations supplying the machines.

Back at home, however, Britain rebranded its exploitative trading practices to an admiring public. In 1851, the British business élite held the Great Exhibition of the Works of Industry of All Nations in a futuristic, million-square-foot metal and glass pavilion called the Crystal Palace. Fourteen thousand exhibitors conducted elaborate demonstrations of the products and promise of the Industrial Revolution. Steam hammers, hydraulic presses, barometers, and diving suits were on display, highlighting the vast yield and majestic power of the new mechanical age.

The Great Exhibition's primary intent was to distract the domestic public from the dark underbelly of international industrial modernity. Through this spectacle, Queen Victoria and the corporations she sponsored disconnected these technologies from the human toll they inflicted on their operators. As if in a shopping mall, people gawked, their jaws dropping, at the steam pipes and gears, utterly unaware of the faces and hands the machines burned and mauled. People saw products and production, but never the producers themselves. If anything, industrial modernity was simpler and cleaner than manual labor. As much a welcome step back as a daring leap forward.

The Great Exhibition was designed to convey precisely this sensibility. Organizers cleverly promoted and organized the event as a celebration of faux-medieval design and dedicated the central hall to an exhibit on Gothic Revival architecture. This was part of a larger effort to disguise the industrialization of Victorian England as a throwback to feudal tradition. The era of the high-tech factory would be rebranded as the romantic revival of medieval monarchy. The Great Exhibition mythologized both free trade and the Industrial Age as a return to the best of pre-Renaissance Europe, when it was actually the extension of its very opposite.

Most significantly, the exhibitions at the Crystal Palace launched a full century of public-relations strategies concocted to disconnect people from one another and to require them to interact with each other through *things* instead. Industrialization meant that labor could now be exploited indirectly, through technology, and from a great distance away. Free-market capitalism meant that class divisions could be enforced through the impersonal movement of the markets instead of by direct repression. The supply-side glut of mass-produced material goods required a new individualism capable of inspiring consumers to purchase as many commodities as they were offered, and experience their social reality through them. And the myth of the meritocracy—that we are all free to compete with one another as individuals for the great prizes our market has to offer—kept people from conferring with one another on just how satisfied they were with the system in which they were living.

In short, mass production led to mass marketing, which in turn required a mass media capable of delivering all that marketing across great nations and beyond. At each step of the way, human relationships were further mediated through capital, products, or myths. Collectivist impulses were shunned in favor of strident individualism and personal achievement. Dreams of achieving status through social participation were replaced by dreams of purchasing status through private acquisition. For corporate industrialism to work as an economic model, people would have to be sold on individuality and personal freedoms as the paramount human goals—even if this actually meant a more isolated and alienated existence.

In America, where Adam Smith's dream of an economy dominated by local, independently run farms and businesses had already been realized to some extent, the transition to an industrial economy would prove a tougher sell. There was no great Gothic era to look back on, no great colonial empire to salute. Life in 1800s America was far from perfect, but the scale of business enterprises and proximity to farms and small factories made for a high level of local awareness and social cohesion. On his tour of America, the French historian Alexis de Tocqueville marveled most of all at institutions like the public library and the New England town meeting. Imposing industrialization on America would have to involve the diminution of these social institutions and a heightening of self.

In the kinds of towns de Tocqueville visited, human relationships dominated the local economy. If you needed oats, you'd go buy them from the general store—just one step removed from the mill—or maybe even from the miller himself. If the oats were bad, you'd know where to find the man responsible. You knew his face and his wife's. His kids might have gone to school with your kids. If his oats were bad, he'd lose more than a customer, for you lived and worked in the same town. You might fix wagon wheels, or even work as the local chemist, mixing his wife's medication. If you ate bad oats, you wouldn't be doing your job as well, either. The miller might end up with a dangerously assembled wheel or, worse, an incorrectly dosed prescription. If the miller supplied a bad product, he had more at stake than your business. You were more than just each other's customers; you were interdependent members of a community.

The Industrial Age brought factories capable of making oats faster and cheaper than the local miller could have ever imagined. (And where industry couldn't succeed in creating economies of scale, lobbyists were sure to tilt the playing field in their favor.) So now, instead of buying oats from a human being you knew, you'd get them from a big factory several hundred or several thousand miles away. It would come in an impersonal big brown box. There was no miller to be seen.

The brand was developed to substitute for the relationship you used to have with the miller. Instead of seeing his face over an open barrel at the mill or the general store, you'd see the face of a Quaker on a box of factory-made oats. Quaker Oats (founded in 1901 and now a unit of the megacorporation PepsiCo) combined the three biggest local Midwestern mills into a single company, and sought to change the way America bought its oats by replacing the human being you knew with a brand. For this to work, you'd have to learn to feel as good or better about the picture of the Quaker as you did about the real person supplying your oats before. The image of a Quaker is a good start; who doesn't feel good about Quakers? They are dedicated to exactly the kind of town meetings and local sharing that a national oats company would seek to replace.

For corporate brands to surpass their corporeal counterparts, they would need to be invested with mythology more compelling than the weight of any genuine social reality. And these mythologies—these brand stories—would need to communicate themselves instantly. The customer had to know who Uncle Ben and Aunt Jemima were just by looking at them once on a store shelf, forcing early marketers to use an overtly stereotypical and highly limited range of images.

Mass media would come to the rescue, giving corporations a way to communicate the qualities they wanted associated with their brands across an entire continent, overnight. This way, the customer would already know who the Quaker was and what he represented before he arrived at the grocery. Make no mistake: radio and television were not created to entertain the American public. RCA and Westinghouse were not working to satisfy Jack Benny's and Lucille Ball's desire for a new technology through which to spread their comedy to the masses. They were addressing the need of mass producers to mass market their goods more effectively to the masses.

But at each stage along the way, the industrialization of the economy required a corresponding desocialization of the people within it. Industrial Age factories reduced the laborers within them to cogs in a machine. From the time clock to the assembly line, the pace of work was dictated by mechanical engines to which the human workers conformed. Rewards were likewise shifted from personal satisfaction, the joy of teamwork, or a sense of accomplishment to the much more symbolic compensation of cash. Instead of using skill to make things they could be proud of, people performed repetitive, meaningless tasks for cash. Their sense of genuine achievement and connection had to be replaced with loyalty to an abstracted corporate parent. Meanwhile, worker-to-worker solidarity (the dreaded unionization) was repressed and derided at every turn. Each worker was to be in this alone, in competition with his fellows, and loyal only to the company.

While mass production desocialized the worker, mass marketing desocialized consumption. Brands had to alienate people from one another in order to replace the human bonds that once characterized commerce with artificial corporate ones. National brand relationships replaced local social relationships. Instead of supplying a neighbor with a particular good, the best one could hope for in an industrial economy was finding a friend loyal to the same brand. When you say Bud you haven't merely said it all—you've said all that can be said. Just as mass production dehumanized workers, mass marketing alienated consumers from one another, replacing the urge to connect with an urge to compare or contrast through consumption.

Finally, mass media's function as brand communicator depended on an isolated target. While the cost of technology initially kept an entire family gathered around its single radio or television set in the evening, the bias of the medium was always toward isolation. It's not a coincidence that televisions spread into every room of the house, so that each family member would eventually watch his own program or niche-marketed channel in his own room. How better to direct targeted marketing directly to its target market?

The isolated audience member provides a better psychological target, as well. Consider any typically hip ad for blue jeans. What universal truth is it attempting to communicate? Something along the lines of "Wear these jeans, and you will attract a lover." Now, who is the best target for such an ad? It is certainly not a young man sitting on a couch next to his girlfriend. He already has a partner, and whichever jeans he happens to be wearing are working well enough in that respect. No, the only appropriate target for the hip jeans ad is the young man or woman sitting on that couch alone and, ideally, friendless. The jeans commercial requires viewers who do not socialize, do not have friends, and believe that new purchases might actually change the situation. More important, the products had better not perform as advertised, delivering friends and satisfaction, or they are likely to reduce your ongoing compliance as an audience member, customer, and worker.

From Subjects to Workers

The premise for an industrial society rested in the ability of corporations to secure cheap and willing labor. Today, this means outsourcing. But originally it meant creating a compliant workforce at home, however coercively it had to be done. In order to be controlled, the teeming masses would be broken down into a mass of teeming individuals.

After the Civil War and the ascendance of the railroad corporations, America changed scale. Local merchants and farmers were consolidated into larger industries. Small businessmen were overwhelmed by big companies and the "robber barons" who owned them. Free enterprise had always meant the right of individuals to pursue their private economic activities in a highly local, human-scaled marketplace. Now it was growing out of control, favoring the interests of a tiny élite of corporate chiefs over everyone and everything else.

The middle class got squeezed as corporations gave away their jobs to low-wage, unskilled immigrant workers flowing in from Europe. Resentment against immigrants swelled (as it has against so-called "illegals" today), and America began its social disintegration into competing interest groups based on race, ethnicity, and wealth. By the 1870s, middle-class Americans were spending most of their money just to cover up their actual poverty. Those who managed to keep their jobs worked, according to contemporary accounts, with an "angry sense of the limited opportunities for a career at their command."

For their part, laborers found themselves much too easily buried in mining accidents, crushed in machinery, or diseased from unsanitary living conditions. With single conglomerates owning entire industries—Rockefeller owned 90 percent of the American petroleum industry—workers had almost no negotiating power.

Sometimes, the government tried to come to their rescue. Every few decades, a progressive such as Teddy Roosevelt would rise to voice the complaints of labor and society against the rising power of corporatism. Roosevelt saw the "masses sinking into degradation and misery," and called out the corporatist bias for "profits over patriotism." Roosevelt may have been the first one to put the opposition between government and corporate interests so bluntly—and this division proved to be the front line in the battle for America's public sentiment. Encouraging the press to expose corporate corruption and injustice, Roosevelt coined the term "muckraker" in 1906, for journalists who did just that, after a character in John Bunyan's *Pilgrim's Progress*. Roosevelt called for "relentless exposure" as long as the reporter "remembers that the attack is of use only if it is absolutely truthful."

Roosevelt's muckrakers had the opposite of the intended effect. Stories about the angry mob scared the middle class off the streets and into their suburban fortresses. Newspapers and magazines became the only way to find out what was actually happening back in the city. As publishers consolidated, local papers became parts of national chains. Large corporations were now mediating reality from a centralized and national perspective, often oblivious to what was actually going on right outside people's front doors—or simply biased against reporting the plights of real people. It was more effective and sensationalist to call them a mob.

Well-meaning progressives read these news reports of angry mobs and found themselves more concerned about calming society and preventing unrest than actually addressing the core problems of industrialization. The reading class believed themselves to be capable of a reflection and self-control that the masses they read about lacked. Gustave Le Bon's tremendously popular book *The Crowd: A Study of the Popular Mind* (1895) warned of the process through which "the voice of the masses has become preponderant." He cautioned against the unpredictable "crowd instinct," and believed that "the divine right of the masses is about to replace the divine right of kings." His audience understood that this meant they'd be suffering under tyranny in either case.

Of course, in the new environment of a national media, there was no such thing as the "masses." As the French social psychologist Gabriel Tarde explained in a series of books extremely influential with early public-relations specialists, Le Bon's "crowd" was really an abstract entity held together by the press. There were no mobs in the streets—there was no herd, only a herd psychology capable of being influenced on an individual basis through the media.

Early public-relations professionals understood what this meant to their craft: they should speak through media, to individuals, as if they were speaking to the masses. By standardizing the public conversation, a national media could address every individual in his home exactly the same way, creating a "virtual" mob with no actual power to do anything. The reading public would passively consume their information, in utter isolation, and do it all at once. A mass of individuals.

Combining this insight with the power of fact-based muckraking, corporate publicists invented the new craft of public relations. They would present "facts" to promote corporate interests to individuals through the national media—and thus direct the group mind, or "public opinion." Ivy Lee was among the very first of these PR men, hired by Rockefeller to do damage control after the Ludlow Massacre in 1914, when five striking miners and their wives and children—a total of twenty people—were slaughtered on behalf of the Colorado Fuel and Iron Company. Ivy placed editorials in Colorado newspapers, using fabricated "facts" about how the dangerous "agitators" lost their lives. Utterly disconnected from real events and absorbed instead in the news stories as individual readers, private citizens had no means to check the claims in these reports. Rockefeller's sponsored reality became reality as far as most of America was concerned.

The more corporatized the media became, the easier this reality was to create. A national media was structurally biased toward the interests of corporate monopolies. When AT&T sought to win public support for a national phone monopoly, it created an information department to disseminate facts supporting its case. The company's argument was that a total, universal system would be cleaner and more efficient than a bunch of local ones. Its job was to break people's local affiliations and get them to relate instead as individuals to one big company. The reality was that regional phone services worked very well, and cross-compatibility for long-distance service was not a problem. AT&T's national media campaign was, predictably, about the superiority of a company that was "national in character." It became an argument for modern cosmopolitanism over backward provincialism.

The readers of national papers saw themselves as modern cosmopolitans, of course, and read AT&T's arguments with an open mind. AT&T wasn't content with just placing ads in papers. The company used its advertising dollars to push newspaper chains into printing its public-relations releases as articles and editorials. The company presented itself through the national media as embodying a new version of the progressive impulse. According to AT&T's president, Theodore Vail, the "private rights" of corporations were dependent on "public acquiescence." The public had to be "educated" toward a greater understanding of these rights. Where that failed, AT&T went in, Wal-Mart style, and undercut regional phone rates until the local companies went out of business. The information department also monitored everything from proposed legislation and dangerous newspaper editors to radical professors and their students' papers.

Finally, for those who remained unresponsive to fact-based arguments, AT&T communicated directly to the heart. The public-relations department came up with the idea of using a woman's voice to represent the whole company. All operators and recordings would be female, making a single, embracing mother out of the whole corporation. Ma Bell.

Facts may have worked well enough alone, but combined with emotional appeals, they were even more powerful. The fledgling public-relations industry was learning that emotional appeals needn't be reserved for crowds—particularly now that there was no such thing. It was government PR specialists who first proved themselves willing to venture into the emotional space.

In 1916 Woodrow Wilson ran for reelection on a peace platform—"He kept us out of the war." A year later, he was trying to get new immigrants to support a war back in Europe. He hired George Creel and his assistant Edward Bernays to form a publicity committee to persuade the country "to make the world safe for democracy." The U.S. Committee on Public Information, or CPI, claimed it did not resort to censorship, but it used the Espionage Act of 1917 and the Sedition Act of 1918 to silence newspapers critical of war policy, and even put journalists in jail with no option for bail. This gave it the freedom to make highly emotional, uncontested appeals to the public, such as a poster of the Statue of Liberty crumbling under German fire, with New York City burning in the background. What seems like de rigueur political advertising to us today was decried by a minority of progressives who might have agreed with Wilson's policy positions, but saw in the "war technique" an undoing of rational society.

Once the war was over, corporate PR departments seized on the new techniques. In the words of the business theorist and statistician Roger Babson in 1921, "The war taught us the power of propaganda. Now when we have anything to sell the American people, we know how to sell it." Ivy Lee, the mastermind behind AT&T's campaign for monopoly, explained that public relations was now "the art of steering heads inside . . . the secret art of all the other arts, the secret religion of all religions . . . the secret [by which a] civilization might be preserved . . . [and] a successful and permanent business built."

Backing all this up was a new, individualistic theory of psychology. While Le Bon had proposed that people faced with great existential quandaries will turn to the "herd" for support, Sigmund Freud argued quite the opposite. What drives the crowd is not some collective mentality, but the unconscious impulses of *individuals*. Not only is each of us an individual, but there is an individual within each one of us that we can't even know! Most important to the would-be controllers of public opinion and consumer behavior, this subconscious individual within the individual could be instructed directly, even secretly, to take actions on our behalf. The distinction between the thoughtful middle class and the irrational working masses vanished.

We were all capable of being controlled the same way, since each of us had the same basic unconscious being within us.

As long as we could be isolated from one another, extracted from the real world, and immersed instead in a sea of emotionally compelling imagery, we could be placed under PR's control. Walter Lippmann, one of Woodrow Wilson's PR men and the first to write about the science of propaganda, realized that the application of Freudianism to public relations would mean disconnecting people from the real fabric of their lives. According to Freud, a psychotherapist should have his patient lie on the couch and look at the ceiling. Removed from the real world of the office and with the actual human therapist out of sight, the patient was believed to be more likely to regress and transfer parental authority onto the disassociated voice of the doctor. To Lippmann this meant that "access to the real environment must be limited, before anyone can create a pseudo-environment that he thinks is wise or desirable." Lippmann saw members of his profession as an intellectual élite, capable of making decisions for a public that would benefit from his better judgment. He simply needed to get them to project themselves into the images he created—to identify with them as strongly as a patient identified with a therapist. This kind of communication could only work on the individual.

For a time, public-relations professionals seemed willing to work for the government and for business interchangeably. American business interests were generally interpreted to be one and the same as American interests, anyway. They both sought to serve the greater national good by swaying the opinions of all the individuals within the nation. And psychology was the new science of the individual. The New School's Professor Harry Overstreet taught a class called "Influencing Human Behavior," in which he demonstrated to the rising ranks of PR specialists that "the secret of all true persuasion is to induce the person to persuade himself. . . . Getting people to feel themselves in situations is therefore the surest road to persuasiveness." William P. Banning, the director of PR for AT&T, shared his admiration for Freud with his shareholders: "The job of the Publicity Directors . . . is to make people understand and love the company. Not merely be consciously dependent upon it—not merely regard it as a necessity—not merely take it for granted, but to love it—to hold real affection for it—make it an honored personal member of their business force, an admired member of the family."

As commercial radio spread from Pittsburgh to the rest of America, families had all the more reason to stay in at night to keep their appointment with *Amos 'n' Andy* and absorb its sponsored programming. Two main networks owned all of radio, and based their business models on advertising. It's not surprising that the medium was biased toward corporate interests—the bigger and more consolidated, the better. Simultaneous with newly centralized top-down electronic media came equally high-tech methods of measuring its results on the public. In 1923, a group of academic psychologists formed the Psychological Corporation to apply their behavioral research to American business interests. Like the newly minted pollsters George Gallup and Elmo Roper, they used "electronic tabulating machines" to record and analyze the purchasing behavior of individuals. For the first time, public-relations firms could gauge the effectiveness of campaigns and retune them toward the single target consumer.

Without any competition, corporatism spread as a national ideology and operating system. Between 1919 and 1930, eight thousand separate businesses in mining and manufacturing disappeared by acquisition. Companies went public, and the public bought shares. By 1929, of the ninety-seven largest corporations in America, only four were operating companies. The rest were some version of a holding company. Government and corporations were on the same side. Calvin Coolidge was convinced that a corporate-driven "universal abundance" was on its way, which makes it fitting that his secretary of commerce, Herbert Hoover, succeeded him as president.

The stock-market crash divided the interests of corporations and government, much as Teddy Roosevelt had foreseen. When his cousin Franklin Roosevelt institutionalized social welfare as part of the New Deal, big business saw only debilitating subordination to federal authority. FDR used public relations, but saw his own manipulation of public consciousness as different from the cynical sort offered by Lippmann and Bernays, who believed that an informed élite needed to direct the sentiments of the ignorant masses to support the free market. Roosevelt held that the free market should always be adjusted and regulated by government to meet the social needs of society.

In his annual message to Congress in 1935, FDR argued that "Americans must forswear the conception of the acquisition of wealth which, through excessive profits, creates undue private power over private affairs and, to our misfortune, over public affairs as well." His

Works Progress Administration, ostensibly a massive employment relief program, also funded films, plays, and art projects dedicated to driving home this new message to a disheartened public. Murals depicted people working together to build bridges and grow food, while movies celebrated the communities and cooperatives that defined New Deal America.

Corporations fought back. Edward Bernays, once an operative for Woodrow Wilson, turned against government and, along with other corporate public-relations men, sought to discredit FDR's collectivism by showing how it threatened the personal freedom of individuals. The National Food and Grocery Committee and California Chain Store Association created the Foundation for Consumer Education to persuade people of the advantages of corporate supermarkets over local grocery stores. A&P hired Carl Byoir, who represented Adolf Hitler's Third Reich in the United States, to create the illusion of a public outcry against federal taxes on chain stores. The American Association of Advertising Agencies campaigned to defend their industry against muckrakers hoping to destroy "public confidence" in advertising. The image industry was in peril as its targets—the American public—attempted to return to reality.

Thanks to the New Deal, personal wealth and employment were up, but the corporate share of wealth was down. Bernays understood that the battle he was fighting was bigger than any single company and argued for businesses to "consolidate their position." Robert Lund, president of Listerine, took over the National Association of Manufacturers (formed in 1895 to reposition worker pensions in the public consciousness as corrupt "handouts"), and enlisted his peers to join in a campaign to cooperate in the advancement of free enterprise. An internal NAM memo reveals their strategy: "Right now Joe Doakes—the average man—is a highly confused individual. . . . We must talk earnestly about our hopes, achievements, and problems with the man in the street—in everyday language he will understand."

Fortune magazine suggested that big business refer to itself as a "public utility," central to the very foundations of American life. Corporations adopted New Deal language and ideology as their own. GM launched its famous "Parade of Progress," a twenty-thousand-mile tour of the United States, in which America's economic and social future was depicted as absolutely dependent on the unimpeded development of automobile technology and free enterprise. DuPont, GE,

Goodyear, IBM, and Westinghouse all followed suit with their own touring exhibitions.

In all these cases, the primacy of the individual was pitted against the dulling effect of collective action. In a 1936 pamphlet, NAM explained that Americans faced a choice between a kind of government in which "the citizen is supreme and the government obeys his will," or "the state is supreme and controls the citizen. The first is individualistic, the second is collectivistic. In the first, man creates machinery to look after him as a separate individual entity . . . in the second, man is but a small cog in the machinery; his desires and will are sacrificed to the state."

The strategy culminated with America's own version of the Great Exhibition, the 1939 New York World's Fair. While the fair was originally supposed to include representatives of the cooperative manufacturing and farming movement as well as consumer advocates, these groups didn't have enough money to buy exhibition space. When the space was finally offered to them at a reduced rate, they realized that the limited participation they were allowed would only lend support to the corporate rhetoric they violently opposed. Still, World's Fair organizers used the names of their organizations in their publicity.

The corporations represented at the fair used it as an opportunity to battle New Deal collectivist propaganda, and they did so by creating highly personal, individualistic exhibits. Westinghouse's promotional film *The Middleton Family* represented America's plight through the experience of one family. While the daughter was seduced by a "radical thinking" boyfriend, corporations offered the family a life of abundance. The film depicts a consumer paradise—not a worker reality—in which machines did all the work and the family could enjoy a world filled with entertainment. GM's "Futurama" exhibit, designed by Norman Bel Geddes, conveyed people through scenes of an automotive utopia characterized by "accident-free" highways and idealized suburbs.

By the time World War II was breaking out in Europe, American businessmen had a hard time deciding which side to support. For the most part, it didn't matter: nations at war were good customers, no matter their political ideology. IBM sold punch-card tabulators to the Nazis, while GE partnered with Krupp, a German munitions firm. GM and Ford, which already controlled 70 percent of the German automobile market, quickly retooled their factories to supply the

Nazis with war vehicles. Putting profits over patriotism, GM resisted requests from FDR to step up military production and preparedness in their plants at home.

American corporatists also saw in fascism a counterbalance to FDR's strong-handed tactics and aggressive social-welfare programs. Henry Ford and other corporate chiefs preferred the top-down, "scientific management" of labor echoed by at least some of the fascist policies of Benito Mussolini. Henry Luce, a cofounder of *Time* magazine, became something of a spokesperson for fascism. He put Mussolini on the cover five times, and traveled the country arguing that corporations, not government, were really in charge of America. Luce convinced many businesspeople that fascism might be corporatism's best hope for organizing and influencing the American public.

The full-fledged war effort against the Nazis, however, made the overt support of fascism impossible for any corporation to maintain. The war even united FDR with industry temporarily—particularly with companies holding military contracts. Many companies had to backtrack or cover up their fascist affiliations. By the war's end, fascism had revealed itself as ruthlessly dehumanizing, and so American industry had to take a different tack. Ford retracted his many publications blaming the "global Jew" for the world's problems, including the anti-Semitic hoax *The Protocols of the Elders of Zion,* especially after his work was revealed to have provided the basis for some of Hitler's beliefs. Standard Oil of New Jersey (SONJ, an ancestor of Exxon-Mobil) created a public-relations department to deflect mainstream media attention over the company's having supplied synthetic fuel to the Nazis (through I. G. Farben) even after the war had begun.

At the same time, corporations that had not directly assisted the Germans or publicly supported their ideology were growing increasingly anxious about how to control a public that had witnessed or even fought in World War II, and come to equate corporate power with fascism. Were Americans capable of the kinds of worker revolts that took place in the Soviet Union? What to do with all the returning veterans? Whose side would they be on?

SONJ convened a series of meetings for the corporate élite to determine what to do next. Earl Newsom, the PR man who had helped Henry Ford restore his reputation after his publication of *The Protocols,* had told corporate chiefs gathered at the Westchester Country Club in 1943 that their only choice was to make corporations more human. The Psychological Corporation insisted that corporate America enact "a transfer in emphasis from free enterprise to the freedom of all individuals under free enterprise. From capitalism to the much broader concept: Americanism."

Through Americanism, postwar corporations would enact a new kind of social control to accomplish what fascism failed to do for them. It would be characterized by voluntary participation, the absence of any visible oppression, and the appearance of a bottom-up economy driven by real people—all the while preventing any civic sensibility from polluting the free market.

This final turn for corporatist public relations—the strategy still in practice today—was to reject both the heartless science of fascism and the equally dark gears of communism by humanizing the corporation. People working in concert, whether in an American work camp or a Soviet factory, were part of the awful totalitarian machine. American free enterprise, on the other hand, offered loyal citizens the opportunity to live "the good life." Soldiers in particular, who had just risked their lives conquering fascism, did not want to return to a country where their identities were defined through their relationships to the companies for whom they worked. Rather than see themselves as workers, Americans would learn to see themselves as consumers.

Corporations made themselves over as the best friends people could ever have: they were empowering people, through their consumption, to become more *themselves*. At its core, the new tactic would be to promote the idea that corporatism restored people's individuality, while collective action and community forced only stultifying conformity. Corporatism would help you be more *you*.

The real problem facing American industry was how good it had gotten at making stuff. Thanks to Ford and his assembly line, production in America had overtaken consumption. Production-based capitalism had always striven to meet the needs of real people. In a virtuous circle of consumption and production, factories made the goods their workers actually used. Now that more products were being produced than people actually needed, manufacturers and their marketers needed to create desire in people whose basic needs were already being met.

Many companies learned how to do this in a purely mechanistic fashion. Car companies developed schemes for "planned obsolescence," through which car parts were manufactured to fail a few years

after the car was purchased. By the late 1970s, that techniq
too obvious—especially in light of the fact that it wasn't
by Japan and Germany, whose cars tended to last much lon
American models. So automobile manufacturers instead de
time lines through which new features could be rolled out in successive years of a particular model. First the regular model, then a sports
coupé, then a bigger engine, then a convertible, and so on, pushing
owners toward frequent trade-ins. Apple uses this strategy on its
phones and MP3 players; early models must be good, while leaving
room for their successors to be even better—or at least smaller.

I once worked at a hair-products company whose celebrity CEO-
stylist could influence beauty trends by coiffing the characters in
major motion pictures. In order to sell more products, she got the
great idea of developing haircutting techniques that intentionally
damaged the hair through excessive heat, stretching, and abrasion.
Once a customer committed to the hairstyle, her hair would be burned
in such a way that it required ample application of one of the
company's products in order to remain shiny and manageable. The
very same effect could have been achieved without damaging the hair
in this way, but then no need would have been created for the product.

People devising these schemes don't feel guilty about any of this
because their stimulation of consumption is understood as a public
good. They are simply extending the deliberate postwar psychological campaign to create desire for products in individuals, all under the
rationale that it could stave off civil unrest. By appealing to people as
individual consumers and stoking their urge to acquire goods, corporations and their advertisers believed they could meet the high level of
factory production while simultaneously addressing problems raised
by the war. A full 49 percent of American vets were experiencing mental breakdowns after leaving combat. Freud's disciples, many of them
European exiles, were convinced that the stress of combat was not
solely responsible for their symptoms, but that it had triggered old
childhood memories of repressed violence. Furthermore, according
to Freud's daughter Anna, the depravity of the Nazis not only revealed the irrationality of groups who surrender judgment to their
leader, it also revealed the dark, libidinal forces within each one of us.
The unleashing of our innermost, repressed "primal fears" had led to
the barbarism of Nazi Germany.

Although America had won the war, corporate leaders in particular now worried that democracy could easily be overwhelmed by the same irrational emotionality that had driven the Nazis and communists to power. What kind of culture might best integrate veterans into society and prevent the civil unrest of which they and everyone else were surely capable?

President Truman was so concerned about such a possibility that he signed the National Mental Health Act in 1946 to address the "invisible threat to society" posed by returning vets. Psychologists, guidance centers, and marriage counselors were set up across the country to help individuals adapt to the world around them. Nowhere was it suggested that the world around them might be changed, instead.

The best, or at least the highest-paid, psychoanalysts were hired by corporations to mold a new American individual. The "depth boys," as they were called in the industry, believed that consumerism could address all of these challenges and more. Instead of presenting Americans, en masse, with propaganda intended to get them on board the corporate bandwagon, marketers could appeal to human beings as individuals, stoke their desires, and then satisfy them, purchase by purchase.

Since they were only of marginal utility, new products would have to stand in for more abstract emotional needs. This way, superfluous merchandise would still have an appeal. It was far easier and more profitable to reproduce cars than psychologists, anyway. Consumption, not counseling, would appease the dangerous and unconscious drives for love, violence, power, and sex. Psychologists put the techniques they had used in therapy at the service of marketers. Dr. Ernest Dichter took up residence in a magisterial stone house overlooking the Hudson River, and opened the Institute for Motivational Research. Corporate chiefs and advertising executives would make the day trip up to Dichter's mansion to watch him conduct "group therapy" sessions with typical people, all in an effort to uncover what he called the "secret self" of the American consumer.

For his first client, Dichter took on Betty Crocker. The new instant cake mixes were failing, but why? Dichter's free-association sessions with housewives revealed that the product's image of ease and convenience made these women felt guilty—as if they weren't really providing for their families, or being adequate mothers. So Dichter suggested that Betty Crocker give housewives a greater sense of participation. By removing egg from the mix, and requiring women to break and add a real egg instead, the company could turn the procedure into an unconscious symbol of fertility and nourishment. After making this change, Betty Crocker saw its sales soar. Dichter became a sought-after consultant and millionaire.

At least Betty Crocker developed a product attribute—however silly—to match the psychological need of its consumer. As television replaced radio in homes across America and Europe alike, the images created for products began to matter as much as or more than the products themselves. Mass-produced goods were interchangeable—but their brand mythologies were not. What differentiated frozen peas was whether they shipped with a green giant or a Birds Eye bird on the package. A consumer chose gasoline based on whether he trusted the man who wore the star (Texaco)—or, more to the point, whether he needed to experience a relationship of trust when he was driving a car. Once a psychological need could be identified, a brand image arose to fill it. The product—the least important link in the chain of production—came only after that.

All that mattered was that people consumed enough to keep up with the pace of production, and that the brands they chose at least temporarily fulfilled the longings that might otherwise make them dangerous to the status quo. Advertising, particularly on television, became the way to communicate those brand attributes. Over its first two decades, TV grew from a few programs with single sponsors (*Colgate Comedy Hour* and *Kraft Television Theatre*) to full days of programming with interstitial advertisements for just about anything. Ads multiplied, taking up more time and costing more money as the years went on. In 1968, American corporations spent $2.2 billion on advertising. In 1984, they were spending $4.2 billion. By 2001, they were already spending $230 billion, $40 billion of which was directed at children. Today, thanks to TV, print, billboards, and Internet banners, the average person sees over three thousand advertising messages a day. And deep down, all those ads are saying the same thing.

CHAPTER FIVE

YOU, YOU'RE THE ONE

Consumer Empowerment and the
Disconnect from Choice

From Worker to Consumer

Advertising doesn't merely mean to suffuse the atmosphere; it means to become the atmosphere. There is no way out, no alternative to the world it depicts. The cumulative effect of all this messaging has less to do with promoting any particular product than it does with promoting the underlying message of advertising itself: you, the individual consumer, matter. You're the one.

The images populating American ads reinforce a national mythology of strident individualism. The Marlboro Man stares out in profile at the western frontier; he has his cigarette to keep him company. This is America's overarching brand identity. The family settles in around its Sylvania television set, safe and entertained, completely independent of the outside world. Even today, as a spokesmodel for Allergan, Inc., the actress Virginia Madsen equates using Botox with self-affirming feminist values: "I work out. I eat good foods. And I also get injectibles." The "army of one" lets you "be all you can be," while McDonald's still insists that "you deserve a break today." It's all you, and you alone. "Just be"—as soon as you purchase some Calvin Klein CK Be perfume.

Even so, no one gets between Brooke Shields and her Calvins. The only way to interact with others, if one still chooses to do that, is through corporate branded products. An ad ridicules a grandmother for daring to knit Christmas presents for her family and shows just how disappointed they will be by her pathetically homemade gifts. Is she that stupid—or just that cheap? Doesn't she know there's a dot-com merchant who lists the presents they already want? Ones labeled with real brand names that people know?

Cagier marketers pull from the other side of the equation, giving people the tools they need to *ask* for the presents they really want. We no longer need to get married or have babies to sign up for a gift registry; many online merchants offer customers the chance to create lists of what they want, fully accessible to other users at any time. Teenage girls on MySpace offer extra pictures and private chats to men who buy the things on their personal registries. Though it's a form of prostitution, perhaps asking for presents instead of cash takes the edge off the transaction. When people relate socially through an Amazon.com "wish list," it's a move in the other direction. We can get the stuff we want from people who don't know us well enough socially to be able to choose something themselves. And that's just the way marketers should want us: dependent on brands for our self-presentation. Even though young people don't expect to actually receive the things on their many wish lists, they use them as a way to indicate to others what they aspire to own—the brands that would define them.

The premise of one Dell computer campaign is that in order to get what you really want from a loved one, you need to enlist the "star power" of Burt Reynolds, Ice-T, or another celebrity to ask for gifts on your behalf. After picking a product and a spokesperson from the Dell website, you are supposed to let Dell spam the people in your address book, who will receive emails from the celebrity beckoning them to the site and your gift request. Not only do our gifts need to be major brands, but we're supposed to communicate *about* our gifts through branded celebrities, as well. As Burt explains, "I can't hear you because . . . you're not famous. If you're a nobody, get a somebody to help you get the Dell you want."

However transparently obvious or even self-parodied this marketing may seem to us, branding works. Contact with the brand or branded celebrity is more real, more trustworthy, and less messily personal than direct contact with another human being—especially one we don't know and don't want to. On a certain level, this is understandable or even useful. If we're traveling in a foreign country where we don't trust the water, a Coke machine with sealed cans is a welcome sight. We trust that a company of Coke's size will have cleaned its water properly, as there's a giant corporation with tremendous assets at stake if it hasn't. I remember how carrying American Express traveler's checks made my parents feel safe when we toured the Arab district of Jerusalem—as if the credit-card corporation were an extension of the U.S. consulate.

An almost existential version of the same fear follows people home, leading them to use brand names as guideposts orienting them to the world. Kids buy National Basketball Association caps, and leave the tag hanging off the button on the top. That tag, complete with holographic NBA logo, proves the hat's authenticity. Is it more convenient to have a little tag flapping around on your head all day? Of course not. But it proves money was spent and creates a sense of connection with the values of the corporation that produced it. An Airwalk or Simple brand sneaker helps a kid define himself as "counter" to the mainstream values of Nike or Adidas, while shopping at Target—thanks to its ads alone—keeps the worried thirty-something closer to shabby chic than at Wal-Mart or Costco.

The brand transcends and in some cases replaces time and space. A Disneyland souvenir used to have some connection to a trip to Disneyland. As commercial as it may have seemed back in the 1960s, Disneyland's "Main Street USA" was at least a part of the theme park, standing just inside the entrance. Its souvenir shops welcomed tourists as they arrived and gave kids a final chance to bring some of Disneyland home with them when they left. Today, a Mickey Mouse doll, "ears," or framed animation image is available at a Disney Store in the local mall. Does a Mickey Mouse hat bought at the mall store have any less connection to Mickey or the Magic Kingdom than one bought in the shop on Disneyland's Main Street USA? Both are manufactured in the same factory in China, under conditions no one really wants to know about. But the hat itself is no longer the souvenir of a place or a trip, but of a more abstract brand. It's an imitation of a souvenir—a souvenir once removed. The brand has replaced what we might call its aura.

The problem with this, as originally pointed out by the German philosopher Walter Benjamin in his seminal essay "The Work of Art in the Age of Mechanical Reproduction," is that by removing something from its original context or setting, we kill the sense of awe that we might attach to its uniqueness. Great works of art were once intrinsically a part of their settings. The stained-glass windows at Chartres are inseparable from the cathedral in which they are set, as is the ceiling of the Sistine Chapel from the basilica, or even Stonehenge from its countryside. According to Benjamin, the pilgrimage to the work of art and the specific location where the encounter takes place makes for a sacred event. Once *The Last Supper* is brought to a generic museum or, worse, replicated thousands of times in a book, it has been removed from its context—from the material processes of its creation. It loses both its religious possibilities and its connection to the labor that created it.

To be sure, the reproduced work of art is much more accessible. Thanks to photographic technology, any schoolchild can see a pretty accurate picture of *The Last Supper* in a book or on the Internet. No expensive airfare or museum admission needed. The reproduction democratizes art. But, according to Benjamin, there's a danger when people mistake that reproduction for the work of art itself, because it is now being presented devoid of its "aura." Influenced by Marx and having witnessed Nazi Germany, he and other members of the Frankfurt School were concerned about disconnecting a work of art too far from the people, places, and processes surrounding it. Once people are relating to mass-produced symbols and imagery as if they were real, they are much more susceptible to mistaking any spectacle for real life. The symbol can be invested with anything.

Worse, according to Frankfurt associates Theodor Adorno and Max Horkheimer, "Under monopoly all mass culture is identical, and the lines of its artificial framework begin to show through. The people at the top are no longer so interested in concealing monopoly: as its violence becomes more open, so its power grows. Movies and radio need no longer pretend to be art. The truth that they are just business is made into an ideology in order to justify the rubbish they deliberately produce. They call themselves industries; and when their directors' incomes are published, any doubt about the social utility of the finished products is removed." And this was in 1944, an era most of us still look back at as predating the corporatization of all media.

The danger is not just the puerile nature of media, art, and products created under this system, but the way a commodity culture perpetuates the interests of industry above all else. Or, to take Walter

Benjamin's language to its logical extreme, the reproduction industry becomes more important than the things being reproduced. Movies serve Warner Bros., cars serve General Motors, and money serves the Federal Reserve. The apparent fidelity of the reproduction—the THX, Dolby Surround, or HDTV resolution—becomes more important than the allegory or narrative, if any, on offer.

Disconnected from any original context, the remaining works of art or cultural products can be *re*connected to any ends the distributor chooses. Iggy Pop's songs sell Carnival Cruises, *The Simpsons* subsidizes the creation of Fox News, or, as Adorno complained, the language of German folk culture could be disconnected from the folk and exploited on nationalist radio to promote the Führer.

The only thing determining whether an image gets to us is whether its sponsor can infiltrate the mainstream commercial media—a public conduit controlled almost entirely by private corporations. While the images they create may be accessible to all audiences, these audiences are not accessible to all creators, or even to one another. The image itself, divorced from whoever created it or whatever it may have once meant, is now in the service of the image-maker. Well, not even that. The image-makers, whether working at Paramount, Pixar, or Publicis, are employees fulfilling a contract to a corporation like Procter & Gamble. And people who may have once interacted directly now do so through the language and imagery of branding. Are you a Mac person or a PC person? Who are you wearing? What's in your Netflix queue?

Of course this deep disconnection from the creation and distribution of products and meaning is recast by the advertising industry as a form of empowerment. Kids have certainly been "empowered" to represent themselves through highly sophisticated brand iconography. The more that companies invest in their brand meaning systems, the more value a kid will get out of wearing Levi's, watching Adult Swim, using a Virgin Mobile phone, or smoking Camel Lights. The brand universe becomes an alphabet through which young people can assemble their own combinations of meaning and identity—and then walk down the street displaying a unique collection of iconography.

A good friend of mine, an advertising strategist and author named Douglas Atkin, developed the science of "cult branding" around this basic insight. It's Atkin's belief that there's nothing inherently wrong with corporations providing people with the systems they use to make meaning and forge identities in the modern world. While in another era a person might have used the Catholic Church's saints as the collection of symbols through which to assemble a meaning system, today a person uses an array of icons created by corporations. What's inherently worse in this? As Atkin writes, "The evidence of my and others' research is that whether we like it or not, brands are being used as credible sources of community and meaning. And I think there's an important reason why they have been elevated to this role."

According to Atkin, corporations have simply stepped in where traditional meaning-makers have failed us. If churches and civic organizations have become incapable of providing people with meaning, why shouldn't corporations provide this necessary human need? What this analysis leaves out is that the failure of churches and civic organizations was not an entirely unaided phenomenon. Corporations, sometimes as a part of misguided government strategizing, intentionally undermined the foundations of community organizations from union halls to credit unions in their effort to promote self-interested consumerism.

Atkin conducted dozens of focus groups with the members of real and "consumer" cults—from Scientology members to Harley-Davidson riders—and found them yearning for the same things: to belong and to make meaning. By investing a brand with the qualities that make cults so compelling, Atkin helped the corporations who hired him build deep connections with consumers. Whether a laptop or a pair of running shoes can actually come close to fulfilling either of these fundamental needs depends on just how disconnected we are from the possibility of their genuine fulfillment in the first place. The more desocialized we are, the more dependent on Atkin's external, prefab meaning systems we become.

The other main difference between brand cults and real religion, culture, or art is the intent. While religious iconography is almost inevitably corrupted by one institution or another, its original intent is to communicate values and meaning useful to human beings. Whether each of the Ten Commandments is valid or appropriate in hindsight is less important than the fact that they were written with the intention of making society more functional and ethical. Some human being somewhere participated mindfully in their creation. The symbols emerging from corporate advertising have no such origins. They are the product of focus groups and brainstorming sessions. They are icons and images tested to evoke a response, and nothing more. If people are using corporate iconography as their meaning systems, then their ability to interact through them will be limited to the kinds of ideas and values that push corporate products. Values that don't resonate with buying things—such as those that actually bring people into direct contact with one another—will be eschewed in favor of those that require corporate-manufactured intermediaries.

The net effect is to reduce our interaction and connection under the guise of increasing our autonomy. We are free to make meaning together, as long as we do it under the auspices of a corporate cult. Atkin argues that this is already an inherent human need; in the focus groups he conducted with consumers over his decades of study, participants naturally gravitated toward cult-like language. They demonstrated a fanatical devotion to certain brands and a revulsion to others. But what Atkin forgets is that these people were not engaged in their real lives; they were participating in focus groups! They were each paid about a hundred dollars, removed from their real lives, put into a conference room, and made to talk with fellow consumers about a particular product category. In these completely alien surroundings, conversing with total strangers, the focus-group participants gravitated toward their common brand interests. That their importance should be magnified is the nature of the focus group. That's why it's called "focus."

Yet this requirement for a target devoid of context also betrays the aim of most brand communication, which is to remove or devalue all meaning systems other than the one the brand can provide. Isolate the target, then advertise to him. Most advertisers justify their craft by casting themselves as pure meaning-makers rather than meaning-takers. They feel that they are working on a blank canvas, a given circumstance, rather than a landscape which their own industry has sterilized, and a consumer who has been quite deliberately individuated in very particular ways.

Kevin Roberts, the CEO of the once colossal advertising agency Saatchi & Saatchi, celebrates the fact that "the consumer is now in total control." Tears well up in the Australian-born charismatic's eyes as he describes the new empowerment. "I mean she can go home, she's going to decide when she buys, what she buys, where she buys, how she buys. . . . Oh, boy, they get it, you know, they're so empowered at every age. They are not cynical, they are completely empowered; they're autonomous. All the fear is gone and all the control is passed over to the consumer. It's a good thing." This control is limited, though, to what can be accomplished from within the role of an individual consumer.

This doesn't dissuade Roberts. "There are many kinds of love and love takes many shapes and forms," he explains. His crowning achievement at Saatchi (announced just two weeks after Saatchi lost the Tylenol account of twenty-eight years) was a selling system he calls Lovemarks. A Lovemark, as Roberts defines it, is "a brand that has created loyalty beyond reason. A brand you recognize immediately because it has some iconic place in your heart." He doesn't mean this in the self-conscious, ironic sense of being cheekily enamored of a certain candy bar or soap. He means really in love. "Tide is not a laundry detergent. It's an enabler. It's moved from the heart of the laundry to the heart of the family."

In developing Lovemark campaigns for his clients, Roberts and those of his ilk invest their brands with the emotionality and meaning they understand to be missing from daily life. "So we have to create for these great Lovemarks wonderful stories that connect past, present, and future, that involve you, that you can participate in, that make you smile, or they make you cry, but what they do is they make you feel." The inference, of course, is that nothing or no one else has that capability anymore. Each major brand—each "super brand"—in our culture lays claim to a transcendent idea capable of generating these highly charged emotions in consumers. For Nike it's transcendence through sports. For Starbucks it's the notion of creating a "third place" that's neither work nor home. Apple has creativity, Benetton has claimed multiculturalism, Ben & Jerry's has hippie conservationism, and Levi's has authenticity.

But there are only so many of these big concepts to go around. As brands look to be the next big thing, they change agencies with increasing speed. The average client-agency relationship in the U.S. was seven years in 1985, and five years in 2001. By 2007, only half of agency engagements lasted more than two years. The loss of a major client weakens any agency, making it temporarily vulnerable to acquisition by one of a few tremendous networks of agencies: Publicis, Omnicom, WPP, and Interpublic. These aren't advertising agencies themselves, but holding companies that have reduced the agencies they own to relatively interchangeable commodities. As a result, more than promoting any particular client, most agencies are left simply trying to differentiate themselves from the competition. First products, then brands, and now the agencies developing the myths behind those brands have become interchangeable.

Finally, psychologists, anthropologists, and sociologists compete to offer agencies an "edge." These well-credentialed folks will reach for (or stoop to) pretty much any tactic capable of persuading a client that they can offer a competitive advantage. This means developing techniques that appear ever more clever, ever more persuasive. They portray the relationship between producer and consumer (or advertiser and audience) as a game of cat and mouse, in which an intellectually superior hunter appeals to the most primitive or unconscious instincts of the prey.

"They're like cockroaches," exclaimed one marketing psychologist who had rented a display booth at the Advertising Research Foundation's annual convention in 2008, referring to consumers. "You come up with one kind of pitch and they evolve a new defense." This gentleman, a Ph.D. from Stanford (whose business card I lost and whom no one at the conference seems to remember), was selling his company's services as "life-cycle" specialists. The idea is to catch consumers when they are most vulnerable to trying something new—to adopting a new myth. This tends to happen along with a major life change or loss: marriage, the birth of a baby, a life-threatening illness, the death of a parent or spouse, menopause, and so on.

"Chances are, the emotional trauma won't be addressed on a personal level. Most people don't have access to counseling or support from a family member," the good doctor explains. "So a new brand has an opportunity to make a connection." Like an opportunistic cult or a pimp sizing up teenagers at the bus station for signs of parental abuse, he sizes up psychographic groups for their vulnerability to a new brand pitch, and then tells corporations where and how to focus their efforts.

Young Gen Xers who thought they had beaten the marketing machine are drawn back in when they become parents. Hip websites capitalize on the psychological side effects of having a baby: Are you still cool? What does it mean when you buy a Sex Pistols T-shirt for your baby? And, more important, which stroller tells fellow still-cool parents you're one of them and not the "other" kind of parent? In a similar way, organized religions target freshmen college students during their very first weeks away from home, hoping to draw lapsed members back with promises of moral certainty, a return to simpler times, or even safe, God-approved sex.

The Fortune 500 member Acxiom churns the data required for corporations to find each and every one of us at the right moment for a pitch. All the applications we fill out, the taxes we pay, the licenses we use, the credit-card purchases we make, and even our credit reports are purchased by or traded to Acxiom, which stores and compares them. The company then creates models—usually about seventy different ones—for each main psychographic type. According to Acxiom, I'm probably a shooting star: "thirty-six to forty-five, married, wakes up early and goes for runs, watches *Seinfeld* reruns, travels abroad, no kids yet, but undergoing fertility treatments." The specificity of detail is scary, as is the ability of the corporation's computer program to reduce human activity and aspiration to predetermined, quantifiable measurements.

The data from companies like Acxiom are responsible for the offers that arrive in our mailboxes, as well as the language that's used in them. This is the data a telemarketer's computer uses to direct him to which of a hundred different possible scripts to use when speaking to each of us. The company doesn't really know anything about any one of us in particular. They don't really care to know. All they need to do is look at our behaviors and then compare them with everyone else's. If they determine that people who travel between six and eight miles to work in the morning will be more likely to vote Republican if their cars have two doors, and Democratic if they have four, then this is all that matters. (Both political parties currently purchase this data when determining whom to pitch and which pitch to use.)

It's a way to treat us as a mob, individually. The programs give corporations direct access to what we may think of as our humanity, emotions, and agency but, in this context, are really just buttons. Addressed in this one-to-one fashion, we respond mechanically. The computer program adjusts and improves, learning to predict our next evasive maneuver and then presenting us with a product, a brand, or even a candidate that embodies our resistance.

Another company featured at the Advertising Research Foundation conference, NeuroFocus, offers advertisers a look at individual consumer brains responding in real time to packaging and pitches. To accomplish this awesome task, the company slides a test subject into a hospital's MRI machine and then watches neurons firing in the person's brain. "We measure attention, second by second; how emotionally engaged you are with what you're watching, whether it's a commercial, a movie, or a TV show; and memory retention," explained A. K. Pradeep, the company's chief executive. NeuroFocus makes recommendations to its clients based on how consumers' brains light up when exposed to a particular product label or spokesmodel. No conscious participation from the consumer is required, as the ads are fine-tuned to speak directly to the individual's cortex.

The neuromarketing industry's advocates are quick to defend their use of medical technology on, or against, the American consumer. When challenged by public-health groups, they claim that they would never "meddle" with a person's "normal, natural response mechanisms." Of course, by announcing their voluntary refusal to use their tools this way they are implying that it is well within their ability to do so if they choose to. In an argument equivalent to "guns don't kill people, people do," they are quick to point out that they're just scientists—messengers, really—selling the brain data to corporations who will use it as they see fit.

As if in a science-fiction movie, the end result of all this consumer research and anthropology-based product and marketing development is a direct feedback loop between corporate computers and individual brains. The opportunities for human intervention in the creation of products and media diminish as a more automatic process takes over. Nowhere is this more evident than in youth programming, where researchers fastidiously research teen culture for clues to what and how to market, while teens themselves scour the teen networks for models of how to dress and act.

Teen-intelligence firms such as Look-Look hire commando squads of teen reporters to do research on their peers. Armed with digital cameras, these marketing "narcs" snap pictures of street fashions and other trends, which then appear on the company's subscription-only website. Corporate clients use the trends—from new body parts kids are piercing to new ways they're tying their shoes—in their ads and product designs. Kids see these ads, and imitate what they see. Then they are photographed by more teen reporters, and so on.

MTV does this sort of research for itself. In the late 1990s the network noticed that its ratings were starting to slide and embarked on a new teen research campaign it calls an ethnography study, which is led by a marketer named Todd Cunningham. "We go out and we rifle through their closets," Todd explained to me as I followed him to the home of one of the teens he was researching. "We go through their music collections. We go to nightclubs with them. We shut the door in their bedrooms and talk to them about issues that they feel are really important to them." At the end of these "ethnography study" visits—for which MTV brings a video camera and a check for the teen—Cunningham and his team translate the visit into a video clip to show to MTV executives. Cunningham said that as far as he is concerned, this is a win-win situation, because now MTV will more accurately reflect kids' styles, concerns, and values.

Sorry, but MTV's research machine doesn't listen to teens in order to make them *happier*—that's not what the column containing "ethnography study" in the MTV balance sheet is named. They are not dedicated to creating new kinds of music and entertainment in order to promote a richer culture. Corporations depend on understanding trends so that they can sell people whatever it is they already have. Amazingly, in becoming the focal point in the mindless feedback loop between production and consumption, corporations have transformed themselves from authority figures into what the media critic Mark Crispin Miller calls "the tacit superheroes of consumer culture." As he explained to me while I was filming a documentary on MTV, "It's part of the official advertising worldview that your parents are creeps, teachers are nerds, and nobody can really understand kids but the corporate sponsor. They are very busily selling the illusion that they are there to liberate the youth, to let them be free, to let them be themselves, to let them think different, and so on. But it's really just an enormous sales job."

Whether or not any of these new and improved techniques work as advertised, they all engender an increasingly hostile and dismissive attitude toward consumers. Practitioners work to sell the idea that people are predictable and persuadable—at least when they are subjected to the latest manipulation systems on offer. So while arguing to themselves, their readers, and their associates that the consumer is empowered, in charge, and gaining control, these same marketing gurus are simultaneously offering their clients tools that they promise will make consumers almost completely programmable. More amazingly, they don't see the contradiction. They believe they are simply helping the consumer get the things she really, truly wants—and she would know what they were if only she were smart and aware enough to see inside herself as well as a good marketer can.

Most of these admen have never read any Bernays or Lippmann.

They might have graduated from communications or advertising programs, but they never explored the assumptions underlying the principles and techniques they were learning. The vast majority of the advertising executives I've interviewed or worked with are really just consumers themselves. They go to work, do their jobs promoting products they don't believe to be any better than any other, and then use their paychecks to buy the stuff that's being advertised to *them*.

This generation of ad strategists and corporate psychologists is well aware of the 1960s advertising legends David Ogilvy and Leo Burnett, but go blank whenever I mention the Creel Commission, Edward Bernays, or NAM. Two generations removed from public relations' founding fathers, they seem oblivious to the biases that were so explicitly a part of their work. They use techniques that assume the primacy of the corporation, the universal benefits of mass persuasion, and the incapacity of average human beings to make decisions in their own best interests. They behave as automatically as the consumers they hope to control, promoting a corporate agenda at the expense of agency.

When push comes to shove, they quote a member of the new intelligentsia, such as the *New Yorker* star Malcolm Gladwell, whose books pretend to offer sociology or more, but really just promote an updated view of the stupid masses with a few marketing tips thrown in. Gladwell's best seller *The Tipping Point* portrays human society as a field of iron shavings moving unconsciously between magnetic poles. All you need to put one over on the crowd is self-confidence, magic, and a few friends. As the novelist and *New York Times* book reviewer Walter Kirn wrote, "Malcolm Gladwell's *The Tipping Point* is a pop-science tribute to the hopeful notion that standing in the right place with the right lever is often all it takes to move the world. Like *Power of Positive Thinking* and *How to Win Friends & Influence People*, the book should have a special attraction for salesmen who need to believe in commercial, secular magic. For while the book's arguments may be academic, their appeal is mystical, alchemical. You *can* get something for nothing, or near enough."

Revealing techniques like website "stickiness" and the power of "word of mouth" to sell products, Gladwell might well have been writing an update to Vance Packard's *The Hidden Persuaders*, which revealed the advertisers' arts to the reading public for the first time back in the 1950s. But Gladwell instead appraises these techniques from

the cool distance of an anthropologist. Though not a scientist himself, he sees simple, scientific adjustments to culture via technology,
media, and marketing as the answer to our biggest problems. Humans
will respond accordingly. It's all just chaos math.

Gladwell's even more disturbing follow-up, *Blink*, appears even
more pointedly directed to the marketers who embraced *The Tipping
Point*. *Blink* insists that human choices—even very important ones—
are made almost automatically, in the blink of an eye. Gladwell
points out the limits to free will and conscious decision, and his book
celebrates automatic, low-level functioning as somehow superior to
considered rumination over things. Gladwell invents terms like "thin-
slicing" to describe what we used to call "skimming," and argues that
these superficial first impressions are not only more influential in our
decision-making, but more accurate as well. Such "rapid cognition,"
as he likes to call this impulsive neural activity, may be more readily
measurable by the MRI technician, but it is the least conscious of the
options available to us. In some sense, it is also the least human.

Gladwell's books and articles offer fewer real techniques than justifications to today's generation of compliance professionals for the way
they treat their subjects. Perhaps unbeknownst to even himself, Gladwell serves as the modern Bernays, offering spiritual and intellectual
rationales for underestimating or intentionally thwarting people's
cognition. "When you walk out into the street and suddenly realize
that a truck is bearing down on you, do you have time to think through
all your options? Of course not," he explains. "The only way that
human beings could ever have survived as a species for as long as we
have is that we've developed another kind of decision-making apparatus that's capable of making very quick judgments based on very little
information." And this kind of decision-making is not altered through
arguments or education, but appeals to the unconscious, the use of
hot-button emotional issues, or the exploitation of social situations
and relationships. Gladwell readily admits that not all decisions made
in the blink of an eye are good ones. Still, the underlying message of
his books and many speeches to marketing conferences is that with the
guidance of well-meaning outside influences, "blink" decisions can be
directed toward almost any ends.

Gladwell isn't alone. Psychologists and linguists from Berkeley's
Dr. George Lakoff to Emory's Dr. Drew Westen advise corporations
and political parties alike to give up on facts and focus on framing is-

sues instead. Accepting the impulsive emotionality of the voting public as a given to be exploited rather than a predicament to be corrected, they implore even the most progressive anti-élitists to give in and adopt Gladwell's "blink" philosophy. They point to the successful Republican strategist Frank Luntz, whose focus groups helped him reword "global warming" as "climate change," "estate tax" as "death tax," and "third-trimester abortion" as "partial-birth abortion." These simple adjustments had a profound effect on public opinion over the issues themselves. But Lakoff uses these examples of successful political marketing to expound a voters-are-idiots hypothesis. He says that people are too stupid to understand that a federal tax cut would only be offset by an increase in local tax or privatization. So rather than attempt to educate the masses, we should simply dispense with facts.

The result is a world in which a few educated experts compete against one another for the "blink" decisions of uneducated and unthinking human beings. Under such a system, the corporations with the most money would presumably have access to the best psychological technicians, and—just as Bernays would have hoped—would direct and control an otherwise unwieldy populace. Even if the best psychologists turn out to be well-meaning manipulators who work for nonprofit organizations instead of for-profit corporations and lobbies, they're still pushing people toward automatic, ill-considered, and often angry behaviors. That these techniques depend on isolating and targeting individuals, psychographic segments, or, at best, consumer tribes is irrelevant. The more we can be made to respond to hot-button issues (as Obama attempted to explain on the campaign trail with his famous guns-and-religion gaffe), the more selfish, fear-based, and individualistic will our behavior be. And it may even feel to us like an exercise of autonomy.

For slowly but surely, the techniques these experts employ for their commercials, packaging, and political slogans eventually seep into the culture at large. Instead of just watching media that acts on us in this devolutionary fashion, we act on one another this way as well. The advent of TiVo and other digital video recorders, combined with better consumer resistance to advertisements (the cockroach principle), has all but neutralized the effect of traditional advertising. TV ads cost more every year, but reach fewer people less effectively. The answer has been to make ads that look like shows, and real life into something like an ad.

The Real World

Back in the 1960s, the psychologist Stanley Milgram was horrified and inspired by the trial of Adolf Eichmann, who engineered the transport of Jews to Nazi death camps. Milgram wanted to know if German war criminals could have been simply "following orders," as they claimed, and not truly complicit in the death-camp atrocities. At the very least, he was hoping to discover that Americans would not respond the same way under similar circumstances. He set up a now famous experiment in which subjects were instructed by men in white lab coats to deliver increasingly intense electric shocks to victims who screamed in pain, complained of a heart condition, and begged for the experiment to be halted. More than half of the subjects carried out the orders anyway, slowly increasing the electric shocks to seemingly lethal levels. (Although the shocks were not real and the victims were only actors, such experiments were declared unethical by the American Psychological Association in 1973.)

Reality TV, at its emotional core, is an ongoing experiment in interpersonal torture that picks up where Milgram left off. Although usually unscripted, reality shows are nonetheless as purposefully constructed as psych experiments: they are setups with clear hypotheses, designed to maximize the probability of conflict and embarrassment.

America's Next Top Model is not really about who wins a modeling contract, but rather about observing what young anorexics are willing to do to one another under the sanctioning authority of supermodel Tyra Banks. Will they steal food, sabotage another contestant's makeup, or play particularly vicious mind games on one another? *Survivor* has never been about human ingenuity in the face of nature, but instead about human scheming, betrayal, and selfishness in the course of competition. *Joe Millionaire* was about the moment that an aspiring millionairess learns, under the glare of the television lights, that the man on whom she performed oral sex isn't really a millionaire at all. Even Oprah Winfrey's feel-good offering, *Your Money or Your Life*, features a family in a terrible crisis, and then offers an "expert action team" to fix up whichever toothless crack addict or obese divorcée begs the most pathetically.

By sitting still for the elaborately staged social experiments we call reality TV, we are supplying further evidence for Milgram's main conclusion: "Ordinary people . . . without any particular hostility on their part, can become agents in a terrible destructive process." But who is the authority figure in the lab coat granting us permission to delight in the pain of others? Who absolves us of the attendant guilt? Why, it's the sponsor, whose ad for a national, wholesome brand interrupts the proceedings at just the right moment and bestows on them its seal of approval. It's a powerful tool for social programming that was recognized as far back as ancient Rome, where gladiatorial contests fought to the death were forbidden within a month of any election. Lawmakers understood how a governor's "thumbs down" execution of a fallen fighter assumed authority for an entire coliseum's urge to see violence committed. He took ultimate responsibility for the mob's desire to see blood. The greater the transference of guilt and shame to the incumbent ruler's authority, the greater the power he seized.

When reality shows are not working to call attention to the sponsor's authority over the proceedings, they are working instead to bury it. Programs ranging from *The Real World* (one of the first reality shows) and *Queer Eye for the Straight Guy* to Donald Trump's *The Apprentice* blend product placement into the fabric of the program itself. Sponsors pay for makeovers to include their cosmetics, or for Donald Trump's contestants to devise a new advertising campaign for their burger chain. While media-savvy viewers will skip over a "real" commercial, they appear more than willing to watch people compete to create a commercial for the very same product.

It's a technique borrowed from an age long before mass media even existed. *The Apprentice* and its corollaries display an environment and lifestyle to which the audience is supposed to aspire. Most people want to live like Donald Trump or Paris Hilton—at least in some respect. Just as Jean-Baptiste Colbert used Versailles as a showcase for the French luxury goods he hoped to export, sponsors from Marquis Jet to Verizon Wireless hope to position themselves as natural elements of the Trump world—a world that twenty contestants are willing to do almost *anything* to be a part of. Universally dubbed "a pioneer of integrated advertising," Trump's program made the competitive materialism inherent to luxury culture an organic part of his show. He is quite literally training people to be alpha members of a consumer society.

And just as in King Louis' era, the promotion ultimately serves no one more than Emperor Trump. The show depicts Trump as an arbiter of luxury and power. It's less an ad for its sponsors than it is for Trump's own properties, investment systems, country clubs, and associated brands. As long as the public associates the Trump name with all the luxury items advertised and given away on his reality show, his brand will increase in value for both investors and consumers alike.

The real difference, of course, is that unlike Donald Trump, King Louis XIV had no mainstream media to broadcast the goings-on at Versailles. His French branding was entirely dependent on the word of mouth spread throughout Europe by visitors. Colbert not only decorated the palace with seven hundred French-made mirrors, but outfitted royals and courtiers in the latest French silks, lace, and fashions, doused them in French perfume, and fed them French wines and cheeses. They were walking, living advertisements, modeling the clothes and products to Colbert's target market.

The final stage in converting real life into a marketing opportunity brings us full circle to Colbert's technique. Only today it's not just members of the Court who are charged with launching these word-of-mouth campaigns, it's you and I.

The term "viral marketing," I must admit with a bizarre mixture of pride and sadness, originated with my early '90s book *Media Virus!*, in which I posited that ideas spread through the interactive media space like viruses. I'm proud to have launched a well-known idea, but I'm disturbed by the direction it took (even more than I am by the fact that I'm not the one who got rich off its exploitation). My own book was concerned with news items and countercultural threads—the Rodney King tape or *South Park*—that trickled up through mainstream media beyond the control of traditional gatekeepers. *Fast Company* magazine saw in the concept a new version of the word of mouth that marketers had used successfully in the past promoting unadvertisable products like cigarettes or alcohol. Marketers would hire pretty girls to go into bars and ask men for a cigarette or vodka by their brand names. With the Internet up and running, a new way to conduct this viral-style marketing was now available.

Thus, the chat rooms in which kids talk about their favorite bands are now populated by the paid shills of companies like the Cornerstone Agency. They pretend to be enthusiastic fans of the groups whose labels pay Cornerstone for publicity. Other professional "trolls" frequent bulletin boards, the comments sections of blogs, and other online social spaces looking for opportunities to spread the word about great new cameras, travel spots, medicines, or even acts of "corporate responsibility."

It didn't take a genius to realize that with enough planning and organization, this process could be extended off the Internet and back into the real world—and not just for products that couldn't be advertised, but anything and everything. It started small, with companies like Sony hiring people to pretend to be tourists on the street, asking passersby to take their picture. Once the target had the camera in his hands, the fake tourist would tout the benefits of the Sony product. Converse hired college kids they had identified as trend leaders to wear Converse shoes. A firm called RepNation hired girls to wear items from Macy's American Rag collection and then talk about them to their friends.

Yes, many brands have true aficionados—true believers who will proselytize the merits of their products. In Apple's earlier days, Macintosh enthusiasts could be counted on to go into CompUSA stores when new products were released and demonstrate their benefits to consumers. But today's brand enthusiasts are paid spokespeople, faking their loyalty for money. It's a big economy. New firms such as Buzz Marketing and industry groups like WOMMA, the Word of Mouth Marketing Association, now conduct word-of-mouth campaigns on a scale unimaginable before. A study by PQ Media, which collects econometric data and researches alternative media, estimates that companies paid outside agencies $1.4 billion for word-of-mouth marketing in 2007, up from less than $100 million in 2001.

This activity isn't limited to fringe electronics gear or kids' fashion; it has become a mainstay for the most traditional corporations and boring products as well. Procter & Gamble's own word-of-mouth marketing armies have swelled to some six hundred thousand adult consumer-marketers, and over two hundred thousand teens. While kids push CoverGirl and Old Spice to their friends online and off, their moms talk up Dawn detergent and Febreze air freshener at work or at the bowling alley. The adult campaign, code-named Vocalpoint, targets women with larger-than-average social networks. These popular moms speak to an average of twenty-five to thirty other women a day, compared to the normal mom, who speaks with just five. Regions where the Vocalpoint campaign has been used sell an average of 17 percent more product than those relying on traditional advertising alone. P&G considers this marketing ethical, especially since its consumer representatives needn't ever disclose to their friends that they were part of a marketing campaign, so no friendships are put at risk. (In other words, as long as you never find out your friends are really marketers, what does it matter?)

Practitioners now like to call this exploitation of community and friendship "social marketing." They don't see it as the destruction of social reality, but as its very rehabilitation. Sufficiently disconnected from the remains of a shared human culture, the amateur marketers believe that they are creating opportunities for people to engage with one another once again. The products they're pitching are just the excuse to start up a good conversation.

Of the scores of people I've spoken to who engage in these campaigns, none of them see any moral hazard. Some advocate only the products they genuinely believe to be beneficial, while others simply feel "empowered" by their ability to influence their peers' purchasing decisions. The consumer chosen to be a product spokesperson gets to step into the role that only a trusted corporation could play before. On a landscape where the exaltation of the "self" is dependent on gaining a competitive advantage over one's friends, how better to gain a leg up than to transcend the role of worker or consumer, and become a living part of a corporation's brand image?

It may as well be considered a form of corporate-enabled self-improvement.

I Am God

I should never have expected a conference entitled "Alliance for the New Humanity" to have been about any such thing. But the invitation to participate on a panel had been signed by both the spiritual healer Deepak Chopra and the Nobel Peace Prize winner Oscar Arias Sánchez. Somehow, it persuaded me that a weekend in Puerto Rico with "confirmed participants" from Al Gore to Ricky Martin might be worth seeing for myself.

I had been hoping that phrases like "the new humanity" were artifacts of bad translation, but I quickly realized that they were anything but unintentional. Panel after panel of chanters, healers, meditators, and spiritualists presented their techniques and aspirations to a crowd of about four hundred paying participants. With all of our help and, presumably, continued paying participation in the presenters' many additional conferences (nearly all of them had colorful tri-fold flyers announcing their upcoming self-help gigs), the new humanity would someday overtake the current culture of violence and pollution.

What none of the participants seemed to notice throughout the proceedings, however, was the television cameras aimed occasionally at them and much more frequently at the most famous of the celebrities who showed up. Nor did they notice the giant satellite dish sitting on the asphalt just outside the main conference hall. These didn't belong to the press, or even to documentary-makers, but to a firm actually hired by the conference to publicize its existence throughout the mediaspace, using a little-known but increasingly popular public-relations tool called the VNR.

The VNR, or video news report, is a complete, prepackaged story made by a company or a cause, which is beamed to news stations around the world for them to broadcast as if it were one of their own reports. VNRs have been used by the pharmaceutical industry to sell new drugs, by the oil companies to present themselves as environment-friendly, and even by the Bush White House in its effort to change public opinion on the postwar effort in Iraq. What makes VNRs ethically questionable is the lack of disclosure. It's one thing to buy a television advertisement; it's another to pass off one's commercial as reported, balanced news. Local TV stations, suffering budget cuts while striving to improve ratings, have little choice but to accept the free, celebrity-rich footage.

So, in its effort to create some buzz for its fledgling civilization, the Alliance for the New Humanity decided to keep up with the times and utilize a form of media that seems destined to be remembered as one of the ways television news helped us lose touch with reality altogether. The panel on which I participated was unfortunately entitled "Publicity for a New Society: Initiating a Publicity Campaign for Humanity," and was supposed to figure out how to "advertise peace." I had been at the conference for two days listening to the worst the New Age had to offer, and I was about to be granted just two minutes to speak. I was no longer in a very good mood.

I explained that advertisements are themselves psychologically violent acts—part of the escalating arms race between public relations and the public—and that "advertising peace" was an oxymoron. Then I asked if anyone onstage or in the audience knew what that big satellite dish was for (no one did), and proceeded to explain VNRs. I went on to argue that the dish only served to underscore the hypocrisy of holding an expensive conference at an exotic resort hotel, and talking about sustainability while eating veal or (endangered) sea bass and drinking water out of individual-sized plastic bottles. When I finished, the moderator closed his eyes and gently asked for twenty seconds of silence, after which my words were all but forgotten and the conversation returned to the great promise of "Buenos Dias Day," when people around the world would spread goodwill through the media, hopefully with Ricky Martin's promotional help.

While you might expect the marriage of progressive sociopolitical goals and the culture of spirituality to ground activism in ethics, it turns out that just the opposite is true. That's because what we think of as "spirituality" today is not at all a departure from the narcissistic culture of consumption, but its truest expression. Consumer materialism and spirituality coevolved as ongoing reactions against the seemingly repressive institutions of both state and church.

The Puritans brought the late-Renaissance ideology of boundless frontiers with them to the new continent as Calvinism. While we associate the Puritan ethic with hard work, proper investment, and devotion to charity, all this insurance for one's soul also promised a totally earthly gratification. Their ascetic renunciation was supposed to yield Puritans a material bounty, and their human prosperity in this world was likewise a sign of their spirit's salvation in the next one. Not surprisingly, then, the brand of Protestantism that developed in America as corporations took hold in the mid-1800s was already consonant with capitalism's requirements for infinite growth and exploitation of material bounty.

John D. Rockefeller saw his monopolies as endowments from the Creator: "I believe the power to make money is a gift from God . . . to be developed to the best of our ability for the good of mankind. Having been endowed with the gift I possess, I believe it is my duty to make money and still more money, and to use the money I make for the good of my fellow man according to the dictates of my conscience." Rockefeller treated his double-entry accounting ledgers as "sacred books that guided decisions and saved one from fallible emotions."

The department-store magnate John Wanamaker saw in American Protestantism an emphasis on how people behaved rather than what they believed. He saw no contradiction, but a complete synergy between the sacred and the worldly—between devotion and consumption. Wanamaker expanded the Bethany Mission Sunday School, funding concerts, classes, and decorations—much the same kinds of innovations he brought to his department stores. He invited an evangelist preacher, Dwight Moody, to hold a revival meeting "tailored more than any that preceded it to the needs of business and professional people who wanted to be freed from the guilt of doing what they were doing." Religion became a way to support capitalism and purge reflection. The poor should not be helped in any case, lest their immorality be rewarded. Books like Charles Wagner's *The Simple Life* criticized the social programs we now associate with churches, because they involve the redistribution of wealth, which was a repudiation of the way God had given it all out. Instead, everyone should just avoid "pessimism" and "analysis," and be "confident" and "hopeful."

Developing parallel to all this were the first stirrings of what we could call the American spiritual movement, or "mind cure," to which Wanamaker's window dresser, L. Frank Baum, belonged. In the 1893 Parliament of Religions at the World's Columbian Exposition in Chicago, the great mind-cure healers were all brought together for the first time. These were the original practitioners of what we could call the "new age," bringing together the values of consumerism with that of spiritual healing. The followers of Baum's own recently deceased guru, the theosophist Helene Blavatsky, were there, right alongside Mary Baker Eddy (the founder of Christian Science) and Swami Vivekananda (the founder of the Vedanta Society). The Russian Blavatsky had confirmed her ethereal stature with earthy demonstrations of power such as levitation and producing objects out of thin air. Mary Baker Eddy healed ailing farm animals as a child, and later taught people how to heal one another through exposure to Christ Truth. Vivekananda introduced yoga to the West, by pairing it with his particularly American-friendly notion that "Jiva is Shiva"—the individual is divine. By completely removing the traditional and institutional undertones from spirituality, they allowed their followers to embrace the here, the now, and, most important, the self as never before, democratizing happiness and, not coincidentally, condoning consumption as a form of making oneself whole.

The new cult of personal happiness through bootstrapping found its way into every arena, most famously into children's literature, where it could take on mythic significance for successive generations. Eleanor Porter's *Pollyanna*, one of John Wanamaker's favorite tomes and a testament of the simple-life philosophy, tells the story of a young orphan who sees gladness everywhere. Regardless of any hardship imaginable, the girl experiences happiness and soon infects others with her irrepressible sense of joy. See it, feel it, be it. The universe will follow. In L. Frank Baum's *The Wonderful Wizard of Oz*, we get theosophy through the lens of a window trimmer. He Americanizes the fairy tale, softening violence and misfortune with color and abundance. The Wizard in the Emerald City can provide anything to anyone, and especially to pure-hearted Dorothy as long as she *believes*. It is mind cure at its best: carpe diem. And it quickly became a foundation myth for the new spirituality of self.

Despite its antiauthoritarian and self-affirming style, the mind-cure movement didn't offer a genuine alternative to American Protestantism, or a break from its manufactured individualism. Both movements focused on the salvation of the self—one through grace, the other through positive thinking. Throughout the twentieth century, personal freedom would become the rallying cry of one counterculture or another, only serving to reinforce the very same individualism being promoted by central authorities and their propagandists. We were either individuals in thrall of the masquerade, or individuals in defiance of it. Corporatism was the end result in either case.

The mind-cure movements of Blavatsky and Eddy launched a self-as-source spirituality that dovetailed ever so neatly with the individualism promoted by corporate marketers and their psychology departments. Freud and his daughter Anna had led corporate psychologists to believe they could tame the irrational secret self by giving people symbols of power in the form of private houses, personal territory, and consumer goods. Another school of psychologists, taking their cue from Freud's former student Wilhelm Reich, took the opposite approach—or so they thought. Reich believed that the irrational inner self wasn't dangerous unless it was repressed, and that the Freuds' techniques did just this. These innermost impulses weren't violent; they were sexual. They should be liberated, according to Reich, ideally through orgasm.

Anna Freud—herself a virgin who had been analyzed by her father for practicing excessive masturbation—was committed to her father's legacy, and determined to take Reich down. She discredited his work and got him kicked out of the International Psychoanalytical Association. He was later treated as a madman and imprisoned. The court ordered that all his books and records be burned. The battle lines in the psych wars were drawn—but both sides were ultimately fighting for the same thing.

By the 1960s, the German philosopher Herbert Marcuse had revived much of the spirit of Reich—this time for an audience already dissatisfied with the spiritual vacuum offered by consumerism. He was the most vocal member of the Frankfurt School, and spoke frequently at student and antiwar protests. Marcuse blamed the Freudians—as well as the government and corporate authorities who used their stultifying techniques—for creating a world in which people were reduced to expressing their feelings and identities through mass-produced objects. He said the individual had been turned into a "one-dimensional man"—conformist and repressed.

Marcuse became a hero to the real counterculture movement, and his words inspired the Weathermen, Vietnam War protests, and the Black Panthers. They saw consumerism as more than a way for corporations to make money; it was also a way to keep the masses docile while the government pursued an illegal war in Southeast Asia. So breaking free of the consumption-defined self was a prerequisite to becoming a conscious protester. As Linda Evans of the Weathermen explained, "We want to live a life that isn't based on materialistic values, and yet the whole system of government and the economy of America is based on profit, on personal greed, and selfishness." But as Stew Albert, a cofounder of the anti-Vietnam movement the Yippies, contended, the police state began in an individual person's mind. People who sought to be engaged in political activism needed first to make *themselves* new and better people.

The counterculture and its psychologists again revived the spirit of Wilhelm Reich in the hopes of freeing people from the control of their own minds. To this end, in 1962 the Esalen Institute was founded on 127 acres of California coastline. The Institute hosted a wide range of workshops and lectures in an atmosphere of massage, hot tubs, and high-quality sex and drugs, all in the name of freeing people from repression. The Human Potential Movement—Renaissance individualistic humanism updated for the twentieth century—began in an explosion of new therapies. Fritz Perls taught people how to kick and scream while George Leonard conducted "encounter sessions" between black and white radicals, and another with nuns from the Immaculate Heart Convent in Los Angeles—a majority of whom discovered their sexuality and quit the order immediately afterward.

Underlying all of this therapy and liberation was a single premise: Esalen hero Abraham Maslow's "hierarchy of needs." The Brooklyn-born psychologist's map for the individual's journey to more liberated states of being held that people needed to fulfill their lower needs for food, shelter, and sex before they could work on higher ones such as self-esteem and confidence. At the very top of Maslow's pyramidal chart sits the ultimate human state: "self-actualization." For Maslow and his followers, the goal of the self-actualizer was autonomy, independent of culture, environment, or extrinsic satisfactions. Agency, personal creativity, and self-expression defined the actualized "self."

Like Dorothy embarking down the yellow-brick road to self-fulfillment, thousands flocked to the hot tubs of Esalen to find themselves and self-actualize. Instead of annihilating the illusion of a self, as Buddha suggested, the self-centered spirituality of Esalen led to a celebration of self as the source of all experience. Change the way you see the world, and the world changes. Kind of. Instead of fueling people to do something about the world, as the Weathermen and Yippies had hoped, spirituality became a way of changing one's own perspective, one's own experience, and one's own *self*. By pushing through to the other side of personal liberation, the descendants of Reich once again found self-adjustment the surest path to happiness. Anna Freud would have been proud. You are the problem, after all.

The self-improvement craze had begun. Instead of changing the world, people would learn to change themselves. Taking this as their central operating premise, the students of Fritz Perls, Aldous Huxley, and the other Esalen elders developed increasingly codified and process-driven methods of achieving self-actualization. Richard Bandler introduced the Esalen crowd to what he called Neuro-Linguistic Programming, or NLP. Part hypnosis, part behavioral therapy, NLP sees the human organism as a set of learned neural patterns and experiences. By reframing one's core beliefs, a person can relearn reality. The NLP practitioner is a kind of hypnotist who can help reprogram his patients by changing their "anchors," "associations," and "body language."

This work trickled down both directly and indirectly to Werner Erhard and Tony Robbins, who democratized these self-actualization technologies even further through their workshops for EST (now the Landmark Forum) and Unleash the Power Within. Erhard based his seminars on an insight he had gained as a used-car salesman: people weren't buying cars from him at all—they were buying something else that they were simply projecting onto the car. When he was doing his sales job properly, he was just selling people back to themselves. So why not do this without the cars at all?

"The purpose of the EST training," we were told when I took it as a college student in the early '80s, "is to transform your ability to experience living so that the situations you have been trying to change or have been putting up with clear up just in the process of life itself." Get it? The point is not to work on the outward circumstances, but on the inner obstacles to experiencing life in a fundamentally different way. Even if the insight had some value for certain people, the benefits of the EST experience were soon outweighed by the tremendous obligation to "enlist" others in the program. Instructors insisted that the only way to "get it" was to bring others into the pyramid. And if one did "get it," why wouldn't one want to share it with friends and family?

Tony Robbins's Unleash the Power Within seminars explicitly married self-improvement with wealth and power. By walking across hot coals, his seminar participants were supposedly demonstrating to themselves the power of mind over matter and, presumably, over money and other people. While the initial focus of this commercial form of NLP may be on self-hypnosis, one only needs as much of that as is necessary to justify the hypnosis of others. That's why the focus of most NLP today is on applying it to sales, advertising, and even influencing jury selection and deliberation.

While the Yippies and Vietnam protesters were becoming self-actualized NLP programmers, Madison Avenue was retooling its campaigns to these new, highly independent consumers. Daniel Yankelovich, a leading market researcher, studied the apparently nonconformist people of the 1960s and 1970s, and realized that they weren't anticonsumerist at all. They simply wanted products that expressed their individuality, their self-direction, their self-actualization. Luckily for American industry, mass production had developed to the point where Detroit could turn out a brand of car for every member of the family, in any number of psychedelics-influenced colors. The Stanford Research Institute hired Abraham Maslow to turn his hierarchy of needs into psychographic categories of American consumers, applicable to marketing.

It's not that the self-help movement sold out. It was sold out to begin with. First imported from the East by mind-cure fans like L. Frank Baum to help rationalize the marketing of illusion as an ethical pursuit, the "religion of no-religion" was nothing more than a change in perspective. A new set of self-as-source glasses through which to see: Pollyanna's.

Making money off the new spirituality is not a corruption of this movement's core truths, but their realization. In that sense, the obligation of Landmark graduates to enlist their friends in multi-thousand-dollar courses really does confirm the teachings of Werner Erhard. In their logic, the refusal to do so indicates a weakness, an inability to master the energy of money, or a difficulty communicating with one's friends from a place of power. The woman taking Km tonic or wearing magnetic jewelry passes it on to others more as a way of confirming her own belief in its efficacy than to help her friends. But it's a win-win, because the friends will be helped, too. A win-win-win, in fact, because she'll get to keep some of the profit as she passes the proceeds up to her supplier.

Every new self-help modality is an opportunity for a new pyramid of wealth-building as it is shared with successive groups of beneficiaries. The patient of a healer first pays to be healed, then pays even more to learn the technique and heal others. Finally, if he's lucky, he can move to the top of the pyramid and charge still others to be healed themselves. Like residents at a teaching hospital, New Age practitioners "watch one, do one, teach one." And at each successive place in the hierarchy, the practitioner has invested more time and money. No one who takes enough courses to become a certified reader of auras will be caught dead saying they don't really exist. Besides, seeing is believing.

Getting past any guilt, shame, or ethics, today's self-help practitioners no longer consider profit to be a happy side effect of their work, but its raison d'être. *The Courage to Be Rich: Creating a Life of Material and Spiritual Abundance*, by the TV wealth advisor and best-selling author Suze Orman, ties psychology, spirituality, and finances together into a single, one-size-fits-all approach to the universe that hinges on our relationship to cash. Esalen, the Omega Institute, and other spiritual retreat centers fill their catalogs with workshops by Malcolm Gladwell on "Being Fearless," Jack Canfield on "Success Principles," and, of course, everyone on The Secret.

Organized religion well understands the new competitive landscape, and offers its congregations just as much personal success as any self-improvement huckster. The televangelist Creflo Dollar (that's his real name) blings the word to his followers: "Jesus is ready to put some money in your pocket. . . . You are not whole until you get your money. Amen." Dollar may be the epitome of the "prosperity gospel," which promotes the "total" enrichment of its followers. Megachurches are megacorporations, whose functioning and rhetoric both foster the culture and politics of the free market. Christian branding turns a religion based in charity and community into a personal relationship with Jesus—a narcissistic faith mirroring the marketing framework on which it is now based. Megastar and multimillionaire televangelist Joel Osteen, "the smiling preacher," prays for raises and bonuses for members of his congregation, and promises that people will find material success through faith. And keep finding it as long as they believe they will.

For it's no longer good enough to make a lot of money. In a society of ever-improving selves, the individual must become a money-making entity all its own. As *Chicken Soup* pusher Canfield says, "The desire for increase is the fundamental. Expansion is the true nature of the universe. More. The soul is attempting to express itself in a higher way." One can't simply earn "enough" and then stop. Like the economy and the universe, a person's wealth must grow. It's only natural.

How does one grow in an ecology defined more by brands and corporations than by whatever it may have once meant to be human? Become a brand and a corporation oneself. Incorporation provides the path to immortality once promised by religion, while branding provides the surest way of communicating one's asset value in a language of imagery that everyone will understand. It's no longer as simple as kids wearing a Nike swoosh or an NBA tag to indicate the brands with which they identify; it's a matter of turning into a recognizable brand icon oneself.

As the consultant Tom Peters explained in an article for *Fast Company*, "It's time for me—and you—to take a lesson from the big brands, a lesson that's true for anyone who's interested in what it takes to stand out and prosper in the new world of work. . . . We are CEOs of our own companies: Me Inc. To be in business today, our most important job is to be head marketer for the brand called You."

Maintaining one's brand means keeping up appearances. Confessing to a neighbor over a beer about the loss of a job or a missed mortgage payment may have once meant enlisting his help. Among branded neighbors, it means admitting vulnerability. How can he recommend you for another job without endangering his own brand? Why would he even want to if he didn't already believe that your brand offered a mystique he couldn't get on his own? What labor unions once earned through solidarity, a society of secreted, branded careerists takes away. Now we can all get paid less for what we produce because admitting to one another how little we're making is bad for our brands.

That doesn't stop this ethos of self-branding from trickling into almost every arena of human interaction, from dating to college applications. Courses in "Speed Seduction" teach NLP hypnosis to nerds hoping to incapacitate bimbos' cognitive functioning for long enough to bed them, while professional counselors rewrite seventeen-year-olds' personal essays with the right emotional hot buttons for admissions officers. Hey, that kid sounds *cool*.

Just like those young businessmen in Bret Easton Ellis's satirical novel *American Psycho* who obsessed over the embossing of their business cards, for us image is everything. We have our signature coats, trademark hats, and other identifiable symbols of our consistent and, hopefully, enviable professional identities. The baker becomes a Baker, the professor a Professor, and an author an Author who must all find styles and personalities to match their professions. Restaurants no longer have enough tables to give every executive his own signature location for daily power lunches. People choose their eateries less by the food they want to eat than the image they want to project. Kids learn how to be doctors, lawyers, or cops by watching *ER*, *Boston Legal*, or *Law & Order* and choosing which branded personality to emulate. And like any outsourcing corporation, the branded personality needn't know how to perform any work himself. The brand alone is the capital through which value from others is extracted.

The successfully branded person makes money just by being himself. Think Paris Hilton. She didn't actually *do* anything to become famous. That's precisely what proved the immense power of her brand. Her signature television show, *The Simple Life*, was about her inability to do anything but watch or complain as other, real people worked around her. In spite of being arrested and jailed for driving violations, Paris was nonetheless offered a million dollars to teach a one-hour course at the Learning Annex called "How to Build Your Brand."

Granted, that may just be the object of the game when it's played in a corporatist landscape and against players who are corporations themselves. The problem is that no matter how well we play, the real corporations will necessarily beat us. This is their realm. Corporations will always be better at being corporations than people will. They don't need to eat, sleep, or, worst of all, feel. They do not age, or suffer doubt. They do not need to be reassured or loved. If we really want to compete effectively, that's the direction we'll have to go.

But it's a difficult moment to try to return to being human again, too. Even that sounds more like a self-help course than a workable strategy. And so human beings go from subjects to citizens, citizens to workers, workers to consumers, and consumers to brands. In the journey toward self-incorporation, market-friendly spirituality provides a momentary release from this uneven fight. All the while, the artificial structures we created—corporations—become bigger players, the true gods of this artificial realm, immortal, utterly impervious to our humanity, and capable of rewriting the rules as they go along.

Our only hope may be to consider the possibility that neither our corporations nor the money on which they thrive are real. They weren't here to begin with. We invented them, together, just as we invented our selves.

CHAPTER SIX

TO WHOM CREDIT IS DUE

Self-Interest and the Disconnect from Currency

Unenlightened Self-Interest

Cindy, a salesperson in a major Chicago department-store jewelry department, got in trouble for helping one of her co-workers.

"That's not your job!" her manager scolded her. "You're supposed to be selling to customers, not helping Anthony with a return."

"But Anthony doesn't know how to ring it up," Cindy explained.

"Then that's Anthony's problem, not yours."

Lisa, Cindy's counter partner in mid-range diamonds, smirked. "Toldja."

Cindy's mistake was innocent enough. After managing a successful independent jewelry store in Evanston, Illinois, for a decade, she understood that when salespeople worked together they achieved better results: more total sales, happier customers, repeat business, better morale, and even fewer sick days. She had studied gemology, not management theory, but she knew how to motivate a sales staff. As far as she understood, helping a co-worker was a good thing, not a bad thing.

But Cindy was no longer working at a successful independent jewelry store. The chain (of three) had been gobbled up by a much larger one, which offered Cindy an equivalent job three hundred miles away. Rather than move, she called what she believed was "their bluff" and they let her go with two weeks' severance. She ended up having to move anyway, and accepted a regular sales position at a well-known department store in downtown Chicago. They assured her there was "room to move up," and that, given her age (forty-five) and her experience, a position off the sales floor in management was a certainty.

Two full years later, Cindy is still on the sales floor, wearing her mandatory heels. She's been called up to human resources at least once a month for breaking store policy by helping her colleagues, working extra hours, or "forgetting" to upsell languishing stock items to her best regular clients. I am not privy to today's reprimand, but Cindy emerges from the elevator in tears. We go to a Starbucks around the corner, where she explains what has happened to the most respected jewelry department in the city after Tiffany.

"They say if Anthony is slow enough with the return, the customer may change her mind. Or think twice about returning something in the future," she explains, exasperated. "The faster he gets done, the more chance he has to sell her something else. But they don't see it that way."

I ask her why salespeople are not allowed to help each other, and she hands me a booklet prepared by a consultancy the store's conglomerate hired to bring their sales figures up to the same rates enjoyed by the discount chains in the portfolio. It's filled with language I've only seen used in the fine print of mortgages or in bankruptcy court documents. Terms like "arrears" and "negative accounts."

The store had changed its compensation scheme from salary plus commission to commission only. But since commission-only full-time jobs violate labor laws, the store created an employee accounting system to accomplish the same thing. Each employee must generate sales that support her salary. So if an employee earns six thousand dollars per month pretax, she must sell $100,000 at a 6 percent commission to cover her salary. If she misses her quota, then her "account" goes into arrears. This means she has to make up the deficit the following month. If she exceeds her quota, however, the surplus isn't carried forward. She must start at zero each month.

By this system, employees end up "owing" the store money—and the debt can accumulate rapidly, particularly in a slow season, or if returns start piling up. A $25,000 sale one month creates tremendous liability for the future. If the item is returned in a different month, it is pure deficit. Worst of all, according to Cindy, the new policy led to a hiring spree of new salespeople, all at much lower hourly rates. They don't have to earn as much to stay out of arrears—which is good for them because now the department is terribly overstaffed.

Most sales activity consists of competing against other clerks for the customers walking in the door. Each salesperson has her own strategy for positioning herself, winding through the counters, and claiming incoming patrons: "I greeted her already." Salespeople quickly learn to say they've already assisted people they haven't even met—leading to great puzzlement from customers. Others attempt to ring up returns under competitors' account numbers, or steal sales by sending off a junior colleague on a fake urgent mission— just before she is about to close a purchase. That's one of the reasons Cindy is not supposed to help anyone: any effort to assist a colleague may as easily be a form of sabotage. The best way to prevent loud battles on the sales floor is to keep the employees from working together at all.

It's also the way to keep the sales staff motivated, energetic, and competitive. At least according to current "performance pay" theory, healthy competition between salespeople leads them to operate more autonomously and effectively. They believe they are independently controlling how much they earn, using their own wits and relative superiority to get ahead. When they see their colleagues as competitors to be beaten rather than as friends to help, they are less likely to relax or socialize. They maintain their edge at all times, ready to fend off a broadside attack from a colleague in arrears.

The whole system is sold to employees as a boon to their independent operation. They aren't mere employees, but entrepreneurs free to use whatever techniques work best. They aren't responsible to the others working alongside them—only to their own accounts. No need to make friends, engage in idle chitchat, or surrender one's personal identity to the brand of the store. This is a miniature free-market economy, so compete! It's every man for himself. Go for it—we've got your back.

By eliminating the possibility of any allegiance between employees, the store ensures that any loyalty will be paid upward instead. Each salesperson is in a direct relationship with the store. Thanks to overstaffing, there are not enough sales to keep everyone's account in good standing. For one salesperson's account to be satisfied, someone else's must go into arrears. By design at least one employee will be in arrears at all times, serving as a motivating negative example. If a salesperson stays in arrears for more than two months, she doesn't have to pay back the money but she is fired with no severance. It's survival of the fittest.

The department-store sales floor is no less coercively biased than the playing field on which free-market competition supposedly takes place today. The store uses the language of free and fair competition to justify near-absolute control over its employees; salespeople fight over a supply of customers made artificially scarce through overemployment, and learn to measure their own success against the failure of others. They are led to believe they are working under a system in which their sole allegiance is to themselves, when their true fealty is to the central authority tallying their credits and debits.

Under the guise of promoting its workers' self-direction, the store manages to pay less for more work. Frequent and unpredictable firings keep workers glad to have a job and health insurance at all—especially in such a "competitive" retail environment. Like union workers who agree to salary decreases in order to compete more effectively with laborers from overseas, the salespeople are fearful, ignorant, and self-interested enough to buy into the myth that their income and benefits are part of the problem. The only bankable outcome is the redistribution of wealth from the person doing the work to the people underpaying them—and, ultimately, the passive shareholders.

The greater competitive marketplace, likewise, works under the presumption of a natural and free contest between self-directed individuals, unencumbered by "senselessly" debilitating regulations. Coddling of the weak or overpaid may provide temporary relief to certain individuals, it is believed, but it only worsens the eventual comeuppance for everyone. American workers get fat while the Chinese learn to work for a fraction of the price. Welfare programs keep young mothers off the streets, but ultimately weigh down corporations with excess taxation. Unions may win workers higher wages, but this only weakens America's last great corporations and their ability to compete in the global marketplace, and weaken self-motivation the way antibiotics weaken our immune system. Like any of nature's real economies, the market economy is best approached as a self-regulating system dependent on lots of freely competing individuals. All this competition doesn't compromise the social fabric; it *is* the social fabric.

And we all now know how well that's working out.

How did we lose our bearings, and surrender social reality to a cynically tilted economic model? The "selves" we so laboriously constructed and revised over the past four hundred years—though decidedly artificial—seemed real enough to twentieth-century economists, especially as they attempted to apply the scientific model to the softer social sciences. At least economics, like physics, could be expressed in numbers. Unlike Freud's unconscious ids, economic actors could be tracked on a balance sheet. As a result, however, the entire theoretical framework for economics was built, at least initially, around the assumption of a profit-maximizing individual. It was a leap, but one supported by the decade's leading psychologists, and one that provided the leaders of the free world with a social model capable of confronting the financial and ideological challenges of managing the postwar industrial economy.

While the Soviets struggled to build a centralized bureaucracy that could administrate the needs of all people, free economies turned to the market. In 1944, an Austrian economist named Friedrich Hayek had just finished his seminal work, *The Road to Serfdom*, in which he argued to his British and American colleagues that all forms of collectivism lead to tyranny. According to Hayek, any central planner will prove incapable of managing resources without resorting to coercive means. The people, desperate for leadership capable of putting bread on the table, would welcome dictatorship and voluntarily surrender their personal and economic freedoms to the promise of greater efficiency. Fascism was not a reaction to communism, according to Hayek, but its necessary outcome.

Hayek's solution was a free and open market. No central authority could ever have enough information to distribute resources effectively. There's just no way to predict what everyone might want, however good the math you're using. Since the information required to make production decisions is inherently decentralized, it should be gathered and reconciled through decentralized means. Adam Smith had already argued that if everyone goes after his own interests, the interests of the greater society will be served. Hayek extended this logic, contending that the price mechanisms of a freely functioning market will naturally synchronize the demands of people with the market's supply. In Hayek's view, this mechanism is not of human design, but a spontaneous "catallaxy": a self-organizing system of voluntary co-operation. As millions of people both rationally and irrationally pursued their goals, a working market would order itself around them. The market was as much a part of human beings as their DNA.

Given the premises he worked under, Hayek's conclusions were intelligent enough, and foreshadowed some of the systems theory to follow. Margaret Thatcher, Ronald Reagan, Tony Blair, and Bill Clinton all based their approaches to the economy on his work, which still forms the theoretical core of free-market theory today. When it's working as designed, the free market can accurately predict and address a wide range of human needs, with a minimum of central planning. Likewise, appeals to self-interest may best motivate human action, at least in the short term. But both principles are operating in a social landscape and economic framework dominated by their own forced implementation. We built this economy from the ground up—at the expense of other social mechanisms—and then used its existence as evidence that this is the way things have always been. Even many of our market economy's most formidable defenders are unaware of the underlying assumptions on which their theories are based.

This is not a case of willful ignorance so much as unconsciously internalized corporatist values. By accepting greed as the foundation and the market as the context of all human interaction, we ended up replacing a complex ecology of relationships with a much simpler and balance-sheet-friendly set of zero-sum equations. More dangerously, by assuming the money we use to be neutral and without bias, we condemned ourselves to the agendas of Renaissance-era financiers whose goals we have long since forgotten.

A Paranoid Schizophrenic's Legacy

"There is no such thing as society."

—MARGARET THATCHER

If our economic theorists seem particularly coldhearted and zero-sum in their thinking about human behavior, we might blame it at least in part on the Cold War. By the 1950s, most of the best mathematicians and social scientists had been hired either directly or through grants to work out America's nuclear-war-game scenarios against the Soviet Union. In a situation where the enemy might be signing a nonproliferation treaty while actually stockpiling an arsenal, paranoia made good sense.

The think-tank logicians at the Rand Corporation called it "the prisoner's dilemma." The scenario went something like this: Two suspects are arrested by the police, who have insufficient evidence to convict either one. If one betrays the other, who remains silent, the betrayer goes free and the silent accomplice receives a ten-year sentence. If both remain silent, they both get six months. If both betray each other, they each get a five-year sentence. What should they do?

The Rand scientists believed that mutual distrust should rule the day. Each prisoner must assume the other will betray him, and then avoid the ten-year sentence by becoming a betrayer himself. They tested their ideas on Rand's own secretaries, creating all sorts of different scenarios in which the women could cooperate with or betray one another. In every single experiment, however, instead of making choices in the self-interested way that Rand expected, the secretaries chose to cooperate.

This didn't deter John Nash, the Rand mathematician portrayed by Russell Crowe in the movie *A Beautiful Mind*, from continuing to develop game scenarios for the government based on presumptions of fear and self-interest. An undiagnosed paranoid schizophrenic, Nash blamed the failed experiments on the secretaries themselves. They were unfit subjects, incapable of following the simple "ground rules" that they should strategize selfishly. Nash remained committed to the rather paranoid view that human beings are suspicious creatures, constantly making strategic assessments about one another and calculating how to gain a competitive advantage in any situation.

Game theory worked quite well in poker, anyway, from which it originated. And what better model existed for the high-stakes nuclear standoff between the United States and the U.S.S.R.? Offering to give up all of one's weapons was impossible, because there was no way of knowing whether the enemy had really done the same or merely bluffed about his holdings. Instead, each nation had to maintain a nuclear arsenal in order to deter the other from using its own, and bringing about what was known as mutually assured destruction, or MAD.

The fact that a nuclear war did not break out served as the best evidence that Nash's theoretical framework was sound.

Encouraged by this success as well as by the voices in his head, Nash applied his game theory to all forms of human interaction. He won a Nobel Prize for showing that a system driven by suspicion and self-interest could reach a state of equilibrium in which everyone's needs were met. "It is understood not to be a cooperative ideal," he later admitted, but—at least at the time—neither he nor Rand thought human beings to be cooperative creatures. In fact, if the people in Nash's equations attempted to cooperate, the results became much more dangerous, messy, and unpredictable. Altruism was simply too blurry.

The young technocrats at Rand believed that Nash's equations presented a way to organize a society of self-interested individuals that promoted their personal freedom. By the 1960s, they had the backing of a counterculture equally obsessed with the personal needs of individuals and the corrupting influence of all institutions—even family. The Scottish psychologist R. D. Laing used game theory to model human interactions, and concluded that kindness and love were merely the tools through which people manipulated one another to get their selfish needs fulfilled. Mental illness was just a label created by the repressive state. So-called crazy people were really evidence of some greater societal problem—a "cry for help" against oppressive institutions. In fact, like the family, the state was just a means of social control that violated the most primal and fundamental urge of human beings to pursue their individual interests. Through Laing, the darkest aspects of game theory were extended to the culture at large and popularized as social truisms: your parents don't really love you and the man is after your money. What look like social relationships are really just "the games people play."

Hippies took these assessments to the streets, but most of them were too distracted by self-actualization for the movement to maintain any cohesion. Within a decade, the counterculture's war against institutional control would become the rallying cry of the Right. The brilliance of Reaganomics was to marry the antiauthoritarian urge of what had once been the counterculture with the antigovernment bias of free-market conservatives. In Reagan's persona as well as his politics, the independent, shoot-from-the-hip individualism of the Marlboro Man became compatible—even synergistic—with the economics and culture of self-interest. No-blink brinksmanship with the "evil" Soviet empire, the dismantling of domestic government institutions, the decertification of labor unions, and the promotion of unfettered corporate capitalism all came out of the same combination of Rand Corporation game theory and the 1960s antipsychiatry movement. Regulations designed to protect the environment, worker safety, and consumer rights were summarily decried as unnecessary government meddling in the marketplace. As if channeling Friedrich Hayek by way of R. D. Laing, Reagan shrank the social-welfare system by closing the public-psychiatric-hospital system.

Almost simultaneously in the U.K., just a few months after becoming head of the Conservatives, Margaret Thatcher explicitly made Hayek her party's patron saint. A colleague had been delivering a speech about the need for a "middle way," when Thatcher interrupted him and held up a copy of Hayek's *The Constitution of Liberty.* "This," she said, "is what we believe," and banged it down on the table. When she became prime minister, she appointed the director of the Hayekian Centre for Policy Studies as her secretary of state for industry. Like Reagan, Thatcher believed that less government and more market would allow the self-interested masses of individuals to get what they needed. Compared with how the Soviet Union was buckling under the weight of its massive and inefficient bureaucracy, it appeared as if the free-market system would become the one true path to individual freedom for everyone.

Reagan and Thatcher extended their market reforms beyond the market itself to include government. If people behaving in a self-interested fashion led to the most equitable distribution of wealth and resources, why not run everything this way? Thatcher and Reagan attempted to dismantle as much state apparatus as possible so that the free market could fulfill these needs instead. Only slightly less Hayekian in their thinking, Clinton and Blair followed by instituting free-market reforms *within* government agencies.

This was not a political compromise, the marriage of traditional opposites, or what Clinton's critics called triangulation. It was a social ideology all its own. As New Labour saw it, game theory could be employed to motivate government workers to perform better. Instead of just paying everyone fixed rewards no matter how well or poorly they performed, why not set workers "free" by letting them achieve the desired results in any way they chose? Government workers should never have been expected to act out of altruism or the social good—whatever that might be. Instead, agencies should appeal to their workers' wallets. To unleash the entrepreneurial spirit lurking within every civil servant, the government established a series of quotas and metrics for its workers to reach—and to get paid for reaching. They didn't realize that appealing solely to people's self-interest might lead to entirely self-interested behaviors.

When given incentives to lower their crime figures, the Lothian and Borders Police reclassified criminal offenses as "suspicious occurrences." The crime rate didn't get any better—except on paper, where it mattered. The National Health Services' performance pay depended on lowering waiting-times statistics, so managers simply took the wheels off gurneys and reclassified them as beds, and reclassified certain hallways as "wards." Target achieved, Nash style.

Game theory's failure to reform government agencies was blamed on the structure of the agencies, not on Hayek's vision of a world self-organized via catallaxy. No, they believed, public institutions were just too old, too steeped in bureaucracy, and too darned artificial to benefit from the functioning of a genuinely complex, natural marketplace. No matter how healthily self-interested their workers, government bureaucracies are themselves so intrinsically controlling and calcified as to make the Hayek effect all but impossible to achieve. A health agency is still an expression of the bureaucratic welfare state, however much it's attempting to imitate the rules by which the private sector operates. Only by removing the safety net altogether—and replacing it with pure market forces—could social engineers hope to restore the full force of nature to public institutions. Privatization was the only way out.

Make no mistake about it: by the late Clinton-Blair years, both the Right and the mainstream Left had accepted the basic premise adapted from systems theory that the economy was a natural system whose stability depended on the government's getting out of the way and allowing self-interested people to work toward a dynamic equilibrium. Gone were the "compassion" and "love" that Mario Cuomo had demanded of government back in his rousing "Tale of Two Cities" speech at the 1984 Democratic convention. In their place were small government and personal accountability. The last heroes of the political age, Reagan and Thatcher, were long gone. In their place, the only rebels capable of dismantling the social-welfare hierarchy were the super-CEOs: Jack Welch, Richard Branson, and Ken Lay, as well as the new breed of free-market theorists advising them.

Thanks to the combined emergence of a computer culture capable of recognizing the power of emergent systems and a rising class of dot-com workers profiting off what appeared to them to be the exploitation of a free-market technology, libertarianism was in ascendance. In reality, the phenomena we were all celebrating in the mid-1990s had little to do with the free market; the Internet had been paid for by the government, and dynamical systems theory was much more applicable to the weather and plankton populations than it was to economics. But as profits and stock indexes rose, the stars themselves seemed to be aligning, and systems theory was as good a way as any of justifying the same options packages that young programmers would have been embarrassed by just a few years before, when they were antiestablishment hackers.

While computer programmers were finding jobs in Silicon Valley, social scientists and chaos mathematicians won contracts at corporate-funded think tanks. The Santa Fe Institute studied complexity theory, and applied its findings to the market. The "four Cs," as they came to be known—complexity, chaos, catastrophe, and cybernetics—now dominated economic thought. Building on the work of Hayek, the new science of economics held that there was no global, central controller in an economy—only a rich interaction between competing agents. Order, such as it was, emerged naturally and spontaneously from the system—the same way life evolved from atoms or organization emerges from an anthill.

For those of us who had witnessed the Internet come to life or who had watched a simple fractal equation render an entire forest or ocean on a computer screen, the case for a bottom-up economy based on nothing but a few simple rules was compelling. If, as the anthropologists and social scientists were now telling us, human beings followed the same sorts of simple rules for self-preservation that ants and slime molds used to build their colonies and distribute scarce resources, then all we needed to do was let nature take its course. A great society would emerge much faster and better than it could ever be legislated into existence by intellectuals or social reformers.

Richard Dawkins's theory of the "selfish gene" popularized the extension of evolution to socioeconomics. Just as species competed in a battle for the survival of the fittest, people and their "memes" competed for dominance in the marketplace of ideas. Human nature was simply part of biological nature, complex in its manifestations but simple in the core commands driving it. Like the genes driving them, people could be expected to act as selfishly as Adam Smith's hypothetical primitive man, "the bartering savage," always maximizing the value of every transaction as if by raw instinct. Even the people who are crazy enough to behave differently end up testing new market strategies in spite of themselves. Best yet, according to Dawkins, "the whole wave keeps moving." In spite of local and temporary setbacks—like what's happening in the United States at the moment—the trend is our friend, and undeniably progressive. Let her rip.

Freakonomics, the runaway best seller and its follow-up *New York Times Magazine* column, applied this model of "rational utility-maximization" to human behaviors ranging from drug dealing to cheating among sumo wrestlers. Economics explained everything with real numbers, and the findings were bankable. Even better, the intellectual class had a new way of justifying its belief that people really do act the way they're supposed to in one of John Nash's game scenarios.

Ironically, while the intelligentsia were using social evolution to confirm laissez-faire capitalism to one another, the politicians promoting these policies to the masses were making the same sale through creationism. Right-wing conservatives turned to fundamentalist Christians to promote the free-market ethos, in return promising lip service to hot-button Christian issues such as abortion and gay marriage. It was now the godless Soviets who sought to thwart the Maker's plan to bestow the universal rights of happiness and property on mankind. America's founders, on the other hand, had been divinely inspired to create a nation in God's service, through which people could pursue their individual salvation and savings.

As the best-selling Christian textbook *America's Providential History* explains, "Scripture defines God as the source of private property. . . . Ecclesiastes 5:19 states, 'For every man to whom God has given riches and wealth, He has also empowered him to eat from them.' . . . Also in I Chronicles 29:12, 'Both riches and honor come from Thee.' " America is God's true nation because it is the bastion of the free market through which He can exercise His divine will. Socialism (and American liberals) set up the state as provider instead of God. Bureaucrats end up intervening in the sacred relationship between the Lord and His creations, usurping His role, and interfering in the process of salvation. Charity is an opportunity for people—not governments—to care for their fellow men. Social-welfare programs, like evolution, implied that God had not created a perfect world in the first place. The free market, on the other hand, gave human beings the opportunity to exercise their free will in pursuit of personal salvation as well as a personal piece of God's good earth. No engineering or central planning was required.

The same right-wing think tanks writing white papers justifying game-theory economics through bottom-up social Darwinism were simultaneously advising conservatives on how to leverage Christian Fundamentalists in support of the resultant ideals. What both PR efforts had in common were two falsely reasoned premises: that human beings are private, self-interested actors behaving in ways that consistently promote personal wealth, and that the laissez-faire free market is a natural and self-sustaining system through which scarce resources can be equitably distributed.

For all the ability of genes and even memes to battle for survival against one another, human beings are just as likely to share and cooperate as they are to cheat and compete. But the ascendance of market rhetoric in America and Britain was accompanied by the assertion of some decidedly antiromantic science. University anthropologists seemed determined to correct the hopeful impressions that so many still clung to of peaceful, vegetarian gorillas enjoying one another's company in the jungle. Like stories of supposedly peaceful aboriginal tribes as yet untainted by corrupt Western civilization, such visions— according to the new social Darwinists—were pure fantasy.

The people-are-actually-really-mean hypothesis was supported by the anthropologist Napoleon Chagnon's observation of violence among the Yanomami people of South America. Chagnon's documentary footage depicted tribesmen attacking one another with machetes. He demonstrated that the seemingly random violence had broken out along complex familial lines, supposedly proving that the tribesmen's genes were still competing for dominance. Buried deeper in his documentation was the real reason for these attacks: Chagnon had distributed a small number of machetes to just one of the tribes. The neighboring tribes wanted the machetes, too. Although the study has been argued over for decades now, the artificially introduced scarce resource was at least part of the reason they were fighting.

Paleontologists and social biologists such as *Lucifer Principle* author Howard Bloom present contagiously popular evidence of violence among competing gorilla and chimpanzee groups, going as far as to describe the steps by which a certain female chimp dashed out the brains of its rivals. That the chimps were fighting over rights to a human garbage dump isn't considered germane. Perhaps predictably, Bloom's follow-up work, *Reinventing Capitalism,* applies these same skewed insights to the market. He is not alone. Volumes could be filled (and actually are) with essays and studies about the violent, self-interested behaviors of monkeys and indigenous peoples, written by prominent scholars and directed to policy-makers and economists.

Just because many participants in leading intellectual forums such as *The New York Review of Books* or Edge.org (a website on which I participate) consider these proudly unromantic views of human nature more consistent with a godless universe doesn't make them any more true. More scientifically gathered evidence points the other way.

A South African archeologist and Harvard professor named Glynn Isaac based his own studies of human behavior less on abstract models or analogies with apes than on hard evidence from fossils and archeological digs. By focusing on the evolutionary record, Isaac showed how social networks and food sharing were the deciding factors in allowing early hominids to succeed over their peers. Researchers at Ohio State University studied sex-based size differences in human fossil remains, concluding that competition between males for mates was much less prevalent than earlier believed. "Males were cooperating more than they were competing among themselves," the researchers concluded.

Studies by psychologists at the University of Chicago in which researchers measured subjects' ability to see problems from the perspective of others demonstrated how "cultures that emphasize interdependence over individualism may have the upper hand." (In their conclusions, the psychologists noted the individualistic bias of Western corporations compared with those of Asia. A Texas corporation "aiming to improve productivity told its employees to look in the mirror and say 'I am beautiful' 100 times before coming to work. In contrast, a Japanese supermarket instructed its employees to begin their day by telling each other 'you are beautiful.' ")

While legends of violent meat-eating *Homo sapiens* vanquishing tribes of Neanderthals still garner rapt attention at dinner parties, there is little evidence that such events ever took place. On the other hand, there's plenty of evidence for the less dramatic assertion that a combination of tools, hunting, gathering, and food-sharing permitted what we now think of as civilization to evolve out of cooperative human activity. In certain circumstances, the tendency toward conflict with neighboring tribes inhibited survival, while cooperation within a social group and beyond promoted it.

We shouldn't be too shocked that the industrial world's intellectuals would be so prone to perceive humanity as driven by instinctual, self-interested violence. This behavior is as old as colonialism itself, and calls to mind wealthy plantation owners arguing that Africans were better equipped anatomically—by the Maker or by evolution—to pick cotton. Today's equivalent, however well masked in scientific jargon, is no better supported by the facts. As a cultural mythology, however, it helps assuage any residual guilt the rich might feel over the inequitable distribution of wealth built into the existing economic order.

Or perhaps the wealthy obsess over what they hope is an entirely dog-eat-dog reality because their participation in the culture of money hasn't ended up making them any happier. According to a study conducted at the height of the market, 23 percent of brokers and traders at the seven largest firms on Wall Street suffered from depression—more than three times the national average. Scientists and United Nations sociologists alike have concluded that affluence produces rapidly diminishing returns on happiness. After achieving an income per capita of about $15,000, any increase in wealth makes little difference to a nation's total happiness metrics.

Among the six articles I found from *Forbes* in 2006 fiercely criticizing this "swath of studies" as well as the whole notion of "happiness research," none mentioned any of them specifically, or their findings. The libertarian think tank the Cato Institute similarly criticized these studies along with any attempt to measure subjective well-being—but concluded that even if they were true and money didn't make people happier, this would only support the libertarian position that wealth redistribution by government was unnecessary. Still others have criticized happiness research because it could lead to the implementation of authoritarian policies by central governments under the pretense that they were trying to make people happier.

But it's disingenuous to equate any critique of the theory of "rational utility-maximization" with efforts to construct a socialist welfare state. And it's especially cynical to do so while marketing and defending financial instruments intentionally designed to take advantage of consumers' *irrationality* when making economic decisions.

Behavioral finance is the study of the way people consistently act against their own best financial interests, as well as how to exploit these psychological weaknesses when peddling questionable securities and products. These are proven behaviors with industry-accepted names like "money illusion bias," "loss aversion theory," "irrationality bias," and "time discounting." People do not borrow opportunistically, but irrationally. As if looking at objects in the distance, they see future payments as smaller than ones in the present—even if they are actually larger. They are more reluctant to lose a small amount of money than to gain a larger one—no matter the probability of either event in a particular transaction. They do not consider the possibility of any unexpected negative development arising between the day they purchase something and the day they will ultimately have to pay for it.

Credit-card and mortgage promotions are worded to take advantage of these inaccurate perceptions and irrational behaviors. "Zero-percent" introductory fees effectively camouflage regular interest rates up to 30 percent. Lowering minimum-payment requirements from the standard 5 percent to 2 or 3 percent of the outstanding balance looks attractive to borrowers. The corresponding increase in interest charges and additional years to pay off the debt will end up costing them more than triple the original balance. It is irrational for them to make purchases and borrow money under these terms, or to prefer them to the original ones. But they do. *We* do. This behavior is not limited to trailer-park renters of the rural South, but extends to the highly educated, highly leveraged co-op owners of the Northeast.

Mortgage lenders lobby Congress for stricter bankruptcy laws, arguing that the vast majority of personal bankruptcies were actually strategic maneuvers by rational and cynical borrowers. Yet these lenders resist all efforts to make the language of mortgage offerings and contracts more transparent, lest their well-tested psychological triggers to irrational financial behavior be neutralized. Lawmakers fighting against mortgage-reform measures argue that regulation of the industry coddles citizens and compromises their freedom to borrow. In their opinion, federal regulation of the lending industry amounts to authoritarian paternalism—anathema to the functioning of a free marketplace.

There is a vast middle ground between attempting to design a socialist welfare state and leaving self-interested individuals alone to spontaneously develop a free-market utopia—especially when the rules of that marketplace have been imposed by forces as powerful as any dictator. To approach that middle ground, however, we must dispense with the assumption that human beings were born to be economic actors or, in Hayek's more nuanced view, that we are all the unconscious arbiters of natural market forces. The principles of the intentionally corporatized marketplace are not embedded in the human genome, nor is self-interested behavior an innate human instinct. If anything, it's the other way around: a landscape defined by the competitive market will promote self-interested behavior. It's the surest path to a corporatist society.

Maybe that was the objective all along.

Central Currency

The economy in which we all participate is no more natural than the game scenarios John Nash set up to test the Rand Corporation's secretaries. It is a model for human interaction, based on a set of false assumptions about human behavior. Even if we buy the proposition that people act as self-interestedly as they possibly can, we must accept the reality that people's actual choices don't correspond with their own financial well-being. They do not act in their own best financial interests. People are either both greedy *and* stupid, or something else entirely.

The only ones behaving rationally under the given circumstances are corporations. And this isn't because corporations have so effectively adapted to the economy; it's because the economy was adapted to them.

We have to go back to the Renaissance just one more time to trace the origins of the stuff we currently call money. The currency system we still use today was invented with very specific biases in mind— ones that promoted the power of central authorities and the assets of the already wealthy, while reducing the ability of smaller groups and local regions to create value for themselves.

This is an almost untold story. History books gloss over or omit entirely the process through which monarchs outlawed certain currencies while promoting others. Contemporary economists, meanwhile, seem oblivious of the concept that other kinds of money with very different biases ever existed. The system they call "the economy" is not a set of natural laws, but a series of observations and strategies based on a very particular game with a carefully developed set of rules. It has simply been in place so long that our business and finance professionals have forgotten there were ever any alternatives. Over the course of my research, I interviewed fiscal strategists at Credit Suisse, Morgan Stanley, and Smith Barney about the biases of the money we use, and not one of them understood what I was talking about. "I'm not an economics historian," one chief economist explained. "There's other kinds of money?" the head of one currency desk asked.

Yes, there are. Or at least there were. The kind of money we use—centralized currency—is just one of them. Moneys are not neutral media any more than guns, televisions, or pillows are neutral technologies. They each favor certain kinds of behaviors and discourage others.

Our money—dollars, pounds, euros, yen, and all those other currencies we can get at the airport exchange or invest in at Forex.com—is lent into existence by a central bank. This bank is usually a private corporation chartered by the government to manage currency. The corporation—be it the Bank of England or the Federal Reserve—lends a certain amount of money to a smaller bank, which then lends it to a company or a person. It has to be paid back, at some rate of interest, to each lender by each borrower. At each step along the way, the lender takes his cut. So if the bank lends a company $1 million to start a business, that company will have to pay back, say, $3 million by the time the original loan comes due. Where does that extra $2 million come from? The money that *other* companies and people have borrowed from the bank. By design, not everyone is going to be able to pay back what he owes.

So the bias of centrally created, interest-bearing money is toward competition. Less money is lent into existence than needs to be paid back, so someone has to lose by going bankrupt. The only other possibility is for the bank to lend even more money to more companies before that happens. More total interest becomes due from businesses and people who have taken on the new, larger debts, which they are obligated to pay back at a faster pace than their predecessors, and so on. As long as the economy keeps expanding and accelerating, this can keep going on. (By the same logic, a gambler can keep paying the interest he owes a loan shark by winning progressively bigger bets. But what if the same loan shark has staked everyone at the table? Eventually, someone will be in trouble.)

Whether we judge it to be a good thing or a bad thing, there's no escaping the fact that the agenda of central currency—the bias of this medium—is to promote competition, require the expansion of the economy, and increase overall indebtedness to the central bank. Central currency favors central authority, because it is created by a central, chartered monopoly, with the provision that it be paid back to that central bank, with interest. Those on the periphery owe while those in the center grow. This, in turn, leads to the redistribution of wealth away from those who actually do work and toward the lending classes. The rules of the currency create a slope of value and authority toward the center.

The more this goes on, the more of our activity and awareness is occupied with servicing the ever-expanding debt. Sustainable business is no longer an option. Everything must grow along with the increasing money supply. The pace at which a business must expand is dictated not by the demand for its goods but by the requirements of its debt structure. And the longer business is done with this priority foremost in mind, the less any of us is capable of distinguishing between the real needs of enterprise and the embedded agenda of centralized currency.

For almost everyone alive today, this is just how money works. But there were once other kinds of money with very different slopes to them. In fact, throughout history, we find the most highly prosperous peoples using more than one currency at a time. It's only when they are conquered by a centralized regime, usually from a great distance, that their regional currency systems are outlawed in favor of a single coin of the realm. Then, prosperity drains from the newly conquered territory to the center, in a fiscal scheme more like the one we use today.

The last time most people enjoyed access to multiple currencies was back in the late Middle Ages, when the bias of money fostered a distribution of wealth much fairer to those who actually create value. Although many of us were taught that the ten centuries preceding the Renaissance constituted the Dark Ages, much of this era was characterized by robust economic activity and widespread prosperity. We remember the poverty, pestilence, and plague associated with the Middle Ages, but tend to forget that these thousand years of human history saw some of the most well-distributed affluence of all time. In fact, the awful years of plague and famine that we associate with the Middle Ages really began in the fourteenth century, once the Renaissance-era revisions to currency had already been made. In order to give chartered corporations authority over the financial realm, monarchs succeeded in crashing Europe's economy. Health and standards of living dropped, disease and famine followed.

But from about the tenth through the thirteenth century—the Age of Cathedrals, as it was once called—most of Europe enjoyed two main kinds of currency: centralized money, used for long-distance transactions, and local currency for daily transactions. Local currency worked very differently from centralized currency. Instead of being issued by a central bank, it was quite literally worked into existence, accurately reflecting the bounty produced. And because of the peculiar bias of this money, the people who used it were the most prosperous working class ever.

In a practice first introduced in ancient Egypt, a farmer would reap his harvest and bring it to a grain store. The grain-store operator would then hand the farmer a receipt, indicating the amount of grain, wine, or other commodity he was storing on the farmer's behalf. This receipt then served as money. In ancient Egypt, the receipt was a shard of pottery—an ostracon—which could be broken into pieces as the farmer "spent" the grain stored in his name. In the Middle Ages, the money was mostly made of precious metal banged into thin foil coins—brakteaten—which could be torn into smaller segments.

This local coinage was not saved for long periods, because it didn't earn any interest. In fact, the longer it was kept, the less it was worth. That's because the person storing the grain had to be paid, and because a certain amount of the grain was lost to water, rats, and spoilage. So once a year on market day, if the grain had not been claimed, the grain-store operator collected his fees by reissuing the money. He didn't devalue the currency itself; the silver content of a unit of money was not reduced or "debased." He simply issued new coins with a new date imprint, and exchanged back, say, three coins for every four he collected. Whoever had possession of the older coins had to pay the recoinage tax in this way.

That's why the bias of local currency was not toward saving but toward spending. Hoarding money meant losing money. Everyone sought to get rid of his or her money before the next recoinage. Capital meant nothing if it wasn't actively invested. So people put their money to work maintaining their equipment, building windmills, and improving their wine presses. The fact that the currency cost money encouraged people to think of other ways to create value over time. On average, at least 10 percent of gross revenue was immediately invested in equipment maintenance—a higher percentage than at any time since.

In the Age of Cathedrals, even small towns invested in tremendous architectural projects to generate tourism spending by pilgrims. Cathedrals were not funded by the Vatican Bank; they were local, bottom-up investments made by farmers and other laborers on behalf of future generations. This was the medieval equivalent of establishing an inheritance—but because the money had to be spent instead of saved, it promoted collective investment rather than private hoarding.

Most people used only local currency for their entire lives because they conducted only local transactions. But what would a German company want with the receipt for some grain stored in Holland? How could England pay ransoms to invading Vikings, or buy luxury goods from France without money that transcended local interests? Luckily for those who needed to conduct long-distance trade, central currencies such as the Byzantine bezant were available. In order to be of use they required the reverse bias, and held their value over long periods of time. So they were not reissued, nor were they representative of some amount of grain rotting in a store. They were valuable because of the precious metal within them, usually gold—the most universally valued substance.

Their bias was toward hoarding—perfectly appropriate for their functional role in the greater economy. As long as people had a bottom-up currency they could use for their local transactions, the existence of this top-down currency for royalty or long-distance merchants was just fine. It didn't threaten local transactions or the flow of money. It even allowed prosperous towns to export and import goods.

One money encouraged spending and recirculation through the local economy; the other encouraged saving and competition through the long-distance economy.

The coexistence of these two kinds of currencies with very different purposes and biases led to an economic expansion unlike any we have seen since. Sometimes called the "first Renaissance," the late Middle Ages offered an enviable quality of life for ordinary people. The working class enjoyed four meals a day, usually of three or four courses. They worked six hours a day, and just four or five days a week—unless they were celebrating one of about one hundred fifty annual holidays. Medievalists from François Icher to D. Damaschke almost unanimously agree that between the eleventh and thirteenth centuries, the quality of life of Europeans was better than at any other period in history, including today. In addition to metrics such as demographic expansion and urban development, measures of health and well-being also surpass our own. Women were taller during these centuries than in any other period. Over the past half century, men have finally surpassed their eleventh-century ancestors—and this only since the advent of meat and milk hormones, which offer us our size as a side-effect, not a feature.

By investing in productive assets instead of bank accounts, people of the Middle Ages built strong businesses, rewarded their workers, maintained the integrity of their equipment, improved the quality of their land, and invested in the research and development of better windmills, waterwheels, ovens, and winepresses. It's when greenhouses were invented, coal was first burned as fuel, eyeglasses were popularized, and London Bridge was built. Meat stopped being scarce for the first time in European history. Money earned did not leach out of the community to some distant central authority, but poured back into local investments aimed at future productivity.

It was during this first Renaissance—not the "real" Renaissance—that many of the innovations credited to the de Medici family and the royal courts actually took place. This was when the first wave of universities was built, when the abstract sciences grew in importance, when economic expansion reached its peak, and when what we now think of as urbanization took off. No matter what the history books say about relative GDP between this era and the Renaissance proper, real people and businesses did the best when prosperity was a bottom-up phenomenon, shared by all instead of just a few. If current economic metrics can't adequately convey the prosperity of the late Middle Ages, this says more about the bias of those metrics toward the rules of a central economy than it does about the relative strength of a distributed one. By most true measures, these people were more prosperous than we are. They ate well, they had plenty of leisure time, and they enjoyed close social bonds.

The Renaissance was never about extending such prosperity but about monopolizing it. Remember, the chartered corporation was at its core a scheme to lock in the recent successes of certain rising merchants. In exchange for receiving full legal monopolies over the industries or territories they controlled, early corporations offered profit participation and symbolic fealty to the monarchs who wrote the laws favoring them. The rising merchant class got full participation in the aristocracy, and the existing aristocracy got to keep their castles. The whole deal promoted stasis and slowed class mobility.

Seizing authority over the issuance of money provided just such an opportunity for monopoly, as well. The rising class of merchants had amassed a whole lot of money and needed a way to invest it—one that didn't require them to personally manage more companies or participate in risky adventures. Likewise, the weakening monarchy needed a way to reinforce its subjects' loyalty, increase its tax base, and centralize value creation. A monopoly currency could do all this, and more.

Interestingly enough, the first and ultimately best of the great European centralized currencies was a reaction *against* a monopoly currency. The florin began as an illegal "people's" money, first minted in 1235 as a silver coin and then in gold in 1252, in a flagrant assumption of power by the people of Florence against Emperor Frederick II. Local municipalities had long been issuing their own currencies, but never in gold and never for long-distance transactions. Now, a comparatively regional power had established the ability to generate a currency that would retain its value over distance and time.

Florence, located on major trade routes, was already an economic center. Royals there, like all monarchs, worked to ensure their stay in power—but they did so by broadening the social base of government. Instead of chartering corporations, Florentine nobles gave merchants a role in legislation, and supported the development of guilds. So much for good intentions; eventually, power was wrested from the royals anyway, and the Florentines established a proud and self-conscious democracy. With the florin, the rising Florentine collective of merchants and guilds could conduct long-distance trade across Europe and beyond without paying tax or homage to the emperor. Florence grew into a dominant regional power—at least in part—by making its own money.

Soon, monarchs from other regions sought to do the same—for themselves if not for their people. It wasn't as natural a fit. Florence was accessible to the Mediterranean Sea. France, Holland, Germany, and Britain were not. The Florentines were a rising democracy, challenging their own monarchs and then the Holy Roman Emperor himself. The kingdoms seeking to copy Florence's fiscal innovations were still run by leaders looking to undermine the many local currencies operating within their realms but beyond their direct control. While the florin expressed the preexisting centrality of Florentine ports to Mediterranean trade, these new competing central currencies would attempt to promote centrality through invented and militarily enforced fiscal policies.

Even this process began rather innocently. When France's King Louis IX got back from the Seventh Crusade in 1254, he found his kingdom in what he believed to be great need of political, economic, and, most of all, moral leadership. To that end, he published several ordinances in the late 1260s establishing the king as the only one who could set monetary policy. The king's money had to be accepted as payment throughout the kingdom, and no one was allowed to test the coins for weight, since the king's imprint was to suffice as a guarantee. Louis forced certain areas to use only his currency, and others to peg their currencies to his.

Louis's ordinances were unprecedented, and angered local barons who had always enjoyed the freedom to mint coins and regulate their value. But the aristocracy was on the decline, and there was only so much authority left to exercise on a prosperous, decentralized late-medieval economy. Besides, pious Louis didn't care as much about economic power as about unifying the kingdom and asserting its Christian framework. Some regions in Louis's realm had gone and adopted the Arab gold dinar, a coin inscribed with Islamic themes. Louis saw the coin as an affront to his own and God's authority, and banned its use on cultural grounds. He wasn't doing this to drain his people's economy, however. Louis's own coinage was gold, stable, and Christian enough to earn the moniker "good money."

Of course, with absolute power to create economic value comes absolute power to siphon it off. Louis's grandson Philip IV used his grandfather's assumption of authority over currency to turn good money into bad.

Young Philip's whole approach to generating wealth was to monopolize internal resources instead of trading with others. He outlawed all local currencies, and forced everyone to use his coin of the realm for both local and long-distance trade—with taxes he established. When the amount of wealth he could extract from his own territories reached its limit, he'd go to war for more territory, then exploit the new lands. To fund these wars, he increased taxes on his subjects. Philip imposed a sales tax on the people in northern towns, and a "subvention," or war tax, on everyone else, particularly the Jews, whom he overtaxed with impunity. His heavy and repeated taxation did not go over well, however, so he hired a few Italian economics experts who offered him more innovative ideas on how to drain his people's resources.

Philip's new, more opaque tactic, made possible by his centralization of money, was to debase his own currency—removing some portion of the gold and recoining it with less precious metal. Philip forced his people to use and value money from which he could extract worth at any time. For these repeated debasements, Dante later pictured Philip in Hell. Philip's wanton currency manipulation led to attacks on royal officials and widespread rioting. By 1306, violence got so bad in Paris that Philip had to take refuge in the house of the Knights Templar and temporarily restore "good money" for his people to use.

Philip had done far worse than simply debase a currency. Taken alone, all that would have done is made it harder for him to purchase foreign goods. His people could still have accepted gold florins for their exports, and used local currencies for their daily transactions. No, Philip's real crime against the people was to outlaw the use of any currency besides his own. Even if they had given up all long-distance trade, the people couldn't conduct efficient local commerce with a currency that was designed for long-term storage instead of short-term exchange. Besides, the long-term-storage capacity of the currency was undermined by Philip's corrupt debasements.

Philip and other European monarchs copying the successful florin

sought to increase their own power by extracting value from local activities. The people no longer had inexpensive currencies that were
grown into existence with each farm's harvest; they now used scarce
currencies coined into existence by a central authority. Instead of
reinvesting excess wealth back into their windmills and ovens, they
hoarded what money they could before it was again debased.

The people's ability to create value had been taken from them.
Central currencies—when they weren't simply debased by corrupt
monarchs—favored the new players on the economic landscape: chartered corporations conducting competitive, international trade, and
speculators who contributed cash and never labor to the enterprise.
By making money scarce and centralized, royals and the corporations they chartered could monopolize savings and investment. As a
result, people who had been in business for themselves, investing and
reinvesting in their own people and equipment, were reduced to laborers. The first Renaissance ended, and the Renaissance we might
better call a dark age had begun.

Between 1000 and 1300, when local currencies peaked in use, the
population of Europe grew at an astonishing pace. The best census estimates we have come from England, where the population more than
doubled over those three hundred years. In the 1290s, England exercised its own changes in the monetary system, outlawing local currencies in favor of a single scarce coin issued by central authorities.
Monarchs extracted wealth and value through constant debasement.
Within ten years, the population increase reversed to a decline as standards of living fell. Another forty years after that, in 1347, came the
first outbreak of the plague.

Historians like to blame the plague for Europe's subsequent loss of
half its people and all its prosperity. But it would be far more accurate
to blame the shift in monetary policy for both the poverty and pestilence that followed. By the time the plague hit, a dramatic decline in
the standard of living and population numbers was already under way.
Unable to earn a living on their farms or in town, people migrated to
cities for jobs as unskilled day laborers in dirty and dangerous workshops. With less money to spare, towns made fewer investments in
basic sanitation. The increase in forced loyalty to central patriarchal
authorities and their particularly Christian traditions led to the repression of pagan practices, folk remedies, and women's access to
work. As a result, people's access to health care diminished as well.

Superstition rose, witches and other suspicious characters were burned, and communities turned against themselves.

Famines and epidemics—which had previously always been highly local, limited events—became widespread phenomena. The price of food went up as the scarcity of commodities matched the scarcity of money. Rural land was purchased by city companies and worked by laborers who didn't enjoy its bounty before it was sent to the urban centers. Farming practices deteriorated along with equipment. The crops suffered. Ten percent of Europe's population had died eating cats, dogs, rats, and in some cases children, before the plague even hit. The plague did not lead to Europe's economic collapse. Rather, Europe's currency-driven economic collapse led to the plague.

Over the next century, as the fully centralized economy locked in gains and institutionalized scarcity, the rich grew richer and the poor grew poorer. Economically, at least, the period we now call the Renaissance wasn't a true renaissance at all. The real, "first" renaissance was a period of bottom-up prosperity and abundance facilitated by the coexistence of multiple currencies. The later Renaissance was really just the end of the plague. At the expense of the lives of more than half of Europe's population, a small group exploited monetary policy to accumulate massive wealth. They then deigned to fund arts and culture to their liking, in a flurry of patronage we now call the Renaissance. This art and culture, in turn, highlighted the individualism, nationalism, ideals, and markets of the economic reality they had created.

To this day, the bias of centralized currency is toward scarcity and hoarding. This slows down the rate at which money circulates, while concentrating wealth at the top. Instead of encouraging cooperation and community, it promotes competition and individuality. Worst of all, instead of supporting a sustainable economy, it depends on an economy that grows forever, accelerating all the way.

That we still look to the Renaissance as a high point and formative template for our civilization attests to its élite's success in institutionalizing their economic reforms and the mythologies supporting them. Our bankers remain woefully unaware that other money systems ever existed, and our economists utterly incapable of imagining the creation of value from the periphery. Those who are aware of the implementation of centralized currencies see it as the end of a dark age rather than the end of decentralized prosperity. Likewise, historians today are more likely to point out that the great art and science of the Renaissance was funded from the top by wealthy patrons, as if to disabuse us of the notion that such an explosion of imagination and inventiveness could have occurred from the bottom up. It did. And only by recovering this ability do we stand a chance of restoring our connection to the value we create.

CHAPTER SEVEN

FROM ECOLOGY
TO ECONOMY

Big Business and the Disconnect from Value

The Market Makers

We base our very survival on our ability to use and accumulate money. So its rules and characteristics can't help but seep into our thinking and behaviors as individuals, as businesses, and as a society.

The more we accept its use, the more we think of our centrally issued money as a natural player in the economy rather than a particular tool with particular biases. But over the centuries of its use, the influence of our money over our interactions has been demonstrated time and time again: a scarce currency designed in favor of competitive corporate behavior will promote such behavior in those who use it. This is not magic; the money is not possessed. It's just biased toward the interests of those in a position to make money by storing it rather than spending it. It's money for capitalists. And they had better use it as it was designed or they'll end up on the wrong side of the currency equation themselves.

Our prevailing ignorance about the bias of the money we use undermines our best efforts at making the economy work better for the many or even the few. Businesses believe they are required to grow, and pick from among their inappropriate acquisition targets as if choosing between the lesser of two evils. Eighty percent of these acquisitions drain value *and* equity from both merging companies. Unions accept the false premise that the new competitive economy demands that they consent to lower wages; they fail to recognize that their wages are making up a progressively smaller portion of corporate profits, or that money paid to them circulates through the real economy, while the money doled out to CEOs and shareholders tends to stay put. As a result, with each cut to union wages, education and health care suffer, and the overall competitiveness of the workforce declines. Businesses, meanwhile, make decisions catering to the agenda of the investing shareholders who seek to extract short-term gains at the expense of a company's long-term stability, research and development, or even basic competence. They outsource core processes, lose access to innovation, and depend on branding to make up the difference. Revenues suffer and growth slows, but there's debt to be paid, so more acquisitions are made and the workforce is slashed or outsourced. All the while, central banks attempt to walk the fine line between stimulating growth through lower interest rates and maintaining the value of their monopoly currencies.

The Wall Street Journal, Fox News, and *The Economist* compete against the BBC, *The Guardian*, and PBS to explain the conflicting interests of workers, investors, and corporations in the new global economy. But no matter whose case they make, they all fail to consider whether the money everyone is fighting over has rules of its own that make such conflicts inevitable. They argue over the placement of the chess pieces without pausing to consider that the board beneath them has been quite arbitrarily arranged to favor players who no longer exist. Neither does the Left-Right divide ever adequately address the income disparity between people caught on opposite ends of the currency spectrum. We can argue labor's cause all we want, add regulations to the system designed to minimize worker exploitation, maximize their participation in corporate profits, or increase the minimum wage. All along the way, management will be dragged along, kicking and screaming, while bankers and investors—the ultimate arbiters of credit—grow more reluctant to fund such handicapped enterprises. It's a lose-lose scenario because it works against the either-or bias of a scarce central currency to promote central authority at the expense of the periphery where value is actually created. Yet this is precisely what the currency we use was designed to do from its inception.

Renaissance monarchs didn't invent central currency, or even the first currency monopoly. Both ancient Egypt and the Roman Republic issued central currencies. In Egypt's case, as best we know from historical accounts, the empire had overextended itself, conquering and controlling territory eastward to Canaan and beyond. In an effort to fund the defense of its borders and the control of its population, successive pharaohs initiated increasingly restrictive and centralized monetary policies—along with centralized religion and culture. Pharaohs outlawed local currencies and forced people to bring grain long distances to royal grain stores in exchange for the central currency. The famous famine depicted in the Bible may have been the result of natural causes or, like the one accompanying the establishment of scarce currency in the Middle Ages, of economic origins. The Roman Republic and later empire issued its own currency to every region it conquered, both to extract value from its new territories and to assert the authority of the emperor. In both historical cases, central currency was a means of control, taxation, and centralization of authority during expansive dictatorships. And, in both cases, after a few hundred years, the continual debasement of currency led to the fall of the empire.

We're fast approaching the limits of our own currency system, instated to benefit corporate interests and adjusted over time to do it ever more efficiently and automatically. If double-entry bookkeeping can be thought of as the spreadsheet software on which businesses learned to reconcile their debits and credits, central currency was the operating system on which this accounting took place. Like any operating system, it has faded into the background now that a program is running, and it is seemingly uninvolved in whatever is taking place. In reality, it defines what can happen and what can't. And if its central premise is contradicted too obviously by world events, it just crashes, taking those without sufficient reserves or alternative assets down with it.

We need to be able to save money for the future, but we also need to be able to spend and circulate it. The money we use is great for the former, but just awful for the latter. Because of the way it is lent into existence, centralized currency draws wealth away from where people are actually creating value, and toward the center, where the bank or lender gets it back with interest. This makes it impossible for those on the periphery to accumulate the wealth created by their labors, or to circulate it through other sectors of their business communities. Instead, the money is used for more speculation. The price of assets increases and inflation looms—but without the wage increases officially blamed for inflation in what is promoted as a "supply-and-demand" economy.

There are two economies—the real economy of groceries, day care, and paychecks, and the speculative economy of assets, commodities, and derivatives. What forecasters refer to as "the economy" today isn't the real one; it's almost entirely virtual. It's a speculative marketplace that has very little to do with getting real things to the people who need them, and much more to do with providing ways for passive investors to increase their capital. This economy of markets—first created to give the rising merchant class in the late Middle Ages a way to invest their winnings—is not based on work or even the injection of capital into new enterprises. It's based instead on "making markets" in things that are scarce—or, more accurately, things that can be made scarce, like land, food, coal, oil, and even money itself.

Because there's so much excess capital to invest, speculators make markets in pretty much anything that real people actually use, or can be made to use through lobbying and advertising. The problem is that when coal or corn isn't just fuel or food but also an asset class, the laws of supply and demand cease to be the principal forces determining their price. When there's a lot of money and few places to invest it, anything considered a speculative asset becomes overpriced. And then real people can't afford the stuff they need. The oil spike of 2008, which contributed to the fall of ill-prepared American car companies, has ultimately been attributed not to the laws of supply and demand, but to the price manipulations of hedge-fund speculators. Real jobs were lost to movements in a purely speculative marketplace.

This is the reality of speculation in an economy defined by scarcity. Pollution is good, not bad, because it turns water from a plentiful resource into a scarce asset class. When sixty-eight million acres of corporate-leased U.S. oil fields are left untapped and filled tankers are parked offshore, energy futures stay high. Airlines that bet correctly on these oil futures stay in business; those that focus on service or safety, instead, end up acquisition targets at best—and pension calamities at worst. Such is the logic of the speculative economy.

As more assets fall under the control of the futures markets, speculators gain more influence over both government policy and public opinion. Between 2000 and 2007, trading in commodities markets in the United States more than sextupled. During that same period, the staff of the Commodity Futures Trading Commission overseeing those trades was cut more than 20 percent, with no corresponding increase in technological efficiency. Meanwhile, speculators have only gotten better at exploiting structural loopholes to engage in commodities trades beyond the sight of the few remaining regulators. Over-the-counter trading on the International Commodities Exchange in London is virtually untraceable, while massive and highly leveraged trades from one hedge fund to another are impossible to track until one or the other goes belly-up—and pleads to be bailed out with some form of taxpayer dollars. Government is essentially powerless to identify those who are manipulating commodities futures at consumers' expense, and even more powerless to prosecute them under current law even if they could. People, meanwhile, come to believe that oil or corn is more scarce than it is (or needs to be), and that they're in competition with the Chinese or the neighbors for what's left.

The speculative economy is related to the real economy, but more as a parasite than as a positive force. It is detached from the real needs of people, and even detached from the real commerce that goes on between humans. It is a form of meta-commerce, like a Las Vegas casino betting on the outcome of a political election. Only in this case, the bets change the costs of the real things people depend on.

As wealth is sucked out of real economies and shifted into the speculative economy, people's behavior and activities can't help but become more market-based and less social. We begin to act more in accordance with John Nash's selfish and calculating competitors, confirming and reinforcing our dog-eat-dog behaviors. The problem is, because it's actually against our nature to behave this way, we're not too good at it. We end up struggling against one another while getting fleeced by more skilled and structurally favored competition from distant and abstracted banks and corporations. Worse, we begin to feel as though any activity not in some way tied to the corporate sphere is not really happening.

Wal-Mart's success in extracting value from local communities, for example, is tied directly to the company's participation in speculative markets beyond the reach of small business, and its tremendous ability to centralize capital. We buy from Wal-Mart because Wal-Mart sells imported and long-distance products cheaper than the local tailor or pharmacist can. Not only does the company get better wholesale prices; its centrality and size lets it get its money cheaper. Meanwhile, because we are forced to use centralized currency instead of a more local means of exchange or barter (and we'll look at these possibilities later), each of our transactions with local merchants is passed through a multiplicity of distant banks and lenders. All of the advantages and efficiencies of local commerce are neutralized when we are required to use long-distance, antitransactional currency for local exchange between people. We must earn the currency from one corporation that has borrowed from the central bank in order to pay another corporation for a product it has purchased from yet another. We don't have an easy way to get the very same product from the guy down the street who knows how to make it better and get it to us ultimately more efficiently than the factory in Asia.

But the notion of purchasing things with some kind of local currency system, bartering for them with members of our local community, or—worst of all—accepting favors in exchange for other ones feels messy and confusing to us. Besides, Wal-Mart is a big company with lots of insurance and presumably some deep pockets we could sue if something goes wrong. When favors replace dollars, who is responsible for what? Too many of us would rather hire a professional rug cleaner, nanny, or taxi than borrow a steamer from a neighbor (what if we break it?), do a babysitting exchange (do we really like them?), or join a carpool (every day? Ugh). Social obligations are less defined than financial ones.

Our successive disconnects from place and people are what make this final disconnection from value so complete and difficult to combat. We have lost our identification with place as anything but a measure of assets, and we have surrendered our identification with others to an obsession with ourselves against everybody else. Without access or even inclination to social or civic alternatives, we turn to the speculative market to fulfill needs that could have been satisfied in other ways.

Even those of us capable of resisting the market for most of our lives can't help but cave in once we attempt to raise families of our own. I was actually looking forward to parenthood as an opportunity to disconnect my family from the consumerist pathology of the market and engage in one of the more natural processes still available to us. I was still under the false impression that there was something going on between mother, father, and baby in which no expert, marketer, or website could interfere.

Of course, it turns out that parenthood means enduring a full frontal assault of marketers trying to make a buck off our guilt, fear, and ignorance. While genetic counselors offer prenuptial evaluations of chromosomal compatibility, an industry of fertility experts offers in-vitro alternatives to worried thirty-somethings after they've been working unsuccessfully to get pregnant for two whole months. Once the baby is born, an army of professional consultants is available to do what parents and their community have done for millennia. Lactation consultants teach new mothers how to breast-feed, while sleep specialists develop the ideal napping schedules. Parents who think they're resisting this trend hire the New Age equivalent of the same professionals—"doulas," midwives, and herbalists perform the same tasks for equivalent fees. For those who don't know which consultant to hire, there are agencies of meta-consultants to help, for an additional fee.

Parenthood—like so much of basic human activity—has been systematically robbed of its naturally occurring support mechanisms by a landscape tilted toward the market's priorities. Towns used to have blocks in neighborhoods with old ladies and large families and neighbors who could watch the baby for an hour while you went out and got some groceries. Now, instead of repairing the neighborhood sidewalks, we purchase Bugaboos—the eight-hundred-dollar stroller equivalent of an SUV, complete with shock absorbers, to traverse the potholes. For every thread of the social fabric worn bare by the friction of modern alienation, the market has risen with a synthetic strand of its own. Refusal to participate means risking that your child will be ill equipped—you guessed it—to compete for the increasingly scarce spots at private prep schools and colleges.

As someone who subsidized his early writing career by preparing high school students for their college entrance exams, I can attest to the competitive angst suffered by their parents—as well as the lengths to which many of them are willing to go to guarantee their children's success. There was a moment in many of my engagements—one that any overpriced SAT tutor will well recognize—when Junior's worried, wealthy parents would sit me down in their Beverly Hills living room, beyond their son's hearing range, to ask me the difficult question: hypothetically, what would it take to get me to sit for the exam in place of their son? While I never agreed to accept the cars or cash offered to me, I still wonder how many steps removed my tutoring services were from any other artificial means through which a generation sought to guarantee their children's place on the speculative side of the economy.

Were these the concerns of Depression-era parents who had experienced lives hindered by the lack of cash, or first-generation immigrants who had escaped from abject poverty, it might be easier to comprehend or excuse their willingness to teach their children to cheat. Their perception of the risks would be understandably magnified. No, the parents in question were hiring tutors to write papers and take tests for children who were already attending thirty-thousand-dollar-a-year private schools, and already in line to inherit multimillion-dollar trust funds. Teachers who challenge the cheating students on their plagiarized work soon learn that parent donors and trustees wield more power than department heads.

The wealthy discount such concerns as needlessly abstract. What does it matter, they ask, when the "real world" is similarly based on cheating and loopholes? (Just to be clear: what's wrong is that kids end up in classes, schools, and jobs for which they are not prepared. Whenever they have trouble on an assignment or a test in the future— even if they are smart enough to complete it—they believe that they are being challenged beyond their ability. Worst of all, on an emotional level, they conclude that their parents don't love them just as they are.) Those who don't count themselves among the privileged classes see it as confirmation of the unfairness of the system, and ample justification for them to do whatever it takes to climb up the ladder themselves. As the arrest of a tiny minority of otherwise identical billionaire stockbrokers, CEOs, and hedge-fund managers teaches us, cheating is wrong only if you get caught.

Kids growing up in such a world inherit these values as their own. This is why American children surveyed will overwhelmingly say they want to grow up to be Bill Gates—the world's richest man—even though almost none of them want to become software engineers. It is why kids can aspire to win *American Idol* without ever caring about singing or even music. The money and recognition they envision for themselves is utterly disconnected from any real task or creation of value. After all, the people who actually create value are at the bottom of the pyramid of wealth.

Sadly, that's not just a perception. The bias of centralized currency to redistribute wealth from the poor to the rich gets only more extreme as the beneficiaries gain more influence over fiscal policy. Alan Greenspan, a disciple of Ayn Rand, repeatedly deregulated markets, leading to the average CEO's salary rising to 179 times the average worker's pay in 2005, up from a multiple of 90 in 1994. Adjusted for inflation, the average worker's pay rose by a total of only 8 percent from 1995 to 2005; median pay for chief executives at the three hundred fifty largest companies rose 150 percent.

The top tenth of 1 percent of earners in America today make about four times what they did in 1980. In contrast, the median wage in America (adjusted for inflation) was lower in 2008 than it was in 1980. The number of "severely poor Americans"—defined as a family of four earning less than $9,903 per year—grew 26 percent between 2000 and 2005. It is the fastest-growing group in the American economy. On a global level, by 1992 the richest fifth of the world was receiving 82.7 percent of total world income, while the bottom fifth received just 1.4 percent. In 1894, John D. Rockefeller, the richest man in Gilded Age America, earned $1.25 million—about seven thousand times the average income in the United States. In 2006, James Simons, a typical hedge-fund manager, "earned" $1.7 billion, or more than thirty-eight thousand times the average income. On top of this, hedge-fund managers' salaries are taxed at "capital-gains" rates much lower than the rate that average workers pay—about 35 percent of everyone else's earnings goes to pay taxes of one form or another, and most of that money goes to pay interest on loans taken out by the government from the Federal Reserve Bank, at interest rates set by the bank.

Unlike money paid to workers, the sums siphoned off by the wealthiest brackets are not used to buy things. These funds do not return to the real economy; they are invested wherever return is the highest. The money itself becomes a commodity to be hoarded, saved, and grown. For most investors, this means either placing it overseas, or in the derivatives and futures that make corn, oil, and money more expensive for everyone.

Since the beginning of currency and trading deregulation in the 1970s (when Nixon took the dollar off even a nominal gold standard), money has left the economy for pure speculation at ever faster rates. Over the same years, with less money in the system, the poor began sending mothers of young children to work—at rates that have doubled since then. Meanwhile, for the very first time, America experi-

enced an overall growth of 16 percent in GDP between 2001 and
2007, while the median wage remained unchanged. The share of total
income going to the richest 1 percent of Americans, on the other
hand, rose to a postwar record of 17.4 percent. Americans work an average of three hundred fifty more hours per year than the average European, and at least one hundred fifty more hours than the average
Japanese.

This means less time for Little League, barbecues, and the Parent-
Teacher Association, and more indebtedness to credit-card companies
and banks to make ends meet. Twelve percent of Americans borrowed
money to pay their winter heating bills; 9 percent of them did so with
credit cards. The neighborhood, such as it is, becomes a place people
struggle to stay in or even to get out of—not a place in which people
contribute their time and energy. It's every family for itself.

This selfishness and individualism reinforces and is in turn reinforced by the avarice that has replaced social relationships in local
communities. Adam Smith's theories of the market were predicated
on the regulating pressures of neighbors and social values. The neu-
roscientist Peter Whybrow has observed that as people meet fewer real
neighbors in the course of a day, these checks and balances disappear:
"Operating in a world of instant communication with minimal social
tethers," he explains, "America's engines of commerce and desire
become turbocharged." As Whybrow sees it, once an economy grows
beyond a certain point, "the behavioral contingencies essential to promoting social stability in a market-regulated society—close personal
relationships, tightly knit communities, local capital investment, and
so on—are quickly eroded."

Instead of working with one another to create value for our communities, we work against one another to help corporations extract
money *from* our communities. When the city of Buffalo, New York,
lost dozens of factories to outsourcing along with their manufacturing
jobs, it became a national leader in bankruptcies, foreclosures, and
urban decay. Over 108 collection agencies have opened to address the
problem in Erie and Niagara Counties, hiring over 5,200 phone operators to track down and persuade debtors like themselves to fix their
credit. As interest rates on these debts rise to upwards of 40 percent,
more wealth is transferred from the poor to the rich, from the real
economy to the speculative economy, and out of circulation into the
banking ether.

It's a system in which there is simply not enough real cash left in circulation for people to pay for their needs. No matter what's happening to the overall economy, the amount of money that consumers owe goes up every year. Again, this is not incidental, but structural, as the total increases every time money is loaned into and then extracted from circulation. According to the Federal Reserve's figures, consumer credit—mainly credit-card debt—went up from $193 billion in 1973 to $445 billion in 1983 to $886 billion in 1993, and $2,557 billion in 2007. As of June 2008, American households have approximately $13.84 trillion in total debt obligations. This is roughly equivalent to the United States GDP for the entirety of 2007.

In order to get people who have lost their access to cash to spend instead through debt, credit-card companies market credit as a lifestyle of choice. MasterCard's "priceless" campaign pretends to appeal to those of us who understand that life's pleasures have become too commodified. It chronicles a day at a baseball game or a beach vacation, and the price of each purchase, presumably achievable only by going into just a bit of debt. Of course, the real joy of the day—the love of a child, or a kiss from a wife—is "priceless," but it comes only after all those purchases.

The Visa card has replaced money in the European version of Monopoly, and the American version of the Game of Life. Having saturated the college and teen markets with promotions and advertisements—often with kickbacks to schools for the privilege of pitching to a captive audience—the credit-card company is now targeting the "tween" market with pretend debt. According to Hasbro (which acquired the game's creator, Milton Bradley), it's meant as an educational experience: "Visa is an opportunity for Mom or Dad to talk to kids about managing money, and that debt isn't a positive thing."

Adults who refuse to use plastic instead of paper are scorned in commercials designed to take any remaining stigma away from debtors by placing it on cash payers instead. In one commercial, a long line of masculine debit-card users waiting to buy refreshments at a sports game groan as a smaller, nerdy man uses time-consuming cash. Actually paying for something with money is depicted as an emasculating fumble for change.

We like to blame corporations for this mess, but many of them are in almost exactly the same predicament. Most of the Fortune 500 companies are just the names on mountains of debt. The total value of any company's shares—market capitalization—can be twenty, fifty, or several hundred times its actual annual earnings. Some multibillion-dollar companies don't actually earn any money per share at all. But because corporations borrow their money from the same institutions the rest of us do, they are subject to the very same rules.

Like towns drained of their ability to create value through local business, many companies find themselves robbed of their most basic competencies by macroeconomic forces that push them toward spreadsheet management and reckless cost cutting. Thanks to their debt structure, corporations are required to grow. This means opening more stores, getting more business, and selling more products (increasing the "top line"), or cutting jobs, lowering salaries, and finding efficiencies (decreasing expenditures). Maintaining a great, sustainable business is not an option—not when shareholders and other passive institutional investors are looking for return on the money they have themselves borrowed and now loaned to the corporation. Stocks don't go up when corporations make a steady income; they grow when companies grow, or at least appear to.

When Howard Schultz, the founder of Starbucks, returned to the helm of his company in 2007, he found his iconic coffee brand watered down by excessive expansion. Opening a Starbucks on every city block had sounded good to investors who hoped they had gotten in on the next McDonald's, but the strategy had damaged the quality and experience consumers sought from a deluxe coffee bar in the first place. As Schultz explained in a candid memo posted on the Internet without his knowledge, by introducing "flavor locked packaging" and automatic espresso machines, "we solved a major problem in terms of speed of service and efficiency, but overlooked the fact that we would remove much of the romance and theatre that was in play with the use of the [La Marzocco] machines." The mandate to open an outlet each day resulted in "stores that no longer have the soul of the past and reflect a chain."

Last year, the president of Ethiopia flew to Starbucks' corporate headquarters in Seattle, hat in hand, to ask the company to credit his country for the export of the beans used in some of their standard coffee flavors. But Starbucks, understanding that helping Ethiopia brand its beans would hurt its own bargaining leverage, refused. From Starbucks' perspective, coffee is a commodity to be sourced from the lowest bidder; once beans have local identity and can be asked for by name, the locality producing them has pricing power. Only when threatened by the possibility of a public-relations disaster did the company relent.

I'm regularly called in by companies looking to improve what they call their "stories"—the way consumers and shareholders alike perceive them. But when I interrogate them about what their companies actually do, many are befuddled. One CEO called me from what he said was a major American television manufacturer. I happened to know at the time that there were no televisions manufactured in the United States. But I went along with the charade.

"So you make television sets?" I asked. "Where?"

"Well, we outsource the actual manufacturing to Korea."

"Okay, then, you design the televisions?"

"Well, we outsource that to an industrial design firm in San Francisco."

"So you *market* the televisions?"

"Yes," he answered proudly. "Well," he qualified, "we work with an agency in New York. But I am directly involved in the final decisions."

Fulfillment and delivery were handled by a major shipping company, and accounting was done "out of house," as well.

Just what story was I supposed to tell? The company no longer did anything at all, except serve as the placeholder on processes that happened in other places.

The problem with all of this outsourcing isn't simply the loss of domestic manufacturing jobs, however painful that might be to those in the factory towns decimated by the movement of these jobs overseas. The bigger problem is that the outsourcing companies lose whatever competitive advantage they may have had in terms of personnel, innovation, or basic competency. During the famous dog-food-poisoning crisis of 2007, worried consumers called their dog-food companies for information. Were the brands getting their chow from the plant in China responsible for the tainted food? Many of the companies couldn't answer the question. They had outsourced their outsourcing to another company in China that hadn't yet determined who had gotten which food. The American companies didn't even do their own outsourcing.

As a substitute for maintaining any semblance of competence, companies resort to branding and marketing. When Paul Pressler—a former Disney executive—accepted his post as CEO of the Gap, he explained at his inaugural press conference that he had never worked a day in the garment industry. He didn't express this as a deficit, but as a strength. Instead, he would bring his knowledge of marketing and consumer psychology to the forefront—as well as his relationships with cultural icons like Sarah Jessica Parker. While Parker made some great TV commercials, they weren't enough to put better clothes on the racks, and under pressure, Pressler resigned in 2007. The company is now struggling to stay alive.

Other companies seek to remain competitive by dismantling the private sector's social safety net—pensions, benefits, and the steady salary increases won by long-time employees. In 2007, Circuit City came under pressure from big box stores such as Wal-Mart and Best Buy, whose young employees earned less than its own. The company decided to dismiss 3,400 people, about 8 percent of its workforce. They weren't doing a bad job, nor were the positions being eliminated entirely. It's just that the workers had been employed for too long and as a result were being paid too much—between ten and twenty dollars per hour, or just around the median of American workers. By definition, to stay competitive, Circuit City would have to maintain a workforce making less than that average. The company blamed price cuts on flat-panel television sets made in Asia and Mexico, which had squeezed their margins.

The corporatist justification for the layoffs, courtesy of McKinsey & Company, was that "the cost of an associate with 7 years of tenure is almost 55 percent more than the cost of an associate with 1 year of tenure, yet there is no difference in his or her productivity." The assertion that a company cannot leverage greater productivity from a more experienced employee is at best questionable and at worst a sign of its own structural inability to properly utilize human competence. That it sees no path to letting employees participate in the value they have created over time for the company is pure corporatism.

Not that this value is even recognized by the spreadsheet. Many assets—like customer and employee satisfaction, innovation, customer loyalty during a crisis, numbers of unsolicited applications for jobs, or contribution to the state of the industry—remain unrecorded in the Excel file, off the quarterly report, and are misjudged as tangential, "feel-good" bonuses, akin to winning the intra-office softball game. Of course, these are some of the most important measures of a company's success both as a business and as a human enterprise.

A few radical business theorists—like Harvard's Bob Kaplan—have promoted the use of "scorecards" designed to measure and include some of these unconventional metrics in the overall appraisal of a company's worth. The traditional spreadsheet, Kaplan believes, is like a supply curve from Microeconomics 101: "It tells you what things cost but not what they're worth. The Balanced Scorecard is like a multidimensional demand curve. It tells you what's creating value." Still, the scorecard itself boils down to more numbers.

Kaplan's former partner, Portland State University's H. Thomas Johnson, thinks the Balanced Scorecard is little better than any other. In his opinion, the reduction of every value to a piece of quantitative information is itself the crime. According to Johnson, human activity, commerce, and creativity are closer to real life than they are to math, and the focus on metrics "contributed to the modern obsession in business with 'looking good' by the numbers no matter what damage it does to the underlying system of relationships that sustain any human organization." Hitting quarterly targets earns CEOs their options bonuses. The "underlying system of relationships" only matters to people who have the luxury of working in a business that isn't stuck on the compounding-interest-payments treadmill.

When it is even considered, creating real, sustained value for customers, employees, partners, or, worst of all, competitors, is less often seen as a plus than a problem. In the zero-sum logic of corporatist economics, creating value for anyone other than the shareholders means taking value *away from* the shareholders. If employees are retiring with money to spare, it means they are being paid too much. If customers get more use out of a car or computer than promised, it means too much was spent on the materials. If a product actually works, then it might solve the problem that a corporation was depending on for its income.

For example, most of us grew up in the era of synthetic insecticides and "crack and crevice" aerosol roach killers. Spraying the kitchen meant poisoning the pets, and the chemicals ended up polluting yards and groundwater. Besides, the formulations worked for only so long before the roaches would become immune, and new, more powerful sprays would have to be deployed. Then, in 1979, some researchers at American Cyanamid in New Jersey came up with a new odorless, tasteless insecticide that was much less toxic to humans and pets, and broke down into harmless ingredients before it could get to any groundwater. The only catch was that roaches needed to eat the ingredient. So the clever scientists dipped communion wafers in the insecticide and waited for roaches to voluntarily eat them. This worked so well that they toyed with the idea of selling the wafers under the name "Last Supper."

Combat, the name they settled on, was so successful at killing roaches that by the end of 2000 *Pest Control* magazine ran the headline "ARE COCKROACH BAITS SIMPLY TOO EFFECTIVE?" After peaking at $80 million in 1995, the market for consumer-grade roach products had begun to shrink. It has gone down by 3 to 5 percent every year since then. Combat has killed its market along with all those roaches. Derek Gordon, a marketing VP at Combat's parent, Clorox, put on a happy face, saying, "If we actually manage to drive ourselves out of business completely, frankly we'd feel like we did the world a service." Clorox execs seemed less impressed by Combat's service record, and sold off the brand to Henkel, of Germany, as part of a larger deal. Even though they had come up with one of the most truly successful industrial-chemical products in modern history, the scientists at Combat were now part of a declining box in the balance sheet and had to be discarded. Their value as innovators—or the value they had created for so many urban dwellers—was not part of the equation.

The less people spend on killing roaches, the worse it is for the economy by corporate and government measures. The universal metric of our economy's health is the GDP, a tool devised by the National Bureau of Economic Research to help the Hoover administration navigate out of the Great Depression. Even the economist charged with developing the metric, Simon Kuznets, saw the limitations of the policy tool he had created, and spoke to Congress quite candidly of the many dimensions of the economy left out of his crude measure. Burning less gas, eating at home, enjoying neighbors, playing cards, and walking to work all subtract from the GDP, at least in the short term. Cancer, divorce, attention-deficit/hyperactivity disorder diagnoses, and obesity all contribute to GDP. The market works against human interest because of the way it measures success. And its measurement scheme has been based on tracking a currency whose bias toward scarcity and hoarding isn't even generally recognized.

Nor do the aggregate GDP figures measure how many people are involved in all the spending. As Jonathan Rowe, director of West Marin Commons, testified at a Senate hearing, "they do not distinguish between a $500 dinner in Manhattan and the hundreds of more humble meals that could be provided for the same amount. A socialite who buys a pair of $800 pumps at Manolo Blahnik appears to contribute forty times more to the national well-being than does the mother who buys a pair of $20 sneakers for her son at Payless." Centralized currency's bias toward the accumulation of wealth by the already wealthy is camouflaged by the measures we use to gauge economic health.

Those who should be our best economics journalists and public educators seem oblivious of the way our business practices and fiscal policies drain value from our society in the name of false metrics. Although free-market advocates such as *The Wall Street Journal, The Economist,* and *Financial Times* are written with the interests of the businessman and investor in mind, their editorial staffs are educated and experienced enough to contend with these very basic contradictions. Instead, they continue to depict the economy as a natural ecology, whose occasionally brutal results are no worse than those of cruel nature herself. That which doesn't kill us makes us stronger, anyway.

Journalists write this way only until the supposedly free and unfettered market comes after the periodical they happen to work for. When AOL bought Time Warner along with its portfolio of magazines, including *Time, People,* and *Sports Illustrated,* writers and editors at those publications complained that their periodicals were being turned into assets. Editorial budgets went down, writers were instructed to become more advertiser-friendly, and the integrity earned by the magazines through years of hard work was being spent all at once on lowbrow television specials and cross-promotions.

The Wall Street Journal didn't shed a tear over such developments. As an independent publication run by the Bancroft family's Dow Jones company since 1902, the *Journal*'s articles described only the process through which Time Warner's "brands" would be updated, its divisions made more efficient, and its overpaid staff trimmed down. Within a few years, however, it was *The Wall Street Journal* fending off an unsolicited $5 billion offer from Rupert Murdoch. A pervasive feeling among investors that print publications were imperiled by the Internet had led to a decline in all newspaper stock prices—making the *Journal* an easy target, even though its website was one of the few profitable online newspaper ventures, earning far more than its print edition.

All of a sudden the tables were turned. Editors who had long argued for free-market principles now saw the benefit in keeping a company small and independent—especially after it had gained over a hundred years of reputation and competency in its field. One of the owners wrote an editorial arguing that "a deal with Rupert Murdoch would not be a deal between partners with shared values. One of Murdoch's stated goals of the purchase is to use the Wall Street Journal to shore up his new business cable channel. By Murdoch's own admission, this so-called business-friendly television channel would shy away from reporting scandals, and concentrate on the more positive business news." In a "wag-the-dog" scenario even more preposterous than the one imagined by Hollywood comedy writers, a corporation buys a business news brand as a public-relations hedge on its investments.

What these editors now understood was that by becoming a part of News Corporation, the *Wall Street Journal* staff would lose its ability to create value through its newsgathering and analysis. News Corp. was buying the newspaper for the value it could *extract* from the venerated media property. *The Wall Street Journal's* name and, for a time, its editors and writers could lend support to Murdoch's effort to build a TV business-news brand. *The Economist* depicted the acquisition of Dow Jones as gaining "the media equivalent of a trophy wife."

Even allies of corporatist culture cannot be allowed to thrive on the periphery. Because it was itself a publicly held company, Dow Jones had nowhere to hide in the open market it had defended for so long. Now the editors—off the record more than on (at least until they were fired or resigned)—were railing against the concentration of global media ownership, warning about the political influence of foreigners on American business, and touting the necessity for family-owned newspapers to maintain their impact and high standards by remaining independent of centralized business interests.

But to do that, they would have had to find a way to remain independent of all centralized media, including the biased medium we call centralized currency.

Let Them Eat Blog

Ironically, it was the threat of competition from a decentralized medium—the Internet—that rendered the *Journal* temporarily weak enough to be conquered by a centralized medium it had unwittingly supported for a century: money.

In one sense, the Internet breaks all the rules imposed by centralized currency and the speculative economy. Value can be created, seemingly, from anywhere. An independent clothing designer can use consumer-grade equipment to shoot pictures of her clothes, post them online, take orders, and even print the postage. No need to pitch the department stores for space on their precious sales floors, to approach major clothing lines for an anonymous position under one of their labels, or to utilize any of the corporate middlemen traditionally extracting value from both the designer and her customers.

Craftsmen from remote regions use communal websites to export products that previously couldn't make it beyond the confines of their own villages. Film students post their low-budget videos on YouTube and earn mainstream attention along with big Hollywood contracts. Politicians use their websites to raise funds from individuals, and amass more capital through many small donations than they would have through a few big ones. A few hundred thousand hobbyists can collaborate on a free online resource, Wikipedia, that beats Britannica in breadth, usage rates, and often accuracy. Another group develops and maintains a web browser, Firefox, that works better and more safely than Microsoft's.

Corporate charters allowed wealthy élites to monopolize industries; the Internet allows competition to spawn anywhere. Only the best-capitalized companies could finance the construction and maintenance of Industrial Age factories; an Internet business can be run and scaled from a single laptop. Monopoly currencies and a few centuries of legislation worked to centralize value creation; the Internet works toward decentralizing value creation and promoting the work of those on the periphery and direct transactions between them.

At the dawn of the Internet era, Marxists, feminist intellectuals, and postmodernists celebrated the decentralization they believed would soon occur on every level of society. They saw in new media the emergence of a truly social and organic human collective. Instead of being controlled and artificially divided by ideologies, class boundaries, nations, or even gender, humans would now become part of what the Frenchmen Gilles Deleuze and Félix Guattari called a rhizome. The rhizome is a peculiarly horizontal and nonhierarchical plant structure—like water lilies or a ginger root—that is capable of producing both the shoot and the root systems of a new plant. New growth and value can come from anywhere. Likewise, a rhizomatic culture would be constantly negotiating meaning and value wherever meaning and value needed to be determined—instead of through some arbitrary central authority.

The Internet and its many hyperlink structures were understood as the true harbingers of this rhizomatic culture. Other metaphors abounded: "cyberia," "fractals," "hyperspace," "dynamical systems," "rain forests"—all described the same shift toward a more organic and bottom-up, outside-in cultural dynamic. Ideas and value could emerge from anyone, anywhere, and at any time.

At least to a point.

While digital technologies may foster the creation and duplication of nearly every kind of value out there, all this value is still measured by most people in terms of dollars and cents. Napster was a sensation because it saved consumers money (while costing some corporations their revenue). Hackers made fewer headlines for coding brilliantly than for selling out and getting listed on NASDAQ. Participation itself is made possible by purchasing equipment and bandwidth from one of a dwindling number of conglomerating megacorporations.

For those with time and money to spend, there's certainly a whole lot of terrific activity occurring online that flies in the face of contemporary corporatist culture. People with rare diseases can find support groups, pregnant women can get free advice, creative types can collaborate on new kinds of projects, amateur drag racers can trade car parts, rock bands can find audiences, nerds can find friends, activists can organize rallies, bloggers can expose political corruption, and people can share their hopes and dreams with one another in forums safer than those available to them in real life.

Still, apart from a few notable and, sadly, declining exceptions to the rule, the energy fueling most Internet activity is not chi (life energy) but cash—or at least chi supported by cash. However horizontal its structure, the Internet rhizome is activated by money: old-fashioned, top-down, centralized currency. As a result, what occurs online is biased toward the very authorities that the Internet's underlying network structure might seem predisposed to defy. Things can feel—or be *made* to feel—novel and revolutionary, even though they still constitute business as usual.

Last year, a student of mine—a clever woman with a good sense of media—sent me a link to a website that had confused her. I clicked on the URL and a video played images from a *Matrix*-like postapocalyptic future. A narrator spoke: "There are those who still remember how it all began. How light and reason had retreated. How greed gave way to great power. How power gave way to great fear. The Great War swept across all the lands, neighbor against neighbor, city against city, nation against nation. The Corporate Lords claimed the world. Creativity and self-expression were outlawed. The Great Darkness had begun. But they speak in low whispers of the legend that One will come. A gifted child. Legend speaks of him finding the Magic Gourd that he will fill with an elixir to restore the soul of mankind."

That elixir, it turns out, is Mountain Dew. The film, directed by Forest Whitaker, is for a web promotion called DEWmocracy. Harnessing the tremendous democratizing force of the Internet, Mountain Dew let its online community select the color, flavor, label, and name of its next sub-brand of soda—from a group of four preselected possibilities. Arriving just in time for the presidential election of 2008, the promotion pretended to encourage democratic thinking and activism on the part of Mountain Dew's young consumers—when it was really just distracting them from democratic participation by getting them to engage, instead, in the faux populist development of a beverage brand.

Maybe the surest sign that the threat of the rhizome has been all but neutralized is corporate America's willingness, finally, to celebrate the Internet's revolutionary potential. Nowhere was Internet culture lauded more patronizingly than by *Time* magazine's 2006 "Person of the Year" issue. We can only imagine the editors' satisfaction at turning the blogosphere on its head: if those pesky bloggers are going to give us hell no matter whom we choose, why not just choose *them*? Let's show the great, unwashed masses of YouTubers that we're on *their* side for a change. A little silver mirror on the cover reflected back to each reader the winner of the award: you.

"Welcome to your world," the article greeted us. Welcome to what? Weren't we online already? "For seizing the reins of the global media, for founding and framing the new digital democracy, for working for nothing and beating the pros at their own game, *Time*'s Person of the Year for 2006 is you." There was something pandering about all this false modesty. It only betrayed how seriously the editors still took their role as opinion-makers: Our liberation from top-down media isn't real until the top-down media pronounces it so.

And where is the evidence that we're actually liberated? Sure, YouTube, Facebook, and Wikipedia constitute a fundamental change in the way content is produced. But for the corporations profiting off all this activity, it's simply a shift in the way entertainment hours are billed to consumers. Instead of our paying to watch a movie in the theater, we pay to make and upload our own movies online. Instead of paying a record company to listen to their artists' music on a CD player, we pay a computer company for the hardware, an Internet-access company for the bandwidth, and a software company for the media player to do all this. And that's when we're doing it *illegally*, instead of just paying ninety-nine cents to Apple's iTunes.

"Silicon Valley consultants call it Web 2.0, as if it were a new version of some old software. But it's really a revolution," *Time* enthused. Peer-to-peer networking is terrific, indeed, but revolutions are those moments in history when a mob storms the palace and cuts off the heads of the people who have been exploiting them. This is something else.

Yes, bloggers and YouTubers have had many successes, particularly against government. They have brought down a Republican senator, an attorney general, and even made headway against the repressive net censorship of the Chinese. YouTube not only embarrassed Barack Obama about his preacher; it also exposed political repression in Myanmar and FEMA incompetence in New Orleans. But this activity is occurring on a platform that has almost nothing to do with the commons. The Internet may have been first developed with public dollars, but it is now a private utility. We create content using expensive consumer technologies and then upload it to corporate-owned servers using corporate-owned conduits, for a fee. More significantly, we are doing all this with software made by corporations whose interests are embedded in its very code.

User agreements on most video sites require us to surrender some or all of the rights to our own creations. iTunes monitors our use of music and video files as keenly as marketers monitor the goings-on at MySpace and Second Life for insights into consumer behavior. Gmail's computers read our email conversations in order to decide which ads to insert into them. Each and every keystroke becomes part of our consumer profile; every attempt at self-expression is reduced to a brand preference.

Microsoft's operating system interrupts users attempting to play

DVDs that the system suspects may not really belong to them by ask-ing whether or not rights to the movie have been purchased and warn-ing of the consequences of owning illegal files. The iPhone is locked to prevent anyone from using a carrier other than AT&T, the majority of our software is closed to user improvement, and most websites accept little input other than our shopping choices and credit-card numbers.

Had *Time* pronounced us Person of the Year back in 1995—before the shareware-driven Internet had been reduced to an electronic strip mall and market survey—it might have been daring, or even self-fulfilling. Back then, however, the magazine was busy deriding the In-ternet with sensationalist and inaccurate stories of online child porn. In the intervening years, Walt Disney and its fellow media conglomer-ates may have cleaned up Times Square, but on MySpace, owned by News Corp., teens were already stripping for attention and for gifts off their "wish lists." *Time*'s hollow celebration meant that corporate America was secure enough in the totality of its victory that it could now sell this revolution back to us as a supposed shift in media power. Let them eat blog.

Yes, we are using media differently, sitting in chairs and uploading stuff instead of sitting on couches and downloading stuff. And there are new opportunities for finding allies and organizing with them. But in the end we're still glued to a tube, watching mostly television shows, arguing too often like angry idiots, surrendering the last re-mains of our privacy, and paying a whole lot more to mostly the same large corporations for the privilege. *Time*'s choice for Person of the Year was announced on Time Warner–owned CNN, in a special pro-gram that may as well have been an infomercial for the user empower-ment offered by Time Warner–owned broadband services AOL and Road Runner. One way or another, each of us anointed Persons of the Year was still just a customer.

Our acceptance of this role along with its constraints is largely vol-untary. We would rather be consumers of unalterable technologies that dictate the parameters of our behaviors than the users of tools with less familiar limits. Technologies resistant to our modification tend to be easier and more dependable for users, but also safer for cor-porations. Who cares if we can't upload our own software into an iPhone as long as the software Steve Jobs has written for us already works well? Likewise, the early Macintosh computer worked so much more dependably than Windows for novice users precisely because

Apple, unlike Microsoft, required its users to use only Apple peripherals. Windows tried to accommodate everyone, so incompatibilities and code conflicts inevitably arose. By attempting to accommodate all comers, Microsoft (the company we like to call monopolist) was actually permitting value creation from the periphery instead of monopolizing it all in the name of hardware compatibility.

Besides, on an Internet where an errant click might introduce a virus to your hard drive or send your banking passwords to a criminal in Russia, the stakes are high. Many of us would gladly surrender the ability to modify our computers or even share music files for the seeming security of a closed and unalterable piece of technology. In exchange for such safety and dependability, we can't use these closed devices in ways their manufacturers don't specifically want us to. We can't change the technologies we purchase to get value out of them that wasn't intended to be there. We can't provide applications for one another's Verizon or Apple cell phone without going to the phone operator's centralized online store and giving it a cut of the money. We cannot create value for ourselves or for one another from the outside in.

But value can still be extracted from the inside out. Technology providers maintain the ongoing ability to change the things they've sold us. Software can be upgraded remotely with or without users' consent; cable television boxes can have their functionality altered or reduced from the home office; the OnStar call-for-help systems in GM cars can be switched on by the central receiving station to monitor drivers' movements and conversations; cell phones can be locked or "bricked" by a telecom operator from afar. In the long run, we surrender the ability to create new value with interactive technologies for the guarantee of getting at least most of what we want out of them as consumers. These sterile technologies generate less new growth, promote a less active role for users, and prevent anyone but the company who made them from creating additional value.

The more we are asked to adapt to the biases of our machinery, the less human we become. In spite of its chaotic and organic propensities, the Internet isn't reversing the Industrial Age role exchange between people and corporations. The Internet provides human beings with an even more entirely virtual, controlled, and preconfigured landscape on which to work and live, while providing corporations with the equivalent of corporeal existence for the very first time. Out on the Web, people have no more substance or stature than any virtual entity—and in most cases, less. We become more virtual while our corporate entities become more real.

The people may as well be the machines. Once high-tech security-minded employers in California and Cincinnati get their way in the courts, they'll be materializing this vision by implanting workers with the same kinds of RFID tags Wal-Mart puts in its products. A central-office computer monitors exactly who is where and when, opening doors for those who have clearance. While implantation isn't yet mandatory for existing laborers, the additional and convenient access to sensitive materials it affords makes voluntary implantation a plus for worker recognition and advancement.

Increasingly, we find ourselves working on behalf of our computers rather than the other way around. The Amazon Mechanical Turks program gives people the opportunity to work as assistants to computers. Earning pennies per task, users perform hundreds or thousands of routine operations for corporate computers that don't want to waste their cycles. There are credits available for everything from finding the address numbers in photos of houses (three cents a pop) to matching Web-page URLs with the product that is supposed to appear on them (a whopping nickel each).

In the constant battle against automated spam, websites require users to prove they are human. In order to register for a site or make a comment, the user must complete a "challenge," such as identifying the distorted letters in an image and typing them into the keyboard. One particularly dastardly spammer has gotten around this by employing people to do what his computers can't: he has created a game that offers pornography to users who complete his computer's challenges. The program copies the picture it can't decode from one location on the Internet and displays it for the porn-seeking human. The human completes the task and is rewarded with a titillating image— the same way a lab rat earns a piece of cheese for ringing a bell.

While this *artificial* artificial intelligence may nudge computers beyond their current limitations, it does so by assigning mechanical tasks to living people in the same way a microchip farms out cycles to its coprocessors.

In the 1950s, visionaries imagined that technology would create a society in which work would be limited to the few tasks we didn't want our machines doing for us. The vast majority of our time was to be spent at leisure—not in boredom, racking up three-cent credits on our laptops, or performing rote operations on behalf of microprocessors in return for some pixels representing a breast.

But these operations are big business—big enough to be outsourced. Workers in massive Chinese digital sweatshops perform the computer tasks that those of us in wealthier nations don't have time to do. A single factory may hold several hundred workers who sit behind terminals in round-the-clock shifts. Amazingly, this work is not limited to data entry, spam evasion, or crunching numbers. In one of the more bizarre human-machine relationships to emerge on the Internet, Chinese day laborers play the boring parts of online games that Westerners don't want to bother with—all the tiny tasks that a player's fictional character must perform in order to earn pretend cash within a game world. People who want to participate in online game worlds without actually *playing* the games will buy game money on eBay from these digital sweatshops instead of earning it. With millions of people now participating in games like Second Life and World of Warcraft, the practice has become commonplace. Current estimates number the Chinese labor force dedicated to winning game points on behalf of Westerners at over one hundred thousand. There are even published exchange rates between game money and U.S. dollars.

This, in turn, has motivated the players within many games to start pretend businesses through which real cash might be earned. The biggest business in the online game Second Life is prostitution. Pretty female avatars engage in sex animations with other players in return for in-game money, which they exchange for real currency on eBay. When players get good or famous enough at this, they move up a level in the business hierarchy, construct bordellos or sex clubs, and then hire other players to do the actual online coupling. Finally, Linden Lab, the corporation that owns Second Life, charges the bordello proprietors for the space and cycles they use on the web server.

The point is not that virtual prostitution is immoral or even unseemly; it's that when we have the opportunity to develop a "second life"—a fantasy realm unencumbered by the same scarcity and tiered system of labor we endure in the real world—we end up creating a market infused with the same corporatist ground rules. If people *pretended* to be prostitutes in an online fantasy realm instead of providing the Internet equivalent of phone sex for money, it might at least indicate a willingness to use an entertainment medium—a play space— for play.

And Second Life is a mere microcosm of the Internet at large. The "open-source" ethos encouraging people to work on software projects for free has been reinterpreted through the lens of corporatism as "crowd sourcing"—meaning just another way to get people to do work for no compensation. And even "file-sharing" has been reduced to a frenzy of acquisition that has less to do with sharing music than it does with filling the ever-expanding hard drives of successive iPods. Cyberspace has become just another place to consume and do business. The question is no longer how browsing the Internet changes the way we look at the world; it's which browser we'll be using to buy and sell stuff in the same old world.

Those of us who don't understand the capabilities of computers are much more likely to accept the limits with which they are packaged. Instead of getting machines to do what we might want them to do, the machines and their programmers are getting us to do what *they* want us to do. Writing text instead of just reading text is certainly a leap forward—but when web publishing is circumscribed by software and interfaces from Amazon and Google, we must at least understand how these companies are limiting our creations and the value we hope to derive from them.

Where does the number of new job applicants or level of worker satisfaction fit in an Excel spreadsheet's bottom line? Does Blogger.com give a person the ability to post something every day, or does the bias of its daily journal format compel a person to write shorter, more frequent and superficial posts at the expense of longer, more considered pieces? Do electronic trading sites encourage certain kinds of trades, at certain frequencies? What does it mean that a person's name and picture in Facebook are posted next to how many "friends" he has accumulated? Why would Facebook choose to highlight this particular number? What are the defaults, what can be customized easily, and what can't? The more automatically we accept the metrics and standards assumed by a program, the more tied we are to its embedded values. If we don't really understand how arbitrarily computer programs have been designed, we will be more likely to look at software as something unchangeable—as the way things are done rather than just one way to do things.

This is not how the Internet's early pioneers and developers saw their network being used. They envisioned the interactive revolution as the opportunity to rewrite the very rules by which society was organized—to reprogram the underlying codes by which we live. In contradiction to popular mythology about them, these researchers had less allegiance to the Defense Advanced Research Projects Agency (DARPA) and the U.S. military than they did to the pure pursuit of knowledge and the expansion of human capabilities. Although their budgets may have come partly from the Pentagon, their aims were decidedly nonmilitary. As seminal essays by World War II technologists Vannevar Bush, Norbert Wiener, and J.C.R. Licklider made clear, the job before them was to convert a wartime technology industry into a peacetime leap forward for humanity. Bush, FDR's former war advisor, wrote of a hypothetical computer or "Memex" machine he intended as an extension of human memory. Wiener, the founder of "cybernetics," believed that lessons in feedback learned by the Air Force during the war could be applied to a vast range of technologies, giving machines the ability to extend the senses and abilities of real people. Licklider's work for DARPA (then called ARPA) was based entirely on making machines more compatible with human beings.

The Internet itself developed around new models of resource sharing. This is why the code was written allowing computers to "talk" to one another in the first place: so that many different researchers could utilize the precious operational cycles of the few early computers in existence at that time. This ethos then extended naturally to the content those researchers were creating. The more access people had to the ideas, facts, and discoveries of others, the better for everyone.

It was a pervasive societal norm, yet one so contrary to the dictates of corporatism that AT&T actually turned down the opportunity to take over the early Internet in 1972. A medium based on sharing access and information was anathema to an economy based on central authority, hoarding, and scarcity. AT&T saw "no use" for it.

Of course, thanks to public money, university interest, and tremendous social desire, the Internet came into being. The software created to run it was developed almost entirely by nonprofit institutions and hobbyists. The urge to gain and share the ability to communicate directly with others was so great that students and researchers wrote software for free. Pretty much everything we use today—from email and web browsers to chat and streaming video—came out of the computer labs of places like the University of Chicago, Cornell, and MIT.

Meanwhile, the emergence of interactive technology was beginning to change the way everyone experienced broadcasting and other top-down media. A device as simple as the remote control gave television viewers the ability to deconstruct the media they were watching in real time. Instead of sitting through coercive commercials, they began to click away or even fast-forward through them. Camcorders and VCRs gave people the ability to make their own media, and demystified the process through which the media they watched was created. Stars lost some of their allure, commercials lost their impact, and newscasters lost their authority.

As computer technology eventually trickled down to the public via consumer-grade PCs, people found themselves much more engaged by one another than with the commercial media being pumped into their homes via cable. The Interactive Age was born. People shared everything they knew with one another. And since computers at that time were still as easy to program as they were difficult to use, people also shared the software they were writing to accelerate all this sharing. Programmers weren't in it for the money, but for the value they were able to create for their fellow netizens, and perhaps the associated elevation in their reputation and social standing.

An early study showed that the Internet-connected home watched an average of nine hours less commercial television per week than its nonconnected counterparts. A people that had been alienated from one another through television and marketing were now reconnecting online in a totally new kind of cultural experience. Something had to be done, and it was.

Mainstream media corporations began by attempting to absorb the assault and assimilate the new content. It wasn't easy. When bloggers like Matt Drudge released salacious news about the president, traditional news gatekeepers struggled to keep up or lose their exclusive authority over the coverage of current events. Major media circled the wagons and became hyper-centralized, debt-laden bureaucracies. The more media empires merged and conglomerated, the less control they seemed to have over the independently created media that trickled up through their empires.

Crudely drawn animations like *The Simpsons, Beavis & Butt-Head,* and *South Park* began as interstitial material or even independent media, but became so popular that they demanded prime-time slots on networks and cable. Although the profits still went to the top, the content flowing through the mainstream mediaspace seemed to be beyond the control of its corporate keepers. Gary Panter, an artist and animator for *Pee-wee's Playhouse,* wrote a manifesto arguing that the counterculture was over; artists should simply make use of the market—turn the beast against itself by giving it entertainingly radical content that it couldn't help but broadcast. His friend Matt Groening followed the advice and sold *The Simpsons* to Fox, making the brand-new, otherwise money-losing TV network a tremendous success. The fact that this may have single-handedly funded Fox News notwith-standing, it appeared that a marriage between radical content and the mainstream media infrastructure might be in the making.

As much as it frightened movie studios and protective parents, a radical content revolution didn't really threaten media conglomerates, as long as they owned the conduit on which all the content was broadcast. *Beavis & Butt-Head*'s wry commentary may have undermined MTV's music-video business, but there was always more content for the network to put in its place. Perhaps the Internet could become an adjunct to the media market rather than its competitor.

To make markets, however, speculators had always sought to exploit or create scarcity. Nothing seemed to be scarce about the Internet. It was an endless and ever-growing sea of data, which everybody shared with everybody else, for free. Abundance wasn't just a byproduct; it was the net's core ethos. But that early study showing how Internet households watched less TV revealed a scarcity that corporate media hadn't considered before: the limits of human attention. Sure, the Internet might be infinite—but human beings only had so many "eye-ball hours" to spend on one medium or another. The precious real estate in the Internet era was not server capacity or broadcasting bandwidth, but human time.

At last, there was a metric compatible with the scarcity bias of corporatism. *Wired* magazine, which had already established itself as the voice of business online, announced that we were now living in an "attention economy" in which success would be measured by the ability to garner users' eyeball hours with "sticky" content. The trick would be to develop websites that people found hard to navigate away from—virtual cul-de-sacs in which users would get stuck. A web marketing company called Real Media took out full-page ads in net business magazines such as *Fast Company* showing Internet users hanging helplessly from a giant strip of flypaper. The caption read: "Nothing Attracts Like Real Media." Corporations would mine the attention real estate of users the same way they mined the colonies for gold centuries earlier. So much for empowering users. We are the flies.

The new mantra of the connected age became "content is king." The self-evident reality that the Internet was about connecting people was conveniently replaced with a corporatist fantasy that it was about engaging those people with bits of copyrighted data. Users weren't interested in speaking to one another, the logic went; they were interested in downloading text, pictures, and movies made by professionals. At least this was something media companies could understand, and they rushed to go online with their books, magazines, and other content.

What they hadn't taken into account was that people had gotten used to enjoying content online for free. By rushing to digitize and sell their properties, corporations ended up turning them from scarce resources into infinitely reproducible ones. Along came Napster, Bit-Torrent, and other technologies that gave former consumers the ability to "rip" movies off DVDs, music off CDs, and TV off their TiVo and then share it anonymously over the Internet. Anything digital, no matter how seemingly well protected or encrypted, was capable of being copied and shared. The bias of the Internet for abundance over scarcity appeared to be taking its toll.

Hollywood studios and record companies began lobbying Congress for laws and enforcement to prevent their entire libraries from becoming worthless. Comcast, a cable company that offers broadband Internet service, began blocking traffic from peer-to-peer networks in an effort to prevent losses to its corporate brethren and subsidiaries. Other corporations lobbied for changes to the way Internet access is billed, making it easier for large companies to support fast content distribution, but much harder for smaller groups or individuals to share their data.

The content wars redrew the battle lines of the net revolution. It became a struggle between consumers and producers: customers fighting to get the products they wanted for free, and doing it by investing in a host of other products that, all told, probably cost them more money anyway. What does it matter if one's iPod contains eighty thousand hours of music? This recontextualization of the net revolution reduced the very definition of winning. The Internet era became about what we could get as consumers rather than what we could create as people. The notion of creating value from the periphery was surrendered to the more immediate gratification of getting free products *to* the periphery.

While corporations could no longer make the same kind of money off their digital content, the massive flow of entertainment and files from person to person was a lot easier to exploit than genuine conversation between people. Every website, every file, every email, every web search, was an opportunity for promotion of a brand.

Genuinely social spaces, from Friendster to Facebook, looked for ways to cash in on all this activity, too. Millions of people were already posting details about themselves, linking up with others, and forming affinity groups. Although corporations couldn't make too much money giving away web space to people, they could try to dictate the metrics people used to describe themselves—and then sell all this information to market researchers.

On social-networking sites—where real hugs can never happen—people compete instead for love in the form of numbers: how many "friends" do you have? The way to get friends, other than inviting people, is primarily to list one's favorite books, movies, bands, and products. This results in a corporate-friendly identity defined more by what one consumes than what one does. Moreover, in cyberspace brands could create pages as human as any person's. And just like people inhabiting these social spaces, they compete for the highest numbers of friends. Do you want to be the "friend" of Chase bank? What if it enters you into a sweepstakes where you might make some money?

Nonprofit groups and social activists got into the act as well, sending out invitations pressuring "friends" to support one another's favorite issues. These issues, in turn, become part of the users' profiles, better defining them for everyone. The ability to attract a hundred thousand fans online goes a long way toward convincing record labels that an independent band may have what it takes to earn a "real" contract. People, companies, brands, and rock groups are all "friends" on the network, even though most of them aren't people at all.

Of course, each of the social networks where all this activity occurs is itself ultimately for sale. MySpace was sold to Murdoch for $580 million. YouTube went to Google for $1.65 billion in stock. As of this writing, Facebook had turned down a billion-dollar offer from Yahoo. These numbers do more than make the head spin; they confirm the mythology underlying the frenzy of Internet investment and activity by corporations: that interactive media technology is the surest path to growth in an era when most everything else is pretty well used up.

While some terrific and socially positive activity is occurring on these sites, they are founded on pure financial speculation, and faith in the same universally "open markets" corporations have been advocating through the World Bank and the IMF. As the Global Business Network cofounder Peter Schwartz argued in his pre-dot-com-crash book, *The Long Boom*, "Open markets good. Closed markets bad. Tattoo it on your forehead." The infinite growth and expansion required by credit-fueled corporate capitalism found a new frontier in the theoretically endless realm of cyberspace.

The myth was enough to fuel the speculative dot-com bubble, which Alan Greenspan belatedly called "irrational exuberance," but which went on long enough to convince investors to lift high-tech issues on the NASDAQ stock exchange beyond even the most optimistically speculative valuations. This was a "new economy," according to *Wired*'s editor Kevin Kelly. A "tsunami," echoed its publisher, Louis Rossetto—one that would rage over culture and markets like a tidal wave. More than simply costing millions of investors their savings, the movement of the Internet from the newspaper's technology section to the business pages changed the way the public perceived what had once been a public space—a commons. The truly unlimited potential for the creation of value outside the centralized realm of Wall Street had been all but forgotten. In its place was an untrue perception that the way to get rich online was to invest in a stock exchange, come up with a compelling business plan, or sell a half-baked enterprise to a venture-capital firm and wait for the IPO.

Places, people, and value again become property, individuals, and money. The evolution of the Internet recapitulates the process through which corporatism took hold of our society. Eyeball hours served as the natural resource that became a "property" to be hoarded. People and groups became "individuals," all with their own web pages and MySpace profiles to be sold to market researchers. Computers—once tools for sharing technological resources—mutated into handheld iPods and iPhones that reduced formerly shared public spaces to separate bubbles of private conservation and entertainment. And value creation—which in cyberspace could have potentially come from anywhere and be measured in units other than dollars—became subject to the rules of the same centralized marketplace that favors existing sectors of wealth. Yes, some people became millionaires or even billionaires, but they did so by entering the game of central capital, not by creating an alternative.

A few did try. PayPal may have come the closest. Online users of sites like eBay needed an easy way to pay one another. They weren't real businesses, and weren't set up to accept credit cards. Besides, some of the exchanges were for such small amounts that a credit-card company's minimum service fees could as much as double the total. PayPal's original plan was to offer its alternative payment service for free. The company would charge nothing, but make money on the "float" by holding on to the cash for three days and keeping the interest earned. This made sense for most users anyway, since PayPal could then even serve as an escrow account—releasing the money only after the product was shipped or received. But the right to make money *from* money was reserved, by corporate charter, to the banking industry. Its representatives demanded that regulators step in and define PayPal's activity as a violation of banking law, at which point PayPal was forced to charge its users a traditional service fee instead. Their original vision dashed, PayPal's owners nonetheless made their millions by selling the whole operation to eBay for $1.5 billion.

In another effort—this one to transcend the polarizing battle over digital content—the legal scholar Lawrence Lessig's Creative Commons project helps content creators redefine how they want their works to be shared; most authors, so far, seem to value getting credit for their contributions over getting paid for them. Traditional publishers still kick and scream, however, forcing some authors and musicians to choose between making money and making an impact—earning central currency or creating social currency. While authors and rock groups who have already succeeded in the corporate system—such as Radiohead or Stephen King—can give away their content for free online and still sell plenty of physical copies, up-and-comers have much less luck.

The battle to unleash the potential of the Internet to promote true decentralization of value may not be over yet. Even on a playing field increasingly tilted toward centralized and moneymaking interests, there are people dedicated to using it for constructive, creative, and common causes. For every bordello in Second Life there is also a public library; for every paid strip show there is a free lecture. Branded "islands" are proving to be a waste of advertising money, while university-sponsored spaces now offer seminars to nonpaying students from around the world. For every company developing a digital-rights-management strategy to prevent its content from being copied, there is a researcher posting his latest findings on Wikipedia for all to learn from and even edit or contest, for free.

On the other hand, for every community of parents, Christians, or environmentalists looking to engage with others about their hopes, doubts, and concerns, there is a media company attempting to brand the phenomenon and deliver these select eyeballs to the ads of their sponsors. For every disparate community attempting to "find the others" on the Internet, there is a social-networking site attempting to sell this activity in the form of a database to market researchers. For every explosion of young people flocking to a new and exciting computer game or virtual world, there's a viral marketer or advertiser attempting to turn their creativity into product placements and their interactions into word-of-mouth promotions. Even a technology that seemed destined to reconnect people to one another instead ends up disconnecting them in new ways, all under the pretense of increasingly granular affinity.

Most of the people at companies exploiting these opportunities believe they are ultimately promoting, not exploiting, social activity. They may even be dedicated to the constituencies they're serving, and simply looking to subsidize their communities' activities with a business plan. But well-meaning or not, these companies are themselves bounded by a corporatist landscape that works against their own best sentiments. The platforms they create are built on borrowed money, and conform to the logic of centralized value creation. Sooner or later, value must be taken from the periphery and brought back to the center.

CHAPTER EIGHT

NO RETURNS

How Resistance Disconnects Us Even Further

Big Blank

There is a way out. But it means getting off the artificial playing field of corporatism and touching terra firma. Only by disconnecting from corporatism and its dehumanizing, delocalizing, depersonalizing, and devaluing biases can we muster the strength and find the tools through which a people-scaled society might be constructed—or reconstructed. Blaming corporations for this mess or trying to unseat their leaders provides only temporary relief for the most superficial symptoms. And in the long run, it may make things worse.

It's just too much like whining, making it easy for defenders of the status quo to frame any effort at overcoming corporatist values as a resentful leftist reaction to successful business; or, in the current mêlée, the knee-jerk reaction of would-be interventionists to a healthy, if painful, market correction.

It adds to corporate entrenchment by continuing to credit these institutions with running and ruining our world, rather than taking responsibility ourselves for ceding to them the landscape on which they operate.

It focuses our attention on the names of artificial entities—particular corporations—and distracts us from the real people making decisions on their behalf and against our collective human interests.

It usually occurs on the corporate-branded playing field. Boycotts and media campaigns take place on the generic, nonlocal landscape where corporations have much more power and grounding than we do. Even a protest against a corporation is usually more of a photo op than a street action, and still taking place in corporate media biased toward corporatist agendas.

Instead of reconnecting people to their local communities, to one another, or to the value that they might be able to create for one another, many well-meaning efforts against corporate power connect people to abstract ideals and highly centralized organizations. This may give us the ability to attack particular offenders, but only disconnects us further from the truly bottom-up networks through which we can restore human-scaled activity.

The "enemy," if we must accept that terminology, is almost never a particular corporation, anyway, but the way commerce, government, and culture have been reconfigured to the corporatist purpose. Bringing down a company—when it can even be achieved—doesn't change that landscape; it only creates a vacuum for a competitor to fill. Chances are, that competitor was an invisible ally to the activists all along. Besides, by blindly following the rules of corporatism that they once fought for, many corporations do *themselves* in. The system is bigger than they are.

Consider General Motors. Once a corporation capable of writing legislation to rezone cities, it is now in a struggle for survival against more efficient manufacturers (of more efficient cars) from Japan. A victim of its own corporatist bias, GM defaulted to short-term solutions and government favoritism.

Addicted to a system in which companies would rather fight against a restriction than calculate its long-term cost or benefit, often spending more on lobbying than they would on any actual change, GM encouraged its favorite members of Congress to water down mileage-standards legislation in 2007. While the company may not be against innovation, it doesn't want to be forced to innovate, either— particularly not by the government or any of the environmentalists who oppose the automobile on principle. But what GM failed to comprehend was that its resistance to fuel efficiency was one of the main reasons it was losing market share to Toyota and Honda.

Moreover, Toyota—whose Prius car gets fifty miles per gallon—

joined with GM in lobbying Congress *against* the tougher fuel standards. These regulations would not affect Toyota, which has already
beat the proposed standards well into the future. No, Toyota was lobbying to keep U.S. standards much lower than its own—and to keep
GM uncommitted to competing on that score. While advertising its
own commitment to energy efficiency, Toyota was actively lobbying to
help the rest of the industry maintain worse fuel standards.

What GM didn't get—what it couldn't get—is that industry-wide
regulation makes it easier, not harder, for it to create value in the long
run. Adhering to fuel-efficiency standards and doing the necessary research and development to meet future targets may cost money in the
short term—but when those costs are mandated by legislation, they
end up costing all competitors roughly the same amount. (Yes, even
foreign competitors if nations maintain some authority over their
trade.) In a highly competitive marketplace, the decision to be the
only company taking a stand on fuel efficiency is a potentially risky
bet. Legislation mandating efficiency spreads that risk to all parties.
No one gets ahead while the other is investing in doing the "right"
thing.

This should be the most compelling logic behind the concept of the
labor union, as well. By negotiating with an entire industry, unions
can win a certain salary or a limit on the length of the workweek without costing any single company its competitive edge. The limits on
what workers can reasonably request are based on the value their
labors create, not the extent to which competitors are willing to go to
undermine another company's bottom line. It's a humane conspiracy,
with great precedents. Ancient Sabbath traditions and more modern
"blue laws" gave stores and workshops a way to close for a day without losing out to some crazy competitor willing to work all the time. It
was a positive conspiracy through which everyone got a day off.

Not surprisingly, however, as corporatism's bias toward colonialism
took hold of the automobile industry, companies that once benefited
from industry-wide labor agreements began to fight for open markets
through which to undercut them. By outsourcing vehicle and parts
manufacturing to nonunion laborers in developing (or, preferably,
nondeveloping) countries, American automobile companies could
now compete with one another in a new way. The problem is, it was by
reducing costs and quality, as well as the population of ready consumers. Instead of accepting a universally civil and humane floor on

how poorly workers could be treated, the industry would now compete against itself for how low it could go.

It was a doomed strategy. As the countries to which manufacturing was outsourced gained more skill and experience, they learned to make and market these goods by themselves. Numerous companies in Asia are now directly marketing goods made in the same plants as major U.S. and European brands—not copies, but the very same products. Their corporations now exploit the same open markets that were once used to exploit them, and cut out (or eventually buy) the middleman.

Thanks to self-defeating competitive strategies like these, many companies are themselves as damaged by the faulty logic of corporatism as their customers and employees. While the actions of certain companies in certain situations are deplorable or even actionably illegal, they are both supported and demanded by the larger corporatist systems to which they belong. In most cases, the corporatist government refuses to intervene, or even actively patronizes the offenders. These are not blameless crimes, but they are perpetrated by large sets of people who rarely understand the effects of their own actions and refuse to consider the big picture. Corporatism now defines the landscape, the activity, and the players, as well as the people and institutions charged with keeping them beneficial to society. While the marketplace may not be a natural system, it is a systemic phenomenon with great inertia and capacity for self-preservation. Plus, it has access to every sector of human activity. Resistance, at least on its own terms, is futile.

Big Energy, Big Agra, Big Pharma, Big War, and Big Government are not easy targets for activists and reformers. They neutralize or absorb efforts to change their practices, leaving would-be resisters confused, weary, or downright cynical.

An Al Gore movie and rising gas prices finally bring the struggle to break Big Oil to public attention. Big Agra seizes on the opportunity to sell corn-based ethanol. Farmers in the depressed Corn Belt cheer. Long-ignored environmentalists and alternative-energy advocates praise the effort too, until they realize that corn is almost as bad a pollutant as oil, and not a particularly efficient substitute fuel. Corn yields only twice the amount of energy it costs to produce. Some other crops without Big Agra support, such as switchgrass and hemp, offer five times the energy output or better.

But by the time these facts begin to surface, corn-industry lobbyists have already secured politicians' commitments to provide new
subsidies for their crop and massive, self-interested farmer support
for their cause. As the commodity value of corn rises to four dollars a
bushel or more, even well-informed farmers are disincentivized to
change to an unsubsidized crop with a lower profit margin. Bigger
companies don't have the mechanisms through which to consider
making such a financial compromise. Instead, they allow the promotion of a single crop to conglomerate their industry even further. As of
this writing, just two companies export over 50 percent of grain from
the United States. The more land used to raise crops for fuel in addition to food, the more valuable the land and crops that Big Agra already controls. A political candidate who sought to provide a subsidy
for a potentially more efficient crop would meet resistance from the
very industry he was attempting to support.

Instead of leading to better land management or a more diversified
crop, evidence of corn's poor performance gives oil-industry lobbyists leverage to push for the opening of more drilling lands. On the
surface—and in TV ads—it seems like a logical enough way to lower
the cost of gasoline at the pump. More supply should mean lower
prices. But the oil industry is happy with high prices, and is already
leasing sixty-eight million acres of land from the U.S. government at
rock-bottom prices that they're not exploiting at all. While a candidate
may get both votes and campaign financing by pushing the oil industry's monopoly over a resource it is making artificially scarce, his support of the "additional drilling" fiction takes us further away from a
sound energy policy.

All this gets so confusingly self-reinforcing that citizens concerned
about energy don't know quite whom to protest against or what to ask
for. Those who do get the full picture—intellectuals reading all about
it in *The New York Review of Books* as they sun with their Dalton-
educated teens on the beaches of East Hampton—can't help but
shrug. The problem is just too big. Concern becomes cynicism, cynicism becomes despair, and despair becomes self-preservation. Maybe
I can earn enough money to insulate my family from the problem.

So we do our part instead by buying organic food and maybe a
higher-efficiency car. But again, if we read the right magazines and
newspapers, we learn that the term "certified organic" has itself been
commandeered by industrial agriculture firms, who have successfully

lobbied government to develop regulations that make it nearly impossible for the small and strictly organic farmer to comply. The required record keeping is designed for large, single-crop farms that exhaust topsoil in ways that more diverse land use by smaller farmers does not. Farmers must use "certified" seed that comes from a few registered and expensive suppliers, and is available only for the small number of crop species favored by larger producers. Larger concerns may also file for "exceptions" through which nonorganic products may be sold under the organic label. In short, small farmers with the very best organic practices do not generally qualify for certification as organic.

Nor do they generally qualify for distribution through today's corporatized version of an organic food store, the multibillion-dollar publicly traded corporation Whole Foods Market, Inc. Seeing an opportunity to generate value from the emerging consumer appetite for organic goods, Whole Foods opened supermarket-sized health-food outlets in organic-friendly cities across America. Offering a worldwide variety, better stock, and a more familiar supermarket experience than traditional health-food stores that depend on small farm suppliers and local deliveries, the chain grew quickly to over 250 stores, putting local health-food stores out of business. Whole Foods operates on a scale that only Big Agra can service. As a result, it utilizes a trucking and warehousing scheme virtually identical to that of its nonorganic competitors, nullifying one of the main reasons people should be shopping organically in the first place. An organic apple shipped across the country does vastly more damage to the environment, including the topsoil, than even a conventionally grown one trucked in from a local farm.

Under current law favoring Big Agra, however, local farms aren't in a position to meet the demand for additional organic food anyway. The only way for them to produce additional fruits and vegetables would be to start using or renting fields that have been designated for subsidy crops like corn and soy. But the commodity-farm program prohibits such use. Farmers planting forbidden crops would lose more than their government subsidies. Thanks to a law written for the national fruit and vegetable growers in California, Florida, and Texas who feared competition from small local farmers, violators would also be penalized for the full value of the forbidden fruits and vegetables. Like the indigenous population of a colonial territory, they are prohibited by law from competing with chartered corporate suppliers who operate from a distance. They may not create value locally, for locals.

Big Pharma is no different. Having spent $855 million between 1998 and 2006, the pharmaceutical lobby is the largest of any single industry. Politicians depending on its contributions have voted to weaken the regulatory powers of the Food and Drug Administration (FDA), block importation of generic drugs, stop postmarket safety studies of already approved medications, and prevent clinical drug studies from going public. And that was all in just one month of 2007. University researchers, meanwhile, receive millions in donations and consulting fees to tilt their findings in favor of drugs' safety and efficacy. In one recent example, two Harvard professors whose studies endorsed the use of certain powerful antipsychotic drugs neglected to disclose the $1.6 million apiece they received from the drugs' manufacturers.

Amazingly, for all of Big Pharma's lobbying to loosen standards, it never seeks to altogether end the system through which drugs must be tested for approval. Not only can the FDA seal of approval relieve them of legal liability for bad drugs, it keeps smaller competitors from bringing drugs to market or, worse, unpatented substances from getting approved to treat real diseases. When it takes upwards of $200 million and one hundred thousand pages of reports to get approval for a single medication, only the largest corporations can afford to engage in the process. The immense cost then helps justify long patent terms and high prices.

But it also maintains the Big Pharma monopoly. When a known substance without a patent shows promise—such as the Alzheimer's treatment vasopressin or the antiaging red-wine ingredient resveratrol—no one has the funds or the profit motive to test it for FDA approval. Instead, pharmaceutical companies attempt to create and patent analogs—molecules close to the promising substances—and then test them in their place. While we're waiting for something similar but more expensive to be developed and patented, the substances that actually work remain unprescribed by doctors afraid to take liability for "off-label" or unconventional therapies. Those who do prescribe unapproved herbs to treat "real" diseases often lose their licenses. With its health care subject to such restrictive centralization, it's no wonder that while the U.S. spends over seven thousand dollars per person a year on medical care, its infant mortality rate, maternal mortality rate, and longevity are among the worst in the industrialized world.

In industry after industry, sector after sector, the same sorts of systems rule, making direct intervention challenging or impossible. Pulling on existing levers or making adjustments to default settings usually just triggers a mechanism through which the entire system manages to maintain its overall inertia. Corporations can't help but resist any maneuvers that threaten the status quo, even if it means sacrificing long-term profitability in order to protect the authority through which they operate. The maintenance of the chartered monopoly system is of greater importance. Like a new form of life, the corporate culture fights for dominance against the humans who created it. Like a cancer, it is willing to bring down its host organism for the sake of growth.

Sometimes the battle over life and death is literal. As the U.S.-U.K. descent into Big War demonstrates, corporatism drives not only military logistics but also foreign policy. When war is outsourced to corporations, short-term profitability ends up trumping long-term regional stability and national interests. Unencumbered by national military codes and unconcerned with internationally negotiated treaties, contractors from Aegis to Blackwater behave with impunity and without consequence. While soldiers who commit crimes in war zones such as Iraq are court-martialed, contractors are sent home. They can return as soon as a week later, working for another company. This allows governments to outsource illegal activities and torture to contractors, with little liability. It's a striking return to the outsourced war practices of the early colonial empires, which has more to do with promoting the profits of the chartered corporations than the long-term success or influence of the nations in their thrall.

In today's version of outsourced war, the blind obedience to the profit motive makes for an incompetent military force. Early chartered corporations actually wanted to win the territories they were fighting for in order to exploit their resources. Most of today's chartered military operatives have a bigger stake in keeping the war going; they simply want to make money through their no-bid contracts. Halliburton has arrangements with the government that are structured so that the more it spends, the more it earns. That's why the company simply destroys any vehicle that breaks, rather than replacing oil filters or tires. Truckers drive empty trucks through the war zone, racking up tremendous bills for the company. Those who tattle to the press or the government are either terminated or effectively bribed with stays at four-star hotels—also billed back to the military at a great markup. Soldiers train contractors to do highly skilled tasks, like fixing radios, and are then put on guard duty to protect their former students—who cost up to hundreds of times more, all told.

But any of us who watch *Frontline* or read *The New York Times* already knows this. The more paralyzing aspect is our seeming inability to do anything about it. Concerned citizens inside and outside government appear impotent. When a Pentagon contract manager, Charles Smith, confronted Kellogg, Brown & Root, at the time a Halliburton subsidiary, about an extra billion dollars of unexplained war billings, he was summarily replaced by—you guessed it—an outsourced auditing company. The more expensive war gets, the less is available for social services and infrastructure at home. The poorer people get, the more easily they can be persuaded that foreign enemies greedy for oil profits and obsessed with religious violence are the real problem. The daily toll of bodies begins to feel less relevant than the escalating price at the pump.

As Naomi Klein amply demonstrated in her book on the extension of war profiteering to other industries, *Disaster Capitalism,* human life is no longer even a valid component of the global business plan. It's not really part of the equation. While privatized war provides direct evidence of the way market forces working within particular institutional structures can end up promoting conflict, with all the human and material waste that this implies, Klein sees the same essential dynamic at play elsewhere. She observes that while in Iraq the people and infrastructure have been devastated by weapons and trade embargoes, "in many other parts of the world, including the United States, they have been demolished by ideology, the war on 'big government,' the religion of tax cuts, the fetish for privatization."

The Hurricane Katrina disaster appeared to confirm the incompetence of big government, while creating $3.4 billion of no-bid contracts for Halliburton, Parsons, Bechtel, and several other Iraq war service providers. It led to a field day for privatization. Wal-Mart signed a disaster-response partnership with the Red Cross and Blackwater provided "green zone" security for contractors in New Orleans against potentially dangerous locals. Corporatized security and emergency relief has become another growth industry.

A management consultant named John Robb, a former Delta Force commander for the U.S. military, wrote a highly circulated manifesto for *Fast Company*, in which he argued, optimistically, that the end result of the war on terror will be a "new, more resilient approach to national security, one built not around the state but around private citizens and companies. . . . Wealthy individuals and multinational corporations will be the first to bail out of our collective system, opting instead to hire private military companies . . . to protect their homes and facilities and establish a protective perimeter around daily life." He predicted that the middle class would eventually develop its own version of "armored suburbs" to defray the costs of security. The more we contemplate Robb's vision of suburban apartheid, the less hopeful we are about developing alternatives.

Lawrence Lessig began a new chapter in his legal career by starting an organization dedicated to exposing the dangerous liaisons between the government and its chartered corporations. His website, change-congress.org, publicizes the distorting influence of money in Washington. While we might all wish for his success, who among us is unaware of the distorting influence of money in Washington? Besides, exposure doesn't really mean anything if people are too concerned with their own short-term assets to care. The transparency Lessig seeks to create will either destroy the corruption it exposes or prove that not enough people care about it to prevent it. Fifty-eight percent of Americans already believe that government corruption is widespread. The major media already report on corporate corruption. But they can't consistently offer an account of why so much of our business is corrupt and prone to criminality. They are even less likely to pay attention to the ways in which we might change things through collective action. Will more lobbyists photographed in handcuffs activate a new generation of democratic participants, or further alienate them from the process? And how do we generally seek to change a system we believe to be corrupted by the influence of money? By raising money of our own to counter that influence.

From newspaper articles published on the same day in the summer of 2008, we learn that the two-million-member Service Employees International Union raised $75 million to help Barack Obama compete in battleground states; Health Care America was planning to spend $40 million on cable-TV ads to promote a national health plan; and MoveOn.org had raised $122 million since 1998 to help pay for political campaigns. All this cash was funneled to cable networks and on-line advertising agencies, themselves subsidiaries of the corporations these efforts are targeted against. Furthermore, by choosing to tangle with corporatism on its own highly branded, emotionally driven land-scape, these efforts are at the very least compromised. They do not serve to reengage people with the reality they have left behind, but to push them further into the ethereal realm of satiric YouTube videos that feed the corporations we think we're resisting.

The Fourth Estate is made up almost entirely of large corporations. And media companies cannot make any distinction between the mar-ket value of information and its importance. Britney Spears's latest breakdown and the invasion of Iraq are both treated as major media events deserving of equal time and space. In the face of all this, the hippest way out is to adopt the attitude of amused and quizzical cyni-cism worn by Stephen Colbert and Jon Stewart.

Besides, no matter how critical of corporatism some entertainers and journalists might be, the impact of their arguments is undercut by their dependence on corporatized media for dissemination. Stephen Colbert and Jon Stewart work for Viacom. Naomi Klein writes for a division of the German publisher Verlagsgruppe Georg von Holtzbrinck, and this book is published by a subsidiary of Bertelsmann. We all have mort-gages to pay. Even most progressive journalism—just like the kind that emerged in the early 1900s—tends to frighten and isolate the middle classes rather than bring them out of their homes to improve their com-munities. Populists such as cable TV's Glenn Beck or Lou Dobbs, speaking on behalf of working stiffs, stoke more rage and discontent than thoughtful engagement. In the isolation of our living rooms and surrounded by bills, the menaces of immigrants willing to take our jobs for less pay and affirmative-action candidates offered our jobs with fewer qualifications feel all too real.

Experiencing all this through the sensationalist lens of Big Media only reduces our connection to the real world in which all this stuff is supposedly occurring. We seek to take on our institutional enemies vicariously through our late-night comedians, or "directly" through our laptops. We get to enter contests through which we can compete to create the most effective video ad for an issue or a candidate. We can make viral documentaries that no matter how painstakingly re-searched end up indistinguishable from ones pushing the most para-noid and baseless conspiracy theories.

The problem with fighting "Big Blank" on its own turf and terms is that it has more money, more access to the government and media through which the battle takes place, better command of the symbols and semantics that sway public sentiment, and much more time to spend waiting for the results it wants. Real people working against it, on the other hand, need to keep alive, employed, and motivated. We need to steer clear of actionable copyright violation and libel, shield ourselves from the emotional damage caused by Internet "trolls" paid to insult or lie about us online, and still manage to maintain an audience willing to listen to what we have to say and then to actually *do* something about it instead of just nodding, passing on a link, and closing the computer for the night.

We cannot market our way out of corporatism. While joining a big cause or a national political campaign may feel good for a moment, it can easily turn immediate, local, and actionable problems into great big abstract ones. The pollution leaching out of the local factory is hard to confront directly, and easier to address instead as part of a bigger environmental movement. Racism downtown can be addressed more painlessly by donating to a black candidate or a scholarship fund online. Carbon offsets, through which a person can pay an online company to counteract the effects of his air travel or air-conditioning, provide a virtual path to personal virtue—and a way for frequent fliers to recontextualize their actions right on their blogs for all to see.

This activity may be well intentioned, but it is chiefly concerned with finding ways to maintain our disconnection while still doing the right thing. Brands were invented to substitute for the real connections we had to people, places, and value. The brand was meant to disconnect, so branded movements and ideologies by their very nature tend toward polarization and extremism. Antiabortion and pro-choice constituencies are pushed to the edges by their highly branded, hotly worded campaigns, and thus less likely to rally around their common cause—reducing the number of unwanted pregnancies. While Saatchi & Saatchi's "loyalty beyond reason" might be great for a cereal's "consumer tribe," it's the surest path away from a reasonable engagement with real life's pressing issues. Activists on MySpace compete for numbers of "friends" willing to become associated with a particular cause, but fail to realize that signing on to a social cause is accomplished with the same mouse click as signing on to be a friend of the Nike Swoosh.

Employing the techniques of marketing to repair the ravages of corporatism is a losing proposition; branding only disconnects us further from the means to rebuild what we have lost. The medium becomes the message as Big Activism becomes just another Big Blank. By attempting to beat them at their own game, we become part of the very thing we should be dismantling.

Inside Jobs

Those with the most experience trying to change the system still seem to feel that the best results can be achieved by reworking it from the inside. Corporations are here to stay, they tell us, like it or not. Real people and local communities are too small and weak to attack them ourselves, but we can create corporate beasts of our own through which to combat them, or turn the ones already out there into better partners of the human species. Maybe, just maybe, we can even create corporations whose mandate is to do good—or, at the very least, like those sci-fi machines programmed with Isaac Asimov's "Laws of Robotics," do no evil.

The nonprofit corporation has been around for a while, but has waned in strength and popularity as the laws of the market dominate thinking about business. More often than not, the regulations on nonprofit activities are seen as an unnecessary hindrance, making it much harder for such companies to maneuver around their stated mandates. Lower salaries and profiles in the nonprofit sector also tended to attract executives with less ambition than their counterparts. Foundations ended up with large bureaucracies, too much middle management, and too many executives looking for a temporary and respectable place to hang their hats while waiting for a cabinet position or an agency post in the next friendly administration.

By the end of the dot-com boom, the sustainable business philosophies of thinkers like Paul Hawken, combined with a fervent faith in the power of the market, led many entrepreneurs to conclude that they could have their cake and eat it, too. High-tech entrepreneurs, wealthy but disillusioned with how they became that way, cashed out of their businesses and were hungry for some meaningful work. Why not create real companies that make real profits by addressing genuine global needs? The world needs wind power, Internet connectivity, private schools, and cures for diseases. There are certainly enough causes that can be addressed by a traditional corporate structure.

A relatively new species of corporation, called the fourth-sector company (meant to combine the best of the public, private, and voluntary sectors), rose to meet the combined challenge of social purpose and financial promise. It would adhere to the new "triple bottom line" of making money, caring for the environment, and treating labor humanely. The problem is, corporations are guided by strict tax and legal rules limiting their investment in anything that can't be tied directly to revenue. While the socially responsible policies of fourth-sector companies might save money in the long run, a lot of the savings are external to the bottom line of the company itself, or too far in the future to be readily quantified.

And 1, a shoe company in Pennsylvania, was committed to maintaining the health of its employees and giving back to its community by funding after-school programs. The company shunned sweatshop practices, provided a gym for its employees, and even hired an independent auditor to monitor its charitable donations. Though the company was privately held, its directors were still under a fiduciary responsibility to its investors and shareholders to maximize their returns. As the company grew too big for its original management to handle effectively, they were obligated to sell the business to a larger company that ended most of And 1's fourth-sector activities.

Ben & Jerry's, another company started by entrepreneurs who genuinely sought to do good, faced an even steeper set of challenges. After opting to become a publicly traded company, the ice-cream maker was at the mercy of shareholders with different agendas than its founders. They voted to sell the company to the food giant Unilever, which now uses what is left of the brand's integrity to strengthen its public image. (Of course, the very notion of operating an ice-cream company as a way to improve the social conditions of an obese nation struggling with runaway diabetes raises questions of its own.) Undermining their foundational premise, corporations that succeed in their initial missions of creating socially responsible but financially profitable enterprises are soon weighed down by their own success. The money has a bias and an agenda of its own.

Wealthy entrepreneurs who understand this seek instead to donate their personal winnings to worthy causes. Without damaging the company's balance sheet, well-meaning directors can contribute their own shares to charitable organizations and even take a tax deduction for the value of the gift. In some cases, however, these donations end up making the donors money while reducing the tax base for regular social services. Less total funding goes to those who need it. A study by the Stern School of Business at New York University revealed that corporate executives often make large gifts of their company's stock to their family foundations shortly before the stock drops. Exploiting a loophole that applies to charitable donations but not to regular stock sales, executives can backdate their donations to a moment in recent history when the stock value was high. This allows them to take a tax credit much higher than the real value of the stock at the time they parted with it. According to the study, which covered about a quarter of all donations made by CEOs and corporate chairmen, these are not isolated incidents but a standard practice.

Most corporate donations also have much more to do with their self-interest than service. In one year, Philip Morris spent $60 million on charitable programs and then another $108 million advertising the fact that they had done so. Specialty firms have arisen to help match corporate donors with charities that meet their specific public-relations needs. Such "context-focused" giving allows corporations to counteract the negative perceptions associated with their particularly noxious behaviors. Companies with bad labor practices can support education, those with bad environmental records can sponsor trash-pickup days, and those making products that make people sick can support disease research. When ExxonMobil pays for a park or Wal-Mart supports a K–12 education program, some of the environmental or social damage their companies create is indeed mitigated. But it is not outweighed. Our sense that "it's better than nothing" just camouflages the underlying causes of the corporation's irresponsibility.

Even the best-intentioned family foundations often find themselves working against their stated purpose. The philanthropic strategy is to siphon off a portion of a family's corporate winnings and invest them in a nonprofit foundation that lasts essentially forever. Bill Gates stunned the world when, after a few decades of low-profile donations, he launched the Gates Foundation and endowed it with 35 billion of his own dollars. As the ultimate software entrepreneur and sometimes-richest man in the world, he restored the nonprofit sector's faith in an entire generation of newly rich dot-com executives.

The foundation's work fighting disease in Africa almost makes our suffering through the Windows operating system seem worth it.

Still, the problem with setting aside $35 billion in cash is that it has to be invested to retain its value. The 95 percent of Gates Foundation holdings that aren't spent on charities each year often work against the very causes the foundation tries to champion. A study by the *Los Angeles Times* revealed that 41 percent of Gates Foundation investments have been in companies that counter the foundation's charitable goals or socially concerned philosophy. These include investments in companies such as Dow Chemical, ConocoPhillips, and Tyco, which are excluded from mutual funds that screen for irresponsible behavior or poor environmental stewardship. As Paul Hawken explains, "Foundations donate to groups trying to heal the future, but with their investments, they steal from the future." The Gates Foundation invests significantly more money in the darkest regions of the corporate sphere than it donates to all its charities combined. It holds $1.5 billion of stock in the very drug companies whose pricing policies are restricting the flow to Africa of medicines that the foundation is supposedly trying to get there.

This is not a mere kink in the system that can be ironed out with a bit more thought. The problem is that amassing a huge wad of cash and then doling it out through a centralized foundation is structurally biased toward exacerbating corporatism, not reducing it. Remember, money isn't real, but at least once removed from the labor, people, services, and goods that earned it. It is not a generic store of energy, but an extremely biased, nationalized, and costly means of exchange. The capitalization and maintenance of a multibillion-dollar foundation is not a neutral event, but one with a tremendous impact on both the economy and the social ecology from which the value has been extracted. Not even the most diligent "triple-bottom-line" approach to corporate and foundation governance takes the biases of operating this way into account.

Instead of participating directly, as human beings, in the restoration of the social fabric, most corporate charities participate by proxy through money, and from a great distance. Even when they're not intended as cynically devised tax breaks or public-relations stunts, these funds function as modern institutional indulgences, offsetting ongoing sins with cash. Like energy and environmental offsets, they give corporations a way to remain as they are.

Corporations may simply be the wrong tools for the job. The way they operate is itself the problem. The Bible's proto-activist, Isaiah, told us to turn our swords into plowshares, but this involves melting them down and transforming them into completely different objects with very different functional biases. Corporations help people and communities create value about as well as swords till the soil. It's not what they were built for. The corporation excels at extracting value from communities and reducing their ability to take care of themselves.

New technologies, new charters, and new personalities don't change this basic fact. The Google corporation may tell its workers that the company lives by the credo "Don't be evil," but its operations and business model are classically corporatist and singularly opportunistic. The company's main claim to virtue is that it fights for "open systems" in all media and on all platforms. Technologically, this means preventing cell-phone companies from locking their phones, Internet providers from blocking certain activities, and wireless carriers from restricting downloads. Practically speaking, open systems mean keeping systems open to Google and its millions of advertisements.

Just as the U.S. and Europe used the "charity" of the World Bank to open markets for their corporate activity, Google uses its goodwill and industry dominance to open systems for its corporate activity. While the rhetoric of open markets seemed to promote an ideology of democracy and equal opportunity, it actually promoted an agenda of resource and labor exploitation. Likewise, Google's push for all competitors to create open systems is really just a way for Google to leverage its existing monopoly into each and every emerging technology. An open system means open to Google.

Famously rejecting its own demand for openness, Google agreed to cripple its search tools for use in China at the request of the government there, which insists on limiting people's access to ideas it deems dangerous or corrupting. Google censored search results as the Chinese government requested. The alternative would have been no Google at all for the Chinese—an unthinkable denial of service for those who really do believe that Google is the next stage of human evolution. But by providing a crippled version of Google to the Chinese people, Google hides from them what is really going on. By refusing them service under the Chinese government's terms, Google would have made a much clearer and more honest communication to everyone. By enabling instead of rejecting Chinese repression, Google also maintains a toehold in the biggest emerging Internet market of all time.

Free-market advocates argue that eventually, perhaps not without some pain, the market will correct any evils of corporate activity. Now that consumers are increasingly aware of the impact of their purchases and willing to vote with their dollars, any corporation behaving inconsistently with market demand will change, get "restructured," or perish. Then, new management, new shareholders, or an altogether new and smarter company will rise in its place, like a phoenix from the ashes, to address the unmet or newly articulated needs. What this analysis leaves out is the collateral damage that may have occurred in the meantime.

For example, after Big Media successfully lobbied for the Telecommunications Act of 1996, the limit on how many radio stations one corporation could own went from forty to no limit at all. Over the next five years, the radio industry consolidated, and Clear Channel Communications emerged as the biggest player, with over 1,200 radio and thirty-nine TV stations. Clear Channel is five times bigger than its closest competitor, and reaches one hundred million listeners daily. It uses this leverage to market over thirty million tickets each year to shows in its forty-four amphitheaters across the United States.

Clear Channel exercised highly centralized control over what had been a highly local form of media. Its central office chose the playlists, wrote the news, and even provided studio space for some of the disc jockeys, who began to broadcast their shows from locations thousands of miles away from the cities where their voices supposedly originated. Diversity of music decreased by every measure, stations lost their local character, songs were chosen for their ability to influence ticket sales, and the culture of radio deteriorated. With no more authority over their playlists and no hope for a direct connection with their constituencies, DJs who weren't already fired left the industry. FM radio stations sold their extensive libraries of music, laid off their staffs, and became remote-broadcasting hubs for content replicated across the country. But radio could not successfully scale this way. As stations became bland, redundant, and delocalized, listeners turned away. Advertising revenues went down, and Clear Channel began selling off its radio assets.

Once dismantled, however, radio's culture can't simply re-form from the ground up. Radio had developed slowly over the course of close to a century. In the single decade that Clear Channel dominated radio, the industry's collective capital and expertise was spent or dismissed. The seasoned staff of an FM music station can't be reassembled any more easily than its collection of out-of-print records can. An audience that may have taken decades to develop cannot simply be called back.

The Clear Channel story, like those of the failed record and automotive industries, reveals the flaw in thinking that the damage caused by corporatism will be corrected by the market. Business is just one part of the social ecology in which it operates. The nonliving part. While a corporation can be replaced by another piece of capitalized paper overnight, a social ecology in a real place takes decades or more to develop. Once destroyed, social capital can't simply be borrowed from the bank by the next corporation, even if that corporation has seen the light and now wants to do the right thing.

CHAPTER NINE

HERE AND NOW

The Opportunity to Reconnect

The Melt-Up

As highly corporatized people, it's only natural for those of us interested in addressing our social and environmental rehabilitation to do so from within our roles as employees, consumers, and maybe shareholders. We rarely relate to one another very directly as it is, so it's a bit much to expect us to engage together in a pursuit as foolhardy as the reinstatement of the social fabric.

Instead, like corporations, we tend to prefer to express our charitable and community impulses from afar. Lord knows there are plenty of people who need our help, and their advocates seem quite happy to accept our donations in whatever denominations we have to offer. So, like Oprah Winfrey setting up a private school for girls in Africa instead of in her native Chicago, we are more ready to write a check for literacy in the ghetto than to go to the projects ourselves and teach a kid to read. We'd rather send a donation to a Middle East peace fund than engage directly with violence-endorsing extremists at our own place of worship. We prefer to PayPal our support of a homeless teen folksinger with a great pitch on his Facebook page than approach those homeless kids we keep seeing in the grocery-store parking lot.

People who actively participate in addressing these problems are considered heroes because their selfless contributions reach far beyond our own capacity to act. Doctors Without Borders volunteers donate their time and risk their lives to fly to war zones, disasters, and refugee camps to save lives. Computer hackers started an organization called Free Geek to wire up schools and refurbish cast-off computers for underprivileged communities. VolunteerMatch connects people with communities that require their skills to repair infrastructure, provide child care, or deliver meals to the homebound. Thank goodness for all of them, but most of them are either wealthy enough, young enough, or simply inspired enough to make such extraordinary efforts.

The rest of us just don't have the time, the energy, or the commitment to take a hands-on approach to anything but work and maybe family. We want to do right by the environment, but we still want to take two adults and two children to Disneyland for under a couple of thousand bucks. The best among us buy some carbon offsets online, as if to compensate for our addiction to oil the way an OxyContin addict snorts a line of speed when he gets to work. By the time we've used the Visa card to buy the offsets, we've involved a dozen corporations with their own biases and agendas in the offsetting of a branded Disney vacation that was itself planned to offset a desocialized and unfabulous life at home.

By donating to charities in the same manner as our corporate equivalents, we succumb to the proxy system that desocializes in the first place. Yes, sharing our cash with the needy is a great thing. If we're lucky enough, we might even end up contributing to the creation of an infrastructure that—against all odds—actually helps people address their basic needs through their own independent activity. But such steps do not address the more basic problem of *our own* disconnection from the real world, and the way that disconnection perpetuates the corporatist drive to disconnect us all further.

Some innovative approaches to charity have emerged that provide money where it is needed while still catering to this impulse for disconnected giving. Kiva.org lets donors lend money to entrepreneurs from the developing world. Visitors to the site can scroll over pictures of craftspeople, bakers, and fishmongers from Mali, Togo, or Bolivia, read their stories, and lend money in twenty-dollar increments. The micro-loans really go to the fledgling businesspeople who need them, and the donor gets a sense of connection to a real human being without ever getting up from the laptop.

Is this good for the developing world? On its own, of course it is. But the whole, heartwarming, electronic process caters to a lifestyle characterized by rushed and disconnected activity. It doesn't stop the way the donor's day job might be causing the problem; it only mitigates a bit of the effect and assuages a bit of the guilt.

DonorsChoose.org has achieved terrific success getting money to classrooms that need it. Teachers post requests for supplies and visitors to the site can choose which pleas to answer. While it's less efficient than simply taking donations and doling them out, first come first served, it gives donors the experience of picking the priorities, objects, and faces that appeal to them. More constructively, DonorsChoose lets users search by location to find out what might be needed in their own or a neighboring community. Still, even local needs are kept at a distance. When I searched for my neighborhood on the site, I found a teacher somewhere in the county looking for funds to start a comic library at her elementary school. I have a few hundred comics I'd like to donate. But because the site keeps the requesters' identities anonymous, I've been unable to figure out who she is.

Fittingly, the first example of a website configured to let potential donors choose between the causes they wanted to support came from the satirical corporate activist group ®™ark in the late 1990s. Exploiting a "market system" made up of activist "mutual funds" and individual "projects," the agitprop performance group let users anonymously support real and imaginary guerrilla activism of sometimes questionable legality, such as raising money to disassemble the Statue of Liberty and send it back to France, or organizing people to shout at movie screens while advertisements play. The distance created between "investors" and pranksters was deliberately calculated to protect donors from repercussions, and to satirize the way the Internet promotes social action by proxy. To the surprise of ®™ark's founders, serious social-action networks have adopted their market-driven methodology as a valid form of participation. If people are given the power to choose their causes, the most important ones are supposed to naturally rise to the top of the heap.

Those of us content to work through proxy certainly have plenty of options available to us. We can vote with our dollars or donate to the political-action groups who we think might restore the social balance.

Today's brands will have us believe that we save the rain forest through our choice of cereal and preserve endangered species with our choice of parka. Websites and magazines teach us how to consume our way to a green world, without acknowledging that their promotion of consumption is itself the core problem. And all of these options offer us the vicarious thrill of contributing to an effort we believe in without disrupting the underlying structures maintaining the status quo—or our own busy schedules.

Political candidates, however boldly they promote change, brand themselves as meticulously as Madison Avenue brands soap powder. We join their movements to help them get elected, and then sit back and wait for them to deliver. Movements, as such, encourage less solidarity than they do individuality. Like brands, they communicate to the masses as individuals, encouraging them to develop what feel like personal relationships with the hero or mythology at the top. When populated by real people willing to take to the streets, they can effectively address or at least publicize collective social causes, from civil rights to AIDS. But in their current form, as media campaigns, consumer tribes, or Internet discussions, they are not an antidote to corporatism.

Too often, the product or candidate hovers above the group, directing all attention toward the distant ideal. Instead of representing our will in the legislative process, they substitute for our true participation in the social and political process. We come out once every four years, get very upset when our plan to change the world by proxy doesn't work out, and then go back to our regularly scheduled programming. Not a great plan for reconnection to the things that matter.

Charity, environmentalism, and politics are all worthwhile endeavors. But practiced this way, they don't change our relationship to the ground, people, and values from which we have become untethered. They do nothing to help us disengage from the myths through which we abdicate responsibility, nor do they help us reclaim our roles as living participants in the creation of the society in which we want to live.

We may not have as much time as we'd like to figure it out. As of this writing, personal bankruptcies, home foreclosures, environmental meltdowns, energy prices, job losses, the national debt, the trade deficit, plant closings, health-care costs, the numbers of uninsured adults, forced evictions, corporate corruption, credit defaults, and school dropouts are at or near record highs. Most of our biggest corporations will be fine; many are already moving operations and assets offshore just in case domestic financial markets take longer than expected to recover, and they're enjoying tremendous tax benefits for their trouble. Even bankruptcy is just a means of "protection." The company gets to reorganize and see another day, free of obligations to health plans and retirees. The only ones in trouble are the humans they leave in their wake.

Widespread pessimism about the state of our economy and social fabric has led to an almost counter-phobic fascination with disaster. Recommendations from local authorities to store a week's worth of water, food, duct tape, and medical supplies call to mind long-forgotten *Twilight Zone* episodes in which families fight over access to bomb shelters. Nightmarish movies in which human survivors hole up in abandoned buildings to weather zombie or vampire pandemics feed the paranoid fantasies of a growing survivalist movement. Websites and radio shows instruct us to buy gold for savings, and smaller silver denominations to trade for food after the economy completely collapses. (Plus a handgun for self-defense and maybe a motorcycle to cut through the traffic jams surrounding our metropolitan areas.)

For many, the apocalypse is less a looming fear than a secret wish. Like Y2K enthusiasts, who predicted that planes would fall from the sky when computers attempted to register four-digit years, we're almost giddy at the thought of our dehumanizing infrastructure crumbling under its own weight. One well-targeted electromagnetic pulse and our debts are erased along with our credit scores. No more Black-Berries. What a relief! We can all go back to the simple life. There's only one catch: all of a sudden, essential skills from which we've been so long disconnected—how to grow food, how to find water, how to build a shelter—will be at a premium. For better or for worse, real people would be called upon to create real value.

Our morbid obsession with doom may hint at something entirely less apocalyptic—something that we hope to gain from a world suddenly devoid of corporatism. If the complex supply chains and economic schemes we use to feed, clothe, shelter, and care for ourselves stopped working, might we possibly develop the ability to provide even some of these basic needs for ourselves and one another? Are we good enough friends with a farmer to ask him for some crops? Do we have anything, as members of his extended community, to offer in return?

The current financial meltdown brings such scenario planning out of the world of fantasy and into the realm of possibility. Financial websites are already advising consumers how illiquidity could affect the ability of a supermarket chain to stock its shelves, a gas utility to keep heating fuel in the pipes, or a medical insurer to make good on its promised reimbursements. Having grown so absolutely dependent on corporations and their debt for our daily functioning and sense of continuity, it's not surprising that our first reaction to Wall Street's implosion is to fund the companies in trouble. So, the public borrows more money from the central banks in order to feed the private sector's credit-vanquished corporations. Instead of merely having value extracted from us in the present, we volunteer our future earnings to keep the system running. Either that, or let the other shoe drop and expose the credit-based, artificial economy and its faulty premise of infinite expansion.

The debate on whether or not to refund the corporate sphere has so far fallen along familiar battle lines. Conservatives see themselves as free-market advocates, and adopt a posture of nonintervention. Regulation and impediments to free trade are what hampered corporations' ability to stay profitable in the first place, they argue. Those arguing for government bailouts and federally sponsored work programs, on the other hand, see this crisis as the opportunity to return corporations to public control, offer funds in return for more socially beneficial products, keep people employed, and restore the corporate sphere to health. They believe the free market has finally been "disproved."

But the distinctions are false. The free market is itself already sloped—highly regulated, in a sense—toward the interests of corporations and away from labor, small businesses, and local activity. If conservatives got their open marketplace and maintained a truly hands-off approach, most of the corporations they seek to liberate from government control would cease to exist. They couldn't survive on a level playing field, because corporations are themselves a byproduct of government regulation. Meanwhile, liberals who promote government investment in corporate debt might as well be arguing for privatizing Social Security. Bailouts, even in the form of recoupable investments, just tie us further to the fortunes of the corporate sphere. We end up with a stake in restoring their future ability to extract value from our society while providing as little as possible in return. These supposedly polarized policy positions are mirror images of the very same corporatism.

The alternative is to let government and business continue their debate about how to mitigate the most painful effects of the speculative economy's cyclical nature. In the meantime, we use the financial stalemate—however long it lasts—as an opportunity to identify the disconnections inherent in our overcorporatized society and try out some new strategies for rebuilding it from the bottom up. The corporate sphere ill serves human needs even when it's working as it's designed to. As corporate insolvency, home foreclosure, and unemployment increase, our financial system may prove incapable of providing us the essentials we need at prices we can afford. Through what mechanisms might we do this for one another, instead of depending on the distant companies who took this responsibility away from us before failing themselves?

We don't all need to move to communes or planned communities; we needn't stake out turf in the mountains for a dream chalet with solar panels. Extreme shifts like that only produce more consumption, waste, and trauma. Nor can we all suddenly quit our jobs working for corporations, sell all the depressed stock in our 401(k) plans, or completely stop using the existing fiscal system to conduct our business. We are dependent on corporations right now, and—however much influence they may lose in the short term—they're not going away anytime soon. We may not even want them to.

But we can't ask corporatized institutions from the private or public sectors to fix this mess for us, either. Just as Malcolm X rejected the help of white liberal groups, understanding that his community needed to learn to help itself, we humans cannot depend on entities biased toward repressing us to assist us in our quest to regain agency. Corporations can't save us, and we have more important business to attend to right now than obsessing over how to save *them*.

Instead, we can look to those who are reclaiming territory, creating value, and reconnecting with others in ways that we might actually be able to try ourselves. Small is the new big, and the surest path to global change in a highly networked world is to make an extremely local impact that works so well it spreads. This may amount to a new form of activism, but it is one without slogans, heroes, or glory. The efforts, and the rewards, are scaled to human beings.

Before her talk at the prestigious 2007 TED conference (an

invitation-only event where industry leaders and visionaries talk to wealthy ticket holders about technology and design), an environmental activist from the South Bronx approached Al Gore. She wanted to know how activists like her were going to be included in his campaign to promote the environmental agenda. He responded that he was developing a grant program. She calmly explained that she wasn't asking for funding—she was making *him* an offer to come to the table and participate in the decision-making process.

The woman, the environmental activist and MacArthur-grant winner Majora Carter, has the direct experience of revitalizing her own polluted ghetto and its forgotten community. Through her group, Sustainable South Bronx, she created opportunities for people to grow vegetables at home, to get paid to do environmental cleanup, and to work through local government to stop New York from using the neighborhood as a dumping site for 25 percent of the city's waste. Her main innovation was to develop a new method of rooftop gardening that provides high yields of organic vegetables for urban dwellers and local restaurants.

Carter engages in sustainable, bottom-up activism, through which ex-convicts, gang members, and the elderly work together to lower asthma rates among children, strengthen the local economy, and reduce residents' exposure to toxic materials. Once trained in landscaping, ecological restoration, green-roof installation, or hazardous-waste cleanup, they can find work elsewhere doing these necessary jobs. Perhaps surprisingly, people who go through the program and then find gainful employment do not move out of the neighborhood. They become the next set of teachers and investors in the Sustainable South Bronx community.

Efforts like these scale up in two ways. First, they are shared with or copied by other groups in other communities around the world. Rooftop gardens can work in any city to lower energy bills and clean the air while providing food and jobs. Sharing the wealth is not a matter of Sustainable South Bronx franchising patented techniques to other cities—there's enough work for them to do in the South Bronx, and they don't need to extract value from other cities in order to achieve sustainability for themselves. By modeling what they do for others, they develop a network through which they too can learn new techniques.

More significantly, the impacts of their highly local efforts trickle up in profound ways. Less pollution means fewer children with asthma, lower medical and insurance costs, and more time in school. Good job opportunities for convicts and gang members means less recidivism and expensive jail time—as well as lower profits for the corporations now providing prison services and less speculative investment encouraging incarceration. Pushing toxic waste out of one neighborhood forces the dumping corporations to find a new place for it; prices on processing garbage go up, and corporations are encouraged to make less trash in order to preserve their bottom line.

While rooftop agriculture may not feed our entire metropolitan population, plenty of other opportunities exist for those seeking a more direct connection with the people and places making their food. Community-supported-agriculture groups, or CSAs, let typical food consumers become members of their local agricultural community. Instead of buying Big Agra produce shipped long distances to the supermarket, people make a commitment to buy a season's worth of crops from a local farm and then either pay up front or by subscription over the course of a year. Some farms require their members to work a few hours during the growing season, others let members work in lieu of payment. In 1990, there were just fifty CSAs in the United States. By 2008 there were over one thousand.

With the commitment of a local population, small farmers can better coordinate against legislative and financial attacks by Big Agra concerns, maintain the environmental integrity of their soil, and promote the efficacy and health benefits of sustainable and organic methods. Members, meanwhile, insulate themselves from the influence of speculators on food commodities' prices, eat a range of foods planned by a farmer and nutritionist rather than a highly lobbied government subsidy, and restore the long-severed connection between urban and agricultural communities. The more demand there is for CSAs, the less there is for mass-produced, highly processed, and long-distance vegetables.

Moreover, it's fun. Members meet people from their community whom they may not already know. They participate in creating value with their time, their hands, or even just their money. Their kids understand that a carrot comes from the ground, not from a plastic bag with a bunny on it. Instead of paying for a convincingly authentic family vacation, they go to the farm and do something real.

The closer we get to the process through which food is grown and cattle are raised, the more direct experience we have of why grass-fed beef is better for all concerned, how rotating crops saves the topsoil, or whether limits should be placed on genetically altered seed. Instead of depending on the latest questionably sponsored news report (or camouflaged public-relations video segment) for our understanding of the issues determining the future of agriculture, we draw on our own successes.

The farmer running my CSA wanted to provide his members with an easy way to sign up for shifts and make special requests for their weekly food shares. An unemployed web designer I knew from the neighborhood built a site for the farmer that offered all this and more—in return he earned a year of crops.

These activities are the most remarkable, however, for the way that they cut out the middleman. People create value for one another directly, rather than paying the corporations that we work for. No one is extracting value from our engagements, separating us from our competencies, or distancing us from one another.

The one exception, of course, is the money we are still using to pay one another. When we aren't coding websites in return for kale, we are cutting the Federal Reserve and its network of banks in on every transaction we make. This extractive force is a drag on the system, particularly at times when speculation or banking-industry incompetence has made money too expensive to get a hold of, or too unstable to use as a means of exchange.

A tiny organic café in my town called Comfort decided to expand to a second, larger location. John, the chef and owner, had been renovating the new space for a year, but—thanks to the credit crisis—was unable to raise the cash required to finish and finally open. With currency unavailable from traditional, centralized money-lending banks, he turned instead to his community, to us, for support. Granted, this is a small town. Pretty much everybody goes to Comfort—the only restaurant of its kind on the small strip—and we all have a stake in its success. Any extension of Comfort would bring more activity, vitality, and commerce to a tiny downtown (commercially devastated in the 1970s by the chain stores and malls on the auto-friendly main strip).

So John's idea was to sell VIP cards, or what I helped him rename Comfort Dollars. For every dollar spent on a card, the customer receives the equivalent of $1.20 worth of credit at either restaurant. If I buy a thousand-dollar card, I get twelve hundred dollars' worth of food: a 20 percent rate of return on the investment of dollars. John gets the money he needs a lot cheaper than if he were borrowing it from the bank—he's paying for it in food and labor that he has in ample supply. Meanwhile, customers get more food for less money.

But wait, there's more: the entire scheme reinvests a community's energy and cash locally. Because our money goes further at our own restaurant than at a restaurant somewhere else, we are biased toward eating locally. Since we have a stake in the success of the restaurant in whose food we have invested, we'll also be more likely to promote it to our friends. By using its own currency, a local business can even undercut the corporate competition. It's not complex or even communist. It's just local business, late Middle Ages style.

Local currencies are now used by several hundred communities across the United States and Europe, giving people the chance to buy and sell goods and services from one another no matter what the greater economy might be doing. Instead of favoring large, centralized corporations, local currencies favor businesses and the community members who own them.

There are two main types of local currency employed today. The simplest, like Comfort Dollars or the BerkShares created for the entire Berkshire Hills region in Massachusetts, have exchange rates for regular dollars. The BerkShares themselves can be spent only at local businesses that accept them, which keeps the currency circulating close to home. Local currencies such as these encourage local buying, put large corporations with no real community involvement at a big disadvantage, and circulate much more widely and rapidly through a community than conventional dollars. Further, the nonprofit bank issuing BerkShares is not an extractive force; no one needs to get rich or pay anyone back. Businesses that refuse to accept the local currency do worse than just brand themselves as apathetic to local development; they cut themselves off from a potential source of revenue.

Townspeople with their own money systems still need conventional currency. The three automobile repair shops in Great Barrington that accept BerkShares must still buy auto parts from Mopar or BMW with U.S. dollars. But they are willing to break down their bills into two separate categories, selling parts at cost in U.S. dollars, and markups and labor in the local currency. The object is not to replace centralized currency altogether, but to break the monopoly of centralized currency and the corporations it supports over transactions that keep money circulating locally. This is why many advocates now call local currency "complementary" currency—because it complements rather than replaces centralized money.

It's not as anarchist as it might sound. Larger businesses have begun to embrace alternative currency systems as well. In October 2008, as the credit crisis paralyzed business lending, companies started signing onto barter networks in droves. One system, called ITEX, which allows businesses to trade merchandise, reported a 37 percent increase in registrations for the month of October alone. Utilizing more than two hundred fifty exchange services now available through the Internet, companies can barter directly with one another, or earn U.S.-dollar-equivalent credits for the merchandise they supply to others. According to Barter News.com, business-to-business bartering already accounts for $3 billion of exchanges annually in the United States. As the credit crisis continues, this figure is growing exponentially.

An even more promising variety of complementary currency, like the grain receipts of ancient times, is quite literally earned into existence. "Life Dollars," such as those used by the Fourth Corner Exchange in the Pacific Northwest, are not exchanged for traditional currency. Instead, members of the Fourth Corner Exchange earn credits by performing services or providing goods to one another. There's always enough money, because money is a result of work exchanged, not an existing store of coin. There can't be too much money, either, since every service provided is a service someone else was willing to be debited for.

These local or complementary currencies, and many others, are as easy to begin as visiting the websites for local economic transfer systems (LETS) or Time Dollars. A local currency system can be as informal as a babysitting club, where parents earn credits for babysitting one another's children, or robust enough to serve as the primary currency for an entire region or sector.

In 1995, as recession rocked Japan, unemployment rose and currency became scarce. This made it particularly difficult for people to continue to take care of their elderly relatives, who often lived in distant areas. Everyone had time, but no one had money. The Sawayaka Welfare Foundation developed a complementary currency by which a young person could earn credits for taking care of an elderly person. Different tasks earned different established credit awards—bathing someone earned more than shopping, and so on. Accumulated credits—Fureai Kippu, or "elderly care units"—could then be applied to the care of one's own relative in a distant town, saved for later, or traded to someone else. Independently of the centralized economy—which thanks to bad speculation and mismanaged banking was no longer supporting them—people were able to create value for themselves and one another.

Although that particular financial crisis has passed, the Fureai Kippu system has only grown in popularity. At last count, the alternative currency was accepted at 372 centers throughout Japan, and patients surveyed said they like the care they get through the Fureai Kippu system better than what they get from professional service agencies. Thanks to the success of the Fureai Kippu and other pioneering models, close to a thousand alternative currencies are now in use in Japan.

Complementary currencies make it easier to record and administrate value exchange in an increasingly decentralized marketplace. They initiate the process through which local regions or specific sectors learn to create value for themselves instead of having it drained unnecessarily by an artificially chartered monopoly entity. They remind us that some of the things we have in abundance are still valuable, even though markets have not yet been created for them. And they give us a way to transact business during a recession or depression, when central banks and treasuries are more consumed with their own solvency and that of the speculative economy than they are with our ability to conduct the basic transactions through which we take care of one another.

Local currencies are just one possible step in the slow subordination of market activity to social activity, and corporate behavior to human behavior. After all, we don't spend time volunteering in our public school because we want to earn local credits; we do it to make the place better for our kids. The psychological hurdle to cross is the inability to accept that ten thousand dollars' worth of one's time spent making a local school better will create more value than thirty thousand dollars of one's money spent on a private school. The money guarantees a great education for our own kid; the time improves the school for everyone's kids. Still plagued by internalized competition and self-interest, most of us are not quite ready to choose the better path, or to convince our neighbors to join us in the effort. Luckily, a desperate lack of funds and employment opportunities can help nudge us toward the more socially beneficial choice.

But the more social we get, the more one voluntary act will encourage another one, and so on. We learn it's more fun and less time-consuming to provide real help to our local elementary school than to take on an extra corporate job to pay for that private one. We reverse the equation through which we calculate how much money we'll need to insulate ourselves from the world in which we live, and instead how much we can get from and give to that world with no money at all. Reciprocity is not a market phenomenon; it is a social one. And when the market is no longer functioning properly, it is a necessary life skill.

This is where the Internet might even be of some help. Instead of just giving existing fringe groups the imagery and anonymity they need to reinforce their secret cynicism, these networks can also connect those looking to reinforce their sense of hope and connection to others. We can share new models that work, collaborate with like-minded members of other communities, and build decentralized constituencies to fight our common battles. Beneath all its flashy, ad-based social networks, the Internet is still a communications medium, after all. We can use it to find the people and ideas deemed unready for corporate media's precious prime time.

Perhaps more important, by restoring our connections to real people, places, and values, we'll be less likely to depend on the symbols and brands that have come to substitute for human relationships. As more of our daily life becomes dictated by the rules of a social ecology instead of those of a market economy, we will find it less necessary to resort to the behavior of corporations whenever things get rough. We might be more likely to know the names of our neighbors, and value them for more than the effect of their landscaping on our block's real-estate prices.

I've offered a few suggestions here, but the ones you'll find will be more particular to your life, your neighborhood, and your situation. That's the whole point: one size does not fit all. Although corporatism offers itself up as a universal answer to our needs, it really just reduces the myriad complexity of human need down to individual selfishness. This monolithic approach to society and its recovery is antisocial in intent, dehumanizing in effect, and, dare I repeat it, fascist in spirit.

It's also entirely temporary. We will either arrest corporatism, or it will arrest us.

Instead of fighting corporations with corporations of our own, or working through corporations to reduce their negative impact on our society, we're better off reinventing ourselves as humans. We live on a terrain and in a dimension they can pollute but to which they will never belong. By working on this human-scaled landscape instead, we can create the changes in our own lives and communities that stand a chance, in aggregate, of trickling up and changing how the big world operates as well.

We can't look for those kinds of changes overnight. The grand expectations we have for ourselves and our achievements are really just the false promises of consumerism, brand culture, and the politics of revolutionary change. This is the ideological heritage of the Renaissance, and what brought us into the cycle of utopian hopes and alienated cynicism we're churning through today.

We'd each like to launch a national movement, create the website that teaches the world how to build community from the bottom up, develop the curriculum that saves public schools, or devise the clever antimarketing media campaign that breaks the spell of advertising once and for all. But these ego trips are the artifacts of the strident individualism we were taught to embrace. The temptation to save the whole world—and get the credit—comes at the expense of steps we might better take to make our immediate world a more fruitful, engaging, sustainable, and satisfying place. A successful movement depends on getting attention from media and institutions that are dead set against recognizing our ability to create value ourselves, and for its own sake. The minute they find out what we're up to, it's their job to dash our hopes and return our attention to the false idols they're selling us.

We'll run into obstacles soon enough. A friend of mine—from the genuinely activist culture fighting to stay in Park Slope—is building bicycle lanes throughout Brooklyn and has fought with enough legislators for zoning changes that he now knows his way around City Hall. A collective in the Midwest outfitting their homes with solar panels is in a battle with the utility company to be permitted to sell the electricity they create back through the power grid. Parents in Pennsylvania got themselves elected to the school board so that they could give themselves permission to teach computer skills to their own public-school teachers, whose union originally resisted teachers' being forced to get online. Once we start reinvesting in our local reality and reaping the returns, the corporatized institutions accustomed to extracting this value at our expense—be they private or public—will do their best to stall our progress.

Finally, we must fight the notion that redirecting our concerns in this fashion represents a retreat into provincial self-interest. The efforts may be local, but the effects are global. Every gallon of gas we don't burn is a few bucks less going to exploit someone in the Middle East. Every student we educate properly has more potential to create value for us all. Every plate of chard we grow is another patch of topsoil saved, another square foot of room on a truck, and another nail in the coffin of Big Agra. Every Little League game we coach is an assault on the obesity epidemic, every illiterate adult we teach to read may become one fewer welfare case to fund, and every hour we spend with friends is that many eyeballs fewer glued to the TV. The little things we do are big, all by themselves.

The best reason to begin reconnecting with real people, places, and value is that it feels good. Happiness doesn't come from the top down, but from the bottom up. The moment we think of ourselves as part of a movement, instead of real people, will be the moment we are much more susceptible to being disheartened or sidetracked by the business page, the terror alert, and the never-ending call to self-interest.

But real people doing real things for one another—without expectations—is the very activity that has been systematically extracted from our society over the past four hundred years through the spectacular triumph of corporatism. And this local, day-to-day, mundane pleasure is what makes us human in the first place.

BUT WAIT: THERE'S MORE

The Life Inc Guide to Reclaiming the Value You Create

Yes, there's hope. A lot of it. The economic crisis has laid bare a lot of what's wrong about the way we work and live. Many people are recognizing that we are running our society on obsolete software—legacy systems of money, government, and commerce that are simply incompatible with the modern, post-colonial world.

But it's hard for people to see past these obsolete systems, or that there's any option besides restoring them. It's hard to imagine how to start a business without a loan, how to get goods and services without dollars, how to work without finding a company to offer employment, or how to invest or save without banks or the stock market. We are so used to working through corporate institutions, we have trouble imagining alternatives for any of our activities.

It's not that we have to get rid of corporations or stop working through them entirely, however. They are great for making smart phones, building bridges, shipping crude oil, or developing medical devices. But they're less effective on the local level, when people might actually be able to serve one another's needs more efficiently, and in ways that encourage transaction, sustainability, and meaningful employment.

After finishing this book, I visited Lansing, Michigan, devastated by the collapse of General Motors. Most people I spoke with wanted to know how they could convince GM to reopen a plant, or a big bank to invest cash in their town. Until then, they believed, they were all out of work. Under the false assumption that money creates jobs (instead of the other way around), they were looking for an external injection to kick-start their economy—even though it would ultimately result in a further extraction of value from their community.

What most of the people I engaged with over this past year couldn't fully grasp was that they already had all the necessary components for an economy: people with needs, and people with skills. Even land. All they were lacking was a means of exchanging the value that they could create for one another. There was plenty of work—just no cash in circulation with which to keep track of who was doing what for whom. All they needed to do was develop a simple alternative currency or barter system and they'd be back in business.

I realize that this suggestion sounds romantic—even old-fashioned. It may seem as if I'm suggesting we return to the Middle Ages, the last time our economy was characterized by peer-to-peer exchange. All I'm actually proposing is that we reinstate a few of the simple social and business practices that were made illegal back then. We don't stop using corporations; we merely re-introduce some other means of getting things done. Just as choosing to walk to work doesn't mean you have to get rid of your car, choosing to work and exchange with other people on a peer-to-peer basis doesn't mean eliminating all corporations from the landscape. We can coexist with them, each offering the other support and a backup plan. Corporations can come through with technology and infrastructure that support local business, while thriving local commerce provides an alternative source of employment and stability when corporations fail, as they did in Lansing.

Some readers, in less dire straits but just as committed to taking back the world from corporatism, felt daunted by how few specific suggestions I made for taking back the world. Joining a CSA (community supported agriculture) group sounds, well, just too easy to fix any big problem, and too inconvenient to bother with. Or a babysitting club? Like that's going to take back the world?

I believe it can. And more important, *you* can.

In the opening chapter of the book, we looked at how each compromise we make to corporatism leads to further compromises. Choosing to purchase her prescriptions at Wal-Mart over the local pharmacy led one mother to stop attending Parent–Teacher Association meetings, for fear of running into her former druggist's wife. When public schools get worse, too many community members think they need to go it alone, and spend their time and energy trying to earn more money to pay for private school when they could be joining with other parents to make the public system better—from the bottom up. Decisions made under the fearful, self-interested presumption of corporatism reinforce one another in a negative feedback loop.

Likewise, each tiny choice we make to take back our world leads to a long chain of *positive* effects. Start a babysitting club and you form closer relationships with neighbors, you get more quality time with your spouse, you learn about your neighbors' kids and give your own kids more role models. You build a support system, a community, a network of friends, opportunities for employment, and you help to counter the isolation intentionally built into the suburban landscape. Join a CSA and you take back your nutrition from Big Agra, reduce your dependence on trucking and oil, challenge the artificial efficiencies of fast food, force reconsideration of zoning laws, and support organic practices—making them cheaper and more competitive in the process. Yes, little ideas and little choices are what matter—especially in a world where the big ones are the province of brands, lobbies, and other highly abstracted and centralized entities.

A young reporter for a major news magazine interviewed me about this book shortly after it came out. She couldn't understand how such big problems could be solved without similarly "big ideas"—as if one kind of problem demanded an equally sized solution. But real people don't engage with the world via big ideas. We engage through activities that are scaled to real life. Big ideas—at least the kind we recognize as big ideas—are for big entities: corporations, countries, continents. If we're going to begin operating on a human scale at least some of the time, then we must abandon the one-size-fits-all way of doing things. That's just another artifact of the Industrial Age and its bias toward highly mechanized, repeatable manufacturing.

By enacting small ideas, often on a local level, we reconnect with the innate power we have as living human beings. We reify the dignity of this scale of existence, and begin to experience the world from the perspective of people rather than that of the Dow Jones Industrial

Average. Plus, we regain our home-field advantage against corporate players that have yet to fully incarnate.

There are as many ways of engaging with the real world as there are real people—and just as many ways of creating and exchanging value, too. The rule book that works for one group in one region may not work for another. Besides—there's no need for us all to approach commerce and community the same way. That's a logic borrowed from corporatism, in which a single company wants to sell lots of the same thing to everyone. In the real world—the one we are restoring—people exchange ideas and models with one another, to use how they please.

So let's spread some of these ideas right here. In order to demonstrate just how accessible so many of these first steps are—as well as to give you some real and ready resources to begin—I have asked some people and organizations that are already taking back the world to share their strategies with you.

Some of the steps we can take to reclaim our world from corporatism may sound crunchy and leftie, while others might sound right wing or crassly commercial. I encourage you to read with an open mind, paying less attention to the political bias of each business or organization, and more to the way its founders solved problems, envisioned solutions, and drew support from other people rather than forming dependencies on banks and other corporations. These are each sustainable enterprises, built from the bottom up to answer real needs, employ real people, and contribute to making the world a better place.

And you could be doing any one of them.

PART ONE: Meet Your Neighbors

How to Start a Babysitting Co-op
by Carrie Tortorella (www.carrietom.com/babycoop.html)

Before having children, I read of moms who networked together to form a babysitting co-op, or a systematic plan to offer parents free and competent babysitting in the convenience of their own neighborhoods. A co-op is useful for appointments, shopping, and general uninterrupted time. It consists of a number of families in a community who decide to share babysitting among themselves without the exchange of money. Members should be able to leave their children without concern for their children's welfare and without financial restrictions.

If you decide to start one, figure out the needs of your community to decide how you'd like to integrate it into what is already in place. In my experience, I've found the following tips have helped with creating and running a successful co-op:

- Solicit interest by posting in free online forums such as Craigslist, put out flyers at churches or doctors' offices, or ask members from a moms' group, such as MOMS Club.
- Keep everyone within a tight geographic area for logistical ease.
- I recommend keeping the size of the co-op between eight and twenty families. Having too few families makes it difficult to find anyone available for your needs; yet too many families makes it less personal, difficult to organize, and can be cliquish.
- Decide on a trade system to use. Some find the "ticket system" is easier and more manageable because there's not a need for a designated monitor—although tickets are easy to misplace, and the trade is not always accurate or fair. The "tally system" used with a spreadsheet is accurate because it takes into account parts of the hour and specialized rules set up for babysitting more than one child; but it needs a designated person to keep score.
- Establish rules or bylaws to avoid confusion and misunderstandings. Examine other sets of club rules that can be found online for ideas and to cover all bases.
- Create an information sheet for all members to complete, including specifics about their family. This helps identify emergency contact information and reveals red flags without having to confront each member (such as guns or pools in the home, location and security of harmful chemicals, and names of other people living in the home, such as a nanny or an extended family member).
- Consider using organizational documents such as a one-page membership list or cheat sheet with phone numbers, children's names and ages, allergy concerns, and email addresses. These are great to post on the fridge for easy access in an emergency.
- Schedule regular meetings so members can get to know one

another and become familiar with family routines. Also, alternate meetings in one another's homes so members can feel comfortable with sending their children there.

- Having a variety of ages in the group makes it possible to match similarly aged playmates and also allow opportunities for older children to practice role modeling.
- Introduce your children to other members and their children beforehand, such as at meetings. Make sure your child knows the family with whom she or he will be spending time.
- Host annual or biannual functions, like a barbecue, and invite all members in each household. This helps reduce what I call the "heebie-jeebies" about having your children in others' homes. It allows members to become familiar with all members in each household.

I've created some resources to help our co-ops function, and uploaded them to my website: www.carrietom.com. Use them to create a co-op in your area, or improve one that you are already in.

Recycle Your Stuff
The Freecycle Movement (www.freecycle.org)
by Deron Beal, Founder

No one could have imagined that what began as a small circle of friends on May 1, 2003, would have evolved into the Freecycle movement of today. It was then that Deron Beal had a bed that he wished to recycle, but he discovered that the local thrift shops did not accept beds. In an effort to protect our planet and recycle a perfectly usable bed, he started a network of friends online and offered the bed. What began with only thirty members in 2003 has now developed into many millions of members worldwide.

The Freecycle Network is the largest environmental Web community on the planet, with nearly seven million members in more than ninety-five countries. This nonprofit gifting movement enables individuals to gift items in their local communities rather than throw them away, thus keeping more than 750 tons out of landfills daily. Freecycle was ranked by Yahoo as the third most searched environmental term on the planet, following only "global warming" and "recycling."

Lending credence to the network's motto of "Changing the world one gift at time," the number of items gifted in the past year is the equivalent of more than ten times the height of Mount Everest when stacked in garbage trucks—over five hundred million pounds.

Freecycle is globally local—each city has volunteer moderators and a unique email group. Anyone living in that city is then welcome to post items to be given away or to seek items that they might be able to use. Whether it is an old door, a pile of dirt, or a computer, it's probably being given away by one of the local groups already up and running as you read this article. Each local group is moderated by a local volunteer. Membership is free. To sign up, visit www.freecycle.org.

When you want to find a new home for something—whether it's a chair, a fax machine, piano, or an old door—you simply send an email offering it to members of the local Freecycle group. Or maybe you're looking to acquire something yourself. Simply respond to a member's offer. After that, it's up to the giver to decide who receives the gift and to set up a pickup time for passing on the treasure.

Liberate a basement near you and keep usable items out of the landfill in the process!

Get Your Food Locally
by the People at LocalHarvest (www.localharvest.org)

Through LocalHarvest, you can find farmers' markets, family farms, and other sources of sustainably grown food in your area, where you can buy produce, grass-fed meats, and many other goodies.

Why Buy Local?
Most produce in the United States is picked four to seven days before being placed on supermarket shelves, and is shipped for an average of fifteen hundred miles before being sold. And this is when taking into account only U.S.-grown products! Those distances are substantially longer when we take into consideration produce imported from Mexico, Asia, Canada, South America, and other places.

We can only afford to do this now because of the artificially low energy prices that we currently enjoy, and by externalizing the environmental costs of such a wasteful food system. We do this also to the detriment of small farmers by subsidizing large-scale, agribusiness-oriented agriculture with government handouts and artificially cheap energy.

Cheap oil will not last forever, though. World oil production has already peaked, according to some estimates, and while demand for energy continues to grow, supply will soon start dwindling, sending the price of energy through the roof. We'll be forced then to reevaluate our food systems and place more emphasis on energy-efficient agricultural methods such as smaller-scale organic agriculture and local production wherever possible.

Cheap energy and agricultural subsidies facilitate a type of agriculture that is destroying and polluting our soils and water, weakening our communities, and concentrating wealth and power into a few hands. It is also threatening the security of our food systems, as demonstrated by the continued *E. coli*, GMO contamination, and other health scares that are seen nowadays on the news.

These large-scale, agribusiness-oriented food systems are bound to fail in the long term, sunk by their own unsustainability. But why wait until we're forced by circumstance to abandon our destructive patterns of consumption? We can start now by buying locally grown food whenever possible. By doing so, you'll be helping preserve the environment, and you'll be strengthening your community by investing your food dollar close to home. Only eighteen cents of every dollar, when buying at a large supermarket, go to the grower. Eighty-two cents go to various unnecessary middlemen. Cut them out of the picture and buy your food directly from your local farmer.

Community Supported Agriculture

Thinking about signing up for a CSA but want to learn more about the idea before you commit? Read on.

Over the last twenty years, community supported agriculture (CSA) has become a popular way for consumers to buy local, seasonal food directly from a farmer. Here are the basics: A farmer offers a certain number of "shares" to the public. Typically the share consists of a box of vegetables, but other farm products may be included. Interested consumers purchase a share (aka a "membership" or a "subscription") and in return receive a box (bag, basket) of seasonal produce each week throughout the farming season.

This arrangement creates several rewards for both the farmer and the consumer. In brief:

Advantages for farmers:
- Get to spend time marketing the food early in the year, before their sixteen-hour days in the field begin.
- Receive payment early in the season, which helps with the farm's cash flow.
- Have an opportunity to get to know the people who eat the food they grow.

Advantages for consumers:
- Eat ultra-fresh food, with all the flavor and vitamin benefits.
- Get exposed to new vegetables and new ways of cooking.
- Usually get to visit the farm at least once a season.
- Find that kids typically favor food from "their" farm—even veggies they've never been known to eat.
- Develop a relationship with the farmer who grows their food and learn more about how food is grown.

It's a simple enough idea, but its impact has been profound. Tens of thousands of families have joined CSAs, and in some areas of the country there is more demand than there are CSA farms to fill it. The government does not track CSAs, so there is no official count of how many there are in the United States. LocalHarvest has the most comprehensive directory of CSA farms, with more than 2,500 listed in our grassroots database. In 2008, 557 CSAs signed up with Local-Harvest, and in the first two months of 2009, an additional 300 joined the site.

Variations

As you might expect with such a successful model, farmers have begun to introduce variations. One increasingly common one is the "mix-and-match" or "market-style" CSA. Here, rather than making up a standard box of vegetables for every member each week, the members load their own boxes with some degree of personal choice. The farmer lays out baskets of the week's vegetables. Some farmers encourage members to take a prescribed amount of what's available, leaving behind just what their families do not care for. Some CSA farmers then donate this extra produce to a food bank. In other CSAs, the members have a wider choice to fill their box with whatever appeals to them, within certain limitations ("Just one basket of strawberries per family, please").

CSAs aren't confined to produce. Some farmers include the option for shareholders to buy shares of eggs, homemade bread, meat, cheese, fruit, flowers, or other farm products along with their veggies. Sometimes several farmers will offer their products together, to offer the widest variety to their members. For example, a produce farmer might create a partnership with a neighbor to deliver chickens to the CSA drop-off point, so that the CSA members can purchase farm-fresh chicken when they come to get their CSA baskets. Other farmers are creating stand-alone CSAs for meat, flowers, eggs, and preserved farm products.

Shared Risk

There is an important concept woven into the CSA model that takes the arrangement beyond the usual commercial transaction: the notion of shared risk. When originally conceived, the CSA was set up differently than it is now. A group of people pooled their money, bought a farm, hired a farmer, and each took a share of whatever the farm produced for the year. If the farm had a tomato bonanza, everyone put some up for winter. If a plague of locusts ate all the greens, people ate cheese sandwiches. Very few such CSAs exist today, and for most farmers, the CSA is just one of the ways their produce is marketed. They may also go to the farmers' market, do some wholesale, sell to restaurants, et cetera. Still, the idea that "we're in this together" remains. On some farms it is stronger than others, and CSA members may be asked to sign a policy form indicating that they agree to accept without complaint whatever the farm can produce.

Many times, the idea of shared risk is part of what creates a sense of community among members, and between members and the farmers. If a hailstorm takes out all the peppers, everyone is disappointed together, and together they cheer on the winter squash and broccoli. Most CSA farmers feel a great sense of responsibility to their members, and when certain crops are scarce, they make sure the CSA gets served first. Still, it is worth noting that very occasionally things go wrong on a farm—as they do in any kind of business—the expected is not delivered, and members feel shortchanged. LocalHarvest, for example, is in touch with CSA farmers and members from all over the country. Every year we hear complaints about a few CSA farms (two to six farms a year, over the last nine years) where something happened and the produce was simply unacceptable. It might have been a catastrophic divorce, or an unexpected death in the family. Or the weather was abominable, or the farmer was inexperienced and got in over his or her head.

In our experience, if the situation seems regrettable but reasonable—a bad thing that in good faith could have happened to anyone—most CSA members will rally, if they already know and trust the farmer. These people are more likely to take the long view, especially if they have received an abundance of produce in the past. They are naturally more likely to think, "It'll be better next year," than are new members who have nothing with which to compare a dismal experience. The take-home message is this: if the potential for "not getting your money's worth" makes you feel anxious, then shared risk may not be for you and you should shop at the farmers' market.

Sometimes we hear complaints from CSA members in situations where it appears to us that nothing really went wrong, but the member had unreasonable expectations. In the hope of minimizing disappointment and maximizing satisfaction, we've prepared the following tips and questions.

Tips

Don't expect all your produce to come from the CSA.
Most CSAs do not provide families with enough fruit to meet their usual intake. Many don't provide any fruit at all, so it is good to ask what to expect in that regard. Depending on the size of your family and how much you cook, you will probably find that you need to supplement the vegetables as well, especially staples such as onions, garlic, and carrots.

If you are not used to eating seasonally, do some research.
You may find that it takes a while to make a transition from eating whatever is at the grocery store (pretty much everything) to whatever

is in your CSA basket (what's in season). It may surprise you to find that tomatoes do not ripen until August in your area. You should expect the season to start off lighter than it finishes. In most areas, the first crops will be salad greens, peas, green onions, and the like. By the end of the season, the boxes should be much heavier, with things like winter squash, potatoes, tomatoes, and broccoli. Many farms provide a list of what produce to expect when. It's worth reading. If they don't offer you such a list, ask.

Quantity varies—it's good to ask up front.

When filling the weekly CSA baskets, farmers try to provide a variety of items, in a reasonable quantity. They don't want to be skimpy, and they don't want to overwhelm their members. Too much of even a good thing ends up going to waste, which makes everyone feel bad. Over time, farmers develop a feel for how much is the right amount for their particular community—what's fair, what's reasonable, what will get eaten. Of course, the weather and other mitigating circumstances can get in the way of their ability to provide the ideal amount, as discussed above. One of the most important questions to ask before you sign up is, "About how much produce do you expect to deliver each week, and how does that vary from the beginning of the season to the end?"

If you want to preserve food for winter, ask.

Some farms allow members to get extra quantities of certain vegetables for canning or freezing. If this is something that interests you, talk to the farmer early in the season.

Make sure you understand the policies.

Farms differ in their policies regarding what happens with your box if you don't pick it up (due to vacation, something-came-up, I forgot, and so on). Make sure you know how these situations are dealt with before the season starts.

Ask questions.

Nothing beats a personal conversation with the farmer. Here are some questions you might ask:

- How long have you been farming?
- How long have you been doing a CSA?
- Are there items in your box grown by other farms, and if so, which farms?
- How did last season go?
- I'd like to talk with a couple of your members before I commit. Could you give me contact info for a couple of "references"?

PART TWO: Turning to People, Not Banks, for Sustainable Business

Let Your Customers Own Your Business
Vox Pop Bookstore and Coffeehouse, Brooklyn, NY
(http://voxpopcafe.com)
by Debi Ryan, CEO and General Manager

Vox Pop, "voice of the people" in Latin, opened a little more than five years ago without a lot of fanfare; that would come later. Vox Pop is a kid-friendly, WiFi-enabled coffeehouse/bookstore/art gallery/music venue/performance space located on Cortelyou Road in the Ditmas Park area of Flatbush, Brooklyn. Our vision is to stand for democracy, equality, and peace in the way we treat one another, our employees, and the community. We strive to be a true community center where everyone's voice is welcome. A space where people are free to speak about their personal beliefs—political, social, and religious—and know that they will be treated with respect for having an opinion. A space where taking an active role in your community is a daily endeavor.

Vox Pop is a café serving Fair Trade coffees and teas, a diverse menu of affordable organic, vegetarian, and vegan choices from local vendors and farms, and an extensive array of microbrewed beers and organic wines.

Recognizing that people find their voices through many different media, Vox Pop strives to provide a supportive, broad platform for them all. It is a great music venue with a full schedule of diverse musical offerings from singer-songwriters to blues to jazz to hip-hop to world music, drum circles, and open-mike sessions. Vox Pop is also an art gallery, exhibiting local artists' work on a revolving four-week show basis, bringing art into the community. It's a forum for screening independent films and documentaries, a venue for book events, spoken-word performances, and poetry slams. Vox Pop is an independent bookstore, carrying primarily non-mainstream published books and children's books. It is also a full-service self-publishing book company, Vox Pop Publishing, helping authors get their work into print. Vox Pop won the Independent Publisher Award (IPPY) for Rebel Bookseller in 2005. We have a great Kids Nook with wonderful children's programming and an award-winning weekly story hour, acknowledging that kids need a voice, too.

When the founders of Vox Pop discovered the Brooklyn neighborhood of Ditmas Park, there were few outward signs of the transformation that would soon take place. Vox Pop took root in this community and it began to grow. Founded on the principles of democratically running the space from the ground up, it encourages all co-workers to take an active role in both the business and the world around them. Vox Pop hopes to set the tone for customers to do the same, soliciting suggestions and allowing the space to grow organically.

Vox Pop pioneered the renaissance of this neighborhood, and during the next five years several restaurants, a wine shop, and two bars would also open. Vox Pop continues to champion the importance of small, independently owned businesses as a way to grow and sustain a community. It has found a way to straddle the line between a for-profit and community-based organization.

As with any good idea, it came with a host of challenges to overcome—a changing community, an economy in flux, undercapitalization, and a very steep learning curve. Having a vision for a place doesn't automatically come with knowledge of sound business practices. With profits plummeting, cash flow became tight and the bills started to pile up. It became hard to make payroll but loyal co-workers stuck it out, eking out a meager living on tips and hoping a miracle would happen. The concept was too good, too fundamentally right, to let it die.

Miracles come in many shapes and sizes. In this case, it came in the form of a city agency. No, the city did not step in to save Vox Pop, at least not intentionally. Instead, it came to shut it down for nonpayment of accrued fines. The food permit was pulled, and Vox Pop would no longer be allowed to sell its Fair Trade coffees and organic foods. People held their collective breath, wondering what would happen to the space that had become such an integral part of the community.

But they didn't hold their breath for long; instead they got moving. Even though Vox Pop couldn't serve food or drinks, it stayed open as a community space, a space where people could gather. And gather they did. People came with their laptops to use free WiFi, musicians continued to perform at the Sunday open-mike, parents and children came to play in the Kids Nook, and books were still available and offered for sale. As great as that was, it wasn't enough to bring in the money needed to pay the fines as well as other costs necessary to reopen the doors.

When the original investors took a hard look at the true financial picture, a sizable amount of debt in addition to the fines owed was discovered. It was time for a difficult decision—declare bankruptcy and close the doors, or try to resurrect Vox Pop. Vox Pop had become a space where neighbors connected. It provided an oasis in the middle of a big, anonymous city to make you feel welcome and accepted. It gave people a true sense of belonging. It grounded people, both long-term residents and newly arrived transplants, in a local community that encouraged participation. The easiest decision would have been to walk away. But the easiest decision isn't always the right one. Walking away would have meant walking away from money owed to local vendors, people dependent upon Vox Pop to make a living, members of the community in need of a space to meet, socialize, network, and study. After much discussion and debate, the decision was made to try to raise the money needed to reopen and work out a plan to pay down debts.

Vox Pop turned to the community. We held town-hall-style meetings, discussing what was at stake to try to reopen the doors, and what was at stake if we didn't. And the community responded in the affirmative; they didn't want to lose Vox Pop. In true Vox Pop fashion, people came together to find a solution. What if everyone who believed in Vox Pop bought shares and became partners in the business? And if we kept the buy-in price low, recognizing that the community was just as harshly affected by the difficult economy, more people would have the opportunity to participate. At a time when the world was looking at "Bail Outs," we looked for a "Buy In." Co-workers, neighbors, customers, friends, and families stepped forward and purchased shares in the business, all becoming owners, and Vox Pop finally became what it was always meant to be—a community-owned space. Over a period of several weeks, enough money was raised to reopen our doors.

Vox Pop transformed itself into a collective. There is no one owner of Vox Pop; instead there are more than 180 shareholders, most of them members of the community we serve, but some living as far away as California. This is both a challenge and Vox Pop's greatest strength. We are still struggling to meet our legacy debt but are meeting our current obligations and have payment plans in place to slowly bring Vox Pop to a profitable status. As an example, we were just able to make a final payment to our pastry vendor, the purveyor of our organic bagels and croissants. We had made an arrangement with him that if he would continue to deliver to us, we would pay for all our orders on delivery plus a small amount toward the back debt that had been accrued. I apologized for having taken almost seven months to pay him back and thanked him for his patience. He said, "No, thank you. When you took over the business, it owed us almost three thousand dollars. We never thought we would ever get to recoup that money. Instead, you gave us a steady stream of income and paid back all that past debt, so, thank you." He and the many other people who have patiently waited and supported us reaffirm that our decision was the right one.

Being a true community-owned company means that the community has input in the way we are run and the projects we undertake. This is evidenced by our diverse programming and partnerships with local nonprofit organizations, and we communicate regularly through a private listserv. There is no obligation as a shareholder to take an active role, but active participation seems to be the rule rather than the exception. Co-workers meet on a monthly basis to discuss what works and what doesn't work, adjusting the business model accordingly. Vox Pop is the best example of what can be achieved if people work together for a common goal.

Please visit our website at http://voxpopcafe.com and, if you find yourself in Brooklyn, be sure to come by for a cup of coffee and experience the place so many people think of as their own.

The Local Art House as Public Good
The Cable Car Cinema, Providence, Rhode Island
(www.cablecarcinema.com)
by Daniel Kamil, Proprietor

If you live outside major urban centers in the United States, there is real difficulty getting to see movies in a theater with other people that doesn't require a lobotomy with your ticket. I essentially view multiplexes as the delivery system for a Hollywood drug that enters our system and transmogrifies us into twitchy, craven, unthinking automatons. Not dissimilar to the zombies depicted in George Romero's *Dawn of the Dead*—minus the viscous fluids, and we can still form sentences, if barely. The sad thing is that everyone knows what to expect at the multiplex, yet we are complicit—we can't help ourselves. Unfortunately, the content available at most theaters is as unhealthy as the GMO popcorn, Day-Glo nacho cheese, and high-fructose corn syrup being ingested, and our culture is paying a high psychic price for the junk food.

Fortunately, there is hope. There is a possibility for resistance. That opposing force is . . . *you!* Because the once insurmountable economics of starting your own cinema are now attainable. Excellent digital projectors can be bought for as little as five thousand dollars, and access to interesting and alternative content has never been easier. Companies such as Emerging Pictures are trying to upend traditional modes of film distribution with HD simulcast of European opera, and, given their network of participating cinemas, seem to be succeeding. I propose that it is time to wrest film culture back from conglomerates and bring it back to the local, independent level where it should be. And I am here to tell you that it is possible. You, too, can start your own art house. And people will come. And your friends, neighbors, and community will share and deeply appreciate your vision, your risk. The work will be hard, you will have doubts, people will doubt you, but if you stick it out and plan well you will become a vital and important part of your community.

In 2003, I started a fifty-seat micro-cinema with my wife called The Revival House in a small coastal beach town called Westerly, Rhode Island. We chose Westerly because we found an old Victorian mixed-use, commercial building in the heart of a small town. It was also the only place we could afford. We were committed to investing our resources and labor in a neglected but charming downtown whose foot traffic had left decades earlier for the convenience of parking and big-box retail. We handled all aspects of construction and lived in a loft above the theater. In fact, I have a scar on my foot from the time I used a sledgehammer to separate two pieces of wood and didn't see the hundred-year-old nail hiding on the other side. Ouch. Tetanus shot aside—looking back, those were halcyon days.

Prior to securing the building, I wrote a business plan with the hope of convincing lenders of the wisdom of opening a movie theater in Anywhere, USA. Bank of America said no. Ditto Citizens. Wells Fargo, no thanks. The routine rejection became almost comical in its repetition. They would always say that they didn't invest in start-ups. That is, unless you're a franchise. So Burger King, yes. Dunkin' Donuts, okay. Local movie theater that intends to show classic films in a unique and interesting environment owned and operated by two people who will live in the building and will personally guarantee the money—absolutely not. Is it any wonder that American commercial life is so bland and homogeneous? In the capitalizing process, I came to understand that big banks were a closed system. And given the current economic climate, I have real doubts about whether any government bailout money is being used for loans like mine. I'm thinking, with a certain degree of hindsight, probably not.

At my lowest point, an auspicious thing happened. I asked my lawyer (but that doesn't really describe the relationship—he was a friend who did legal work for me and was paid with my wife's art) if he knew any commercial lenders that might be willing to back this project. He pointed me to a local credit union. This particular financial institution was founded in 1920 and was originally created as a member-owned, not-for-profit organization. Russell, the man responsible for commercial lending, was dedicated to serving both the mission whose mandate was to customer service and the belief that the role of the credit union was to help stimulate the local economy. Unlike commercial banks—which are beholden to shareholders who may or may not keep their assets in the bank—credit unions invest members' money and are thus inherently more conservative.

Russell believed in the project. He believed in us. He believed that we would create a commercially viable business that would also en-

hance the quality of the cultural life in the community it was serving. Russell rolled the dice. He took a risk. And he became a regular
patron. Had it not been for our local credit union, this project would
not have happened. I have come to understand on an intimate level
that business is all about personal relationships. All small-scale
businesses, including running a cinema, are about human inter-
connection. Thanks, Russell. We couldn't have done it without you.
We will keep your seat warm. Popcorn and beers are on the house.

In 2007, after four years of running Revival House and with the
real-estate market "frothing," we were made an offer we couldn't refuse and sold the building. We were fortunate to get out when we did.
That sale and what we accomplished in Westerly led us to our next
endeavor and current project, The Cable Car Cinema in Providence,
Rhode Island. It was voted one of the 10 Best Cinemas in the country
by *Entertainment Weekly.* The cinema has 105 seats.

We project movies on 35mm, 16mm, and digital video formats. The
establishment has been showing foreign, independent, and classic
movies since 1976 and is known as the "theater with the couches."
Located across the street from the Rhode Island School of Design, the
cinema and accompanying café are embedded in Providence's cultural life. Every year, the Cable Car hosts several film festivals: the
Providence French Film Festival sponsored by Brown University,
the Providence Latin-American Film Festival, and the Magic Lantern
Screening Series, which is devoted to screening avant-garde and ex-
perimental work exclusively.

I have owned and operated the business since 2008 and have come
to understand its public importance. The Cable Car will never be able
to compete with national theatrical chains that also own major film
studios. We also cannot compete with Netflix, video-on-demand, or
BitTorrents for convenience and accessibility of content, all of which
erodes our potential customer base. But what The Cable Car provides
that these other experiences do not is community. Not faux Facebook
networked community. But the Good, the Bad, and the Sometimes
Awkward community. As when our meth-addicted regular, who lives
in his car, occupies the same space as a former U.S. senator—and they
have a conversation. The scale is real. It is personal. Those interactions have value for me. They are meaningful in a way that money exchange isn't and could never be. So to further this small-scale
pleasure, I invest when I can in Rhode Island businesses. I do my best

to keep vendors local. Our baker is up the street, in the same building as our coffee roaster, which also happens to host our winter farmers' market. Paying these vendors at the end of the month gives me a real sense of gratification. It is a contentment based on knowing that my money is helping their businesses grow. If money is energy exchange, then my goal is to use that dynamic as efficiently as possible.

Barter for Art and an Education

OurGoods and Trade School (http://ourgoods.org)
by Caroline Woolard, Co-founder

OurGoods is a New York online barter network for independent artists citywide. It revitalizes economic opportunities for cultural producers and creates a strong, integrated community of support. The site matches barter partners, provides accountability tools, and offers technical assistance resources. On OurGoods, an artist can find all the resources s/he needs to complete a project outside the cash economy.

We offer an innovative economic model for artists by marrying an old idea—barter—with cutting-edge technology. We shift the focus from "How can artists get more money?" to the deeper question, "How can artists get more resources?" In so doing, we offer more than cash funding offers. OurGoods is a sustainable model in which art can be made regardless of economic climate. It increases networking and collaboration among artists. It offers access to new resources, expanding the scope of each individual's work. And it forms relationships that create a resilient network to meet future challenges. The foundation funding model puts artists in competition with one another. On OurGoods, a benefit to one user expands resources for all users.

The OurGoods FAQ

Tell me about OurGoods.
OurGoods is a barter network for creative people. Members of the OurGoods network barter skills, spaces, and objects, organizing creative projects with "haves" and "needs." OurGoods matches barter partners, tracks accountability, and helps the business of independent, creative work. The site can be used to find collaborators, see

emerging interests, or just execute projects without cash. For example, I can help you write a grant if you make my costumes. OurGoods is a new model for valuing creative work. It fosters interdependence and strong working relationships. You will get your independent work done with mutual respect instead of cash (see http://ourgoods.org for more information).

And how does OurGoods relate to Trade School?

The virtual component of OurGoods is necessary because artists and designers make up a transient community, always on the move. In some ways, OurGoods.org is simply a directory of available creative people ready to connect in real space to share skills and head toward a barter negotiation. In-person meetings are incredibly important. This is why we jumped on the opportunity to occupy a storefront on the Lower East Side for five weeks.

On a seasonal basis, the OurGoods group runs a storefront at 139 Norfolk Street in the Lower East Side. This space is called Trade School and will help OurGoods members get to know one another while sharing resources.

By day, Trade School is a shop. People can drop in to barter with artists, designers, and craftspeople on a range of products and services. They can peruse the trading board for things they want, and leave a contact card for things they have to offer. Skilled staff help make connections. By night, Trade School is a school. People can take a class with a range of specialized teachers in exchange for basic items and services, and they can secure a spot in a Trade School class by meeting one of the teacher's barter needs.

Trade School allows a generous and rigorous creative community to grow organically. If you teach a class at night, you can share the Trade School space during the day. Trade School is only open to the wider public (as students) at night, so the shared office, or common studio, fosters deeper relationships for Trade School teachers. This day office also encourages enthusiastic students to engage with the Trade School/OurGoods network more fully by teaching a class to spend more time with the group during the day. Everyone has something to share.

See the current classes at http://tradeschool.ourgoods.org and reports on past classes at http://blog.ourgoods.org.

How did you come up with the idea?

I must say that the idea is less important than its realization. Jen Abrams [a dancer-choreographer] and I met because we were both talking about a resource-sharing site for artists, but OurGoods only became possible when it collided with Rich [Watts, an artist], Louise [Ma, an artist-designer], and Carl [Tashian, a developer-engineer]. The OurGoods idea came into form when we five co-founders committed to developing it.

At one point, I wondered: Why can't I get my favorite band to play in my studio? Is cash the only way to pay for a labor of love? I didn't know the band members personally, but hoped we'd have a mutual understanding of the passion and respect that motivates labor. I wanted to work hard for them because I love their work. We decided that they'd play if I gave the lead singer one of my "Work Dresses" [a cross between a tool belt and an apron that the author makes for barter] and the guitarist a day of spackling and sanding help in his studio.

Creative people often work for free, expanding the public imagination while trafficking in a murky labor-value exchange. Rather than complain about limited funding and access to resources, OurGoods shows that we already have a community of resources at our fingertips.

What has the response been like so far?

The enthusiasm for OurGoods is shocking. Most classes are full (with waiting lists) and students come from all over the city. I've been asking teachers why they are interested in Trade School, and each teacher refines my understanding of the power of peer learning.

Describe the typical participant—or someone who's participated that's really surprised you.

There is no typical participant. Trade School brings out the multiple identities of creative individuals because classes are based on enthusiasm rather than professionalism or expert knowledge. At the beginning of each class I say, "If you'd like to teach a class, talk to me later." I could teach classes about mushrooms, conceptual furniture, grant writing, or running an LLC. Teachers become students and vice versa. We've had students from Washington Heights and the West Village, future forecasters from Nokia, private chefs, art historians, former real-estate developers, and vegan dumpster divers, and I'm sure there's one person who is a former real-estate developer, vegan dumpster diver, private chef, and art historian. Creative people often live multiple lives.

Who funds it and how much did it cost to get going?

Rich Watts bartered design work with Grand Opening in exchange for the storefront space we're using for Trade School. Grand Opening collaborated with us on the design for Trade School and has been instrumental in helping us broaden our reach.

OurGoods received fifteen thousand dollars through The Field's Economic Revitalization for Performing Artists grant and fifteen hundred dollars from the Brooklyn Arts Council for outreach. With five co-founders working on OurGoods for more than a year, however, most of the OurGoods labor is not remunerated in cash.

How do we support public works today?

The site will eventually have a point system (an online currency to assist indirect barters) that could pay individuals who work for OurGoods, but the point system cannot exist without a robust network and a communal acknowledgment of the site's value. Just as our national currency only works because we all agree to use it, we cannot implement a point system until a community of trust is established.

What have you learned that you didn't know how to do beforehand?

1. People really like fulfilling Trade School teachers' obscure barter requests. I think going through a teacher's barter requests (in exchange for a class) allows students to get a sense of who they are.

The composting teacher, Amanda Matles, was wooed, for example, by a trombone solo. I am getting running shoes for grant writing, and Emcee C.M., Master of None, received handwritten stories about wildness. People are incredibly thoughtful and responsive.

2. I had no idea that I would love organizing a storefront and running public programming. I hope this becomes my paid day job!

Start a Biodiesel Collective

Piedmont Biofuels (www.biofuels.coop)
by Lyle Estill, Founder

We never had a plan at Piedmont Biofuels. Instead, we began with a handful of passionate individuals making biodiesel out of used cooking oil in the backyard. Biodiesel is a cleaner-burning renewable fuel that can run any diesel engine. And it can easily be made in the corner of the garage.

Piedmont Biofuels began with us simply wanting to get our hands on more gallons of fuel. When co-founder Rachel Burton and I got our first ten-gallon batch of biodiesel to separate properly thanks to the heat of the woodstove, there were six people ready to receive fuel. Everyone got a gallon and a half.

From these humble beginnings as a backyard brewing setup, Piedmont Biofuels became a cooperative fuel-making operation, and then a million-gallon-per-year chemical plant. We accidentally created a model for community-scale biodiesel, in which Moya collects used cooking oil from area restaurants, Jeremy spins it into fuel, Xiaohu certifies that it conforms to our specification, and I put it on a truck and deliver it to the B100 Community Trail, where hundreds of long-suffering members fill up their cars and trucks. We sell the rest to oil companies, which blend it with petroleum and sell to thousands of consumers across the region.

Many biodiesel co-ops have formed and folded. Many biodiesel collectives have come and gone. People fall to fighting, money comes to the fore, and someone takes their reactor and goes home. Things come apart. If all we had to deal with was renewable energy—just BTUs—it would be simple. But because there were people involved, it was trickier.

People used to ask us how we managed to stick together, and we always told them that we tried to do what was in the best interest of the fuel. And while it is true that many of us have subjugated our self-interest in the name of the fuel, I think we had that part wrong.

It's not about the gallons. It's not about the fuel. It's about people.

We envisioned a world in which the stuff we needed to make our fuel would come from within a hundred miles of our plant, and where the fuel would be sold within that same hundred miles. It's easy. We simply wanted to upend the overarching top-down energy infrastructure that ruled our lives. We wanted to get free of the petroleum grid. We saw a world of micro-nodal energy production, where energy would be harnessed at the place it was used. That's all.

We accidentally formed a relationship between people and their fuel. Which meant we formed relationships with a larger group—those of us who cared about our fuel.

We made the same mistake when it came to food.

When you are obsessed with the production of local fuel, it is a small step to take to focus on local food. So we formed a farm in the front yard. And when we wanted to expand food production, we launched another farm in town, on the vacant lot that surrounds our chemical plant.

When we were shipping trucks and trailers full of food, we thought it was about sustenance. We mistakenly believed it was about growing calories. But in fact it was about interacting with those people who were intent on eating locally produced, sustainable food.

On our quest for sustainable biodiesel, we found ourselves immersed in ways to improve the "energy balance" of our fuel. We had fuel makers who were riding their bikes to work, and we obsessed over the "life cycle analysis" of our plant. That aligned us squarely with the solar installation community, as we deployed solar thermal and photovoltaic systems to get our work done.

Along the way we took on like-minded tenants, one of whom was distributing organically grown produce. Another started making nontoxic bug repellent using biodiesel as its start point.

Suddenly we were what the economic developers call a "cluster," and with seventy-some people employed on our project we were having a material impact on our small southern town's economy. One day I got a call from a gentleman at Standard and Poor's who wanted to talk to me about our county's credit rating. What? Because we had emerged from the community college, the county pointed to us as one of their successes, and wanted our existence to provide a demonstration of what they did with their debt instruments.

I said to Rachel, "Back when you and I were standing around a fifty-five-gallon drum with a canoe paddle trying to make biodiesel for the first time, did we ever think it would lead to a role in public finance?"

She replied, "Probably. But at the time I just wanted you to add more lye . . ."

Years later, we hung a canoe paddle in the control room. For me it is a reminder of E. F. Schumacher, who came up with the notion of "appropriate technology." It hangs over the heads of a bunch of design-build guys who engineer manifolds and methanol recovery systems, and who are sought after the world over for their expertise in biodiesel technology. Piedmont Biofuels accidentally ended up as experts in small-scale biodiesel production.

Seven years before there was a "stimulus package for green jobs," during the first W. Bush administration, we were calling for an "energy regime change." One of our members coined the term "Hometown Security."

Having accidentally built critical mass in our small southern town, our interest in self-reliance increased. We were fueling ourselves. We were feeding ourselves. But we were having trouble financing ourselves.

In the spring of 2008, my book *Small Is Possible: Life in a Local Economy* hit the bookstores. In it I mentioned a local currency effort called the PLENTY—which was an acronym for Piedmont Local Economy Tender. It had nothing to do with us, really, except we traded in it. And we paid our interns with PLENTYs.

That book restarted an interest in the PLENTY, a new board of trustees was formed, and the currency was relaunched with new vigor in the fall of 2008, just as the rest of the world was melting down. Our locally owned Capital Bank started accepting PLENTYs at par, and the headline, LOCAL BANK ACCEPTS LOCAL CURRENCY, became international news.

Before we knew it we had film crews from Poland, CNN, and Fox, and crews from shows that I had never heard of, like *Inside Edition,* running around our small town filming people spending PLENTYs at the grocery store.

I don't have a TV. And I don't get out much. But for a moment there we were big news.

Ironically, the PLENTY has a much smaller role in our local finance efforts than the peer-to-peer financing that also rose from an experiment I outlined in *Small Is Possible.* I took ten thousand dollars of my kid's college savings and lent it to a local cabinetmaker at 4 percent so she could pay off her credit cards that were charging 28 percent.

And it worked. She got back on her feet. Micro-loans started popping up everywhere. When the "credit crunch" of 2009 set upon us, money started coming out of the woodwork. Landlords were lending to tenants for capital equipment necessary to keep small businesses alive. The Abundance Foundation started a revolving credit program out of static "restricted funds." Neighbors started lending to neighbors.

What began as a ten-thousand-dollar experiment swelled to hundreds of thousands of dollars of loans. Today I am aware of about $350,000 worth of personal "notes" in our community, each bearing between 4 and 6 percent interest, and to date I am aware of zero defaults. Peer pressure is the glue that holds micro-finance together. If I want to default on a loan from Mrs. Ferguson in this town, I best move away.

And the beauty of it is that 4 percent micro-loans have outperformed the S&P 500 of late.

Just as the fuel wasn't about the gallons, and the food wasn't about the calories, the local currency and the loans aren't about the money. They are about the people who use the money for the new mechanic's garage, or a new table saw. They are not even about the "stuff" the money can buy. They are about the human who is going to use the stuff to create a living.

We were once dubbed "the most exciting renewable energy project on the eastern seaboard." And while we liked the moniker, it was incorrect.

It turns out that everything we do is about people. And about how we interact with people. People just want to be "in on things." And people just want to have a say in how they can govern their own lives. People just want to be supported. And cared for. And more important, people want to have something they can care about, too.

At Piedmont Biofuels, we have encountered mental illness. We have felt the sting of departure from those who have moved on. We've faced death. And terminal illness. We've had weddings (one couple actually got married at the chemical plant), and we've had births. We've had ribbon cuttings, and politicians speaking, and accidents and explosions, and potlucks and games tournaments and quarrels over dogs and cats and when all is said and done, it's just about us. And how we hold together. As a project. And as people. Just trying to find our way.

For more information about our project, see www.biofuels.coop. For a look at how we are re-engineering our food shed, see http://sustainablegrub.wordpress.com. And for those who still like to read things in print, there is *Biodiesel Power: The Passion, the People, and the Politics of the Next Renewable Fuel* (New Society, 2005). And *Small Is Possible: Life in a Local Economy* (New Society, 2008).

Grow a Sustainable Business by Going Nonprofit

Open Books, Chicago, Illinois (www.open-books.org)
by Kevin Elliott, Store Manager, and Stacy Ratner, Founder and Executive Director

In 2006, Open Books Ltd. set out to form the city's first nonprofit literacy bookstore. The vision included fifty thousand used books for sale in a colorful, creative, collaborative place where all proceeds would go to support a unique spectrum of in-house and partner literacy programs. The organization now proudly serves more than two thousand students of all ages each year through four signature reading and writing programs plus a slate of opportunities with partners across the city. It is run by a staff of nine, powered by a volunteer corps of three thousand, and dedicated to changing lives every day through reading, writing, and the *unlimited* power of the more than three hundred thousand used books (and counting) that fuel its operations.

In the hierarchy of human needs in a major urban center like Chicago, perhaps only food and shelter rank above literacy. Life literacy skills such as reading a food label, filling out a job application, or decoding a bus schedule are vital. To be limited in one's ability to read, write, and communicate is to be silenced and subjected to a life in the margins, and it is a massive threat not only to the individual, but to society and its future as a whole. Fifty-three percent of Chicago's adults read at or below the fourth-grade level. Sixty-one percent of low-income households do not own a single children's book, and 37 percent of the city's residents could not read such a book if they had one. But Chicago is more than just these daunting statistics, most of which are unknown to residents not directly involved in the issue. It is also a world center of academic and cultural activity, and therefore it is awash in a currency uniquely suited to change the face of literacy: used books.

At Open Books, about twelve thousand donated books each month are processed by type and value. Many of them then go straight to the multicolored shelves of the store (which also features two comfortable lounges, a literacy awareness pavilion, an extensive children's section with book-shaped furniture, and an event stage) for sale to the general public, while others are listed online for sale nationwide. Visitors to the store come for many reasons: to drop off donated books, find great reads, hold book club meetings, enjoy story time with their children, attend author events, and so on. But what they find, in addition to what one publication called "the most beautiful bookstore in Chicago,"* is an awareness of the challenge and the role they can play in fighting it, from buying books and spreading the word to volunteering their time in the store or the organization's programs citywide.

Open Books' programs begin with Buddies, a one-on-one opportunity for volunteers to share an hour of reading with an elementary school student once each week. The pairs work on fluency, vocabulary, and comprehension, but the experience of having a dedicated mentor who proves that reading is fun is at least as valuable as the pedagogic components. "The students I work with lag behind their classmates in reading ability and I am not sure that they get enough much-needed individual attention in the classroom," wrote one Buddies volunteer recently. "Whenever they struggle with a word, I am ready to provide encouragement and support. As a result, my buddies have become more competent and confident readers. Perhaps as important are the relationships I have developed with the students. After talking with them, I've learned that their circumstances do not afford much interaction with positive role models. I'd like to think that through my time with them each week, the students gain a trusted friend who can offer valuable life lessons and broaden their perspectives." In one hour a week, this volunteer has changed the course of a child's life through reading. And the experience is repeated each week in ten schools around Chicago, reaching two hundred students each year and providing more than five thousand hours of reading time.

Next on the list of programs comes Adventures in Creative Writing field trips, which bring classes of fourth- through twelfth-grade students to Open Books for two-hour workshops in nonfiction prose, poetry, slam, and fairy-tale writing. Students share tables with volunteer writing coaches who help them think through their life experi-

---

* www.examiner.com/x-416-Chicago-Literary-Scene-Examiner~y2009m11d20-Open -Books-unveils-most-beautiful-bookstore-in-Chicago.

ences, choose a moment to write about, and put the story down on paper, then join in the applause as the writers take the floor—in the distinctive pencil costume—to read their work to the group. Some students choose to share stories about amusement parks or birthday parties. Others write about gang violence, drugs, abuse, and death. For many students, the trip is the first time they have shared a particular experience with the group. For all of them, it is a chance to make writing an exciting, relevant, participatory adventure instead of a rote academic assignment. "Open Books made me feel like I can be a great writer and you gave me the confidence to do it," wrote one student. "I had a great time and I can't wait to come back!! You made me express myself in a way I can't ever imagine. You made me feel good about my writing and not ashamed." When the trip is over, each student gets a published booklet of the entire class's work (and photos of the trip) to keep. In 2009, more than twelve hundred students—and over forty schools—came to the program. In 2010, that number will more than double.

VWrite, the third of Open Books' programs, matches high school juniors with volunteer mentors to work on professional reading, writing, and communications skills. Pairs meet in person at the beginning of the program, then communicate by phone and email about college essays, job applications, interview etiquette, and more, forming what *The New York Times* describes as "a full-scale mentoring relationship with the potential to change lives."* WeWrite, the last of the current signature offerings, provides creative and professional writing classes for adults. And in summer 2010, Open Books will launch Wordshops, a series of workshops in everything from short-story writing to zine production and ESL enrichment activities. Like all the organization's programming, Wordshops will focus on the big picture: not simply to boost reading and writing skills for students, but to help them understand the intrinsic value of being literate individuals who can think critically about their world and use their voices to shape their communities for future generations.

Literacy is a pressing, a crucial, and an imperative challenge. But it is also a cause where one person can make a difference, where incremental gains are significant, and where the rewards are both fun and fundamental. Volunteering for an hour a week can be the inspiration a

---

* www.nytimes.com/2010/01/15/education/15cncbooks.html.

child needs to make books a central part of his or her life, and thus to break the cycle of low literacy and improve prospects for each successive generation. Serving as a mentor for a high school junior can turn him or her onto a career or academic path that might not have been under consideration. A coach at a writing workshop can convince kids that their story is worth telling, and that they have the talent to tell it. Donating a book—or several hundred of them—can bring the world, one page at a time, toward literacy instead of landfill. Book drives help. Reading to kids helps. Spreading the word so that other people are inspired to join the cause helps. If you can read this page, you can make a difference. Your community and the world need you to do so.

PART THREE: Take Back Your World

The Accidental Activist

Streetsblog, Brooklyn, New York (www.streetsblog.net)
by Aaron Naparstek, Founder

Streetsblog is a news source, online community, and political mobilizer for people who are working to reclaim their cities by reducing dependence on automobiles and improving conditions for cyclists, pedestrians, and transit riders.

I'm an accidental activist. Back in 2001, after a near-death experience with a maniacal Brooklyn motorist, I decided I needed to take a stand. Every day, a nonstop armada of horn-honking, gas-guzzling, exhaust-spewing, planet-broiling motor vehicles made life in my neighborhood far more miserable than it had to be. But as one guy with limited resources, what could I do about it? I stepped back, took a deep breath, observed the problem . . . and decided to write a haiku poem about it. This was my first one:

> *You from New Jersey*
> *Honking in front of my house*
> *In your SUV*

I called it a "Honku." I printed fifty copies and went out late one night taping them to lampposts up and down my street. The act of doing that felt great. Though I didn't think it would do much of anything to stop Brooklyn drivers from continuing to act like raging sociopaths, it gave me a strange feeling of power over the traffic. Every couple of weeks I'd sneak out around midnight and tape up fifty copies of my latest Honku, honking back in my own quiet way.

On the evening of my third lamppost publishing run, a woman walking her dog approached and asked excitedly if I was the Honku poet. Feeling embarrassed that I'd been caught, I confessed that I was. She extended her hand and said, "My kids and I love your work! We put them up on our refrigerator. We call you the 'Bard of Clinton Street'!" As I made my way down the block I noticed that a handful of new Honku had appeared on the lampposts, written by others. Some of them were really good.

Oh, Jeezus Chrysler
What's all the damned honking Ford?
Please shut the truck up!

Over the next few weeks, dozens of Honku spontaneously popped up around the neighborhood. Clearly I wasn't the only one being driven crazy by all of the honking. I created a Honku.org website and organized a neighborhood meeting. Our city council member took up our cause. Soon, the local precinct was handing out $125 tickets to honkers and, for the first time in years, I was sleeping past 6 AM without being woken up by pissed-off, aggressive maniacs horn-blasting their way into Manhattan.

The media latched on to Honku, and stories appeared in *The New Yorker*, *The New York Times*, and on NPR. From there, it rapidly spread to newspapers in far-off lands like England, Sweden, and Minnesota. Suddenly we were a "movement." The New York City Department of Transportation eventually retimed the traffic lights, installed traffic-calming measures, and vastly improved conditions for cyclists and pedestrians throughout our neighborhood. The gridlock, honking, and road rage haven't disappeared, but my old street is much better now. That first, seemingly embarrassing and trivial action I took of writing a haiku poem and taping it to a lamppost—it worked! Honku made people stop, take notice, and laugh. It raised consciousness. It brought the neighborhood together. It solved problems. It made things change.

As I set out to solve the problems in my own neighborhood, I quickly realized that my local issues were, in fact, systemic, citywide problems requiring solutions on a much larger scale than just having the local precinct handing out summonses. The endless horn-honking on Clinton Street was the result of too many cars trying to pile onto the Brooklyn Bridge. That was the result of too many cars on the Brooklyn–Queens Expressway, which was the result of, well, it goes on and on. Ultimately, all of these problems were the result of seventy years of planning, design, and engineering aimed at accommodating the needs of automobiles over human beings and just about everything else. The honking was, of course, just the tip of the iceberg. In addition to destroying my neighborhood's quality of life, America's overwhelming automobile dependence makes us obese, it turns farmland into suburban sprawl, it requires us to defend a vast supply of foreign oil, and it's melting our polar ice caps and changing our planet's climate.

So I launched Streetsblog.org at the start of 2006. At that time, New York City transportation policy was stalled in complete gridlock. While cities such as London, Paris, Chicago, and Portland were rolling out innovative transportation reforms and ambitious long-term sustainability plans, New York's streets were still mostly ruled by a 1950s traffic-engineering mind-set aimed at maximizing the city's capacity for motor vehicles. While other world cities were building new bike infrastructure, pedestrian plazas, bus rapid transit, and congestion pricing systems, New York City government still treated motor vehicle traffic as something akin to the weather—a force beyond the control of mere mortals. Though few issues touch New Yorkers' lives more personally on a more regular basis, transportation was a third-tier issue at City Hall. No one, it seemed, was even paying attention to it.

With Streetsblog I set out to change that. I launched the blog with four goals in mind: First, I aimed to create a new journalistic beat covering a range of stories from the intense neighborhood-level battles over new bike lanes and parking spaces to the big questions around how New York City planned to address the challenge of peak oil and climate change. Second, I wanted Streetsblog to serve as a watchdog for the New York City Department of Transportation, an agency that no one was holding to account. Third, Streetsblog would educate New York City's policy makers, press, and regular citizens about urban planning and transportation best practices that were emerging in other cities. Finally, the blog would function as a gathering place and discussion forum for livable-streets advocates. If it succeeded, I figured, Streetsblog would, at best, help get New York City moving slowly in the right direction.

Streetsblog succeeded beyond my wildest expectations. It quickly emerged as a daily must-read among advocates, the press, policy wonks, and City Hall insiders. Daily newspapers and TV news picked up and ran with our stories. Our coverage helped to generate unprecedented crowds at community board and city council meetings where transportation and planning issues were being discussed. More funding poured in.

In addition to informing and educating, Streetsblog connected and empowered New Yorkers to take action on their own. Within minutes of posting the license plate number of a hit-and-run driver, Streetsblog commenters had run the plate, found his name and address, posted a Google Street View photo of his home (offending SUV parked in the driveway), and emailed him to ask about the incident. By showing off urban planning and transportation best practices from all around the world via Streetfilms, we helped make new ideas spread from city to city. Our Streetsblog Network brought together more than three hundred local livable-streets bloggers from across the United States to share information, resources, and support one another's work.

In New York City, Streetsblog helped to hasten the departure of Mayor Bloomberg's first DOT commissioner and create a new, more ambitious set of expectations for her successor. Today, with Janette Sadik-Khan at the helm, New York City's DOT is pushing a bold program to create "sustainable streets" through the prioritization of pedestrians, transit, and bicycles. Concepts that were considered "crazy" and politically impossible—a car-free Times Square and physically separated bike lanes, for example—are now being planned, designed, and built. New York City DOT is not just reformed, it is *transformed,* and widely considered a leading example for transportation agencies in other U.S. cities to follow. People who contributed to Streetsblog in the early days are now working in the DOT commissioner's office. With editions up and running in San Francisco, Los Angeles, and on Capitol Hill, Streetsblog is also helping to make change happen in cities beyond New York and at the federal level. This all started with a haiku poem taped to a lamppost.

Looking back at Streetsblog's first four years, I'm reminded of Danish urban designer Jan Gehl's famous quote: "How nice it is to wake up every morning and know that your city is a little better than it was the day before." If you want to see your city get a little bit better every day, you just have to take one small, incremental action and see where it leads. There are plenty of resources out there to help you do that. Here are a few to get you started:

Streetsblog Network (www.streetsblog.net)

Find and connect with a local livable-streets blogger in your own community. Streetsblog Network brings together more than three hundred blogs from all regions of the United States and beyond and highlights their best work every day.

Planetizen (www.planetizen.com)

Planetizen is the top Internet source for news, analysis, and discussion of urban planning, design, and development issues. If you're looking for daily news on issues like transportation, climate change, architecture, infrastructure, and community development, you need to be reading Planetizen.

Alliance for Biking & Walking (www.peoplepoweredmovement.org)

Alliance for Biking & Walking creates, strengthens, and unites state and local bicycle and pedestrian advocacy organizations. If you want to know who the bike, pedestrian, and transit advocates are in your community—or if you want to start an advocacy effort in a community that does not already have one—call the alliance.

Blueprint America (www.pbs.org/wnet/blueprintamerica)

This ongoing PBS series is doing an incredible job of shining a spotlight on America's decaying and neglected infrastructure. If you really want to get a better understanding of how federal planning and policy impacts our lives at the local level, the high-definition, Web-streamed documentaries at *Blueprint America* are very much worth your time.

Post Carbon Cities (www.postcarboncities.net)

How is your local government preparing for climate change and energy uncertainty? Post Carbon Cities provides an array of research and resources to help local economies make a smoother transition to a world no longer dependent on hydrocarbon fuels or emitting climate-changing levels of carbon.

SeeClickFix (http://seeclickfix.com/citizens)

A great tool for enhancing civic engagement, SeeClickFix empowers citizens to use their computers and mobile phones to identify and report problems in their communities, and track their progress (or lack thereof). With user-friendly mobile apps, mapping tools, and problem trackers, concerned citizens can keep tabs on the civic problems in their communities and make sure their local officials do, too.

Remap the Roads
Reclaiming Our Transportation: Three Thousand Miles of East Coast Greenway
The East Coast Greenway (http://greenway.org)
by Dennis Markatos, Co-founder

The East Coast Greenway Alliance is a nonprofit dedicated to giving people a safe and accessible route to get around in the urban corridor of the eastern United States. Today, mobility is 90 percent dependent on burning fossil fuels that harm our bodies and the environment. We waste valuable land for parking spaces and send money out of our communities every time we fill up our gas tank. By completing the three-thousand-mile East Coast Greenway (ECG), we will empower people to walk, jog, skate, or bicycle from point A to point B.

Ever since the early 1990s, the East Coast Greenway Alliance has been working with community organizers, local transportation planners, and elected officials to complete this trail through eastern cities. Our route goes right through urban neighborhoods so that people can take the greenway for their daily commute, weekend recreation, and even long-distance trips between Maine and Florida. Whether ECG participants are avid cyclists or children biking or jogging for the first time, the greenway will make active transportation safe in a transportation system that currently favors the automobile.

Like most good things, the East Coast Greenway was the brainchild of a few committed citizens who wanted to make a positive impact in their communities. After the 1991 East Coast Bicycle Conference in Cambridge, Massachusetts, nine people got together at New York City's American Youth Hostel on Amsterdam Avenue to develop their dream of a greenway from at least Boston to Washington, D.C. This group of planners and cycling advocates decided to start a nonprofit to house the advocacy and became incorporated in 1995 as the East Coast Greenway Alliance (ECGA). They held exploratory rides along the route, eventually settling on a greenway all the way from Canada to Key West, Florida. By 2010, the ECGA had five staff and more than five thousand members from all over the United States.

The early years were focused on establishing viable corridors for the route—both an interim travel route that includes on-road stretches and the permanent long-term route of public multiuse trails. Now our staff and our thousands of members engage transportation leaders and elected officials from the federal to the state and local level to get approval and funding for our project. A recent collaboration with local partner organizations in the Philadelphia region resulted in the East Coast Greenway route of Pennsylvania receiving the largest bike/ped federal stimulus grant in the country at $23 million (which goes directly into construction of many miles of trail).

We envision the ECG as a model trail to inspire Eisenhower 2.0—an interstate network revolution throughout the country based on green and healthy modes that enrich communities. Improved bike/ped infrastructure can help all of us effectively tackle two of the biggest challenges of the twenty-first century—global warming and expensive oil.

We have established a route from the Canadian border at Calais, Maine, down to the tip of Key West, Florida. As of early 2010, our route is 25 percent on greenways that are separated from traffic and 75 percent on the safest roads we could find (many including wide shoulders, bike lanes, and other improvements).

The East Coast Greenway is partnering with each of our fifteen states and D.C. to fully sign this route by 2016. In 1999, the Clinton

White House named the ECG one of sixteen National Millennium Trails. Within a few years, the National Park Service may integrate the East Coast Greenway into its national system of trails.

The two key challenges we face are obtaining the necessary land and funds to complete the project. Even though we already have an interim travel route that many people have taken from Maine to Florida, there remain small stretches of our route that are gap areas because we have yet to determine optimum routes for our permanent trail. And like any transportation corridor, this route requires serious capital investment. The 2,250 miles we have yet to build necessitate more than two billion dollars in federal, state, and local funds—a large sum, though it is equal to the amount it took to build one seven-mile bridge on I-95 across the Potomac River. We get past these hurdles by showing decision-makers the strong public support our trails have and the many benefits our trails bring—such as improved air quality, reduced greenhouse gas emissions, a healthier society, lower transportation bills, and economic development and jobs to construct and then service this ecotourism corridor.

With your help, we can complete the greenway and catalyze a green transportation revolution where our food gives us the clean, efficient energy to get from place to place. Please consider joining the effort even if you live away from our route as we aim for the ripple effect of ECG success to help empower the active transportation movement across the globe.

You can find us and our maps at http://greenway.org.

Start a Radio Station
How the Prometheus Radio Project Is Taking Back the Airwaves—and How You Can, Too
Prometheus Radio Project (http://prometheusradio.org)
by Brandy Doyle, Regulatory Policy Associate

Imagine a national forest valued at $800 billion, worth more than Bill Gates, McDonald's, the U.S. military budget, and Medicaid spending combined. Like other national resources, this forest is regularly logged and looted by the usual cast of corporate criminals who profit off our shared treasures. Unlike most other public resources, however, imagine that this particular forest is everywhere around us—but invisible.

This elusive public resource is the radio spectrum. The radio spectrum is used not just for radio and television (both analog and digital), but for other communication tools, including satellites, mobile phones, and a growing number of wireless devices. The park rangers who manage this resource for us are the lawyers, engineers, and bureaucrats at the Federal Communications Commission (FCC), a poorly understood agency with a tremendous responsibility of stewardship. The FCC is obligated to serve the public interest when setting rules on spectrum use, and when allocating chunks of the spectrum to license holders—who lease the rights to use our airwaves but can never own them.

Although we all use the radio spectrum more regularly than most people visit national parks, we can't easily see the speculators getting rich off that spectral real estate. What we do notice, however, is that our media doesn't seem to reflect the diversity of viewpoints and values in our communities.

We notice that radio stations rely on uninspired, repetitive playlists programmed by corporate headquarters instead of local DJs. We notice that TV stations have cut their news teams and focus more on driving profits than driving public debate. We notice that the "digital divide" widens the gap between richer and poorer areas with unequal access to broadband. The spectrum itself may be invisible, but we notice the effects of bad spectrum policy all the time.

At the Prometheus Radio Project, we work to demystify the radio spectrum and the esoteric system that governs our media. Prometheus was founded in 1998, soon after the 1996 Telecom Act brought an era of unprecedented consolidation in media ownership. Think back to the rise of Clear Channel—by removing limits on national ownership, the Telecom Act raised the financial stakes of broadcasting and set off an acquisition frenzy that resulted in mega-networks with increasingly standardized programming and centralized personnel. Media owners had more power than ever before. Activists, including those at Prometheus, began to fight for spectrum access as a fundamental right and a condition of a truly democratic society.

Some of our founders had been involved in the pirate radio movement in the 1990s, when hundreds of unlicensed broadcasters protested the crisis in media ownership by taking to the airwaves directly. We recognized, however, that those excluded from media access shouldn't have to take the legal risks of unlicensed broadcasting in order to access the airwaves. Alongside thousands of others, Prometheus pressured the FCC to free the public airwaves. In one protest, media activists marched to the FCC in droves, flooding their offices with unlicensed broadcasts from hidden backpack transmitters; later the radio "pirates" ran the Jolly Roger up the flagpole at the National Association of Broadcasters building. Faced with legal challenges to the ban on pirates and a nationwide defiance of its rules, the FCC created the low-power FM (LPFM) radio service in 2000.

LPFM stations are run by neighborhood groups, schools, churches, labor unions, arts organizations, and other noncommercial groups. Prometheus has helped hundreds of community organizations to apply for licenses and build their stations, and we have hosted twelve intensive radio "barn raisings" in which hundreds of volunteers build a radio station over three days. In 2003, we partnered with the Coalition of Immokalee Workers to build Radio Conciencia, which was key to successful boycotts of Taco Bell and other corporations that resulted in better wages for Florida's tomato pickers. In 2006, Prometheus helped Pineros y Campesinos Unidos del Noroeste (Northwest Treeplanters and Farmworkers United) build Radio Movimiento in rural Oregon. During the 2008 election season, the station helped to register fifteen hundred and educate seventy-five hundred Latino voters.

Over the years, we have worked with stations as diverse as Maryland's WRYR (dedicated to conserving the Chesapeake Bay), Louisiana's KOCZ (committed to preserving the region's indigenous zydeco music), and Kentucky's WMMT, which connects prisoners in Appalachia with their families with a weekly call-in show. Although our media policies are designed to benefit a powerful few, at Prometheus we have learned that participatory radio can be a powerful tool for social justice organizing and community expression.

To make this a reality for more of us, however, we have to fight for it. The broadcasting lobby won't give up a sliver of the spectrum without a struggle. Want to take back the airwaves from corporate control? Here are some ideas to get started:

1. Start Your Own Radio Station!
At one hundred watts or less, low-power FM stations are inexpensive and easy to operate, allowing new voices on the airwaves. Licensed only to locally focused nonprofits, an LPFM station's success depends

not on professional broadcasting experience or tons of start-up capital, but on the strength of the community organization behind it. By building an inclusive, participatory organization that offers media access to those in your community who need it most, an LPFM station can empower a neighborhood or even a movement. Learn more about low-power radio at http://prometheusradio.org.

Unfortunately, you can only apply for an LPFM license when the FCC opens an application window, and that hasn't happened since 2000. The FCC is waiting on Congress, which restricted the LPFM service as soon as it was introduced (thanks to lobbying from incumbent broadcasters that don't want to share the spectrum). Until Congress lifts the restrictions, there won't be many more LPFM opportunities in most of the country anyway, and the FCC won't act. Which brings us to . . .

2. Support the Local Community Radio Act
This bill would open the airwaves to hundreds of new low-power radio stations, bringing community radio to urban areas for the first time. By removing restrictions created by Congress in 2000, the Local Community Radio Act would return authority to the FCC to license low-power stations on more channels. Along with a broad bipartisan coalition of religious groups, civil rights organizations, media reform organizations, and others, Prometheus has pushed this bill forward in 2005, 2007, and 2009, each time with more success. It's been an uphill struggle against the powerful broadcasting lobby, and when the bill passes, it will be the most significant victory in the fight for community media in a decade. Get involved at www.expandlpfm.org!

3. Make Your Voice Heard at the FCC
The FCC is required to consider public comment when making decisions, but mostly it hears from industry insiders. The technical and bureaucratic complexity of spectrum policy prevents most people from participating in the process, which means that decisions end up enriching current license holders instead of benefiting the public.

But the FCC does make better choices when it knows people are watching. When first considering the low-power radio service, the FCC received more than thirty-five hundred formal comments—at that time a new record for public participation in an FCC rulemaking. It's not the most exciting tactic, but filing comments with the FCC does help to stake the public's claim to the airwaves.

Developing technologies offers new ways to use the spectrum with greater efficiency and flexibility, and with the right policy decisions, these advances could allow innovation and greatly expanded public access to the airwaves. But broadcasters are fighting to keep out competitors—meaning the vast majority of us who don't already have licenses. Tell the FCC how you think the spectrum should be used, and let it know that the public has a right to share in the promises of a digital future.

To file comments with the FCC, go to www.fcc.gov. Click on "Filing Public Comments" in the left-hand column to find rule-makings that are currently open for public comment. You can also go to http://reboot.fcc.gov for more information, including live and archived footage of FCC workshops and events.

4. Make Your Own Media

Even if you don't have a community radio station in your neighbor-hood (yet), you can still distribute your own media by submitting con-tent to independent media sites, creating an online radio station, or starting a podcast or blog. Producing short radio pieces or Internet radio shows is also a great way to build your station and train station volunteers even before you're ready to launch.

5. Support Universal Broadband Access and Net Neutrality

Both of these are key for economic development and self-determination in poor communities, rural areas, and communities of color. Digital inclusion means closing the gap between those who can afford to access the Internet and those who cannot. As we develop new technologies and tools, we continue to rely on the radio spectrum to communicate. That spectrum, like the right to communicate, belongs to us all. Sup-port policies at the local, state, and federal level that close the digital divide.

6. Get Involved with the Prometheus Radio Project!

Volunteer with Prometheus, attend a radio barn raising, make a dona-tion, or learn more at http://prometheusradio.org.

Team Up to Compete
Super CTAs: How a New Kind of Contractor Can Serve the Greater Good
ReddixGroup (http://reddixgroup.com)
by Chris Charuhas

Big corporations can cause big problems. They often exploit people and destroy value in the private sector, and they do damage in the public sector as well. Big corporations working under federal contracts waste billions of dollars, impede the functioning of government, injure citizens, and obstruct progress in public policy.

Large federal contractors defend this with arguments like, "You can't complete big projects without big contractors." In other words, big may be bad, but it's a necessary evil. Is that true? Perhaps it was at one time, but a new kind of contract team is poised to prove that in the world of federal contracting, smaller is better.

That's why a dozen or so small companies have formed what we call a "Super CTA" to bid on new federal information technology contracts. This team-up is based on the premise that a group of small companies can outperform a single large contractor—doing large projects faster, cheaper, and better than the "big boys."

Big contractors form their own Contract Teaming Arrangements when necessary, but these teams are organized hierarchically, like a military unit, with the "prime" contractor commanding and controlling its subcontractors. A Super CTA is very different: It's organized as a peer-to-peer network, like a modern software development team. It's a partnership of equals; in a Super CTA, one company handles the team's communication and coordination functions, but no company in the team dictates to any other.

A Super CTA is a contracting democracy, and, like democracy in general, it requires checks, balances, and good communications to function well. It's more complex than a hierarchical team, but that increased complexity brings higher performance and potentially greater benefits to society. Compared with a single big contractor or traditional prime-plus-subcontractors team, a Super CTA can do much more to serve the common good. For example:

- It can focus on doing useful work instead of just making money. The unspoken mission of many large federal contractors is to suck as much money out of our government as possible; the work they do is merely a means to that end. This is unlikely to change—their overriding goal of maximizing profits is too strongly ingrained. A Super CTA composed of small, privately owned firms, by contrast, can focus on the work itself. The first Super CTA is doing just that. "If we do great work, the money will come," says Joe Reddix, the team's chief facilitator and a longtime federal project manager. "What's most important is fulfilling our public trust."

- It can create value for our government, instead of extracting value from it. Big contractors have typically tried to tie federal agencies to their proprietary IT systems, achieving "lock-in" and creating a dependent relationship that they can then exploit. This ensures high profits for the contractor while sticking agencies with high costs and technological stagnation. The smaller companies that make up a Super CTA are much more likely than big firms to use open-source software, and they also tend to favor open standards. Anyone can fix, improve, and connect to the systems they create, which lowers costs and makes upgrades easy.

- It can create more and better jobs. Small businesses create two out of every three new jobs, but large federal contractors try to keep them from creating too many. Forced by government to subcontract to small firms, big contractors give them only low-value work, and thus avoid funding and training potential competitors. Small companies in a Super CTA, by contrast, have an interest in helping one another grow. The capabilities of each member firm complement those of the others, so the more work a member firm gets in its specialty, the more work its team members can do. As the team becomes capable of undertaking bigger projects, it must hire more people to complete them.

When the Obama administration released a request for teams of small companies—CTAs—to participate in its twenty-billion-dollar health care IT initiative, Joe Reddix saw an opportunity to employ a new model. "When I saw what the government was doing with Web 2.0, how they were promoting transparency, I thought it might be ready for something new. When it began canceling big companies' contracts for nonperformance, I knew it was. That's when I created the Super CTA."

This new breed of business is being built right now. More than a dozen companies have joined the Super CTA that Joe founded, and the team is online at www.reddixgroup.com. If it's selected to work on the huge health care IT initiative, the team intends to serve as the model for what federal contracting can and should be in the future. "We want to be the poster child for a new way of working with government," Joe says. "But at the very least, we should be able to keep some big contractors honest."

PART FOUR: Print Your Own Money

Alternatives to Bank-Issued Money
Life Dollars
Fourth Corner Exchange (www.fourthcornerexchange.com)
by Francis Ayley, President

Have you ever wondered why, when millions of people have been working for positive change for so many years, the world is still in such a mess? Does it seem like no matter how much good work is done, the destructive juggernaut of modern culture steams ahead regardless, intent on destroying the planet and the quality of people's lives?

There is an invisible but powerful underlying structure in our lives and our culture, one that supports and rewards antisocial behavior, the destruction of the environment and our communities, and the exploitation of people and resources. At the same time, it penalizes altruistic, social, cooperative, and community-oriented behavior. The vast majority of people accept this structure without question, never realizing how deeply it affects their lives and their world.

What is it? The bank-issued money system. The one we use every day.

Surprised? Bank-issued money is something most people simply accept as a given. It's there, we use it, and it never occurs to us to question it. It seems so simple. The only real issue for many of us is making sure we have enough of it.

In fact, money is far from being a "neutral medium of exchange," as it is often claimed to be. The structure of any financial system, the rules by which it operates, inevitably condition the behavior of those who use it. The money system we use directly affects the quality of our lives, our communities, our culture, and our world.

In our present monetary system, everyone is competing for an artificially scarce resource (money). This scarcity-based system inevitably creates a fear of not having enough. It encourages, even forces people to behave competitively, against their natural instincts. Greed, selfishness, competitiveness, and antisocial behavior are encouraged and often rewarded financially. Cooperation, altruism, and community-building activities typically go unrewarded, and those who engage in them must often limit them to their "spare time." Money is issued by private, profit-driven banks as interest-bearing debt, an inherently flawed and unsustainable model (visit our website and watch the excellent animated video *Money as Debt* to learn more). As a result, more money must always be repaid than has ever been put into circulation, reinforcing the (accurate) perception that there is "not enough," so you had better be ruthless if you want to be sure to have all the money you need.

Some would argue that this competitive attitude is simply human nature. In fact, some studies now suggest that it is cooperative behavior that is instinctive and natural for human beings, and competitive behavior that is learned (see Alfie Kohn, *No Contest: The Case Against Competition*, or the work of Glynn Isaac). The truth is, if you place people in an environment that demands they compete to survive, nearly all of them will compete. If the influence of the environment remains unseen, such behavior can seem like human nature when in reality it is being invisibly conditioned.

The conventional money system, the one we use every day, intrinsically supports and rewards competition, antisocial behavior, the destruction of the environment, and the exploitation of people and natural resources. It undermines democracy, as without economic democracy our political democracy can be sold to the highest bidder. It forces people to behave competitively when they don't want to and would choose not to if they had a real choice. Money is issued through privately owned banks whose fundamental goal is to create profits for their shareholders, not serve the common good of the people. Banks create money as and when they can profit from it, forcing citizens into wage slavery to repay the bank for money it created out of nothing (unbelievable, but true). The expansion and contraction of the money supply locks us into a "boom and bust" cycle of never-ending, unsustainable growth. At some point, a crash is inevitable, and vast amounts of suffering ensue.

A healthy, sustainable money system would operate quite differently. It would be non-usurious, as any financial system based on interest is inherently unsustainable. It would be based on abundance instead of scarcity, and would place the power to issue currency into the hands of the people rather than banks. It would create a healthy trading environment, giving people a genuine choice to behave competitively or cooperatively, and holding people and organizations accountable for their behavior. It would facilitate the exchange of goods and services among its members and would give people access to the resources they need for the trades they need to do. The amount of currency in circulation would be linked to the actual goods and services being exchanged, not to a scarce physical resource or the creation of profits for a bank.

Fourth Corner Exchange Life Dollars are a sustainable and equitable alternative money system. Using Life Dollars empowers people and communities to take back economic power into their own hands.

A Life Dollar is valued at one hour of time. Time is a universal currency; an hour of time is the same length for everyone, no matter who you are or where you live. Unlike time banks, however, we do not impose an "hour for an hour" equivalence on exchanges. We recognize that differences in value do exist, and that the "hidden" hours someone spends in order to offer one hour of service must be taken into account for a trade to be fair and for an economic system to function universally.

In thinking about exchanging time, we ask questions like: How much of someone else's life energy am I asking for in exchange for what I have to offer? How much of my own time and energy has gone into being able to provide this service or this item? What is a fair exchange of life energy for what I want to buy or sell?

In this way, we move beyond the usual concepts of how much "money" something is worth to a more just and equitable assessment of value. We eliminate artificially created inequalities among the currencies of different nations, and normalize economic transactions among communities. We are creating a world of economic justice and sustainable prosperity for all.

Life Dollars are non-interest-bearing, sustainable, and completely stable. They are not linked to any national currency and are not subject to inflation or deflation. They are an unlimited supply of currency, electronic and printed, issued by citizens themselves in sufficiency as and when they need them. The trading environment created by the use of Life Dollars is cooperative rather than competitive, and people often remark upon how different it feels. Based on our experience, the overwhelming majority of people do choose to behave cooperatively and act responsibly toward other members and the environment, given a healthy monetary system in which to trade.

The Life Dollar cooperative economy connects people with one another. It facilitates mutually beneficial exchanges, helps to rebuild and strengthen communities, and fosters a culture of goodwill and trust. By removing artificial incentives toward competition, building in accountability, and rewarding expressions of goodwill and socially responsible action, Life Dollars enable our members to remove their support from the dysfunctional financial structures that keep so many destructive practices in our world in place.

Members of Fourth Corner Exchange, the Pacific Northwest organization that developed Life Dollars, began trading in January 2004. We have grown consistently since then and now have many hundreds of members who have made thousands of exchanges, trading a vast variety of goods and services. We are spreading to other communities and other parts of the world.

Our vision is a world of economic freedom and justice for all, where all communities have access to a fair and equitable universal medium of exchange, issued by the people in sufficiency to meet their own needs and the needs of their communities.

Our mission is to create this world of economic democracy by rebuilding communities through teaching people how to use our sustainable currency in a socially just and responsible manner.

We warmly invite you to join us. *Join the revolution! Be part of the solution.* Visit www.lifedollars.org to join us in bringing Life Dollars to the world and your community.

Start a Local Energy Trading System
Sydney LETS (www.auslets.org/sydney)
by Annette Loudon, Assistant Coordinator

In Paul Grignon's enlightening animation *Money as Debt*, Anton the baker explains that money is just a way of measuring value. If money is just a measurement, how can it become scarce? Anton points out that "No one is ever stopped from building a house due to a shortage of inches."*

If our community has an abundance of skills and goods to offer, why should trading be limited by a shortage of regular currency? If money is tight, why not find another way to trade?

How Does LETS Work?
LETS members advertise their goods and services via a trading post (this may be in print or online). Offers in Sydney LETS include babysitting, massage, personal training, gardening, holiday accommodation, mending, business services, DVDs, books, clothes, dinners, cakes, cookies, et cetera . . .

When members see an interesting offer, they contact the member to arrange a trade. After the trade is completed, the seller charges the buyer. Some systems keep track of trades by sending paper checks to an office for processing. In Sydney, we use an online trading system that allows members to charge one another directly.

How Does LETS Keep Track of Trades?
In LETS, the total of all balances is always zero. Some members are in credit, others are in debit. As one person must spend for another to earn, it's not considered a bad thing to hold a negative balance for a while. Of course it works best when all members give and take evenly over time, so members are always encouraged to focus on earning units if they've held a negative for a while.

---

*Grignon, Paul. *The Essence of Money: A Medieval Tale*, www.digitalcoin.info/The_Essence_of_Money.html.

Here is a very simple example of how LETS trading works. Mike, Amy, and Sarah all start with balances of 0.

Mike, Amy, and Sarah already have 90 units' worth of good stuff without any "money" changing hands. They may be short of cash, but as long as they have something valuable to offer, and some spare time, there's no need for them to go without.

LETS is not a utopian solution. There's the occasional bad trading experience, some members have trouble earning, others have trouble spending. Despite the occasional glitch, most members appreciate the opportunity to put their talents to use earning (and spending!) in the local community.

ACCOUNT BALANCES AND TRADES	MIKE	AMY	SARAH	TOTAL OF ALL ACCOUNTS
ALL ACCOUNTS START AT 0	0	0	0	0
MIKE BUYS BOOKS FROM AMY FOR 40 UNITS	-40	+40		
UPDATED BALANCES	-40	+40	0	0
AMY PAYS SARAH 20 UNITS FOR BABYSITTING		-20	+20	
UPDATED BALANCES	-40	20	+20	0
SARAH PAYS MIKE 30 UNITS FOR A YOGA CLASS	+30		-30	
UPDATED BALANCES	-10	20	-10	0

Engage in Open-Source Economic Solutions
How New Kinds of Currencies Can Solve Social and Economic Problems
MetaCurrency.org
by Arthur Brock, Co-founder

Modern technology makes it realistic for us to perform the accounting and transaction functions that banks have traditionally done for us. We have the means to put an end to the money monopoly and currency monoculture that they have fostered to make it easier for them to control the economy and channel wealth into the hands of the few.

Contrary to traditional economic dogma, currencies are not neutral measures of value. Every currency embodies specific values through the nature of its design, which ignores certain things and elevates others. For example, the single largest sector of health care providers is never discussed in our health care debates because mothers don't charge for their caregiving. Vital things such as breathable air and drinkable water have no monetary value until they become scarce. This is not an inherent behavior of markets, only for markets designed to revolve around artificially scarce currencies. Different currencies incentivize different behaviors and, hence, yield different economies.

Information Age economies will replace commercial markets with more efficient, high-trust, self-organizing social networks that immediately channel appropriate resources where they are needed. Just as factories and finance were high-leverage tools of the Industrial Age, social software and reputation currencies that fuel these new social markets are the tools of the new economy. And yes, these markets move real value. It is already happening with software (open source), accommodations (couchsurfing), knowledge (MIT open courseware), and many domains.

There is a family of projects fostering these new economies and wielding currencies as something more powerful than money. They recognize currencies as formal symbol systems for shaping, enabling, and measuring currents—currents of time, attention, participation, resources, sharing, trust, giving, information, knowledge, goods, and services—as well as tools for exchanging value. These projects are specifically geared to help you learn currency design principles so you can invent and implement well-targeted currencies of all types tailored to the needs of your community.

The MetaCurrency Project: Building the Platform for the Next Economy

We are creating the means and standards for new currencies to interoperate, to provide transparency about the rules they operate by, and to run in a decentralized manner. "Open sourcing" money requires that we eliminate power imbalances inherent in modern technology systems (for example, system admins are all-powerful and users can only do what the admins permit). By separating data integrity, security, and access, our protocols enable fractal sovereignty at every level (which also provides new alternatives to the endless political/ideological debates over who gets control).

Find out more about our ridiculously ambitious projects at www. metacurrency.org.

Start a Time Bank, Save a Community

One Blue Dot (www.onebluedot.com)

by Jessica Harris

What Is Time Banking?

Time banking is a system of exchange where members trade services for hours instead of money. The hours that members earn can be spent on any other service offered within the time bank. For example, Asli babysits for Marge and earns four hours. Asli then spends two hours getting her lock fixed by Sarah and the other two hours on a German lesson from Nia. Because the value of all services is equal, most transactions are considered a gift and are therefore tax-free.

What Is the Value of Time Banking?

While time banking is an effective way to save money, the real value of time banking is in the formation of new relationships and social engagement within a community. Time banking has been shown to be a remarkable tool for revitalizing communities and helping reduce rates of mental health disorders. By sharing services, members are engaging in co-production, the act of creating together. Unlike co-consumption, the social model that our current economic system supports, co-production fosters mutual trust and positive action, and increases local resilience by weaving together the needs of a community. There is no scarcity within a system of time banking; rather, abundance is generated by the activity of its members. The more transactions there are, the more value is generated and circulated within the community.

How to Join a Time Bank

There are more than a hundred time banks in the U.K. and over sixty in the United States. To find a time bank near you or to learn how to start a time bank, visit Time Banks USA, the national organization of time banking, at www.timebanks.org.

New York is home to one of the most active time banks in the country, the Visiting Nurse Service Community Connections TimeBank. VNSNY Community Connections TimeBank has more than twelve hundred members and has facilitated over eight thousand transactions, generating more than thirty-two thousand hours of exchange services. To learn more about the VNSNY Community Connections TimeBank, visit www.vnsny.org/timebank, email timebank@vnsny.org, or call 212-609-7811.

New York is also home to Time Interchange New York (TINY), a newly formed time bank that has grown to more than five hundred members in the first six months. Visit www.timeinterchange.com to learn more.

The Future of Time Banking

One Blue Dot is a company formed by TINY members to develop design tools that strengthen and expand the possibilities for community building. Currently, one of its projects is to create open-source software that will support a global network of time banks, as well as to consolidate complementary systems that allow people to reduce consumption and share resources. One Blue Dot is committed to utilizing complementary currencies to facilitate the creation of community design tools. To learn more, visit www.onebluedot.com.

Join a time bank to start weaving your community today.

Break Up the Big Banks

A New Way Forward (http://anewwayforward.org)
by Tiffiniy Cheng and Donny Shaw, Co-founders

In the spring of '09, as it was becoming clear that the big banks would continue their domination over public policy under the Obama administration, an email was circulated to a small group of friends say-ing, "OK, it's time to do something." Of course, we had no idea *what* to do. But as the giant AIG bonuses were getting paid out and the Bush bailout policies were getting extended, we decided that we couldn't do nothing. We were a few friends looking to pick a fight against the biggest industry in the country; one that, according to Senator Dick Durbin, "owns" the Congress. We knew the Internet was the platform, we knew this was a pinnacle issue of political power for our generation, and we just had to be ingenious to do something big. It was exciting.

So, we thought we'd have a protest. Actually, we thought we'd have dozens of protests all across the country. And we thought we'd see if we could keep the protests focused on super-wonky economic policy in order to get our point across that the public was going to wage a real battle against the collusion of the banks and the government—specifi-cally, that all "too big to fail" banks should be resolved through nor-mative bankruptcy procedures, divided up, and then sold back to the private market with new rules in place that keep them from getting huge again. For two months straight, co-founder Donny Shaw and I did almost nothing other than send emails, blog, talk to people, learn the ins and outs of protest planning, and work out logistics. We had a few close friends help us pull all the pieces together—language, design, Web development, old open-source code, and organizing strategy. We launched our website with a one-month organizing dead-line. People began to come out of the woodwork. All kinds of people from all kinds of backgrounds stepped in to ramp up the energy. On April 11, 2009, people held sixty protests against the big banks across the country. Four hundred in Portland, Oregon, three hundred or so in San Francisco, two hundred in Seattle and Los Angeles, a hundred or so in dozens of other cities, a dozen or so in several rural locations.

The protests were the beginning of a local organizing model and the spawning of local groups that could continue as a volunteer effort and completely unfunded for the next year. All this showed that our national bullhorn could serve as a catalyst for local organizers, whom we could then support with organizing processes and materials, no matter their level of prior experience. This coming together was excit-ing then and continues to be exciting as the campaign grows greater local group engagement into a larger public discussion and platform across the country. With a common purpose and under a consolidated action plan, ordinary people are coming together to talk about the economy and what can be done to make it work better for people and the preservation of the public good, not corporations. An organizers' mailing list has served as an asynchronous space for those wanting to do more to stay informed and to discuss next steps and policy issues. We hope to help develop more local mailing lists that help people organize themselves and work on their ideas with strangers in their area. Some local groups hold regular meetings; do research and create organizing materials, public educational forums, and phone and email banks; distribute informative flyers; protest foreclosures; work on getting their local governments to divest from large banks; and more.

It's a decentralized movement of people making sense of the economy in their area and fighting to transform it into a level playing field for everyone. It's a fight for structural change of the economy and the financial sector in order to create the strategic footholds the public needs to attain a real quality of life for all. In the same way that corporate greed has organized to make itself heard in the political process, the public is carving out ways their policy positions come to matter.

Over time, our volunteer efforts have focused on reforms that are broad and structural, with a particular focus on how the economy relates to political power. Our goal has been to see firm caps enacted to limit the size of financial powerhouses, especially the big banks, in order to limit their power over our political process, the economic landscape, and the policies that affect every element of this country. When these giant, totally unaccountable financial corporations imperil our public institutions, destroy our neighborhoods, and eliminate our jobs, all because they made some mistakes with their absurd profit-making schemes, we need to extend our sense of the scope of democracy to include the financial sector. Finance has grown so big in recent years that it now controls 40 percent of all profit that is generated in the U.S. economy. We need to start viewing finance as an extension of public policy that can either improve our lives by creating security and sustaining growth, or harm it by inflating debt bubbles that pop and put our livelihoods in jeopardy.

In the last year, economics has become a part of people's daily discourse. This is probably the only upside to the financial crisis, and we are very happy to encourage and help facilitate this conversation. As a group, we're continuing to craft campaigns that anyone can join easily. Here are a few simple ways to get involved:

1. Break up with the big banks. Cut up that big-bank credit card, borrow money from friends or family, bank with a local, community-oriented bank.

2. Find your local A New Way Forward group and get involved. Help build a local mailing list by inviting friends and other groups and get local activities started. If there isn't a local group or list in your city, start one up: http://www.anewwayforward .org/og.

3. Join us in flyering in your city about the big banks and their destructive effects. A Bank of America ATM is a great place to start, or we have hundreds of events across the country listed (and a downloadable flyer) on our events page. Join us in organizing a local event in upcoming national campaigns: http:// www.anewwayforward.org/events.

4. Donate money or your time. This is a 100 percent unfunded effort, which means that we rely on individual donations and volunteerism to keep it running. It is important to maintain a truly grassroots, decentralized effort that anyone can participate in. To do so, we need a technical infrastructure that makes joining easy and the organizing support to help people keep it going. If you can donate money—or your organization can— that will help us get Web assistance. If you can help with Web design, programming, or just about anything else you have a special talent in, that will be immensely helpful, too. Email us at tyc@anewwayforward.org or donate through PayPal at donate@anewwayforward.org.

PART FIVE: DIY Activism—From the Bottom Up

Engage in Micro-Lending
by the staff of Kiva.org

In 2004, Matt Flannery and Jessica Jackley took a trip to East Africa, where they witnessed the power of micro-finance. Jessica was conducting impact evaluation surveys for Village Enterprise Fund while Matt filmed interviews with small-business entrepreneurs, and they saw and heard how grants had been used to build small businesses, which could then support a family.

They were inspired to find a way to facilitate loans to small-business owners in the developing world and began developing the concept of an Internet-based fund where socially minded individuals could loan directly to these deserving entrepreneurs. They spent the next year researching and creating a business plan to make Kiva a reality.

In 2005, Kiva.org launched as the world's first micro-lending website for the working poor, empowering individuals to lend to entrepreneurs across the globe. By combining micro-finance with the Internet, Kiva created a global community of people connected through lending.

Today, anyone with an email address can create a Kiva account, and anyone who can make payments using a credit card or PayPal account can be a Kiva Lender. With as little as twenty-five dollars, users can make a huge difference.

Kiva was born of the following beliefs:

- People are by nature generous, and will help others if given the opportunity to do so in a transparent, accountable way.
- The poor are highly motivated and can be very successful when given an opportunity.
- By connecting people, we can create relationships beyond financial transactions, and build a global community expressing support and encouragement of one another.

Kiva promotes:

- Dignity: Kiva encourages partnership relationships as opposed to benefactor relationships. Partnership relationships are characterized by mutual dignity and respect.
- Accountability: Loans encourage more accountability than donations where repayment is not expected.
- Transparency: The Kiva website is an open platform where communication can flow freely around the world.

How Kiva.org Works

1. Field Partners disburse a micro-loan.
   - The process starts with Kiva's Field Partners, which are micro-finance institutions operating around the world.

- Field Partners typically approve and disburse a micro-loan to an entrepreneur in their community at the same time they seek funding through Kiva.
- Disbursals can happen up to thirty days before or thirty days after a loan request is uploaded to the Kiva website. Field Partners use their knowledge of local business conditions to determine when it is best to disburse the loan and ensure success of the business.

2. An entrepreneur profile is uploaded to Kiva.org.
   - The Field Partner works with entrepreneurs to create a profile that tells potential lenders about their background, their business goals, and their funding needs—either the new investment they seek, or the amount of the loan already disbursed by the Field Partner.

3. Lenders choose an entrepreneur to support and make a loan.
   - Lenders browse the collected set of entrepreneur profiles on www.kiva.org and choose an entrepreneur they want to help.
   - Lenders provide their funds to Kiva using PayPal or a credit card in amounts of twenty-five dollars or more.

4. Kiva provides the funds to the Field Partner.
   - Kiva processes the payments from all its lenders, and sends the appropriate funds to each of its Field Partners to support the entrepreneurs the lenders have chosen.
   - Field Partners use the funds from Kiva as the capital needed to disburse loans to the selected entrepreneurs, or to replenish the capital used to disburse the loan already made to the entrepreneurs.
   - The entrepreneur's obligation to repay becomes directly tied to the Kiva lender.

5. The entrepreneur repays his or her loan.
   - The Field Partner collects repayments on behalf of Kiva and its lenders.
   - Field partners report repayments to Kiva, which reports them to the lenders.
   - Lenders are repaid their principal when the loan is paid off. Lenders do not earn interest.
   - Field Partners retain the option to cover both currency losses and entrepreneur defaults, so they can respond appropriately to changing local economic and other conditions.

As of March 2010, more than 680,000 people have joined Kiva, and over 430,000 Kiva lenders have loaned more than $125 million to better than 315,000 entrepreneurs in fifty-four countries. As of March 2010, loans made through Kiva.org have a 98 percent repayment rate. Kiva.org is headquartered in San Francisco. To learn more, or to become a Kiva lender, visit www.kiva.org.

Simply Evolve the Species

Evolver (www.evolver.net)
by Ken Jordan, Co-founder

Evolver is a global network of inspired evolutionaries—the growing movement of people who know that the expansion of awareness and consciousness is a necessary part of social change. Evolvers are hope fiends, ecological activists, and utopian pragmatists who see this time of creative chaos as an opportunity to rethink, reconnect, and reinvent our lives. Meeting both online and offline, Evolver is an experiment in the creation of a new society with communities and institutions that favor collaboration over competition, sustainability over throw-away consumerism, spirited engagement over spectator entertainment, and transparency over opaque hierarchy. The effort itself is a kind of living artwork; in the words of Joseph Beuys, it is "a social sculpture."

A great many of us are aware of the critical challenges that face us, and of the inadequacy of society's institutions to adequately address them. Through Evolver, members of the transformational community are connecting to find one another, share knowledge and resources, and participate in projects that are models for change that others may follow.

This movement began with a Web magazine, Reality Sandwich. Launched in May 2007, Reality Sandwich gives voice to the consciousness community, covering topics from sustainability to shamanism, alternate realities to alternative energy, remixing media to reimagining community, holistic healing techniques to visionary technologies. Writers range from established and bestselling authors—such as Daniel Pinchbeck, Starhawk, and Stanislav Grof—to emerging voices—like Charles Eisenstein, Anya Kamenetz, and Adam Elenbaas, to college students publishing their first articles. Reality Sandwich has no "editorial positions" to uphold. Rather, the site offers a variety of perspectives on subjects that matter to its readers, and which are largely ignored, even disdained, by the mainstream media. It is a platform of possibilities and alternative realities meant to de-hypnotize readers from the deadening drumbeat of the corporate culture machinery.

Reality Sandwich quickly grew a loyal readership. Not only were people attracted to the articles, but they also wanted to connect with one another. So the comments area on the site gave birth to a dynamic online community. That community was given its own long-awaited home in the summer of 2009 on Evolver.net, an online social network for conscious collaboration. It provides a platform for individuals, communities, and organizations to discover and share the new tools, initiatives, and ideas that will improve our lives and change the world.

Soon after the Evolver.net site launch, the community felt it was as important (maybe even more so) to meet in physical space as to connect in digital space, which led to the creation of Evolver Regionals. By early 2010, more than thirty active groups had been founded in cities from Boston to Seattle, Cape Town to Sydney, Baltimore to Long Beach. Each month, they hold Evolver Spores: presentations, panel discussions, and film screenings about the topics discussed on Reality Sandwich. Once the Regionals were established, Evolvers came together to hold Evolver-themed festivals, develop permaculture gardens, and establish community spaces, among other projects.

Looking ahead, our aim is to build this movement into a powerful force by providing platforms where people can connect and take action. By uniting our voices into a larger movement, we can create a "tipping point" that shifts the debate on climate change, the War on Drugs, corporate overreach, economic disparity, renewable energy, preservation of wilderness and natural resources, and more. We will keep improving Evolver.net's online tools to enable collaboration, while giving support to grassroots initiatives taken by the Evolver Regional groups. Other activities include publishing books, offering educational programs, and producing media (including podcasts and videos) and events.

A project of this kind, which emerged organically from the unique community it serves, should not be expected to have a conventional organizational structure. Following the public radio model, it is made possible by paying members in an Evolver Social Movement (E+SM). Their contributions cover operating costs so that most offerings are available for free to all comers. A small paid professional staff handles the editorial and administrative tasks that maintain and grow the Evolver movement's infrastructure (such as managing the flow of content and information on Reality Sandwich, Evolver.net, and the monthly Spores), while hundreds of volunteers provide content for the websites and take part in grassroots initiatives. The staff act as facilitators, coordinating efforts and consulting with the community about how resources should be channeled, which grassroots projects to support, and how best to grow the movement.

As the community expands, Evolver will offer new services—modeling cooperative systems aimed at shifting society away from an endless emphasis on competition and the abuse of the natural world. These include the introduction of a complementary currency, the cooperative acquisition of socially responsible goods and services, as well as barter and exchange networks. We will also produce more ambitious events, including conferences, regional festivals, and Evolver shamanic retreats in South America. Unlike many mission-driven operations, Evolver is incorporated as a socially responsible business rather than as a not-for-profit. This is a deliberate attempt to transmute the extraordinary ability of the corporation to act with speed and efficiency to effect change, redirecting its energies toward serving the public good. In this way, Evolver is an alchemical enterprise, with a firm commitment to transparency and to being responsive to the movement we serve.

Start a Religion
Reverend Billy and the Church of Life After Shopping
(http://revbilly.com)
by Reverend Billy Talen and Savitri D, Director

Let's talk about the Devil. Corporate Commercialism has sped up to a roar, virtually unopposed. Consumerism is normalized in the mind of the average person; sometimes we even refer to ourselves as consumers, forgetting that we are also citizens, humans, men, women, animals. We forget that we share many resources, public spaces, and histories with one another. The subjugation of these resources and these laws to the forces of the market demands a response.

We are a post-religious church, a radical performance community. We hold "services" wherever we can, in concert halls, theaters, churches, community centers, forests, fields, parking lots, mall atriums, and perhaps most important, inside stores, as close to the cash register as we can get, within spitting distance of the point of purchase.

We have identified particularly egregious corporate practices: Starbucks blocking Ethiopian coffee farmers from adding value to their coffees by trademarking their ancient coffee names, Victoria's Secret clear-cutting virgin forest to send out a million catalogs a day for a 2 percent return, Disney and its sweatshop labor, Wal-Mart and its union busting. We study their ad campaigns and their marketing strategies, and we invent and shape a counterstory, a fresh narrative. Then we go into the retail environment armed with this new message, The Anti-Ad. The Truth.

We sing, we dance, we preach, sometimes we perform small "interventions," invisible plays, acts of ritual resistance. We exorcise cash registers and remythologize the retail environment; we illuminate the Devil. We make media and send it out around the world. We get hassled by security guards and sometimes get arrested.

Above all we try to complexify the moment of purchase, to snap people out of their hypnosis and back into the mystery of being human. We remind people that things come from somewhere, that products have a resource past, a labor past. Someone made It, and It is made of something. We trace the route a product took to get on the shelf, the life it might have when we throw it away. We animate the objects that surround us and in so doing we reanimate ourselves. We become citizens again.

Liberation is a radiant process; it spreads. We think freedom from consumerism is virulent, contagious. Tell your neighbor you stopped shopping and it gives her permission to do the same. One day we can all live in richly varied and consistently surprising neighborhoods, with people who seem to have invented themselves, and so are endlessly fascinating, something beyond entertainment. Yes, there *is* a life after shopping!

Naturally, people wonder how this all works. Do we live in the bushes? Do we forage for food? Spin our own wool? Have we stopped our shopping? Where did I get my underwear? We are organized like a not-for-profit theater company and we support this work by teaching, lecturing, and performing, with generous donations and grants. Most of all, we depend on the volunteerism and skill sharing of the church's singers and musicians and activists. We try to spread whatever resources we have as far out in our community as we can. Among us there are scientists, filmmakers, teachers, musicians, dog walkers, hairdressers, executives, painters, and bakers. We are all ages and many races and we are definitely not Puritans, so sometimes we do shop, but carefully and locally if at all possible.

This is not a Utopian vision, or maybe it is and our Utopia just looks less like the biosphere and more like a healthy neighborhood. We know the health of the planet is depending on us and on the degree to which we can create healthy neighborhoods. Everywhere. My healthy neighborhood depends on your healthy neighborhood, and your healthy neighborhood depends on the health of a neighborhood in rural Peru or Calcutta. What we need now are more people in more neighborhoods spreading that radiant freedom, teaching other people to turn their backs on the billboards and back away from the product. Please join us, somehow someway. There are all kinds of resources at our website http://revbilly.com, conversations to join, plays to perform, songs to learn, campaigns to replicate.

Above all, we invite you to start your own church. Start with what you have. We build performances and rituals with songs and prayers and dancing and an updated kind of preaching because that's what we know how to do. If what you know how to do is bake, then we suggest you start a cake brigade. People who join us "bring forth" what they have in the way of skill, talent, and chutzpah. That is the beginning of the independence that corporations know we have, but hope we never discover. The corporations can just keep holding their breath. We have work to do.

Rewrite the Law: Change the Constitution to Protect People Over Corporations
The Environmental and Social Responsibility Amendment to the U.S. Constitution
by Rabbi Michael Lerner (http://tikkun.org)

Preface
The intent of this Amendment is to provide democratic control over the economic life of our society to the citizens of the United States, to encourage the development of locally controlled businesses and

corporations and cooperative enterprises controlled by the people engaged in those enterprises, to require that corporations serve the public good and not just their own private ambitions, to ensure that corporations make decisions that enhance the ecological/environmental well-being of the Planet Earth and all its people, to control and reduce the power of corporations and other limited-liability entities, and to ensure that our economic life reflects our understanding of the importance of kindness, generosity, cooperation, the fostering of solidarity and caring for other people, our mutual interdependence with all Americans and with all people on the planet; that it enhances our capacities to find meaning and purpose in work that truly contributes to the well-being of others and the well-being of the planet.

This Amendment is intended to apply to all aspects of economic life in the United States including new forms that may develop in the future. Because many of the forces shaping U.S. economic life are or may in the future derive from other countries, all parts of this Amendment, unless otherwise specified, shall apply to any entity operating within or impacting upon the economic life in the U.S., and the Congress shall be enjoined to develop whatever legislation is necessary to ensure that the standards of social and environmental and ethical behavior mandated herein are applied also to any foreign economic, political, or media entity operating within, selling its products within, or advertising and promoting its products or services within the U.S.

For purposes of this Amendment, all monetary figures listed below are to be adjusted annually in accord with rises or falls in the cost-of-living index, so figures cited are meant to indicate the values as of 2010. The word "stakeholders" below refers to all citizens in the communities in which the corporations in question have their offices, advertise or market their products or services, or are impacted by the operations of those services or products, as well as representatives of environmental organizations, unions representing the workers of that corporation, and human rights and civil rights organizations representing the interests of those affected by the operations or investments of that corporation. Stakeholders shall not include organizations that are created directly or indirectly by the corporation or members of its governing bodies, its corporate leadership and their assistants, or by anyone else acting in consort with that corporate leadership or corporate managerial groups. Stakeholders as defined here shall have standing to sue in federal court should any part of this Amendment be ignored or not fully implemented toward the purpose of creating greater democratic control over the economy by citizens of the United States, and the courts are hereby empowered to issue injunctions and assess penalties should any legislative or judicial body or corporation or media outlet seek to impede or frustrate the intent of this Amendment or its speedy implementation.

Article One

Corporations and any other for-profit business form or limited-liability association or economic entity developed in the United States and either operating in the U.S. or based in the U.S. but operating in other parts of the world are not and shall not be considered "persons" or given the rights of individual human beings under the terms of the U.S. Constitution or the constitutions of any state in this Union, nor shall Congress or the courts give them similar rights or protections. All corporations or limited-liability associations or for-profit businesses shall be responsible first and foremost to the communities in which they operate and the communities in which their sales, products, and advertising have an impact, then to the people of the United States as a whole, and then finally, and only after fulfilling these primary responsibilities, to their stockholders. Corporations are created by the decisions of the people of the United States, not by private contract, and any aspect of existing contracts that impedes a corporation from serving the public good shall be declared null and void.

Article Two

It is the right of the people of the United States to democratically shape and control the economic life of this society and to protect the environmental/ecological well-being of the Planet Earth and all of its peoples, and any attempt to limit that right by the courts, the presidency, the Congress, the media, or state and local legislative bodies shall be deemed a violation of the rights of American citizens and doing so or conspiring to do so shall be punishable by fine or imprisonment. Any aspect of this Constitution or laws or interpretations of laws by the courts that currently function to limit the right of the people to democratically shape and control the economic life of this society are hereby declared null and void.

Article Three

Any corporation or limited-liability economic entity functioning within, selling its products within, or incorporated within the territorial boundaries of the United States or its territories, and having a gross income exceeding twenty million dollars per year (adjusted for future inflation or deflation), shall be required to seek a new corporate charter from the state or territory from which it has been chartered (or, in the case of corporations incorporated in other countries but operating in the U.S., a corporate charter must be granted by the U.S. government) every five years. That new charter shall be granted only to those corporations that can prove a satisfactory history of social responsibility to a jury of ordinary citizens selected in the same manner as any jury hearing capital crimes in the state or federal jurisdiction in which these hearings are to take place. The state and federal government must supply the jury with subpoena power, plus financial assistance to make possible a thorough investigation of the societal, environmental, and ethical impact of that corporation, and shall hear the testimony not only of the corporation's own staff but also of the people who work for that corporation in the lowest-paid jobs and middle-income jobs, and the testimony of all of the stakeholders including any communities within which that corporation operates or whose activities have a demonstrable impact on the economic, environmental, societal, and ethical life of that community.

The jury reviewing the social responsibility of the corporation shall be empowered to require specific changes in the corporation's governance, practices, products, and services, which must be completed within three years' time. If that jury finds that there are prima facie reasons to believe that the changes are not done in a satisfactory manner, the jury will reconvene and be empowered to transfer ownership of that corporation to the workers of that corporation who would hold a majority of the seats on its board of directors, and to a group of community stakeholders representing the interests of the environment, the communities in which the corporation operates, and the communities in which the corporation's products, activities, and services have a demonstrable impact on their economic, political, cultural, or ethical life. This new governing body will then have five years to prove to the jury that it has taken appropriate steps toward the goal of dramatically increasing the social, environmental, and ethical responsibility of the corporation while continuing to make it economically viable. If the jury determines that it has failed to do so, it can then turn the governing body over to another corporation or to a group of individuals who can convince the jury that it could run the corporation under review and provide for it to continue to provide its public benefits while increasing its level of social responsibility. At that point the jury has fulfilled its function, and after another five years a new jury will be impaneled to consider the social and environmental responsibility of the corporation in question.

Among the issues that the jury must consider:

- Does the corporation pay its lowest-paid workers a living wage in the community in which those workers live?
- Does the corporation seek to avoid living wages and environmental protections in the United States by moving or having some of its operations in countries where the living wage is lower or environmental protections less stringent?
- Does the corporation provide for democratic participation by all employees in its decision-making?
- Does the corporation treat its employees with adequate respect?
- Is the corporation producing services and/or products that are beneficial or destructive to the environment of the planet?
- Does the corporation make investment decisions that enhance and promote the economic, social, and ethical welfare of the communities in which its products may be produced, sold, or advertised?
- Does the corporation seek to advertise in ways that manipulate consciousness, or does it seek to present honest information about the value of its products without providing subliminal messages or in other ways manipulating people into buying products or services, for example by raising fears, providing ungrounded hopes, using women's bodies or sexual overtones, or suggesting ungrounded possibilities for success or material reward or appreciation by others for consuming the product or

service being advertised? Does the corporation promote in advertising or in other ways a culture that fosters violence, insensitivity to others, or the consumption of products such as cigarettes, alcohol, or guns that have been proven to be detrimental to the health of American citizens? Does the corporation's advertising enhance or undermine the values articulated in the Preface to this Amendment?

- Does the corporation contribute to the economic, ethical, and environmental well-being of American society and the well-being of people around the world?
- Does the corporation encourage and reward its employees in participating in nonprofit volunteer activities by allowing at least five hours of paid time each week to be spent in such activities to be chosen by the employees themselves and without direct or indirect pressure from their supervisors or the corporate hierarchy?
- Does the corporation provide adequate health care and retirement benefits for its employees?

Article Four

Corporations or any other limited-liability entity selling products or goods or services in the United States, whether based in the U.S. or not, are prohibited from engaging in any effort to influence the electoral process or to influence the votes of Congress, state legislatures, or the policies of the courts or presidential administration. Officers and members of governing bodies of corporations may provide information to congressional committees as requested by the majority or minority of the Congress, but only through written reports submitted exclusively to the majority and minority and not through personal contact with any elected official. The intent of this article is to reduce the ability of corporations to shape public policies. Attempts to do so by the corporations, either directly through lobbying or indirectly by fostering or supporting nonprofit organizations or media or by attempting to influence the shaping of education or media or public discourse, or conspiring to achieve those ends in new ways not yet envisioned by the drafters of this Amendment, shall be subject to jail sentences not less than five actually served years in a federal penitentiary.

Article Five

Any corporation providing information on or analysis of American politics, including but not limited to newspapers, television, radio, Internet, handheld communication devices, or new forms yet to be developed and not yet fully anticipated by the drafters of this Amendment, shall be required to ensure the free and equal access to this information source by all candidates running for public office. These sources of information shall provide greater amounts of time for those running for the nomination of major parties (any party that received at least two million votes in the last election nationally) for the presidency, U.S. Senate, U.S. Congress, gubernatorial, and mayoral elections than for the other elected offices, but anyone running for those offices from a major party shall be given an equal amount of time to present a case in a way that the candidate herself or himself deems fair and not with the media's spin or commentary preceding or following it. Every source of information must provide at least the equivalent of five free hours of prime-time exposure to each candidate for the offices specified above and allow that candidate to determine how s/he is presented. Moreover, each such corporation must provide at least four hours of time for a debate among the major candidates, and must provide information to the public each day in the week before the election informing and reminding the public of those candidates who refused to participate in that debate.

Article Six

Stakeholders in any corporation with gross incomes of more than twenty million dollars per year (adjusted for inflation or deflation) shall be allowed to elect 51 percent of the members of the board of trustees of that corporation, and the corporation must provide funds to ensure full participation of those stakeholders in an impartial and adequately publicized election for those seats. The corporation must make all information available to those stakeholder representatives, and failure to do so shall be a felony punishable by not less than five years in federal penitentiary by anyone involved in withholding any information deemed necessary by the stakeholder representatives.

Congress shall encourage through financial support and legislative assistance the creation of worker cooperatives, community-owned corporations, and federally owned corporations. These entities must also meet all conditions for social and environmental responsibility.

Article Seven

Every corporation with gross annual income of fifty million dollars or more per year (adjusted for inflation or deflation) shall donate at least 10 percent of its gross profits to one of the following:

- A fund established by the U.S. government to fund a Global Marshall Plan aimed at eliminating global and domestic poverty, homelessness, hunger, inadequate education, inadequate health.
- Global environmental funds to repair the damage already done to the environment.
- A fund established to provide funding for a National Bank in the United States that would provide interest-free loans (that is, paying back only the principal plus adjustments to account for inflation or deflation) to people with incomes under $100,000 or to small businesses with gross annual incomes under $5 million per year. The funds for that bank would be distributed based on a determination of how those funds might assist the needy and those straining under economic difficulties, and/or to provide for the funding of projects that can demonstrably improve the lives of people in local communities around the U.S.

Article Eight

In order to provide for democratic control of the economy and environmental responsibility, all officials elected to city councils, county boards of supervisors or comparable office, state legislatures, the governorship of the several states, the House and Senate of the U.S. Congress, and the presidency of the United States shall not receive any funding from any source, including their own incomes or wealth, except as will be appropriated to major candidates for that office by the respective legislative bodies and in accord with the following principles:

- All major candidates for that office shall receive equal funding, and no funds may be expended by them or by any other body supporting their candidacy or supporting any of their principles in the three months immediately preceding the election. "Major candidates" are those who receive support from at least 5 percent of the potential electorate in a set of five public opinion polls taken three months before the election in question. Any group seeking to find a way to financially support the candidacy of anyone seeking public offices stated above or to use funds to influence public opinion about that candidate shall be punished by fines of not less than $10,000, and any corporation by not less than $200,000, and the person may be imprisoned for not less than five years and corporate directors imprisoned for not less than seven years if convicted of using those funds or conspiring to do so for electoral purposes.

- Any media corporation or media source using the public highways or public airwaves or telephone lines or other means of communication that have been partially subsidized or aided by use of public land or public funds must make available to all candidates for any of the offices stated above at least two hours of free time during prime-time hours in the three months before elections, and at least five hours to candidates for the House or Senate and eight hours to candidates for the presidency, and all of these during prime time (between 6 PM and 11 PM). Moreover, any such media reporting on the words or deeds of any candidate must give that same candidate equal space to present his or her own perspective on the facts reported or perceptions or editorial views stated, and the same shall be granted to other major candidates seeking that office.

- All elections to the offices listed above shall be governed by the principle of instantaneous runoffs. This works in the following way: voters are required to list their choices in priority order for at least their first three highest choices. Then, if no candidate gets a majority vote for that office, the lowest vote getter will be eliminated and the second-place votes of that candidate will be assigned according to the specifications of their voters, and this process will continue through the other votes of other candidates, until one candidate has received a majority of all the votes being counted.

If you'd like to work on this project, please contact its author, Rabbi Michael Lerner (RabbiLerner@tikkun.org), or visit www .spiritualprogressives.org to learn how to get involved in supporting the Environmental and Social Responsibility Amendment.

ACKNOWLEDGMENTS

This book would not have been possible without the advice, support, and research of many people. The ones who come to my compromised mind at the completion of this project follow, but I'm sure I am leaving a great many of you out. Thank you all.

Katinka Matson
John Brockman
Will Murphy
Dan Hind
Shawn Kittelsen
Janine Saunders
Sally Marvin
Ramona Pringle
Nick Hasty
Lian Amaris
Ari Wallach
Andrew Mayer
Bernard Lietaer
Howard Rheingold

Richard Metzger
Jay Babcock
Steven Johnson
Eamon Dolan
Amy Hertz
Gillian Blake
Bálazs Szekfü
Media-Squatters
Suzan Eraslan
David Lanphier, Jr.
Felipe Ribeiro
Fernando Cervantes
Armanda Lewis
David Pescovitz

John Merryman

Propaganda

John Leland

Darren Sharp

Amy Sohn

Jason Liszkiewicz

Kevin Werbach

Timothy Mohn

Matthew Burton

Josh Klein

Jeff Gordiner

Getachew Mengistie

Justin Vogt

Nancy Hechinger

Benjamin Kirshbaum

Ken Miller

David Feuer

Jonathan Taylor

Lance Strate

John Rogers

Jules Marshall

Christina Amini

Jeff Newelt

Xeni Jardin

Anaid Gomez-Ortigoza

Max Brockman

Russel Weinberger

Helen Churko

Courtney Turco

Joost Raessens

Rachel Dretzen

Barak Goodman

Naomi Klein

Kate Norris

and, most of all, Barbara and Mamie Rushkoff

NOTES

CHAPTER ONE
Once Removed: The Corporate Life-Form

4 **Most history books recount** For the best descriptions of late Middle Ages and Renaissance life and commerce, see Fernand Braudel, *The Wheels of Commerce: Civilization and Capitalism, 15th–18th Century* (Los Angeles: University of California Press, 1992), and Carlo M. Cipolla, *Before the Industrial Revolution: European Society and Economy, 1000–1700*, 3rd ed. (New York: W. W. Norton & Company, 1994).

8 **A Child Is Born** For a comparison of perspectives on the agendas behind the birth of the corporation, refer to the following scholarly books and articles that formed the basis for my own inquiry:

George Cawston and A. H. Keane, *The Early Chartered Companies: 1296–1858* (New York: Burt Franklin, 1968).

Ann M. Carlos, "Principal-Agent Problems in Early Trading Companies: A Tale of Two Firms," *The American Economic Review* 82.2 (1992): 140–45.

Ann M. Carlos and Stephen Nicholas, "Giants of an Earlier Capitalism: The Chartered Trading Companies as Modern Multinationals," *The Business History Review* 62.3 (1988): 398–419.

Ann M. Carlos and Stephen Nicholas, "Agency Problems in Early Chartered Companies: The Case of the Hudson's Bay Company," *The Journal of Economic History* 50.4 (1990): 853–75.

Ann M. Carlos and Stephen Nicholas, "Theory and History: Seventeeth Century Joint-Stock Chartered Trading Companies," *The Journal of Economic History* 56.4 (1996): 916–24.

S.R.H. Jones and Simon P. Ville, "Theory and Evidence: Understanding Chartered Trading Companies," *The Journal of Economic History* 56.4 (1996): 925–26.

S.R.H. Jones and Simon P. Ville, "Efficient Transactors or Rent-Seeking Monopolists? The Rationale for Early Chartered Trading Companies," *The Journal of Economic History* 56.4 (1996): 898–915.

Shaw Livermore, "Unlimited Liability in Early American Companies," *The Journal of Political Economy* 43.5 (1935): 674–87.

Janice E. Thomson, *Mercenaries, Pirates, and Sovereigns: State-Building and Extraterritorial Violence in Early Modern Europe* (Princeton, N.J.: Princeton University Press, 1994).

8   **"The state ought to rejoice"** John Brathwaite and Peter Drahos, *Global Business Regulation* (New York: Cambridge University Press, 2000), 445.

12   **"The class of citizens who provide"** James Madison, *Letters and Other Writings of James Madison* (Philadelphia: J. B. Lippincott & Co., 1865), 476.

13   **"The defendant corporations are persons"** Thom Hartmann, *Unequal Protection: The Rise of Corporate Dominance and the Theft of Human Rights* (New York: Rodale Books, 2002), 105.

15   **The anti-Semitic diatribes Ford published** Adolf Hitler, *Mein Kampf,* translated by Ralph Manheim (Boston: Houghton Mifflin Company, 1939), 639, and Steven Watts, *The People's Tycoon: Henry Ford and the American 15* (New York: Knopf, 2005).

15   **American corporations from General Electric** Graeme Howard, *America and the New World Order* (New York: Charles Scribner's Sons, 1940), and Max Wallace, *The American Axis: Henry Ford, Charles Lindbergh, and the Rise of the Third Reich* (New York: St. Martin's Press, 2003).

16   **Although he had run for reelection** Edward L. Bernays, "The Marketing of National Policies: A Study of War Propaganda," *Journal of Marketing,* Vol. 6, No. 3 (1942).

16   **Instead of letting them rule themselves** Edward L. Bernays, *Crystallizing Public Opinion* (New York: Kessinger Publishing, 2004), 19.

16   **Consumers are easier to please** Edward L. Bernays, *Propaganda* (1928) (Brooklyn, N.Y.: Ig Publishing, 2004), 51, and Larry Tye, *The Father of Spin: Edward L. Bernays and the Birth of Public Relations* (New York: Holt Paperbacks, 2002), 92.

18   **"be, if not literally worldwide"** Niels Bjerre-Poulsen, *Right Face: Organizing the American Conservative Movement 1945–65* (Copenhagen: Museum Tusculanum Press, 2002), 117.

CHAPTER TWO
Mistaking the Map for the Territory

30   **Henry did not personally expand** Clifford D. Conner, *A People's History of Science* (New York: Nation Books, 2005), 190–95, and Peter Russell, *Prince Henry "the Navigator": A Life* (New Haven: Yale University Press, 2001), 372–74.

30   **Reductionism promoted a fragmented view** Clive Ponting, *A Green History of the World* (New York: Penguin, 1991), 154.

31   **By selling their lands** Fernand Braudel, *Afterthoughts on Material Civilization and Capitalism* (Baltimore: Johns Hopkins Press, 1977), 60.

33   **In Bengal, for example** Arnold Pacey, *Technology in World Civilization: A Thousand-Year History* (Cambridge, Mass.: MIT Press, 1991), 102.

34 **"By preferring the support of domestic"** Adam Smith, *The Wealth of Nations, Books IV–V,* Penguin Classics Edition (New York: Penguin Classics, 1999), 32.

35 **For one, the economic globalization** David Korten, *When Corporations Rule the World,* 2nd ed. (San Francisco: Berrett-Koehler Publishers, 2001), 39.

37 **As a result, debt payments** Ibid., 64.

42 **In the 1970s, for example** Dean Foust and Maria Mallory, "The Boom Belt: There's No Speed Limit on Growth along the South's I-85," *BusinessWeek,* September 27, 1993: 98–104, and Korten, *When Corporations Rule,* 132.

42 **In 1993, South Carolina** Foust and Mallory, "The Boom Belt," 98–104, and Korten, *When Corporations Rule,* 132.

44 **As of 2000, by utilizing** Wal-Mart Watch, http://walmartwatch.com/ (accessed March 20, 2008).

44 **After peaking at more** Anne D'Innocenzio, "Wal-Mart Scales Back Expansion in Tough Economy," *USA Today,* October 28, 2008.

CHAPTER THREE
The Ownership Society

46 **Before the twentieth century** Steven Johnson, *The Ghost Map: The Story of London's Most Terrifying Epidemic* (New York: Riverhead, 2006).

46 **Emerson wrote of** Kenneth T. Jackson, *Crabgrass Frontier: The Suburbanization of the United States* (New York: Oxford University Press, 1985), 16.

47 **"sinking into degradation and misery"** Stuart Ewen, *PR! A Social History of Spin* (New York: Basic Books, 1996), 49.

47 **"society is not friendly"** Ibid., 52.

48 **To serve this new market** Jackson, *Crabgrass Frontier,* 22.

48 **"unabashedly the instrument"** Ibid., 37.

48 **"Somerville, Medford, and Woburn"** Ibid.

49 **"Much of life was inescapably public"** Ibid., 47.

49 **"A man is not a whole"** Ibid., 50.

49 **"It is strange how contentedly"** Ibid.

49 **"Introduce me to the people"** Ibid.

50 **"chaining the worker"** Andy Merrifield, *Metromarxism: A Marxist Tale of the City* (New York: Routledge, 2002), 45.

50 **"Give him hope"** Jackson, *Crabgrass Frontier,* 50.

50 **The "great country estate"** Jessica L. Malay, "Building with Words: Architectural Metonymy in Early Modern Literary Texts," APPOSITIONS: Studies in Renaissance/Early Modern Literature & Culture, http://appositions.blogspot.com/2008/01/jessica-malay-buildings-with-words.html (accessed March 20, 2008).

51 **In Boston's Brookline** Jackson, *Crabgrass Frontier,* 100.

52 **The economist Richard Hurd** Ibid., 120.

53 **While GM's role in dismantling** For a detailed chronicle of this process, see Edwin Black, *Internal Combustion: How Corporations and Governments Addicted the World to Oil and Derailed the Alternatives* (New York: Macmillan, 2007).

54 **According to Senator Gaylord Nelson** Dennis R. Judd and Todd Swanstrom, *City Politics: Private Power & Public Policy* (New York: HarperCollins, 1994), 204.

54 **This was intended to keep poor** Langdon Winner, *The Whale and the Reactor: A Search for Limits in an Age of High Technology* (Chicago: University of Chicago Press, 1986), 2.

55 **In 1935, General Electric** Jackson, *Crabgrass Frontier,* 187.

58 **Green was the best** C. Lowell Harriss, *History and Policies of the Home Owners' Loan Corporation* (New York: National Bureau of Economic Research, 1951), 41–48, and Jackson, *Crabgrass Frontier,* 197.

58 **Appraisers learned to see** Stanley L. McMichael, *Appraising Manual: A Real Estate Appraising Handbook for Field Work and Advanced Study Courses* (New York: Prentice-Hall, 1931).

59 **In one startling example** Jackson, *Crabgrass Frontier,* 209.

59 **"to private industry the feasibility"** Jackson, *Crabgrass Frontier,* 221.

60 **"It is likely that a desperation"** Barbara M. Kelly, "The Houses of Levittown in the Context of Postwar American Culture," Hofstra University, http://www.nps.gov/nr//publications/bulletins/suburbs/Kelly.pdf (accessed March 20, 2008).

60 **Housing starts boomed** Jackson, *Crabgrass Frontier,* 233.

61 **"No man who owns his own"** Ibid., 232.

62 **At the request of** Kelly, "The Houses of Levittown."

63 **Having paved over the country** For Levittown turnover figures and characteristics compared with the rest of the United States, see Herbert J. Gans, *The Levittowners: Ways of Life and Politics in a New Suburban Community* (New York: Columbia University Press, 1982).

66 **"This particular problem"** Daniel Gross and Jon Meacham, "The Oracle Reveals All: A Candid Conversation with Greenspan," *Newsweek,* Web Exclusive, September 24, 2007, http://www.newsweek.com/id/41390 (accessed September 25, 2007).

66 **Banks found willing customers** Julia Werdigier, "Debt-Gorged British Start to Worry That Party Is Ending," *The New York Times,* March 22, 2008, Business section.

67 **As of this writing, 6 percent** Peter Gumbel, "The $915B Bomb in Consumers' Wallets," *Fortune,* October 30, 2007.

68 **But credit-rating agencies** Mark Pittman, "Moody's, S&P Defer Cuts on AAA Subprime, Hiding Loss," Bloomberg.com, posted on March 11, 2008, http://www.bloomberg.com/apps/news?pid=20601109&sid=aRLWzHsF16l Y&refer=home (accessed March 20, 2008).

68 **Goldman Sachs and other** Ben Stein, "Tattered Standard of Duty on Wall Street," *The New York Times,* December 23, 2007, Business section.

69 **Thirty-nine percent of Americans** "30% of Recent U.S. Homebuyers Have Negative Equity: Report," *CBC News,* posted on February 12, 2008, http://www.cbc.ca/money/story/2008/02/12/homeequity.html (accessed February 14, 2008).

70 **Mr. Greenspan and the federal government** Edmund L. Andrews, "Fed and Regulators Shrugged as the Subprime Crisis Spread," *The New York Times,* December 18, 2007, front page.

71 **While Goldman Sachs was underwriting** The Daily Reckoning website has the best narrative accounts of Goldman Sachs's short-selling strategy during the subprime-mortgage meltdown: Adrian Ash, "Goldman Sachs Escaped Subprime Collapse by Selling Subprime Bonds Short," Daily Reckoning, October 19, 2007, http://www.dailyreckoning.com.au/goldman-sachs-2/2007/10/19.

71 **For help predicting the extent** Gregory Zuckerman covered the Paulson-

Greenspan relationship for *The Wall Street Journal*. Start with Gregory Zuckerman, "Trader Made Billions on Subprime," *The Wall Street Journal*, January 15, 2008, Business section.

72 **Membership in civic organizations** Robert D. Putnam, *Bowling Alone: The Collapse and Revival of American Community* (New York: Simon & Schuster, 2000).

78 **The Chinese restaurant offered** Ada Louise Huxtable, *The Unreal America: Architecture and Illusion* (New York: The New Press, 1999).

78 **An Austrian architect named Victor Gruen** Douglas Rushkoff, *Coercion* (New York: Berkley Publishing Group, 1999).

82 **The more a town** Elizabeth Currid, *The Warhol Economy: How Fashion, Art, and Music Drive New York City* (Princeton, N.J.: Princeton University Press, 2007).

CHAPTER FOUR
Individually Wrapped

91 **This idea inspired many poets** Stephen Greenblatt, *Renaissance Self-Fashioning* (Chicago: University of Chicago Press, 1980).

91 **Perspective painting meant**

Jan Goldstein, *The Post-Revolutionary Self: Politics and Psyche in France* (Cambridge: Harvard University Press, 2005).

Jan R. Veenstra, "The New Historicism of Stephen Greenblatt: On Poetics of Culture and the Interpretation of Shakespeare," *History and Theory*, Volume 34, No. 3 (October 1995).

John Martin, "Inventing Sincerity, Refashioning Prudence: The Discovery of the Individual in Renaissance Europe," *The American Historical Review*, Volume 102, No. 5 (December 1997).

Geoff Baldwin, "Individual and Self in the Late Renaissance," *The Historical Journal*, vol. 44, No. 2 (2001).

Lewis P. Hinchman,"The Idea of Individuality: Origins, Meaning, and Political Significance," *The Journal of Politics*, vol. 52, No. 3 (August 1990).

Steven Lukes, "The Meanings of 'Individualism,' " *Journal of the History of Ideas*, vol. 32, No. 1 (Jan–March 1971).

While there's some evidence Stuart Ewen first called my attention to Colbert. My research comes principally from Charles Woolsey Cole, *Colbert and a Century of French Mercantilism*, vols. I–II (New York: Columbia University Press, 1939).

94 **"With our taste"** Stuart Ewen, *All Consuming Images: The Politics of Style in Contemporary Culture*, rev. ed. (New York: Basic Books, 1999), 30.

96 **The Great Exhibition's primary** Richard Barbrook, *Imaginary Futures: From Thinking Machines to the Global Village* (London: Pluto Press, 2007), 22–28.

96 **The Great Exhibition was designed** Jeffrey A. Auerbach, *The Great Exhibition of 1851: A Nation on Display* (New Haven: Yale University Press, 1999), 119.

98 **On his tour of America** "De Tocqueville: Jared Sparks's Correspondence About the United States," *The New York Times*, January 21, 1899, Review of Books and Art section, BR41.

101 **"angry sense of the limited"** Ira Steward, *Annual Report on the Statistics of*

Labor by Massachusetts Dept. of Labor and Industries, Division of Statistics, Massachusetts Bureau of Statistics of Labor (1873), 414.

101 **"relentless exposure"** Theodore Roosevelt, *The Autobiography of Theodore Roosevelt, Condensed from the Original Edition, Supplemented by Letters, Speeches, and Other Writings,* Centennial edition, 1958, ed. Wayne Andrews (New York: Charles Scribner's Sons, 1913), 246–47.

102 **Early public-relations professionals** Gustave Le Bon, *The Crowd* (1895) (Whitefish, Mont.: Kessinger Publishing, 2004). Also see Gabriel Tarde, *The Laws of Imitation* (1890), trans. E. C. Parsons (New York: Henry Holt, 1903).

104 **"The war taught us"** Stuart Ewen, *PR!: A Social History of Spin* (New York: Basic Books, 1996), 131.

104 **"the art of steering heads"** Ibid., 144.

105 **Walter Lippmann, one of** Walter Lippmann's work predated that of his colleague Edward Bernays: Walter Lippmann, *Public Opinion* (New York: Harcourt, Brace and Company, 1922); Edward Bernays, *Crystallizing Public Opinion* (New York: Boni and Liveright, 1923).

105 **"access to the real environment"** Lippmann, *Public Opinion,* 43.

105 **"the secret of all true persuasion"** Ewen, *PR!,* 175.

105 **"The job of the Publicity Directors"** Ibid., 194.

106 **"Americans must forswear"** Franklin D. Roosevelt, "Annual Message to the Congress, January 4, 1935," from *The Era of Franklin D. Roosevelt, 1932–1945: A Brief History with Documents,* ed. Richard D. Polenberg (New York: Palgrave Macmillan, 2000), 49.

107 **"Right now Joe Doakes"** Ewen, *PR!,* 305.

108 **"the citizen is supreme"** Ibid.

109 **Putting profits over patriotism** Michael Dobbs, "Ford and GM Scrutinized for Alleged Nazi Collaboration," *The Washington Post,* November 30, 1998, A01.

109 **American corporatists also saw** Benjamin L. Alpers, *Dictators, Democracy, and American Public Culture* (Chapel Hill, N.C.: University of North Carolina Press, 2002).

109 **The full-fledged war effort** "Why Mussolini Charms the American Business Man," *Literary Digest,* LXXVII (June 9, 1923), 72–74.

109 **Standard Oil of New Jersey**
G. William Domhoff, *The Higher Circles: The Governing Class in America* (New York: Vintage, 1970); Josiah E. Dubois, Jr., *Generals in Grey Suits* (London: The Bodley Head, 1953); Nuremberg Military Trials, *Case VI: United States of America v. Carl Krauch et al. (I.G. Farben Case), 1946–1949,* National Archives Microfilms Publication M892, 1264–1311; and Anthony C. Sutton, *Wall Street and the Rise of Hitler* (San Pedro, Calif.: GSG & Associates, 1976), 104–17.

110 **"a transfer in emphasis"** Ewen, *PR!,* 360.

110 **People working in concert** See academic articles from the period, such as Henry F. Ward, "The Development of Fascism in the United States," *Socialism, Fascism, and Democracy,* vol. 180, Annals of the American Academy of Political and Social Science (July 1935).

CHAPTER FIVE
You, You're the One

116 **Today, a Mickey Mouse doll** All of America's Disney Stores, except for the flagship location in Manhattan, have actually been owned and operated by a different corporation, the Children's Place, LLC, under a long-term licensing agreement. As of this writing, Disney is working to buy them back, and to close a third of them so as not to dilute the Disney brand any further.

116 **The problem with this** Walter Benjamin, "The Work of Art in the Age of Mechanical Reproduction" (1936), *Illuminations* (New York: Harcourt, Brace, Jovanovich, 1968).

117 **Influenced by Marx and having witnessed** Actually, Walter Benjamin's colleagues Theodor Adorno and Jürgen Habermas would argue this much more forcefully. Benjamin was himself torn on this issue.

117 **"Under monopoly all mass culture"** Theodor Adorno and Max Horkheimer, *The Culture Industry* (1944) (New York: Routledge, 1991).

118 **What's in your Netflix** Netflix is an online DVD-rental service that lets users list the movies they will be renting in the future.

119 **"The evidence of my"** Douglas Atkin, *The Culting of Brands: When Customers Become True Believers* (New York: Portfolio Books, 1994).

120 **"the consumer is now in total"** Kevin Roberts, in an interview with me for *PBS Frontline*, "The Persuaders" (2004). Available online: http://www.pbs .org/wgbh/pages/frontline/shows/persuaders/.

121 **"There are many kinds of love"** Ibid.

121 **"So we have to create"** Ibid.

121 **The average client-agency relationship** American Association of Advertising Agencies, "Longevity of Accounts in the Advertising Agency Business 2001" (2001).

121 **By 2007, only half** Reardon Smith Whittaker, "A Client's Perspective About Agencies," 2007 New Business Report (2007).

124 **"We measure attention"** Stuart Elliot, "Is the Ad a Success? The Brain Waves Tell All," *The New York Times*, March 31, 2008, Business section.

124 **"normal, natural response mechanisms"** Ibid.

125 **"the tacit superheroes of consumer culture"** Mark Crispin Miller, in an interview with me for *PBS Frontline*, "The Merchants of Cool" (2001). Available online: http://www.pbs.org/wgbh/pages/frontline/shows/cool/.

126 **When push comes to shove** Malcolm Gladwell, *The Tipping Point* (New York: Little, Brown and Company, 2000).

126 **"Malcolm Gladwell's *The Tipping Point*"** Walter Kirn, "Viral Culture," review of *The Tipping Point*, *New York*, February 21, 2000.

127 **"When you walk out into"** Malcolm Gladwell, *Blink* (New York: Little, Brown and Company, 2005), 11.

128 **TV ads cost more** See my *Frontline* documentary "The Persuaders" for more on the decline of traditional advertising and the emergence of new methods.

130 **"Ordinary people . . . without"** Stanley Milgram, "Behavioral Study of Obedience," *Journal of Abnormal Social Psychology*, vol. 67 (1963): 371–78.

131 **The real difference, of course** Charles Woolsey Cole, *Colbert and a Century of French Mercantilism*, vols. I–II (New York: Columbia University Press, 1939).

132 **A study by PQ Media** Nara Schoenberg, "She's a B.M.O.C. Meet Alex,"

Commercial Alert, May 13, 2008, http://www.commercialalert.org/news/featured-in/2008/05/shes-a-bmoc-meet-alex (accessed May 28, 2008).

132 **Procter & Gamble's own** Robert Berner, "I Heard It Through the Grapevine," *BusinessWeek,* May 29, 2006.

132 **P&G considers this marketing** Cliff Peale, "P&G Targets Teenage Buyers," *The Cincinnati Enquirer,* October 27, 2002.

135 **The Puritans brought** For the original, and still best, account of the marriage of capitalism to early American Christianity, see Max Weber, *The Protestant Ethic and the Spirit of Capitalism* (1904), trans. Talcott Parsons (Mineola, N.Y.: Courier Dover, 2003).

135 **"I believe the power"** Ron Chernow, *Titan: The Life of John D. Rockefeller, Sr.* (New York: Random House, 1998), 46.

136 **"tailored more than any"** William Leach, *Land of Desire: Merchants, Power, and the Rise of a New American Culture* (New York: Vintage Books, 1994), 201.

136 **Instead, everyone should just avoid** Ibid., 204.

138 **"We want to live a life"** *Century of the Self,* dir. Adam Curtis (United Kingdom: BBC Four, 2002).

138 **To this end, in 1962** For a detailed history of Esalen, see Jeffrey J. Kripal, *Esalen: America and the Religion of No Religion* (Chicago: University of Chicago Press, 2007).

139 **The Brooklyn-born psychologist's** Abraham H. Maslow, *Toward a Psychology of Being,* 3rd ed. (New York: Wiley, 1998).

139 **For Maslow and his followers** Abraham H. Maslow, "A Theory of Human Motivation," *Psychological Review,* 50 (1943), 370–439.

140 **The Stanford Research Institute hired** Edward Hoffman, *The Right to Be Human: A Biography of Abraham Maslow* (New York: McGraw-Hill, 1999), and Abraham H. Maslow and Deborah C. Stephens, *The Maslow Business Reader* (New York: Wiley, 2000).

142 **Dollar may be the epitome** Carol Costello, "Don't Miss Televangelist Refuses to Turn Over More Financial Documents," CNN.com, December 7, 2007, http://www.cnn.com/2007/POLITICS/12/07/prosperity.preachers/index.html (accessed February 16, 2008), and Michael Luo, "Preaching a Gospel of Wealth in a Glittery Market, New York," *The New York Times,* January 15, 2006, http://www.nytimes.com/2006/01/15/nyregion/15prosperity.html (accessed February 16, 2008).

142 **Megastar and multimillionaire televangelist** Mara Einstein, *Brands of Faith: Marketing Religion in a Commercial Age* (New York: Routledge, 2008), 123.

142 **"The desire for increase"** Jack Canfield, "Keynote Speech," The Learning Annex Wealth Expo (Jacob Javits Center, New York, N.Y., November 18, 2007).

142 **"It's time for me"** Tom Peters, "The Brand Called You," *Fast Company,* Issue 10, August 1997.

143 **Hey, that kid sounds *cool*** Joseph Berger, "Blurring the Line Between a College Application and a Slick Sales Pitch," *The New York Times,* November 28, 2007, U.S. section.

CHAPTER SIX
To Whom Credit Is Due

147 **"performance pay" theory** This is a big field, with a wide array of opinions and research. See David H. Autor, Lawrence F. Katz, and Melissa S. Kearney, "The Polarization of the U.S. Labor Market," *American Economic Review*, vol. 96, No. 2 (May 2006), 189–94; Edward E. Lawler, "Pay Practices in Fortune 1000 Corporations," *WorldatWork Journal*, vol. 12, No. 4 (4th Quarter 2003), 45–54; Thomas Lemieux, W. Bentley Macleod, and Daniel Parent, "Performance Pay and Wage Inequality," Departmental Working Papers from McGill University, Department of Economics, at http://econpapers.repec.org/paper/mclmclwop/2006-08.htm (accessed May 1, 2008); and, most important to my own argument, Alfie Kohn, *No Contest: The Case Against Competition* (Boston: Houghton Mifflin, 1992).

149 **In 1944, an Austrian economist** Friedrich Hayek, *The Road to Serfdom* (Chicago: University of Chicago Press, 1947).

151 **A Paranoid Schizophrenic's Legacy** Robert Boyd and Peter J. Richerson, "Solving the Puzzle of Human Cooperation," in *Evolution and Culture*, ed. Stephen C. Levinson and Pierre Jaisson, 105–32 (Cambridge, Mass.: MIT Press, 2005).

151 **The think-tank logicians at Rand** Rand corporation, or Research and Development Corporation, is a global policy think tank created originally for the U.S. Air Force in 1943, and then spun off as a nonprofit corporation in 1948. The official Rand site is http://www.rand.org/.

151 **They tested their ideas on** Oliver Burkeman, "Cry Freedom," *The Guardian*, March 3, 2007.

152 **"It is understood not to be"** John Nash spoke to filmmaker Adam Curtis in the BBC documentary *The Trap*, dir. Adam Curtis (United Kingdom: BBC Two, 2007).

152 **The Scottish psychologist R. D. Laing** Laing had some evidence on his side. In the infamous "Rosenhan Experiment," fake patients went to psychiatric institutions and managed to get faulty diagnoses as suffering from mental disorders. Worse yet, when the experiment was revealed, psychiatrists began identifying real patients as participants in the experiment. Psychiatry seemed to be exposed as a sham in which supposed experts had no real tools with which to determine a person's sanity. For more, see R. D. Laing, *The Politics of Experience* (New York: Pantheon, 1983).

153 **"This," she said, "is what"** John Ranelagh, introduction to his book *Thatcher's People: An Insider's Account of the Politics, the Power, and the Personalities* (London: HarperCollins, 1991), xi.

155 **Just as species competed** The "meme," as coined by Richard Dawkins, is the cultural equivalent of a gene. For more, see Richard Dawkins, *The Selfish Gene* (Oxford, Eng.: Oxford University Press, 1976).

156 **Right-wing conservatives turned to** Gordon Bigelow, "Let There Be Markets: The Evangelical Roots of Economics," *Harper's Magazine*, May 2005.

156 **"Scripture defines God as the source"** Mark A. Beliles and Stephen K. McDowell, *America's Providential History*, 2nd ed. (Charlottesville, Va.: The Providence Foundation, 1991).

157 **The same right-wing think tanks** People for the American Way and Americans for Tax Reform, to name just two groups with such contradictory stances.

158 **Volumes could be filled** Richard W. Bloom and Nancy Dess, *Evolutionary Psychology and Violence: A Primer for Policymakers and Public Policy Advocates* (New York: Praeger Publishers, 2003).

158 **By focusing on the evolutionary** Glynn Ll. Isaac, "The Harvey Lecture Series, 1977–1978: Food Sharing and Human Evolution: Archaeological Evidence from the Plio–Pleistocene of East Africa," *Journal of Anthropological Research*, vol. 34, No. 3 (Autumn 1978): 311–25.

158 **"Males were cooperating"** "Early Hominids May Have Behaved More 'Human' Than We Had Thought," *Science Daily*, August 7, 2003, http://www.sciencedaily.com/releases/2003/08/030807075457.htm (accessed July 1, 2008).

158 **Studies by psychologists** Boaz Keysar and Shali Wu, "The Effect of Culture on Perspective Taking," *Psychological Science*, vol. 18, Issue 7 (2007): 600–606.

158 **"cultures that emphasize interdependence"** Roxanne Khamsi, "Self-centered cultures narrow your viewpoint," NewScientist.com News Service, July 12, 2007, http://www.newscientist.com/article/dn12247-selfcentered-cultures-narrow-your-viewpoint.html (accessed September 15, 2007).

159 **23 percent of brokers** Landon Thomas, Jr., "Depression, a Frequent Visitor to Wall St.," *The New York Times*, September 12, 2004, Business section.

159 **Scientists and United Nations sociologists** See Geoffrey Miller's work on evolutionary psychology applied to marketing: Geoffrey Miller, "Consciousness as a Corporate Pep Rally," essay for *Edge* (February 2004), http://www.edge.org/documents/archive/edge144.html#miller, and Geoffrey Miller, "Social Policy Implications of the New Happiness Research," essay for *Edge* (June 2000), http://www.edge.org/3rd_culture/story/contributions.html#miller.

159 **After achieving an income** Bruno S. Frey and Alois Stutzer, *Happiness and Economics: How the Economy and Institutions Affect Human Well-Being* (Princeton, N.J.: Princeton University Press, December 2001), 10.

159 **Still others have criticized** Rana Foroohar, "Money vs. Happiness: Nations Rethink Priorities," *Newsweek*, Web Exclusive, April 29, 2007, http://www.newsweek.com/id/35108 (accessed December 15, 2007).

160 **These are proven behaviors** Susan Block-Lieb and Edward J. Janger, "The Myth of the Rational Borrower: Rationality, Behavioralism, and the Misguided Reform of Bankruptcy Law," *Texas Law Review*, vol. 84 (2006): 1481–565.

160 **Lowering minimum-payment requirements** Robert D. Manning, *Credit Card Nation: The Consequences of America's Addiction to Credit* (New York: Basic Books, 2000).

164 **In fact, the awful years** This chapter would not have been possible without the research of Bernard Lietaer, whose books first exposed me to these ideas and many, many examples which I subsequently researched myself. Bernard Lietaer, *The Mystery of Money* (Munich: Riemann Verlag, 2000); Bernard Lietaer, *The Future of Money* (London: Random House, 2001), full text available online at http://www.lietaer.com/books/futureofmoney.html; and Bernard Lietaer and Stephen M. Belgin, *Of Human Wealth: Beyond Greed and Scarcity*, Galley Edition Version 2.1 (Boulder, Colo.: Human Wealth Books and Talks, 2004).

167 **The florin began as** Luca Fantacci, "The Dual Currency System of Renaissance Europe," *Financial History Review* 15.1 (2008): 55–72.

167 **So much for good intentions** Gene Adam Brucker, *Florence: The Golden Age, 1138–1737* (New York: Abbeville Press, 1984), 70–77.

169 **For these repeated debasements** Fantacci, "Dual Currency," 60.

170 **Monarchs extracted wealth** One ruler in Poland changed his coins four times every year. The Duke of Saxony reminted his currency eighty-six times in eighteen years. Lietaer, *The Mystery of Money*, 173.

170 **Another forty years after that** Referenced in Lietaer, *The Mystery of Money*, 166; see also Christopher Dyer, *Standards of Living in the Later Middle Ages: Social Change in England Circa 1200–1520* (Cambridge, Eng.: Cambridge University Press, 1994), 101.

171 **Ten percent of Europe's population** Referenced in Lietaer, *The Mystery of Money*, 172; see also Henry S. Lucas, "The Great European Famine of 1315–1316," *Speculum*, vol. 5, No. 4 (October 1930), 343–77.

CHAPTER SEVEN
From Ecology to Economy

176 **Between 2000 and 2007** Senator Dick Durbin, "Report to Senate Appropriations Subcommittee on Financial Services and General Government, Thursday, June 12, 2008," official Senator Durbin home page, http://durbin.senate .gov (accessed June 17, 2008).

180 **No, the parents in question** I've interviewed teachers at three of New York's top private schools, who tell me that an increasing number of papers turned in each year are the obvious work of tutors and professional writing services. The teachers have learned to specify extremely specific subjects to prevent students from buying prepared papers over the Internet, but parents now hire writers to do custom work. When one teacher—a friend of mine—challenged a student over work that used words and sentences the student didn't himself understand under questioning, the parents (good funders of the school) had the headmaster suspend the teacher from his job for a semester.

181 **Alan Greenspan, a disciple** Leo Hindery, Jr., "Why Obama, Congress Must Curb CEO Pay," *BusinessWeek*, November 5, 2008.

181 **Adjusted for inflation, the average worker's** Ben Stein, "In the Boardroom, Every Back Gets Scratched," *The New York Times*, April 6, 2008, Business section.

181 **The top tenth of 1 percent** Robert H. Frank, "In the Real World of Work and Wages, Trickle Down Theories Don't Hold Up," *The New York Times*, April 12, 2007, Business section.

181 **The number of "severely poor Americans"** "Report: In U.S., Record Numbers Are Plunged Into Poverty," *USA Today*, February 26, 2007, http://www .usatoday.com/news/nation/2007-02-25-us-poverty_x.htm (accessed March 1, 2007).

181 **Meanwhile, for the very first time** Greg Ip and John D. McKinnon, "Bush Reorients Rhetoric, Acknowledges Income Gap," *The Wall Street Journal*, March 26, 2007, Business section.

182 **Americans work an average** Robert Reich, "Totally Spent," *The New York Times*, February 13, 2008, Opinion section.

182 **"Operating in a world"** Peter Whybrow's ideas have been promoted most recently and successfully by Bill McKibben. For this quote and more, see Bill McKibben, "Reversal of Fortune," *Mother Jones*, March/April 2007.

183 **This is roughly equivalent** "Federal Reserve Flow of Funds Report, June 2008," The Federal Reserve, http://FederalReserve.gov (accessed June 14, 2008).

183 **"Visa is an opportunity"** Eileen Ambrose, "Kids' game now takes plastic," *The Baltimore Sun*, October 9, 2007.

184 **"we solved a major problem"** Daniel Gross, "Starbucks' 'Venti' Problem," *Los Angeles Times*, March 4, 2007, Opinion section, M-1.

185 **Only when threatened by** Joint Statement, "Starbucks and Ethiopian Intellectual Property Office (EIPO) Partner to Promote Ethiopia's Coffee and Benefit the Country's Coffee Farmers," Ethiopian Intellectual Property Office, June 19, 2007.

186 **The company blamed price cuts** David Leonhardt, "One Safety Net Is Disappearing. What Will Follow?" *The New York Times*, April 4, 2007, Business section.

186 **"the cost of an associate"** Ibid.

187 **The traditional spreadsheet** Art Kleiner, "What Are the Measures that Matter?" *strategy+business*, Issue 26 (First Quarter, 2002), 16–21.

187 **"contributed to the modern obsession"** H. Thomas Johnson and Anders Bröms, *Profit Beyond Measure: Extraordinary Results Through Attention to Work and People* (New York: Simon & Schuster, 2000), 58.

188 **Then, in 1979, some researchers** Sam Schechner, "The Roach That Failed," *The New York Times Magazine*, July 25, 2004, 20.

188 **"If we actually manage to drive"** Ibid.

188 **Even the economist charged with developing** Jonathan Rowe, testifying before the Senate Committee on Commerce, Science, and Transportation, Subcommittee on Interstate Commerce, March 12, 2008. "Our Phony Economy," *Harper's Magazine*, June 2008, 17–24.

188 **"They do not distinguish"** Ibid.

190 **"a deal with Rupert Murdoch would"** Jim Ottaway, Jr., and Jay Ottaway, "Statements by Jim, Jay Ottaway on News Corp. Bid for Dow Jones," *The Wall Street Journal*, May 6, 2007, Business section, Web edition, http://online.wsj.com/article/SB117847597734093670.html (accessed May 6, 2007).

190 **"The media equivalent of a trophy"** "Why Rupert Murdoch Wants the WSJ," *The Economist*, May 5, 2007, Media section, North American.

191 **Instead of being controlled** Gilles Deleuze and Félix Guatarri, *A Thousand Plateaus: Capitalism and Schizophrenia*, 8th printing, trans. Brian Massumi (Minneapolis: University of Minnesota Press, 2000).

193 **"There are those who still remember"** *DEWmocracy*, dir. by Forest Whitaker (United States: PepsiCo, 2008).

193 **"Welcome to your world"** Lev Grossman, "*Time*'s Person of the Year: You," *Time*, December 13, 2006.

194 **"Silicon Valley consultants"** Ibid.

195 **Back then, however, the magazine** *Time* published a cover feature about net porn and children on July 3, 1995. The articles that made up the special feature were widely critiqued, discredited as sensationalist, and eventually largely retracted. But the damage was done.

196 **These sterile technologies** Jonathan Zittrain, *The Future of the Internet and How to Stop It* (New Haven: Yale University Press, 2008).

197 **Once high-tech security-minded** Patrick McGreevy, "Senate Blocks Mandatory ID Implants," *Los Angeles Times*, August 31, 2007, B-3.

198 **Current estimates number the Chinese labor** David Barboza, "Ogre to Slay? Outsource It to Chinese," *The New York Times,* December 9, 2005, Technology section.

200 **As seminal essays by** Copies of all these essays, and more, are collected in Randall Packer, Ken Jordan, and William Gibson, eds., *Multimedia: From Wagner to Virtual Reality* (New York: W. W. Norton & Company, 2001).

CHAPTER EIGHT
No Returns

209 **Addicted to a system in which** Thomas L. Friedman, "Et Tu, Toyota?" *The New York Times,* October 3, 2007, Opinion section.

210 **While advertising its own commitment** Staff, "Et Tu, Tom Friedman," *Edmunds AutoObserver,* October 4, 2007, http://www.autoobserver.com/2007/10/et-tu-tom-friedman.html (accessed October 5, 2007).

213 **In short, small farmers** Michael Pollan, *The Omnivore's Dilemma: A Natural History of Four Meals* (New York: Penguin Group, 2006), 136.

213 **publicly traded corporation Whole Foods Market** Though swinging wildly along with the stock market, Whole Foods' stock price multiplied by total number of shares issued has stood between $2 and $5 billion.

213 **Thanks to a law written** Jack Hedin, "My Forbidden Fruits (and Vegetables)," *The New York Times,* March 1, 2008, Opinion section.

214 **Having spent $855 million** Ken Dilanian, "Senators Who Weakened Drug Bill Received Millions from Industry," *USA Today,* May 11, 2007, News section.

214 **In one recent example** "Hidden Drug Payments at Harvard," *The New York Times,* June 10, 2008, editorial page.

214 **Not only can the FDA seal** Johnson & Johnson obscured evidence that its Ortho Evra birth-control patch delivered dangerous amounts of estrogen, but has successfully argued that FDA approval preempts legal liability for deaths and injuries associated with the patch. David Voreacos, "J&J Hid Safety Risk Data on Birth-Control Device, Women Claim," Bloomberg News, April 5, 2008, http://www.bloomberg.com/apps/news?pid=20601202&sid=aINZlEE D4Z6E (accessed November 14, 2008).

214 **When it takes upwards** Michael R. Ward, "Drug Approval Overregulation," *Regulation,* No. 4 (1992).

214 **Those who do prescribe unapproved herbs** See the case of Dr. Serafina Corsello, for just one example, in the Townsend Newsletter, August/September 2002, online at http://www.townsendletter.com/ (accessed November 1, 2008).

216 **Soldiers train contractors** *Iraq for Sale: The War Profiteers,* dir. Robert Greenwald (United States: Brave New Films: 2006), and "Private Warriors," *PBS Frontline,* prod. Marcela Gaviria and Martin Smith (United States: WGBH Educational Foundation, first airdate June 21, 2005).

216 **When a Pentagon contract manager** "Mr. Smith Goes to War with KBR," *The New York Times,* June 19, 2008, editorial page.

216 **"in many other parts of"** Naomi Klein, *The Shock Doctrine: The Rise of Disaster Capitalism* (New York: Macmillan, 2007).

217 **"armored suburbs"** Ibid., 420.

217 **Fifty-eight percent of Americans** CBS News/New York Times Poll, Oct. 27–31, 2006; N=932 registered voters nationwide, MoE ± 3. http://www.pollingreport.com (accessed June 20, 2008).

221 **A relatively new species of corporation** Stephanie Strom, "Businesses Try to Make Money and Save the World," *The New York Times*, May 6, 2007, Business section.

222 **A study by the Stern School** Stephanie Strom, "Study Says Gifts of Stock Precede Sharp Price Dips," *The New York Times*, March 5, 2008, U.S. section.

222 **In one year, Philip Morris** Lori Dorfman, "Philip Morris Puts Up Good Citizen Smokescreen," Alternet, November 27, 2000, http://www.alternet .org/story/10129 (accessed November 27, 2000).

222 **Companies with bad labor practices** Jeff Miller, "Corporate Donations: Generosity Is Often Part Altruism, Part Goodwill Hunting," *Long Island Business News*, October 20, 2006.

223 **A study by the *Los Angeles*** Charles Piller, Edmund Sanders, and Robyn Dixon, "A Times Investigation: Dark Cloud over Good Works of Gates Foundation," *Los Angeles Times*, January 7, 2007, National News section.

223 **"Foundations donate to groups"** Ibid.

225 **Advertising revenues went down** Damien Cave, "Inside Clear Channel: How the Company's Domination Has Made the Airwaves Blander and Tickets Pricier," *Rolling Stone*, August 13, 2004, http://www.rollingstone.com/news/ story/6432174/inside_clear_channel (accessed October 31, 2007), and Clear Channel press release, "Clear Channel Announces Plan to Sell Radio Stations Outside the Top 100 Markets and Entire Television Station Group," November 16, 2006, http://www.clearchannel.com/Corporate/PressRelease .aspx?PressReleaseID=1825 (accessed November 10, 2007).

226 **Once dismantled, however, radio's culture**
Peter DiCola, "False Premises, False Promises: A Quantitative History of Ownership Consolidation in the Radio Industry," December 13, 2006, http:// www.futureofmusic.org/research/radiostudy06.cfm (accessed November 8, 2007).
Vincent M. Ditingo, *The Remaking of Radio* (Boston: Focal Press, 1995).
Future of Music Coalition, "Radio Deregulation: Has It Served Citizens and Musicians?" November 18, 2002, http://www.futureofmusic.org/research/ radiostudy.cfm (accessed November 8, 2007).
Paul McLane, "10 Years Later, Business as Usual," *Free Press*, January 17, 2007, http://www.freepress.net/news/20503 (accessed November 9, 2007).
The Media Bureau, "The Public and Broadcasting," Federal Communications Commission, http://www.fcc.gov/mb/audio/decdoc/public_and_broadcast ing.html (accessed November 7, 2007).
Sanford Nowlin, "Clear Channel Earnings Jump 51% in 3Q," *San Antonio Express-News*, November 8, 2007, http://www.mysanantonio.com/business/ stories/MYSA110907.01C.ClearChannel110907.2b446dc.html (accessed November 10, 2007).
David Sedman, "Radio Regulation," *The Radio Broadcasting Industry* (Boston: Allyn and Bacon, 2001).
David Siklos, "Changing Its Tune," *The New York Times*, September 15, 2006, http:// www.nytimes.com/2006/09/15/business/media/15radio.html (accessed November 10, 2007).
Kristin Thomson, "Media Ownership Fact Sheet," January 17, 2006, http:// www.futureofmusic.org/articles/MediaOwnershipfactsheet07.cfm (accessed November 7, 2007).

Celia Viggo Wexler, "The Fallout from the Telecommunications Act of 1996: Unintended Consequences and Lessons Learned," Common Cause Education Fund, May 9, 2005, http://www.commoncause.org/atf/cf/%7BFB3C17E2-CDD1-4DF6-92BE-BD4429893665%7D/FALLOUT_FROM_THE_TELECOMM_ACT_5-9-05.PDF (accessed November 9, 2007).

CHAPTER NINE
Here and Now

228 **Kiva.org lets donors** For more on Kiva.org, visit its site, http://www.kiva.org.

238 **One system, called ITEX** Mickey Meece, "The Cash Strapped Turn to Barter," *The New York Times*, November 13, 2008.

238 **There can't be too much money** Thomas H. Greco, Jr., *Understanding and Creating Alternatives to Legal Tender* (White River Junction, Vt.: Chelsea Green Publishing Company, 2001).

238 **These local or complementary currencies** Learn more about them through LETSystem: http://www.gmlets.u-net.com/; Time Banks: http://www.timebanks.org/; and Transaction.Net: http://www.transaction.net/money/timedollars/.

INDEX

DOUGLAS RUSHKOFF is a widely known media critic and documentarian. He has written ten books, and his documentaries include *Frontline*'s award-winning "The Merchants of Cool" and "The Persuaders." He teaches media studies at the New School, hosts *The Media Squat* on radio station WFMU, and serves on the board of directors of the Media Ecology Association, the Center for Cognitive Liberty and Ethics, and the National Association for Media Literacy Education. He has won the Marshall McLuhan Award for Outstanding Book in the Field of Media Ecology and was the first winner of the Neil Postman Award for Career Achievement in Public Intellectual Activity.

http://www.rushkoff.com

ABOUT THE TYPE

This book was set in Ehrhardt, a typeface based on the original design of Nicholas Kis, a seventeenth-century Hungarian type designer. Ehrhardt was first released in 1937 by the Monotype Corporation of London.